Tale of the Waning Moon

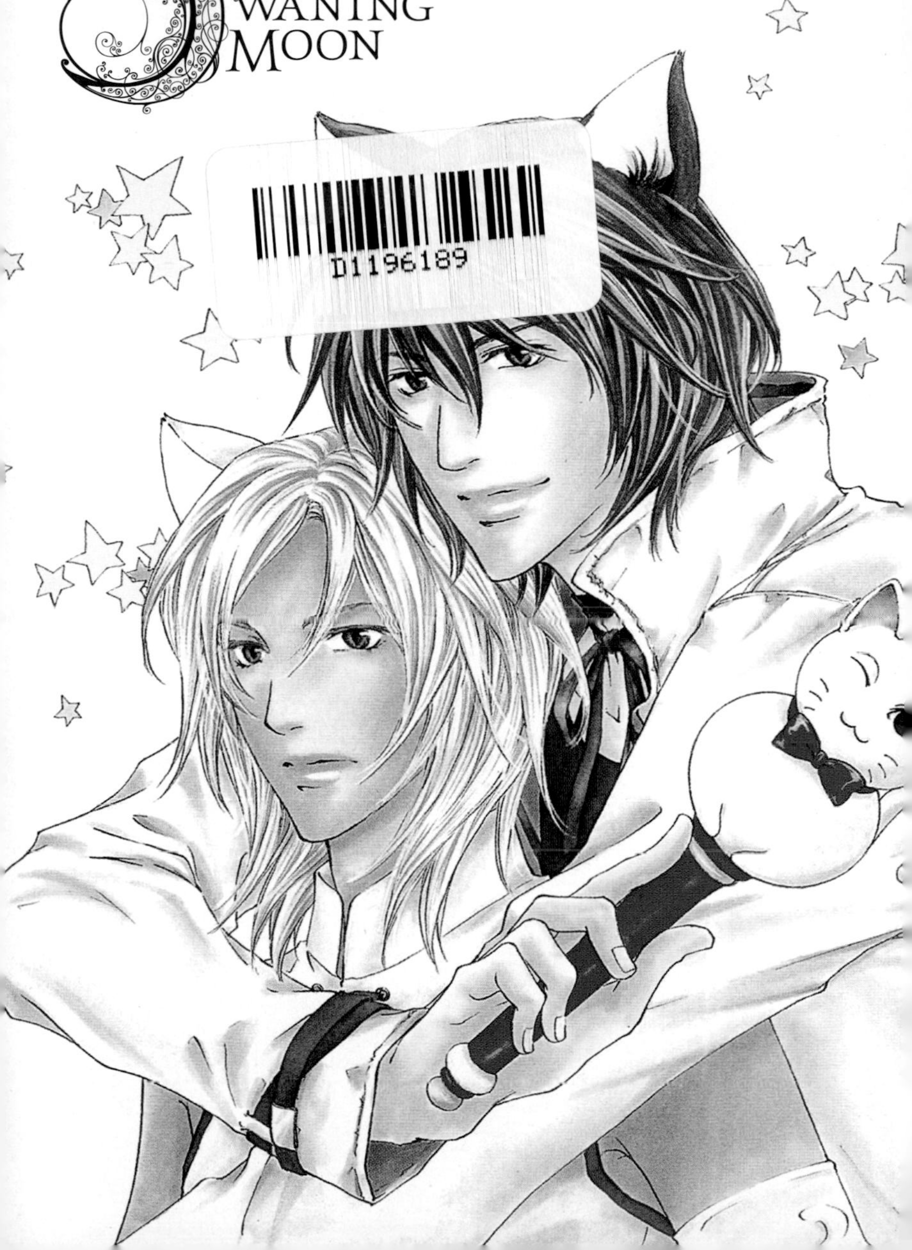

TALE OF THE WANING MOON ②

CONTENTS

TALE OF THE WANING MOON ②

HYOUTA FUJIYAMA

Translation: Tomo Kimura • Lettering: Keiran O'Leary

KAGEN NO TSUKIYO NO MONOGATARI Vol. 2 © 2010 Hyouta Fujiyama.
All rights reserved. First published in Japan in 2010 by HOUBUNSHA
CO., LTD., Tokyo. English translation rights in United States, Canada, and
United Kingdom arranged with HOUBUNSHA CO., LTD., through Tuttle-
Mori Agency, Inc., Tokyo.

Yen Press
Hachette Book Group
237 Park Avenue, New York, NY 10017

www.HachetteBookGroup.com
www.YenPress.com

Yen Press is an imprint of Hachette Book Group, Inc. The Yen Press name
and logo are trademarks of Hachette Book Group, Inc.

First Yen Press Edition: June 2011

ISBN: 978-0-316-17801-3

10 9 8 7 6 5 4 3 2 1

BVG

Printed in the United States of America

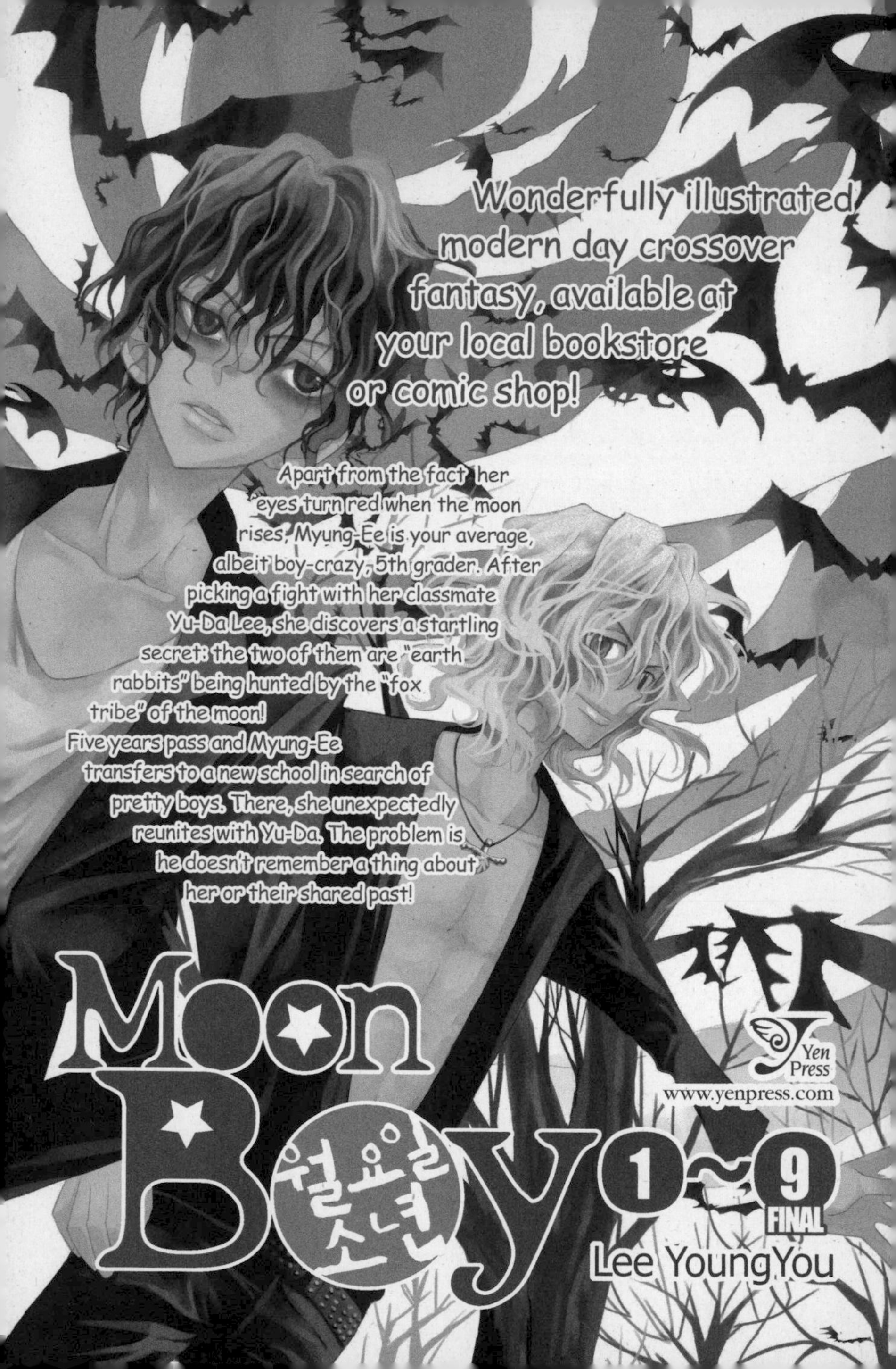
Wonderfully illustrated modern day crossover fantasy, available at your local bookstore or comic shop!
Apart from the fact her eyes turn red when the moon rises, Myung-Ee is your average, albeit boy-crazy, 5th grader. After picking a fight with her classmate Yu-Da Lee, she discovers a startling secret: the two of them are "earth rabbits" being hunted by the "fox tribe" of the moon!
Five years pass and Myung-Ee transfers to a new school in search of pretty boys. There, she unexpectedly reunites with Yu-Da. The problem is he doesn't remember a thing about her or their shared past!
Moon Boy
월요일 소년
1~9
FINAL
Lee YoungYou
Yen Press
www.yenpress.com

A totally new Arabian nights, where Scheherazade is a guy!

Everyone knows the story of Scheherazade and her wonderful tales from the Arabian Nights. For one thousand and one nights, the stories that she created entertained the mad Sultan and eventually saved her life. In this version, Scheherazade is a guy who disguises himself as a woman to save his sister from the mad Sultan. When he puts his life on the line, what kind of strange and unique stories will he tell? This new twist on one of the greatest classical tales might just keep you awake for another ONE THOUSAND AND ONE NIGHTS!

Yen Press

www.yenpress.com

Available at bookstores near you!

One thousand and one nights 1~11 final

Han SeungHee · Jeon JinSeok

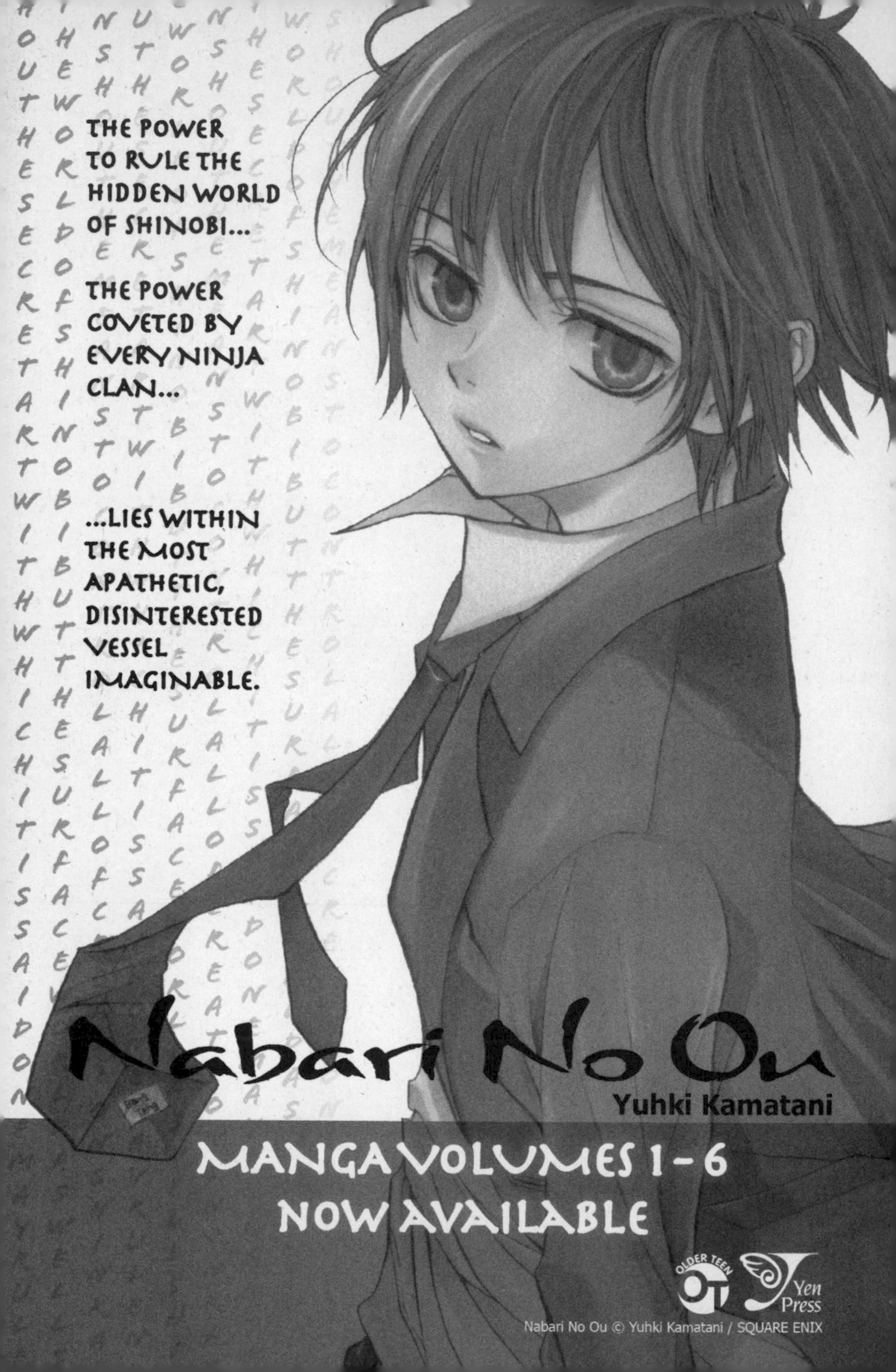
THE POWER TO RULE THE HIDDEN WORLD OF SHINOBI...
THE POWER COVETED BY EVERY NINJA CLAN...
...LIES WITHIN THE MOST APATHETIC, DISINTERESTED VESSEL IMAGINABLE.
Nabari No Ou
Yuhki Kamatani
MANGA VOLUMES 1-6 NOW AVAILABLE
OLDER TEEN OT
Yen Press
Nabari No Ou © Yuhki Kamatani / SQUARE ENIX

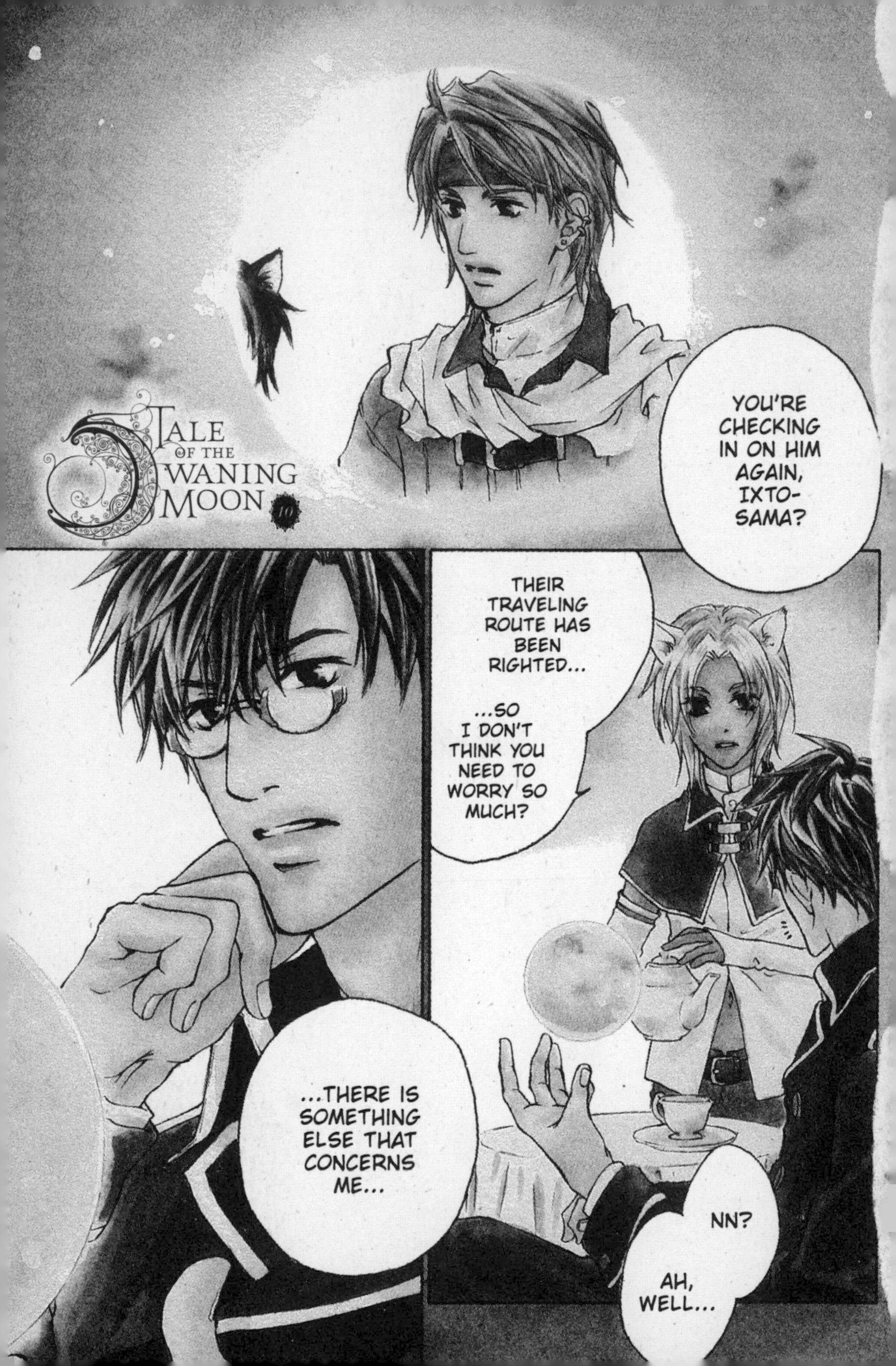
TALE OF THE WANING MOON
10
YOU'RE CHECKING IN ON HIM AGAIN, IXTO-SAMA?
THEIR TRAVELING ROUTE HAS BEEN RIGHTED...
...SO I DON'T THINK YOU NEED TO WORRY SO MUCH?
NN?
AH, WELL...
...THERE IS SOMETHING ELSE THAT CONCERNS ME...

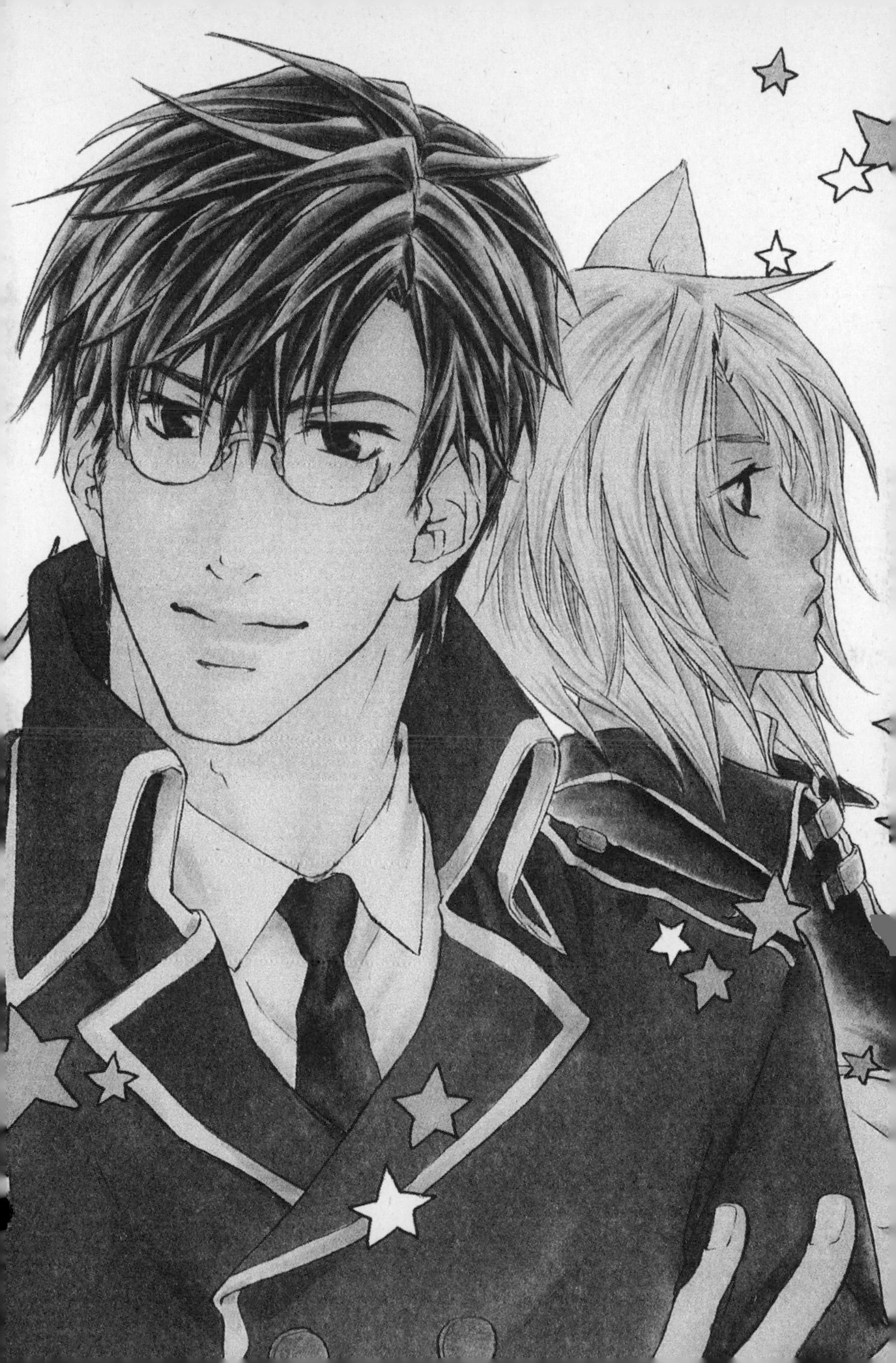

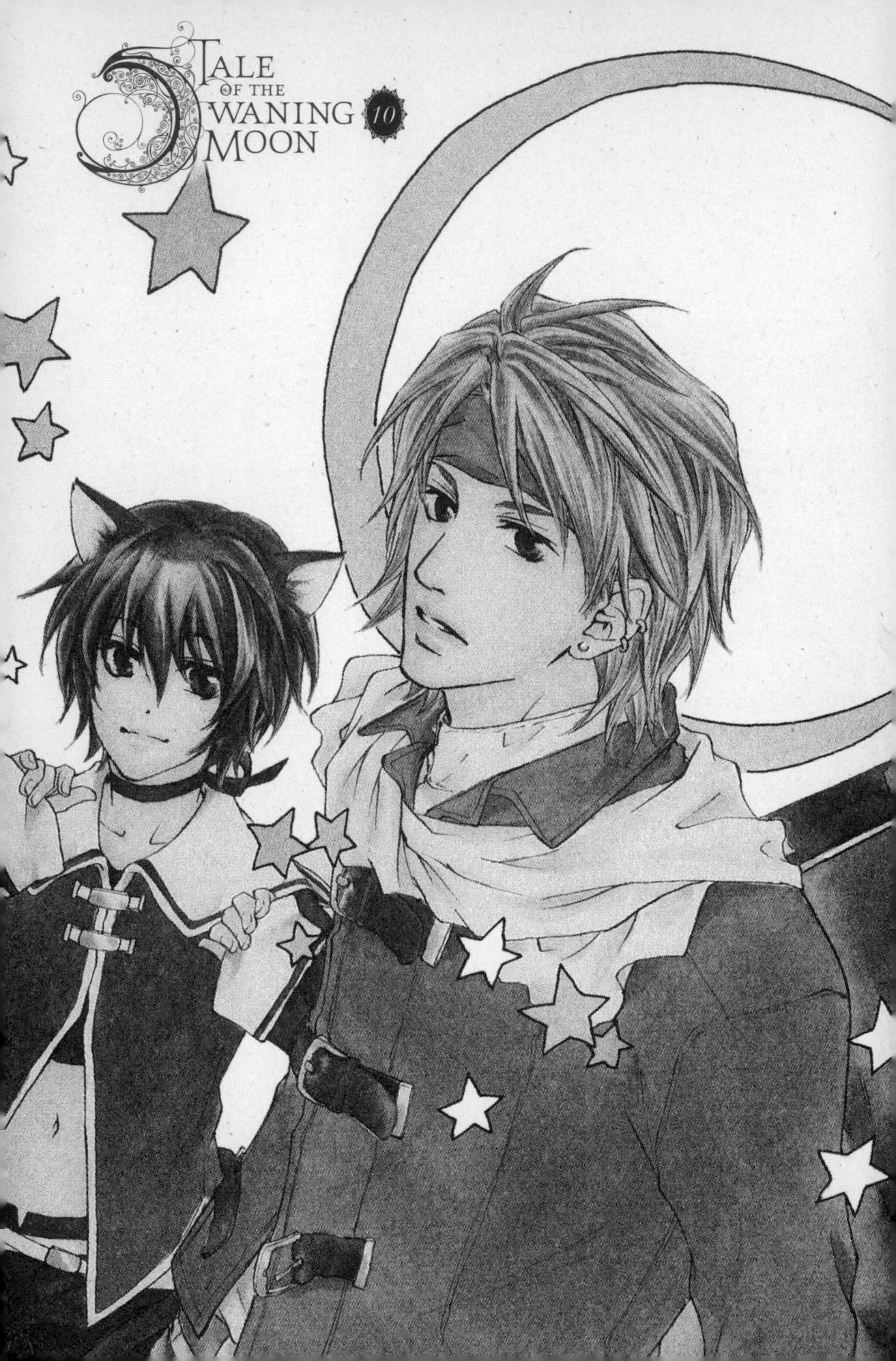
TALE
OF THE
WANING
MOON
10

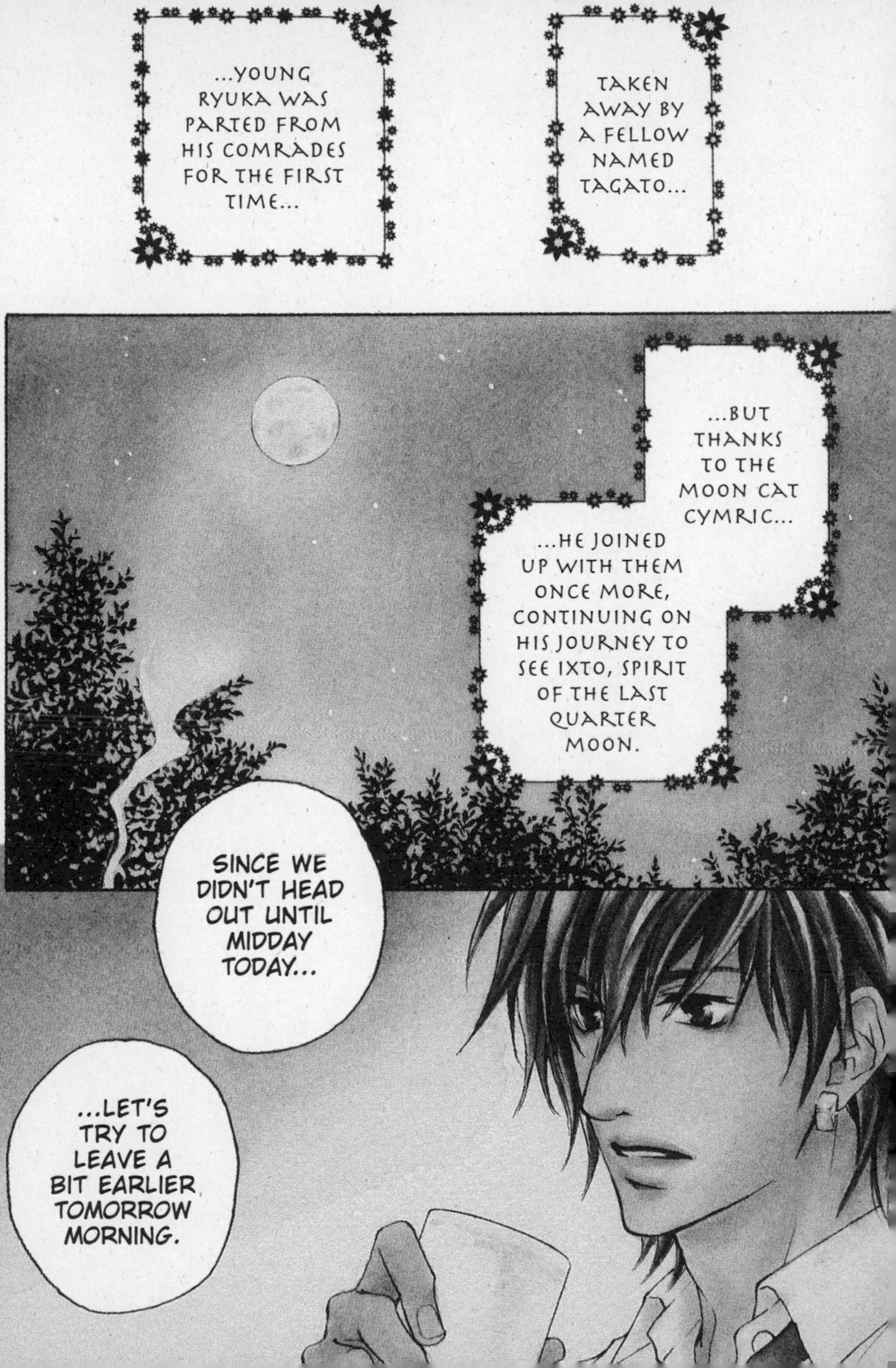
TAKEN AWAY BY A FELLOW NAMED TAGATO...
...YOUNG RYUKA WAS PARTED FROM HIS COMRADES FOR THE FIRST TIME...
...BUT THANKS TO THE MOON CAT CYMRIC...
...HE JOINED UP WITH THEM ONCE MORE, CONTINUING ON HIS JOURNEY TO SEE IXTO, SPIRIT OF THE LAST QUARTER MOON.
SINCE WE DIDN'T HEAD OUT UNTIL MIDDAY TODAY...
...LET'S TRY TO LEAVE A BIT EARLIER TOMORROW MORNING.

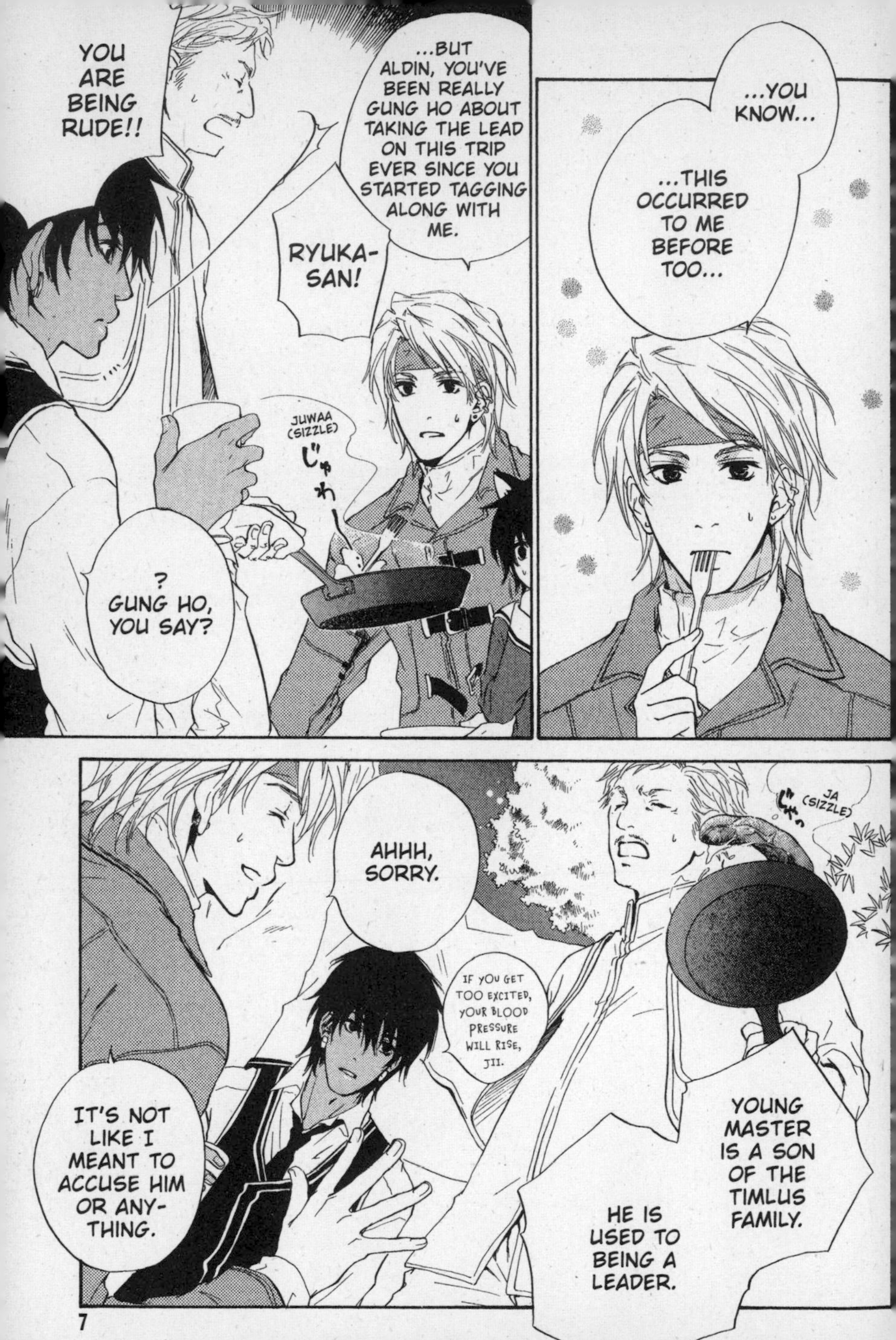
...YOU KNOW...
...THIS OCCURRED TO ME BEFORE TOO...
...BUT ALDIN, YOU'VE BEEN REALLY GUNG HO ABOUT TAKING THE LEAD ON THIS TRIP EVER SINCE YOU STARTED TAGGING ALONG WITH ME.
YOU ARE BEING RUDE!!
RYUKA-SAN!
JUWAA (SIZZLE)
じゅわ
? GUNG HO, YOU SAY?
JA (SIZZLE)
じゃ
AHHH, SORRY.
YOUNG MASTER IS A SON OF THE TIMLUS FAMILY.
IF YOU GET TOO EXCITED, YOUR BLOOD PRESSURE WILL RISE, JII.
HE IS USED TO BEING A LEADER.
IT'S NOT LIKE I MEANT TO ACCUSE HIM OR ANY-THING.

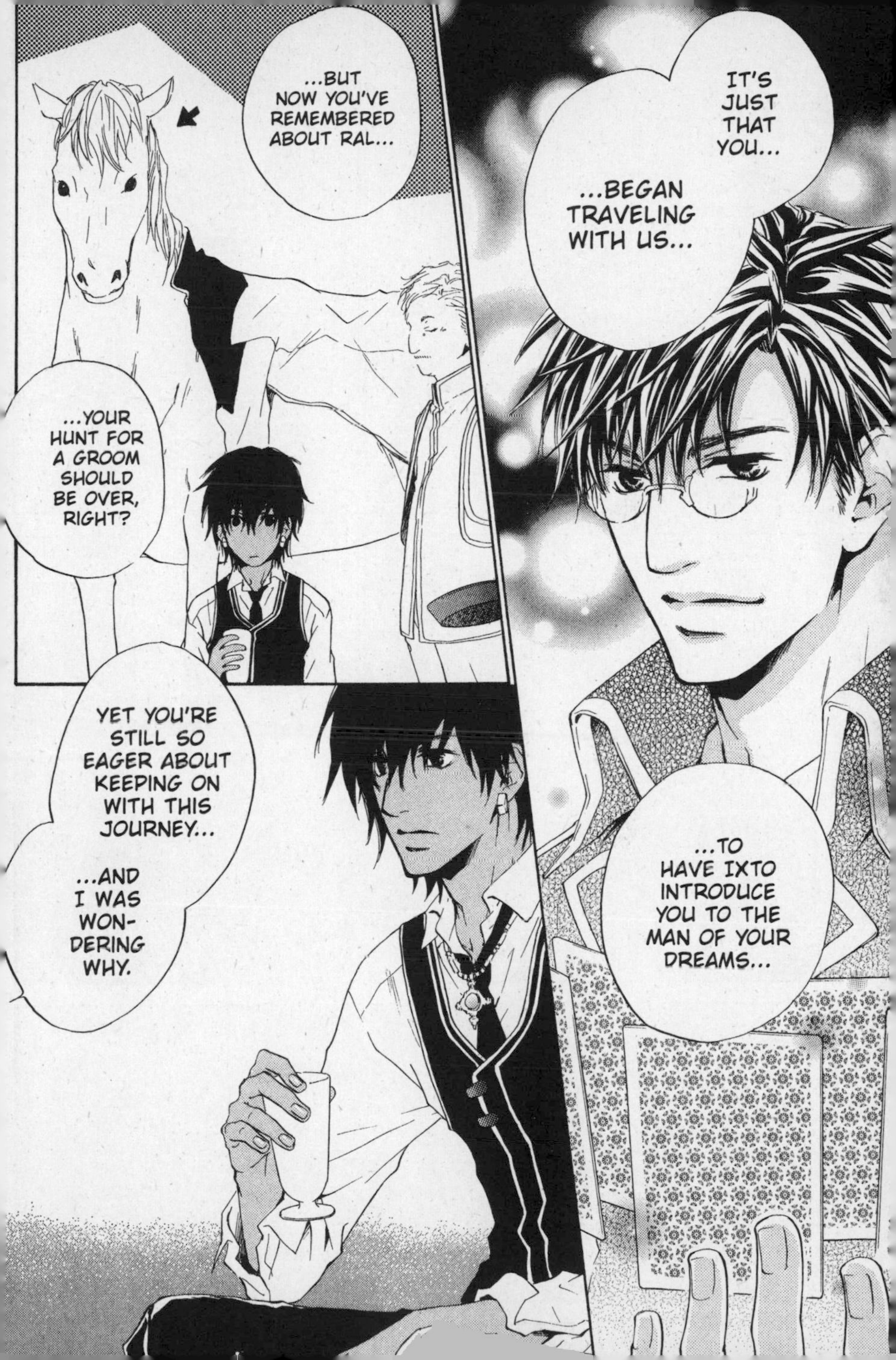
IT'S JUST THAT YOU...
...BEGAN TRAVELING WITH US...
...TO HAVE IXTO INTRODUCE YOU TO THE MAN OF YOUR DREAMS...
...BUT NOW YOU'VE REMEMBERED ABOUT RAL...
...YOUR HUNT FOR A GROOM SHOULD BE OVER, RIGHT?
YET YOU'RE STILL SO EAGER ABOUT KEEPING ON WITH THIS JOURNEY...
...AND I WAS WON-DERING WHY.

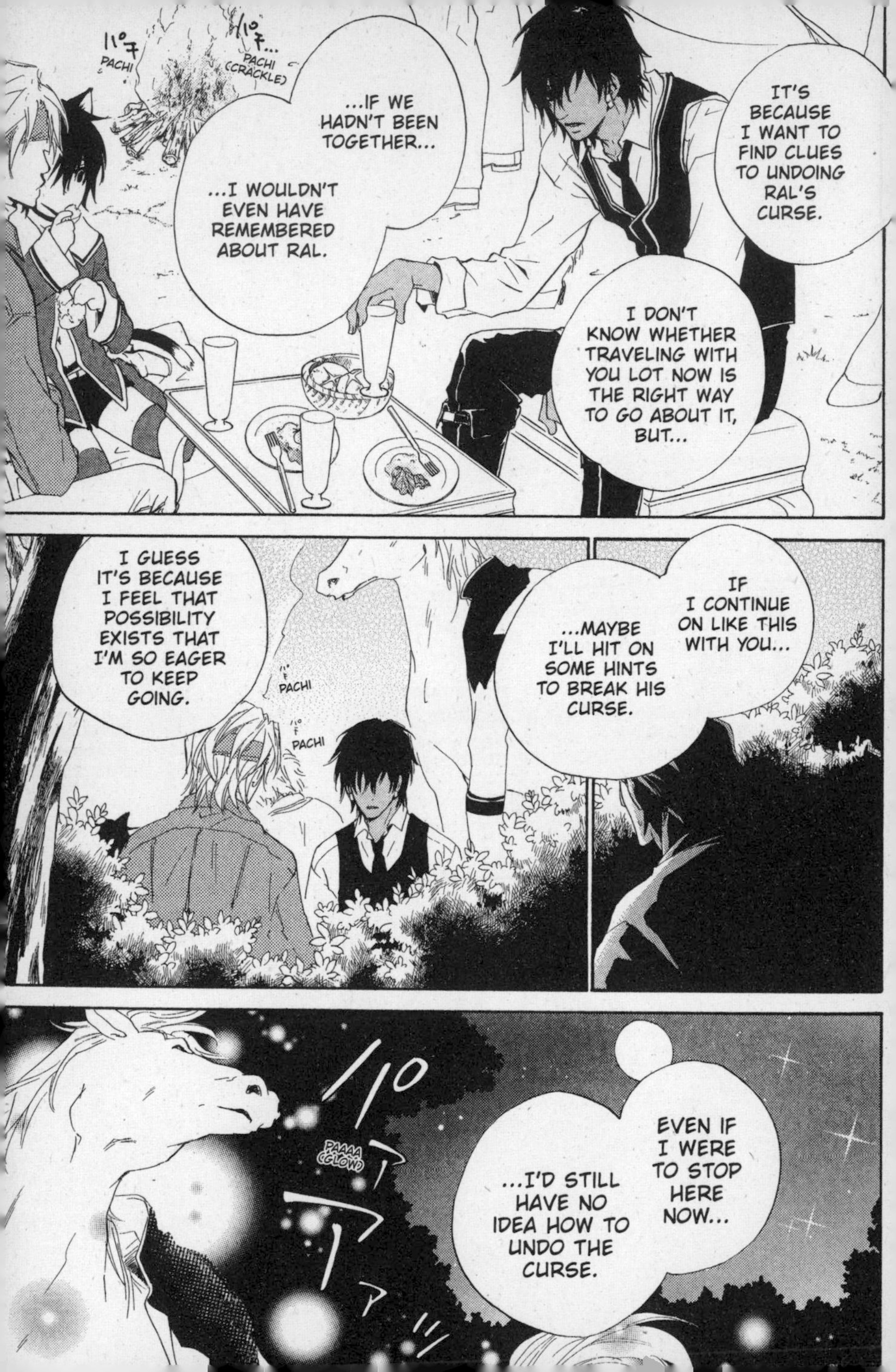

IT'S BECAUSE I WANT TO FIND CLUES TO UNDOING RAL'S CURSE.
I DON'T KNOW WHETHER TRAVELING WITH YOU LOT NOW IS THE RIGHT WAY TO GO ABOUT IT, BUT...
...IF WE HADN'T BEEN TOGETHER...
...I WOULDN'T EVEN HAVE REMEMBERED ABOUT RAL.
パチ... PACHI (CRACKLE)
パチ PACHI
IF I CONTINUE ON LIKE THIS WITH YOU...
...MAYBE I'LL HIT ON SOME HINTS TO BREAK HIS CURSE.
I GUESS IT'S BECAUSE I FEEL THAT POSSIBILITY EXISTS THAT I'M SO EAGER TO KEEP GOING.
PACHI
PACHI
EVEN IF I WERE TO STOP HERE NOW...
...I'D STILL HAVE NO IDEA HOW TO UNDO THE CURSE.
PAAAA (GLOW)

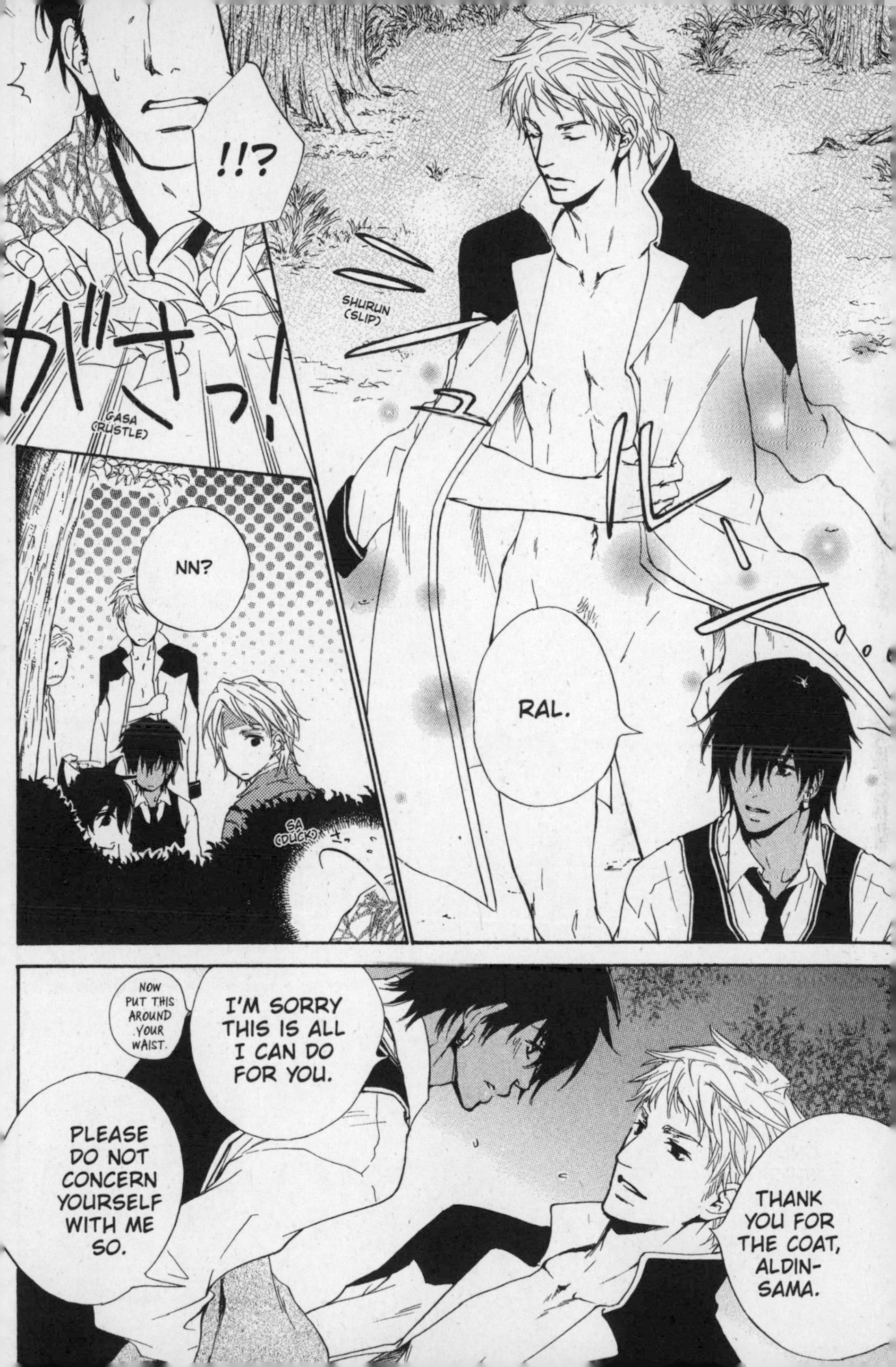
SHURUN (SLIP)
RAL.
!!?
がさっ!
GASA (RUSTLE)
NN?
SA (DUCK)
THANK YOU FOR THE COAT, ALDIN-SAMA.
I'M SORRY THIS IS ALL I CAN DO FOR YOU.
NOW PUT THIS AROUND YOUR WAIST.
PLEASE DO NOT CONCERN YOURSELF WITH ME SO.

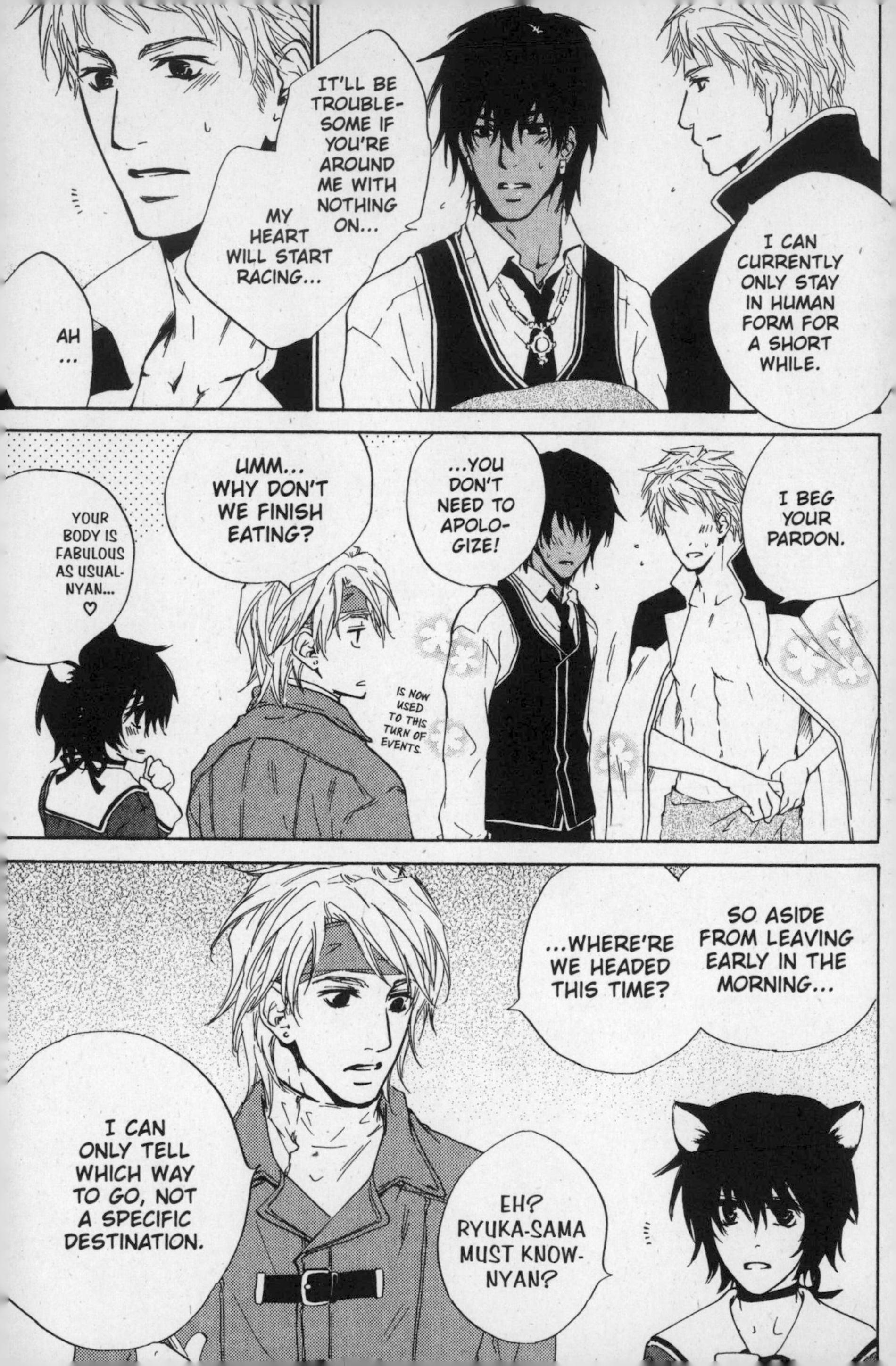
I CAN CURRENTLY ONLY STAY IN HUMAN FORM FOR A SHORT WHILE.
IT'LL BE TROUBLE-SOME IF YOU'RE AROUND ME WITH NOTHING ON...
MY HEART WILL START RACING...
AH ...
I BEG YOUR PARDON.
...YOU DON'T NEED TO APOLO-GIZE!
UMM... WHY DON'T WE FINISH EATING?
IS NOW USED TO THIS TURN OF EVENTS.
YOUR BODY IS FABULOUS AS USUAL-NYAN... ♡
SO ASIDE FROM LEAVING EARLY IN THE MORNING...
...WHERE'RE WE HEADED THIS TIME?
EH? RYUKA-SAMA MUST KNOW-NYAN?
I CAN ONLY TELL WHICH WAY TO GO, NOT A SPECIFIC DESTINATION.

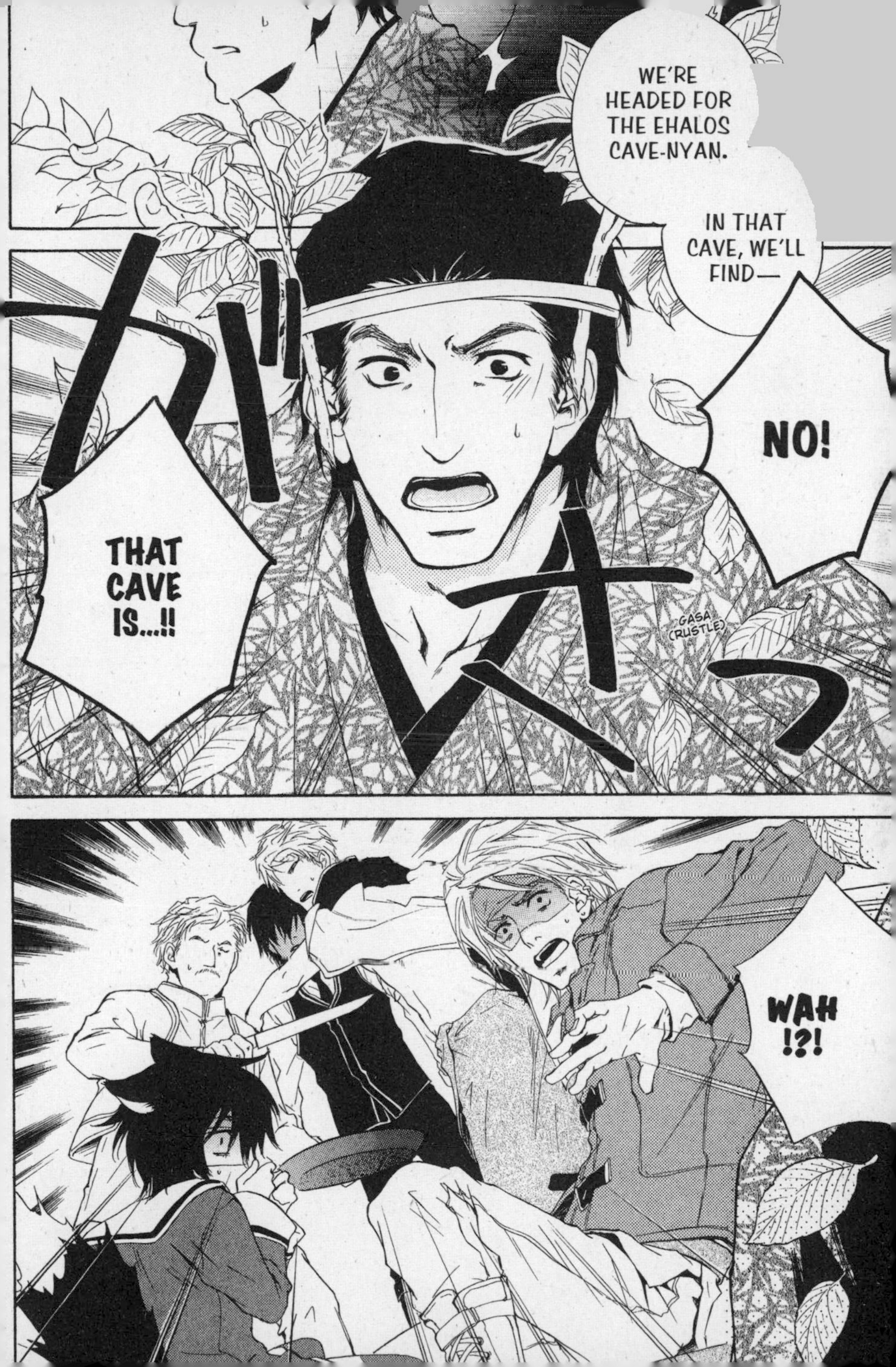
WE'RE HEADED FOR THE EHALOS CAVE-NYAN.
IN THAT CAVE, WE'LL FIND—
NO!
GASA (RUSTLE)
THAT CAVE IS...!!
WAH !?!

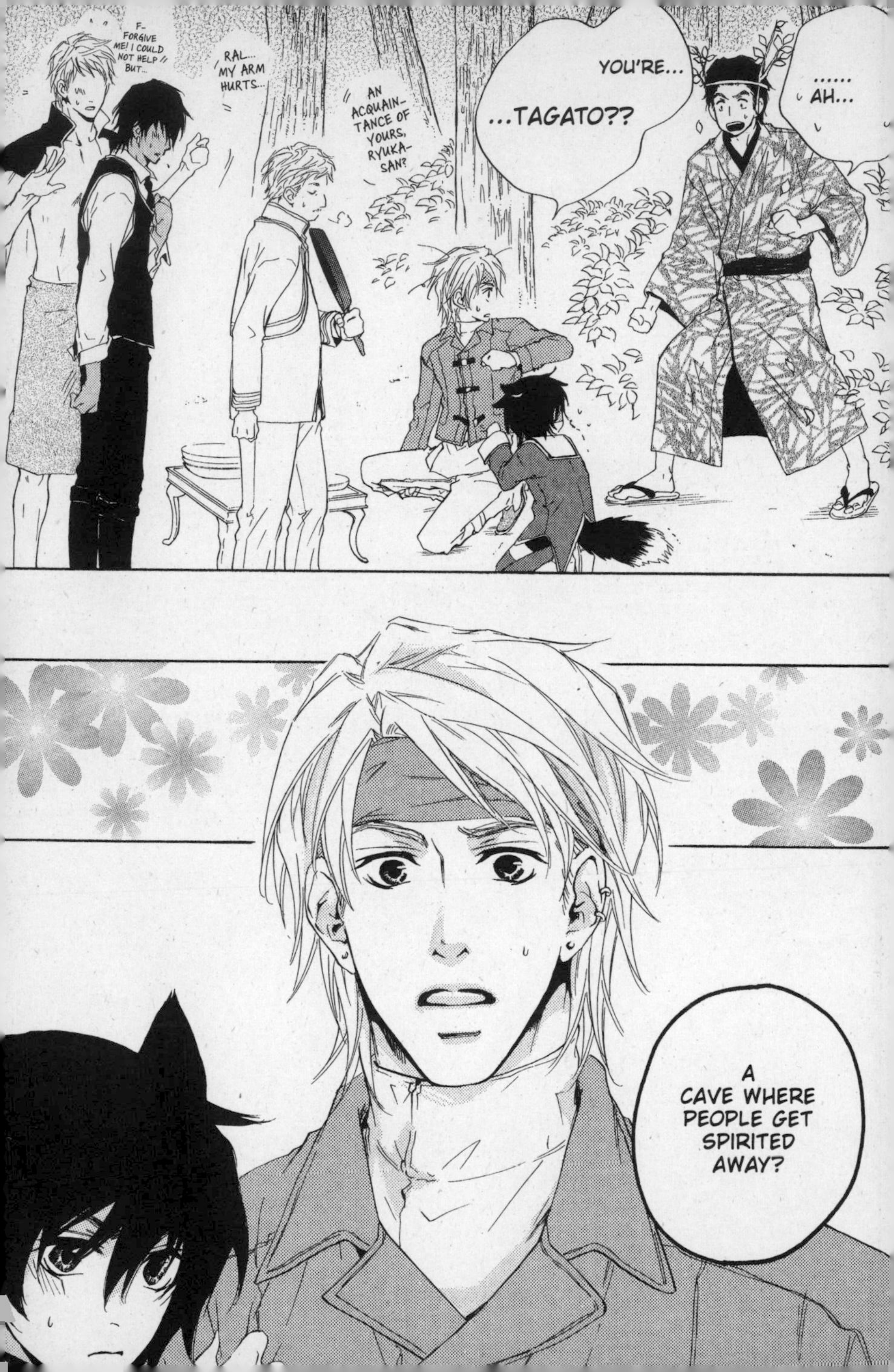
......
AH...
YOU'RE...
...TAGATO??
AN ACQUAINTANCE OF YOURS, RYUKA-SAN?
RAL... MY ARM HURTS...
F-FORGIVE ME! I COULD NOT HELP BUT...
A CAVE WHERE PEOPLE GET SPIRITED AWAY?

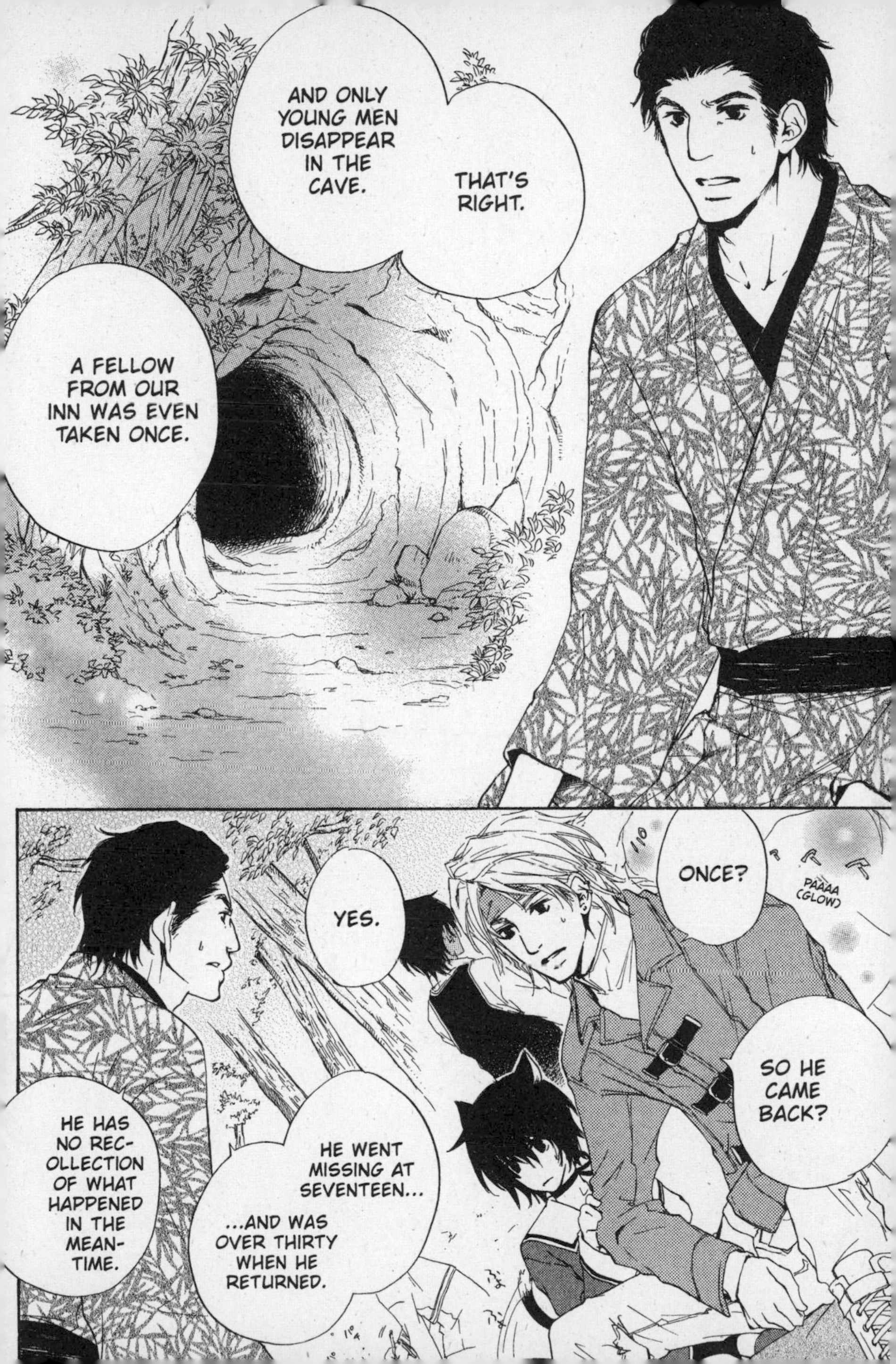
THAT'S RIGHT.
AND ONLY YOUNG MEN DISAPPEAR IN THE CAVE.
A FELLOW FROM OUR INN WAS EVEN TAKEN ONCE.
ONCE?
PAAAA (GLOW)
YES.
SO HE CAME BACK?
HE WENT MISSING AT SEVENTEEN...
...AND WAS OVER THIRTY WHEN HE RETURNED.
HE HAS NO REC-OLLECTION OF WHAT HAPPENED IN THE MEAN-TIME.

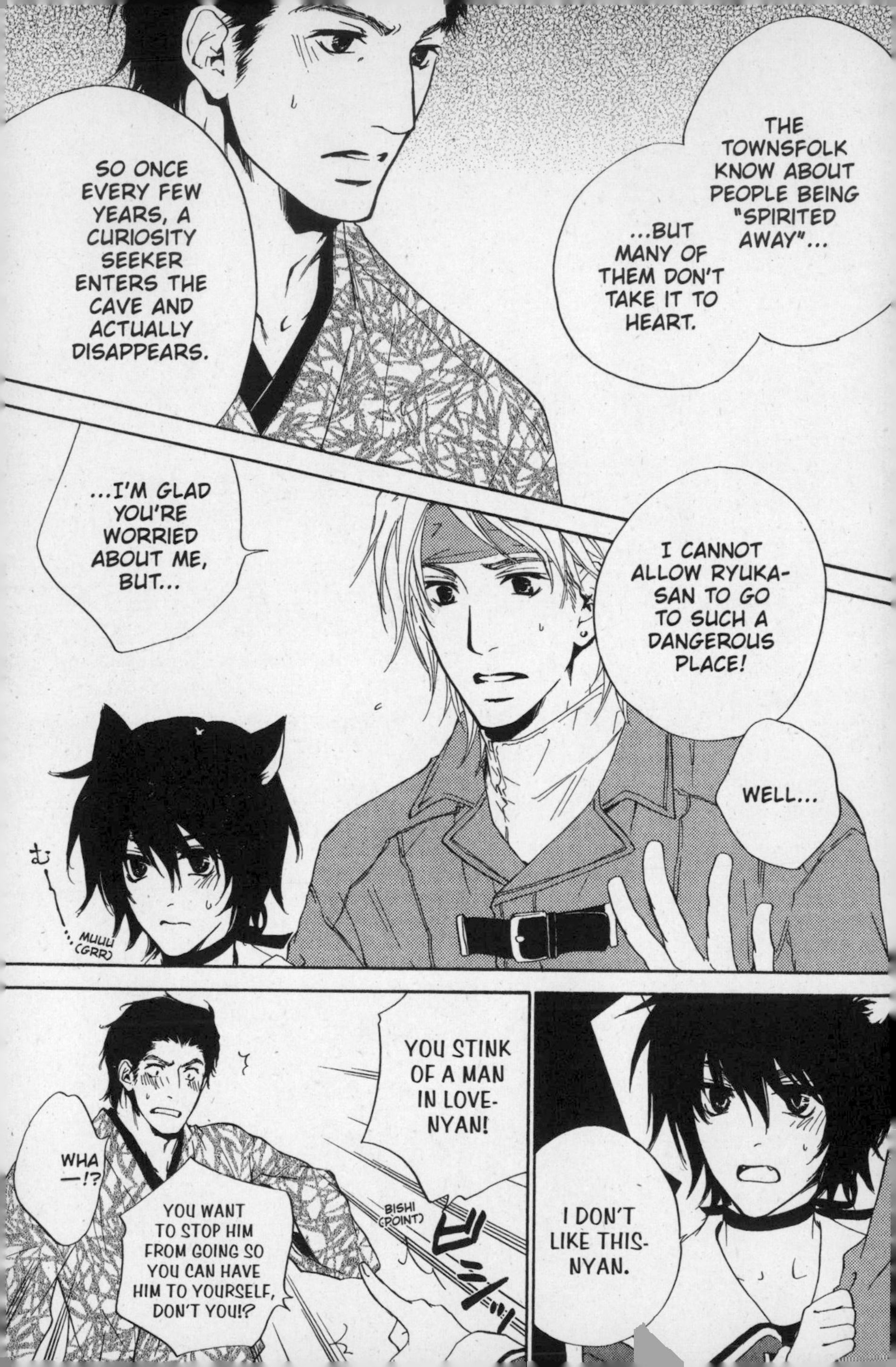
THE TOWNSFOLK KNOW ABOUT PEOPLE BEING "SPIRITED AWAY"...
...BUT MANY OF THEM DON'T TAKE IT TO HEART.
SO ONCE EVERY FEW YEARS, A CURIOSITY SEEKER ENTERS THE CAVE AND ACTUALLY DISAPPEARS.
I CANNOT ALLOW RYUKA-SAN TO GO TO SUCH A DANGEROUS PLACE!
...I'M GLAD YOU'RE WORRIED ABOUT ME, BUT...
WELL...
む
MUUU (GRR)
I DON'T LIKE THIS-NYAN.
YOU STINK OF A MAN IN LOVE-NYAN!
BISHI (POINT)
WHA—!?
YOU WANT TO STOP HIM FROM GOING SO YOU CAN HAVE HIM TO YOURSELF, DON'T YOU!?

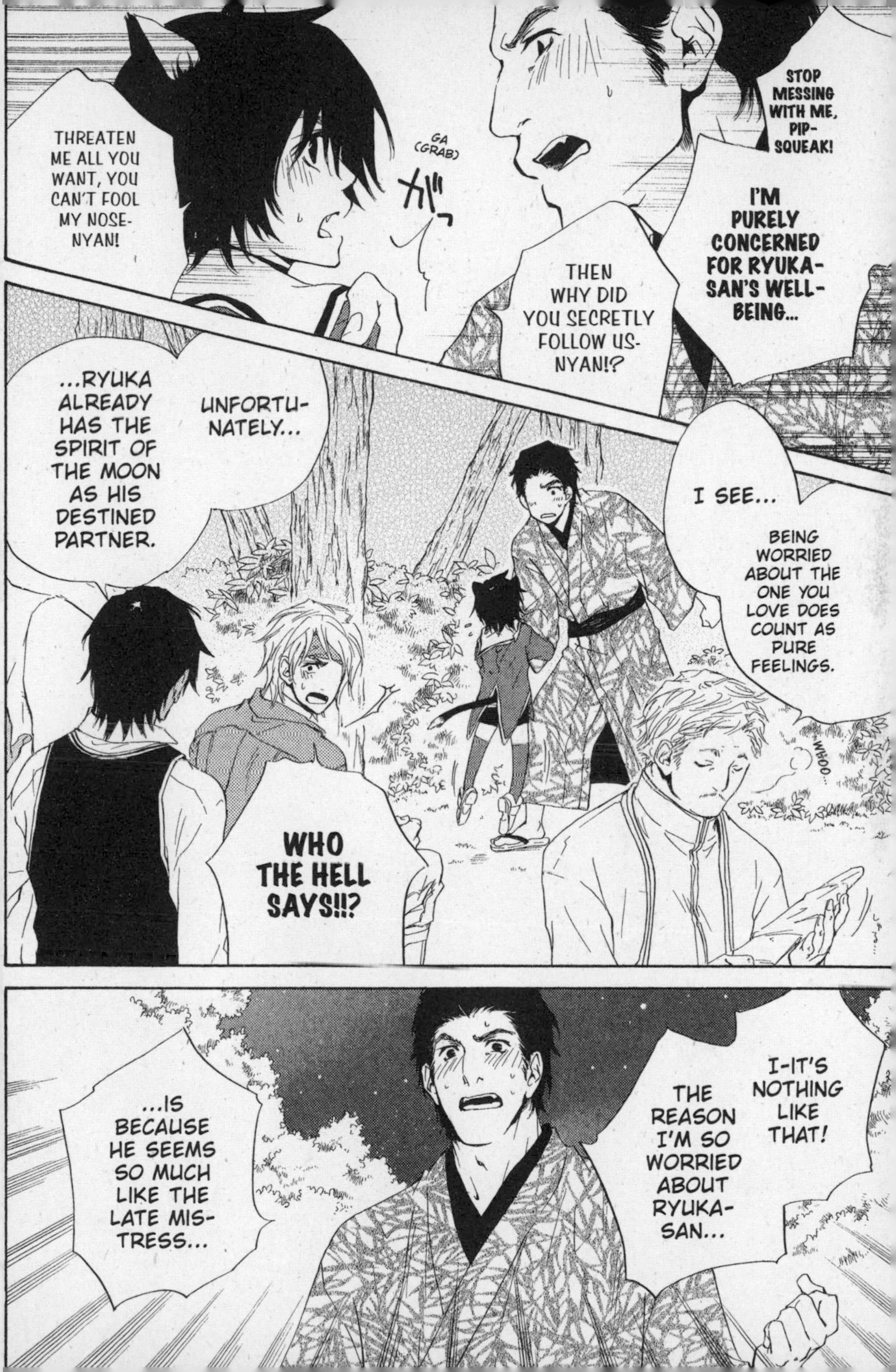
STOP MESSING WITH ME, PIP-SQUEAK!
GA (GRAB)
THREATEN ME ALL YOU WANT, YOU CAN'T FOOL MY NOSE-NYAN!
I'M PURELY CONCERNED FOR RYUKA-SAN'S WELL-BEING...
THEN WHY DID YOU SECRETLY FOLLOW US-NYAN!?
I SEE...
BEING WORRIED ABOUT THE ONE YOU LOVE DOES COUNT AS PURE FEELINGS.
OOHH...
UNFORTU-NATELY...
...RYUKA ALREADY HAS THE SPIRIT OF THE MOON AS HIS DESTINED PARTNER.
WHO THE HELL SAYS!!?
I-IT'S NOTHING LIKE THAT!
THE REASON I'M SO WORRIED ABOUT RYUKA-SAN...
...IS BECAUSE HE SEEMS SO MUCH LIKE THE LATE MIS-TRESS...

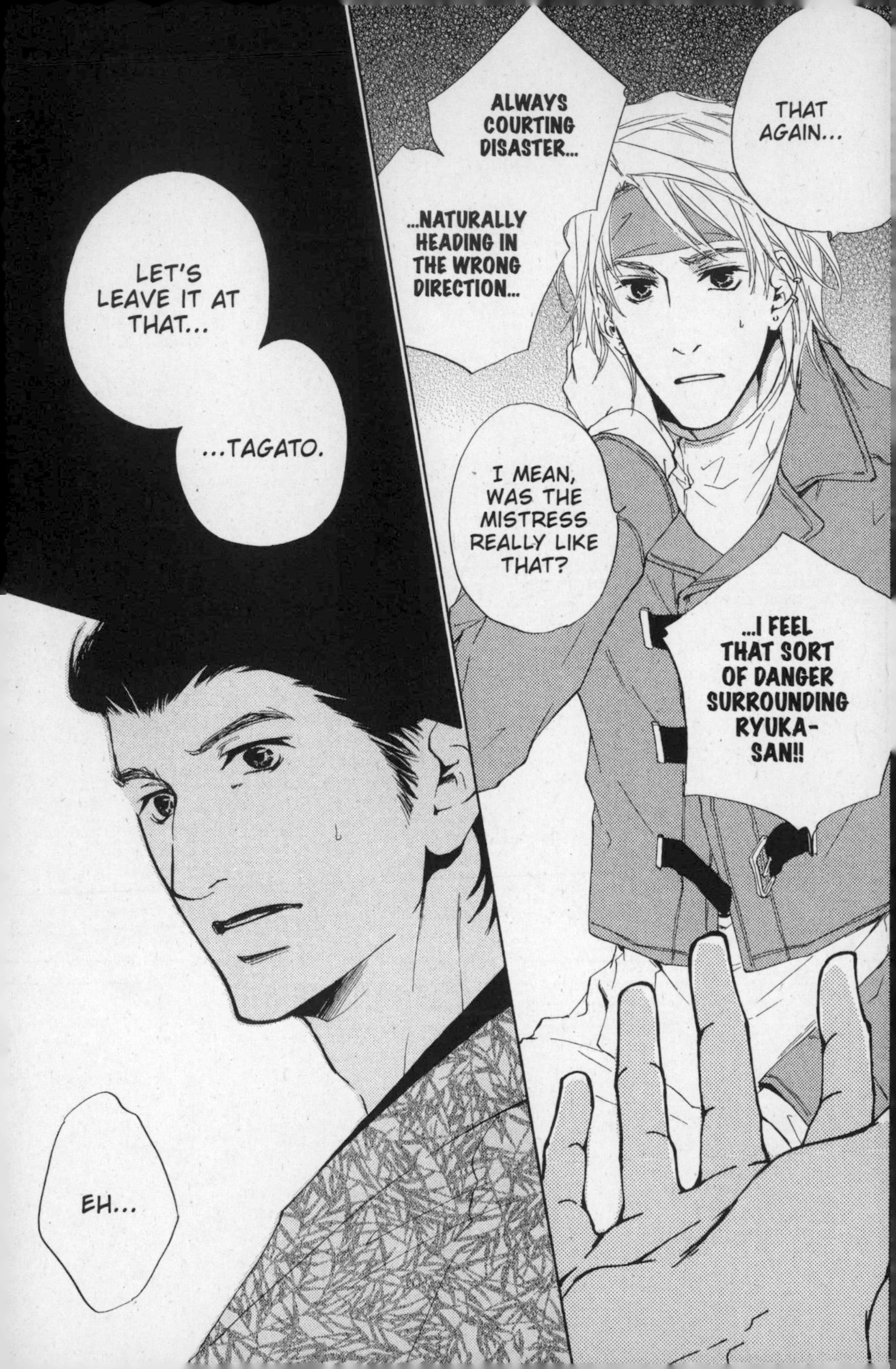
THAT AGAIN...
ALWAYS COURTING DISASTER...
...NATURALLY HEADING IN THE WRONG DIRECTION...
I MEAN, WAS THE MISTRESS REALLY LIKE THAT?
...I FEEL THAT SORT OF DANGER SURROUNDING RYUKA-SAN!!
LET'S LEAVE IT AT THAT...
...TAGATO.
EH...

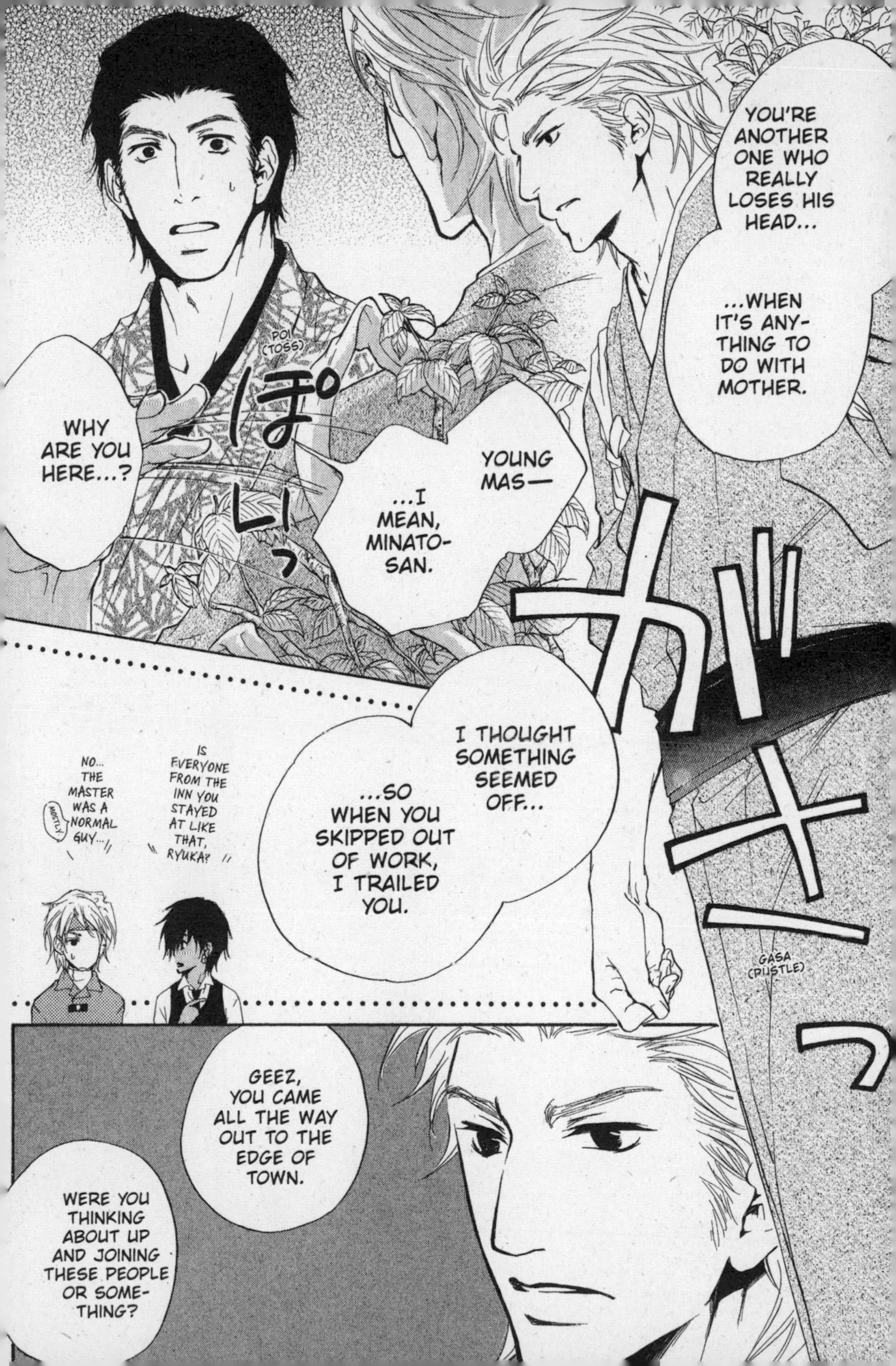
YOU'RE ANOTHER ONE WHO REALLY LOSES HIS HEAD...
...WHEN IT'S ANY-THING TO DO WITH MOTHER.
YOUNG MAS—
...I MEAN, MINATO-SAN.
ぽいっ
POI (TOSS)
WHY ARE YOU HERE...?
ガサッ
GASA (RUSTLE)
I THOUGHT SOMETHING SEEMED OFF...
...SO WHEN YOU SKIPPED OUT OF WORK, I TRAILED YOU.
IS EVERYONE FROM THE INN YOU STAYED AT LIKE THAT, RYUKA?
NO... THE MASTER WAS A NORMAL GUY...
MOSTLY
GEEZ, YOU CAME ALL THE WAY OUT TO THE EDGE OF TOWN.
WERE YOU THINKING ABOUT UP AND JOINING THESE PEOPLE OR SOME-THING?

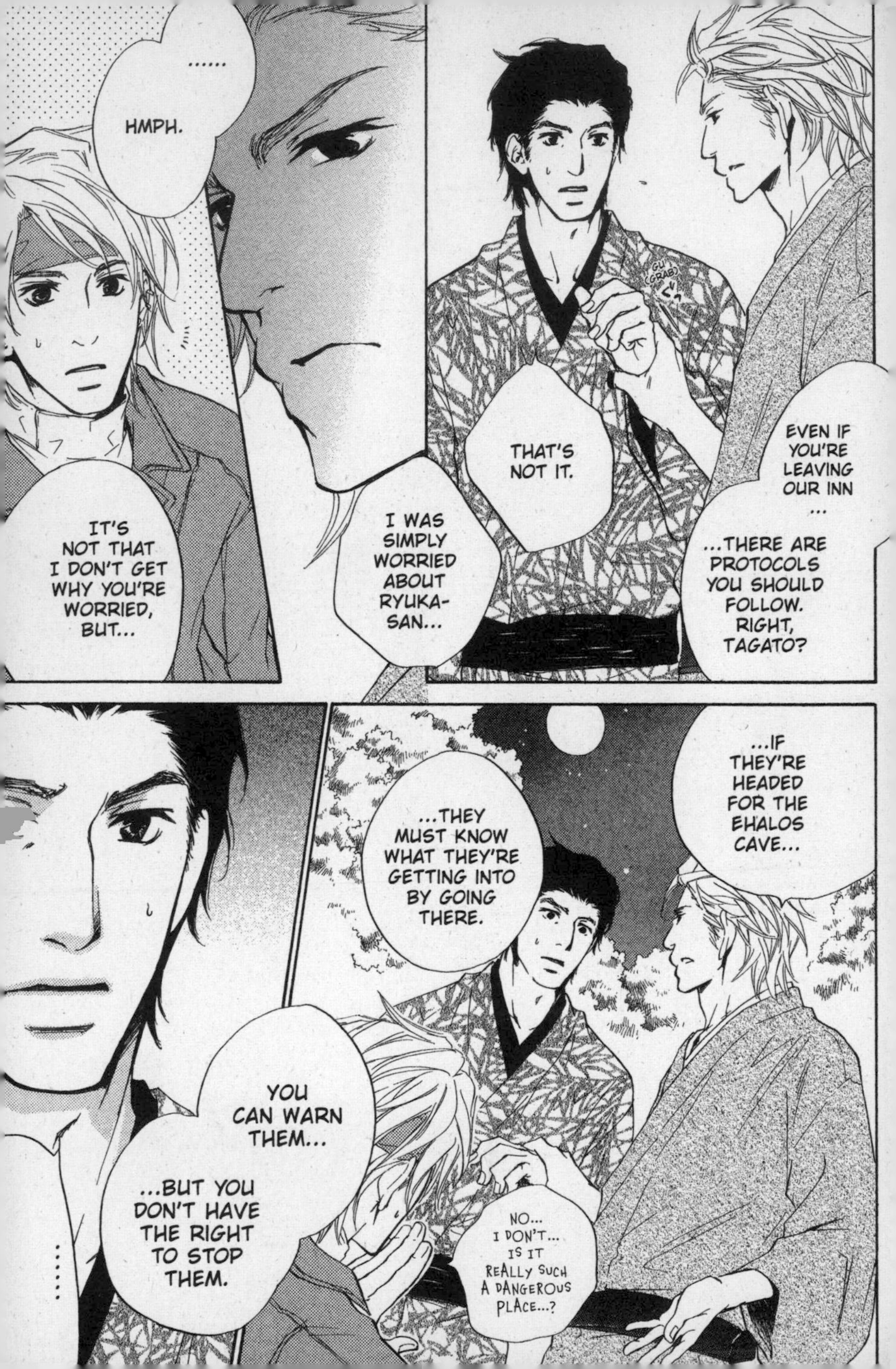
EVEN IF YOU'RE LEAVING OUR INN ...
...THERE ARE PROTOCOLS YOU SHOULD FOLLOW. RIGHT, TAGATO?
GU (GRAB)
THAT'S NOT IT.
I WAS SIMPLY WORRIED ABOUT RYUKA-SAN...
......
HMPH.
IT'S NOT THAT I DON'T GET WHY YOU'RE WORRIED, BUT...
...IF THEY'RE HEADED FOR THE EHALOS CAVE...
...THEY MUST KNOW WHAT THEY'RE GETTING INTO BY GOING THERE.
YOU CAN WARN THEM...
...BUT YOU DON'T HAVE THE RIGHT TO STOP THEM.
NO... I DON'T... IS IT REALLY SUCH A DANGEROUS PLACE...?
......

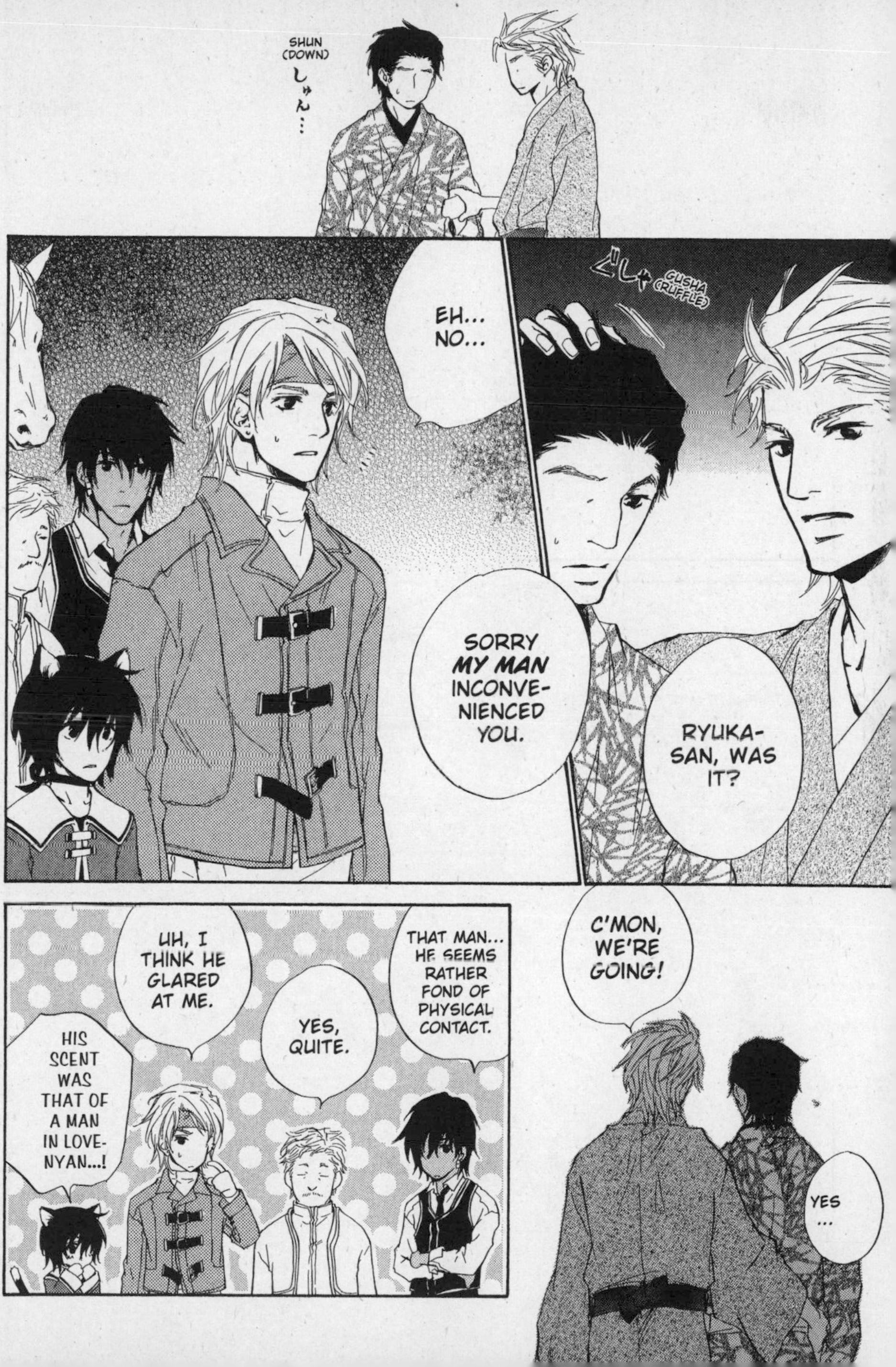
SHUN (DOWN)
しゅん…
ぐしゃ
GUSHA (RUFFLE)
RYUKA-SAN, WAS IT?
SORRY *MY MAN* INCONVENIENCED YOU.
EH... NO...
C'MON, WE'RE GOING!
YES ...
THAT MAN... HE SEEMS RATHER FOND OF PHYSICAL CONTACT.
YES, QUITE.
UH, I THINK HE GLARED AT ME.
HIS SCENT WAS THAT OF A MAN IN LOVE-NYAN...!

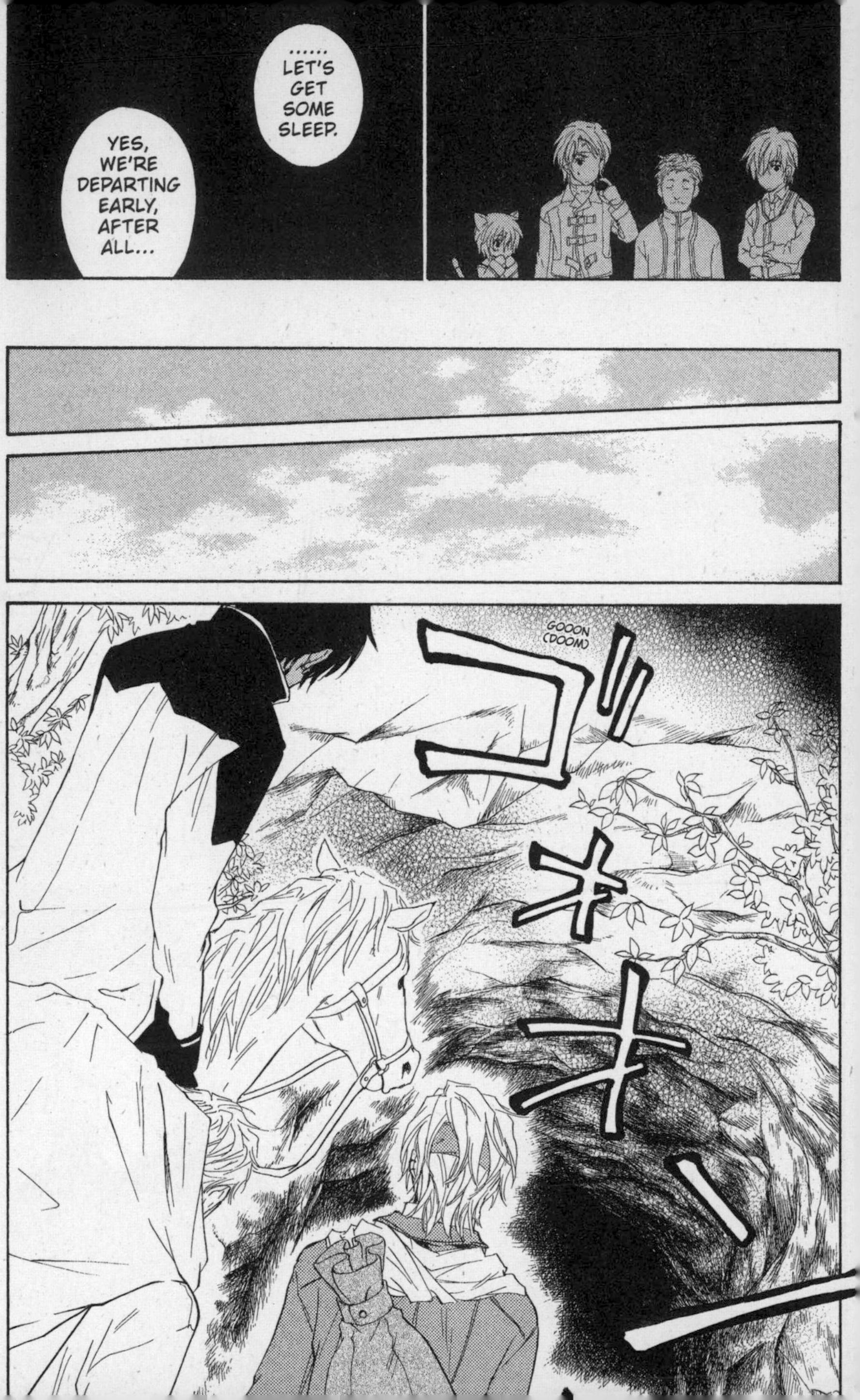
......
LET'S GET SOME SLEEP.
YES, WE'RE DEPARTING EARLY, AFTER ALL...
GOOON (DOOM)
ゴォォー

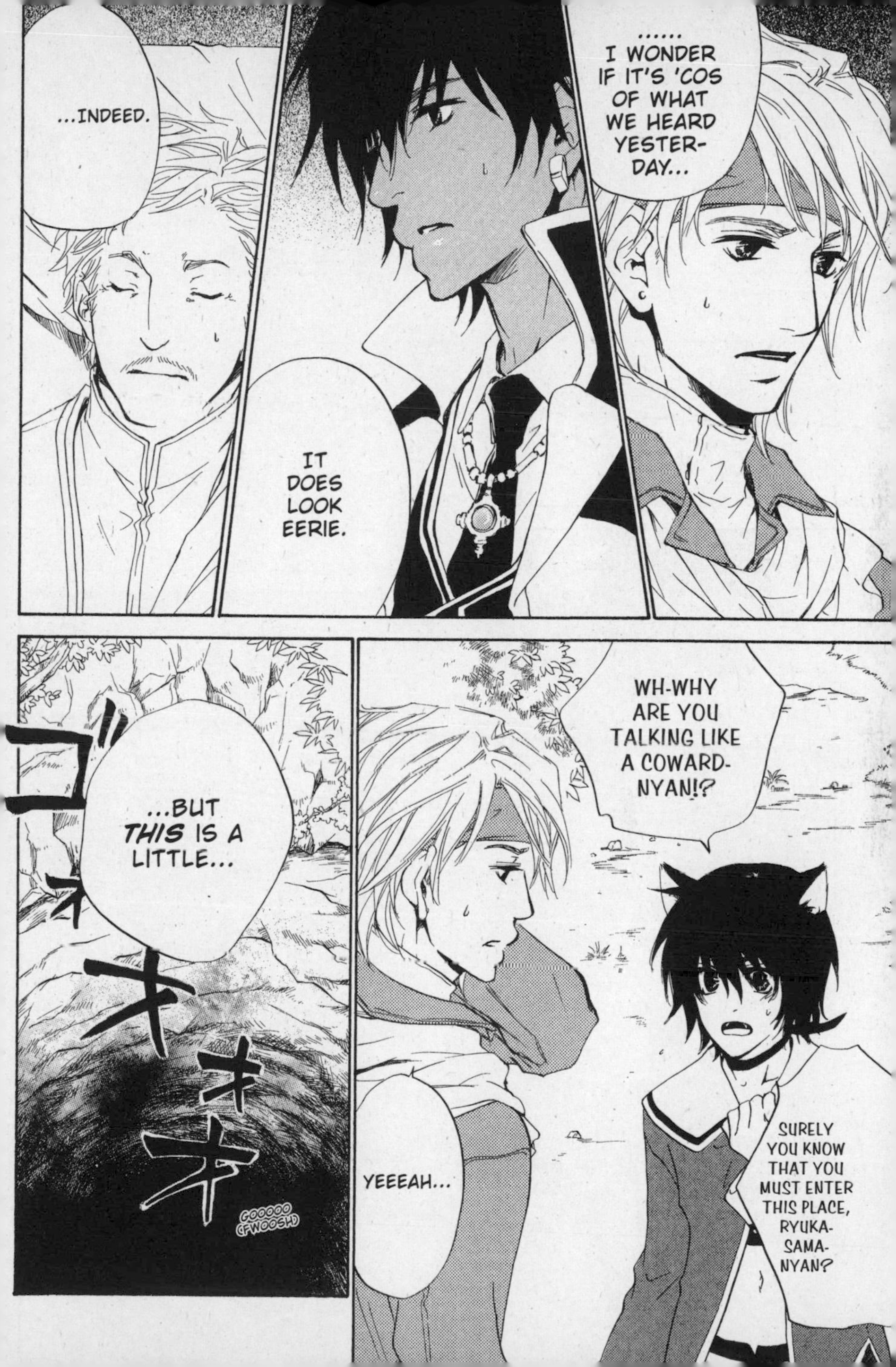
......
I WONDER IF IT'S 'COS OF WHAT WE HEARD YESTERDAY...
IT DOES LOOK EERIE.
...INDEED.
WH-WHY ARE YOU TALKING LIKE A COWARD-NYAN!?
SURELY YOU KNOW THAT YOU MUST ENTER THIS PLACE, RYUKA-SAMA-NYAN?
YEEEAH...
...BUT *THIS* IS A LITTLE...
GOOOOO (FWOOSH)

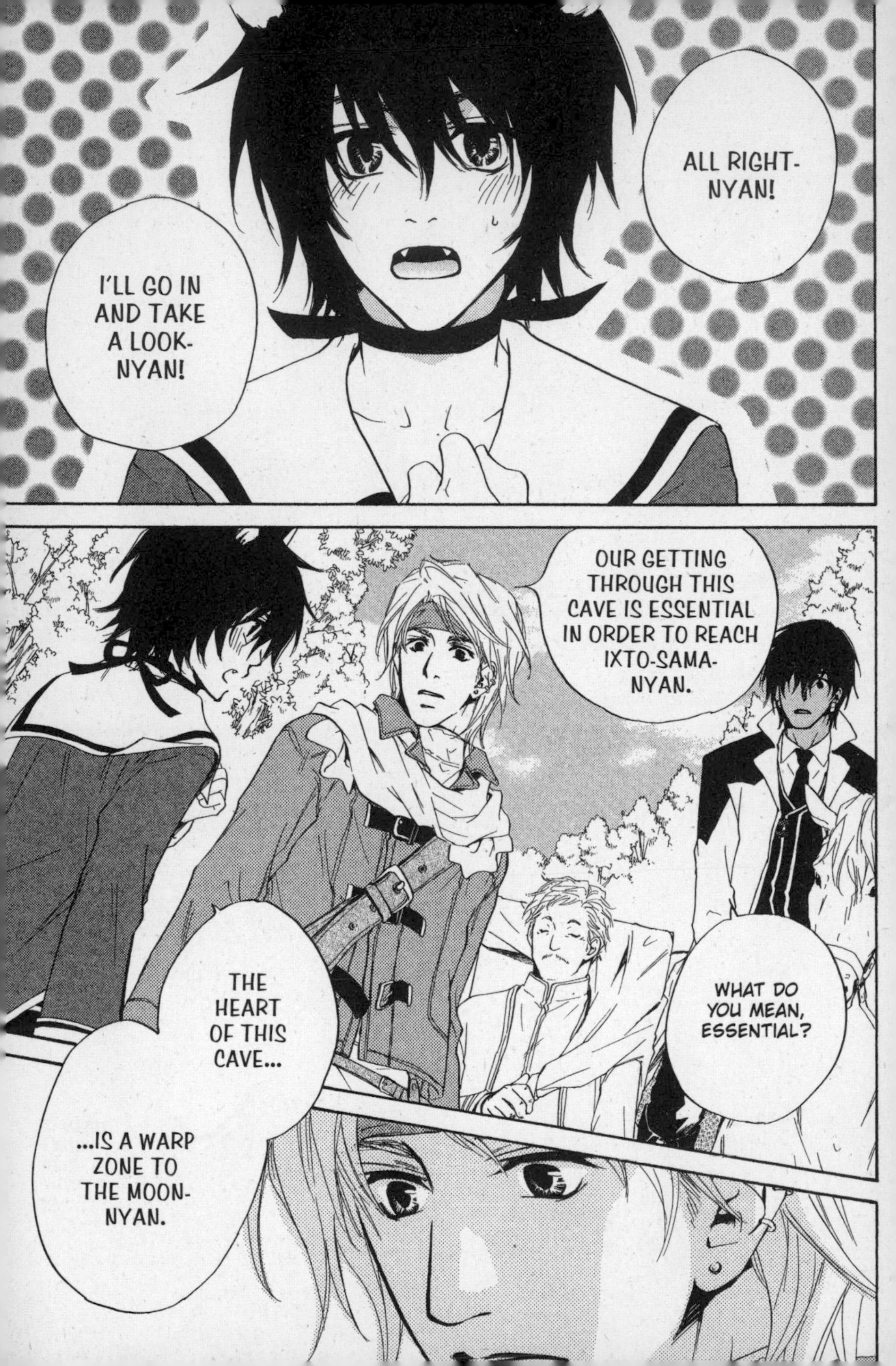
ALL RIGHT-NYAN!
I'LL GO IN AND TAKE A LOOK-NYAN!
OUR GETTING THROUGH THIS CAVE IS ESSENTIAL IN ORDER TO REACH IXTO-SAMA-NYAN.
WHAT DO YOU MEAN, ESSENTIAL?
THE HEART OF THIS CAVE...
...IS A WARP ZONE TO THE MOON-NYAN.

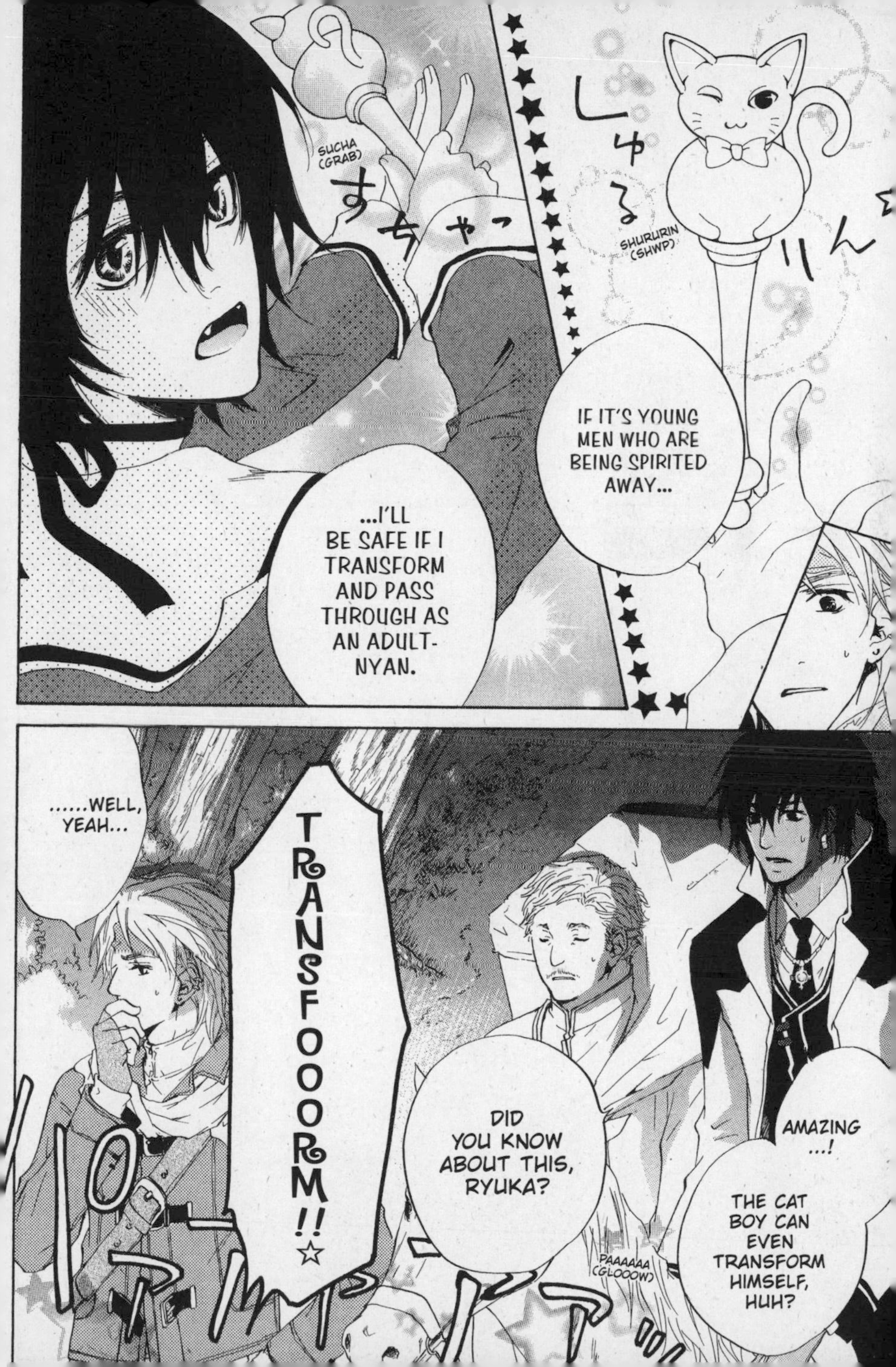
しゅるりん
SHURURIN (SHWP)
IF IT'S YOUNG MEN WHO ARE BEING SPIRITED AWAY...
すちゃっ
SUCHA (GRAB)
...I'LL BE SAFE IF I TRANSFORM AND PASS THROUGH AS AN ADULT-NYAN.
AMAZING...!
THE CAT BOY CAN EVEN TRANSFORM HIMSELF, HUH?
PAAAAAA (GLOOOW)
DID YOU KNOW ABOUT THIS, RYUKA?
TRANSFOOOORM!!☆
......WELL, YEAH...

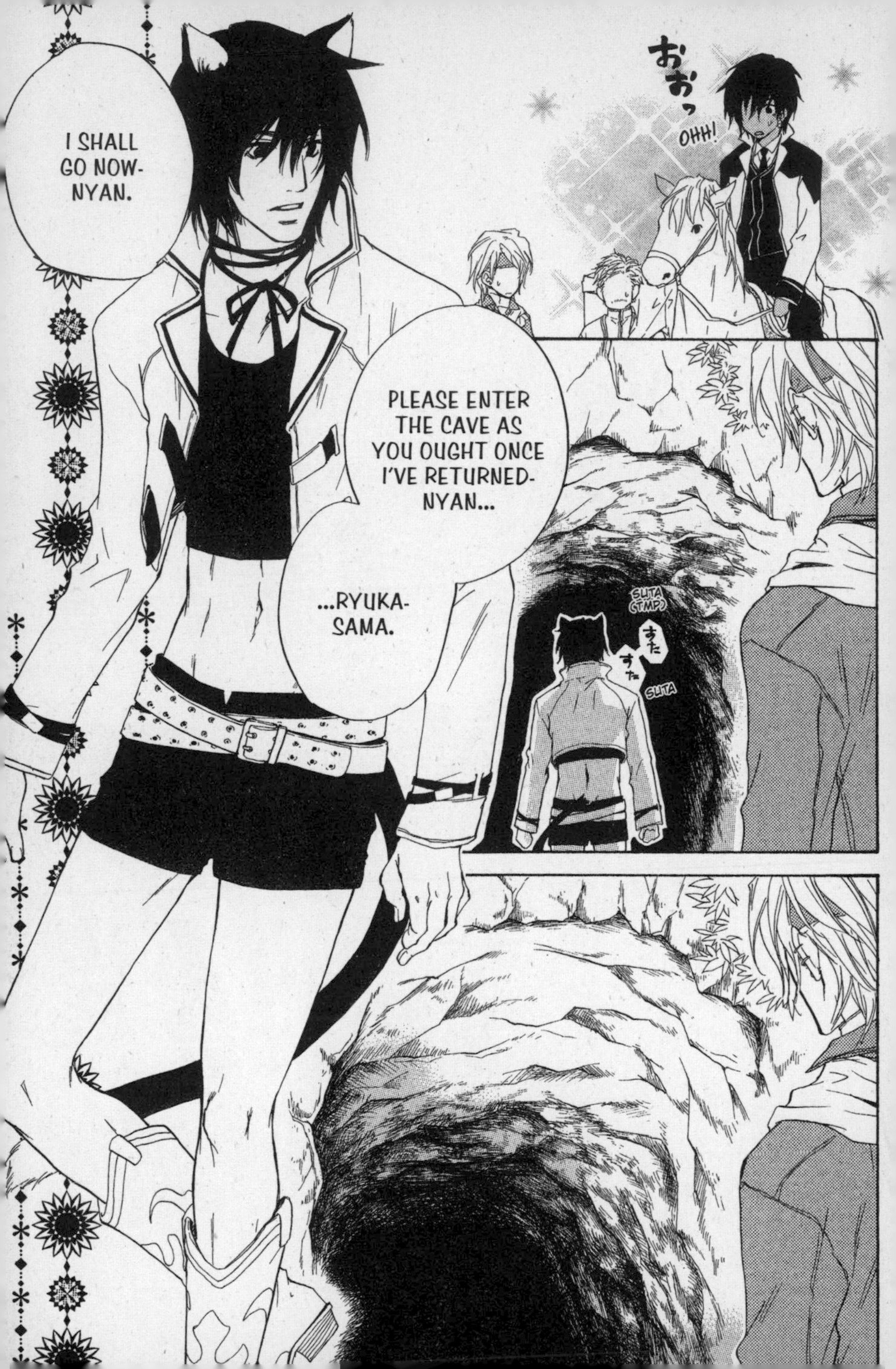
おおっ
OHH!
SUTA (TMP)
すた
すた
SUTA
I SHALL GO NOW-NYAN.
PLEASE ENTER THE CAVE AS YOU OUGHT ONCE I'VE RETURNED-NYAN...
...RYUKA-SAMA.

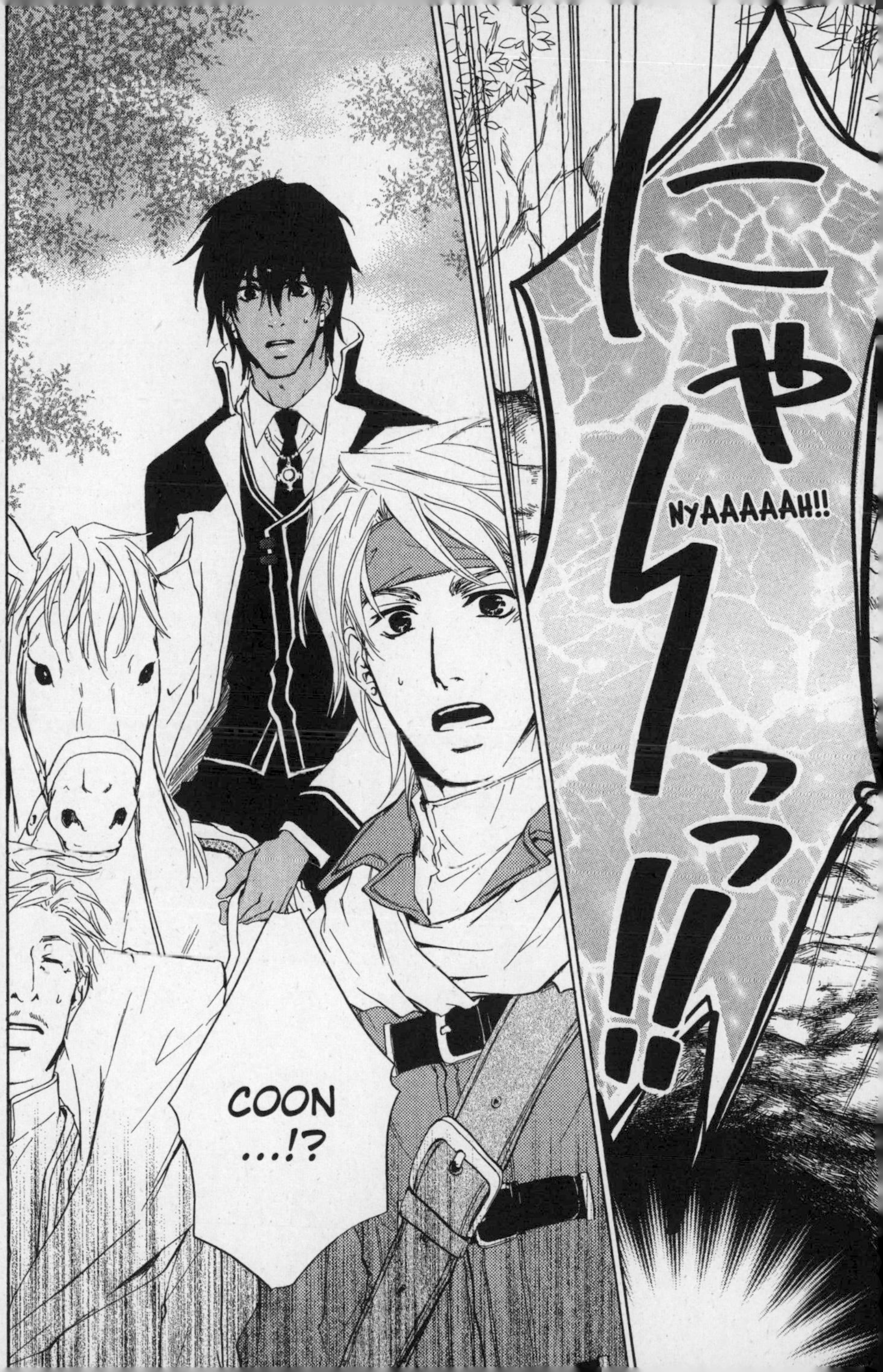
NYAAAAAH!!
COON ...!?

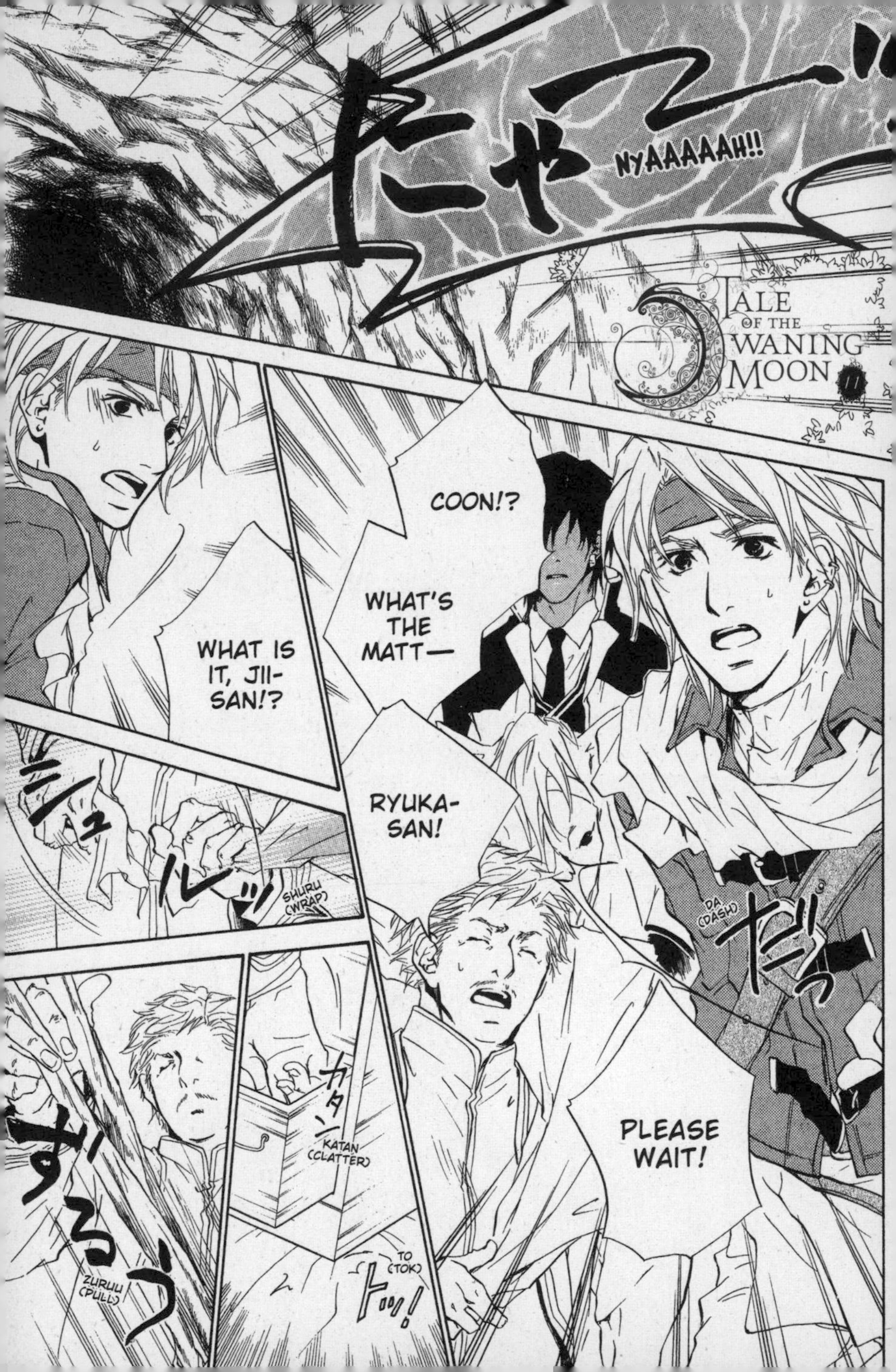

にゃーっ
NYAAAAAH!!
TALE OF THE WANING MOON
11
COON!?
WHAT'S THE MATT—
WHAT IS IT, JII-SAN!?
シュルッ
SHURU (WRAP)
RYUKA-SAN!
だっ
DA (DASH)
PLEASE WAIT!
カタン
KATAN (CLATTER)
トッ!
TO (TOK)
ずるう
ZURUU (PULL)

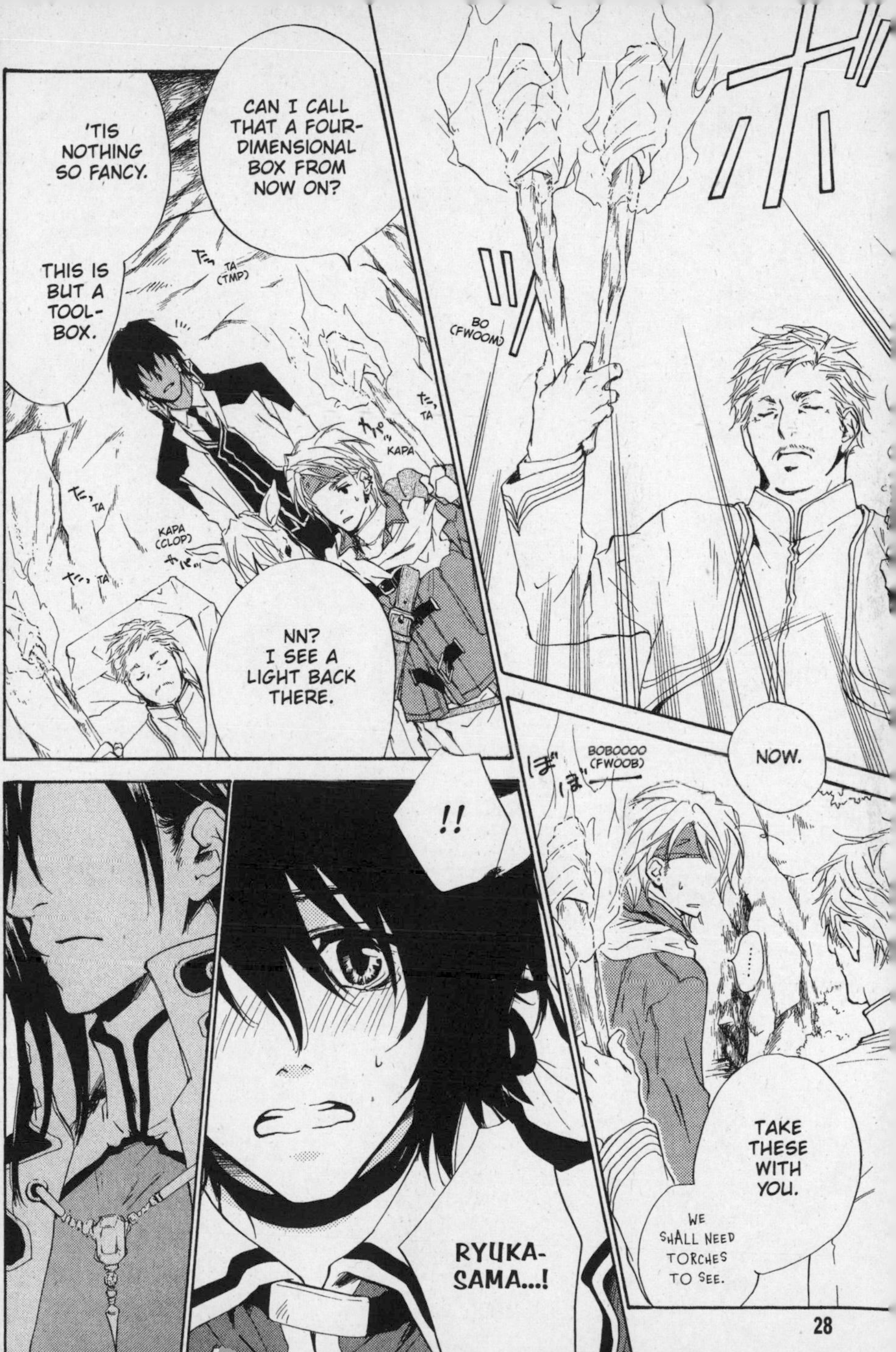
CAN I CALL THAT A FOUR-DIMENSIONAL BOX FROM NOW ON?
'TIS NOTHING SO FANCY.
THIS IS BUT A TOOL-BOX.
TA (TMP)
TA
KAPA
TA
KAPA (CLOP)
TA
NN? I SEE A LIGHT BACK THERE.
BO (FWOOM)
NOW.
BOBOOOO (FWOOB)
...
TAKE THESE WITH YOU.
WE SHALL NEED TORCHES TO SEE.
!!
RYUKA-SAMA...!

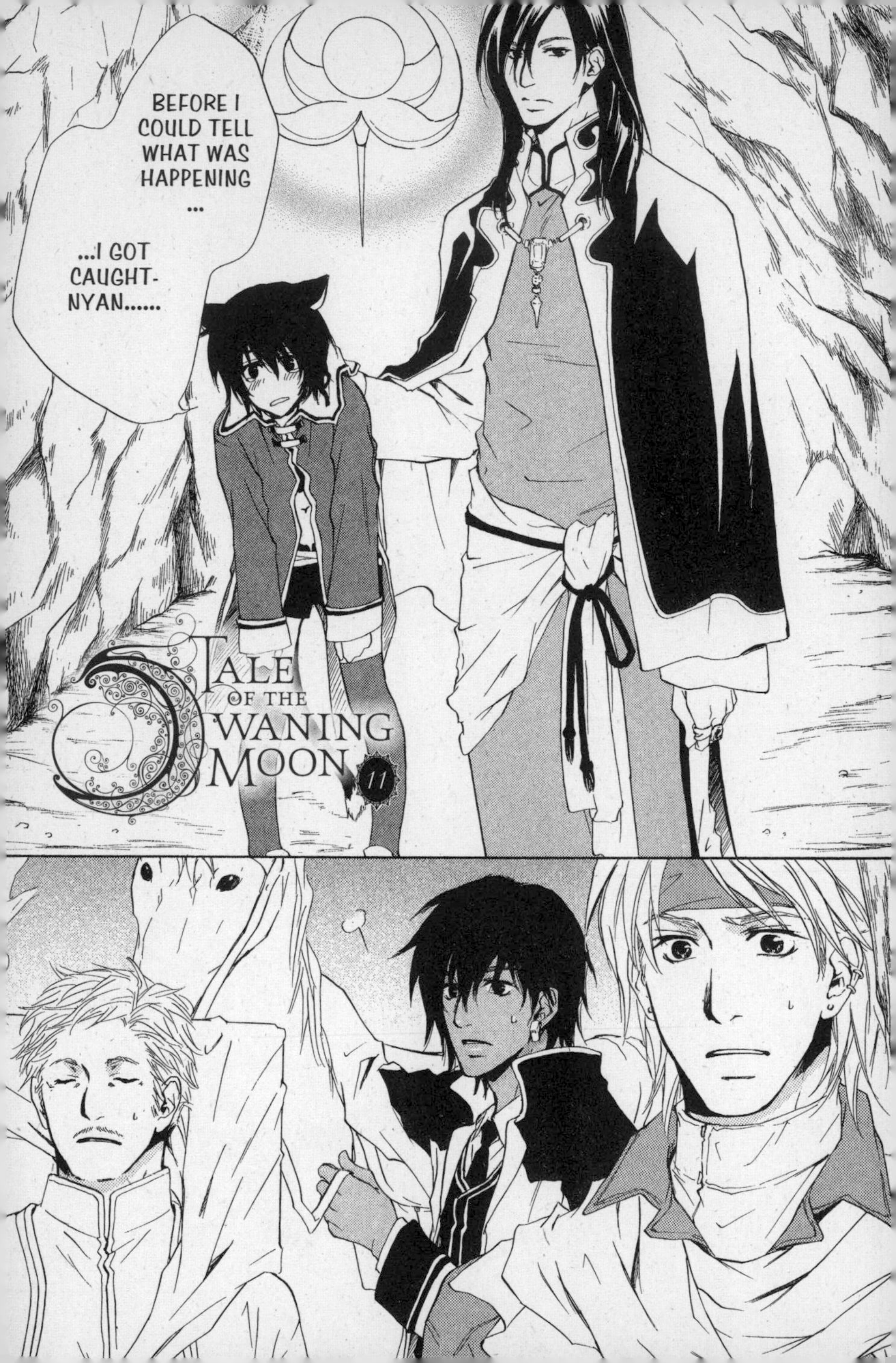
BEFORE I COULD TELL WHAT WAS HAPPENING ...
...I GOT CAUGHT-NYAN......
TALE OF THE WANING MOON 11

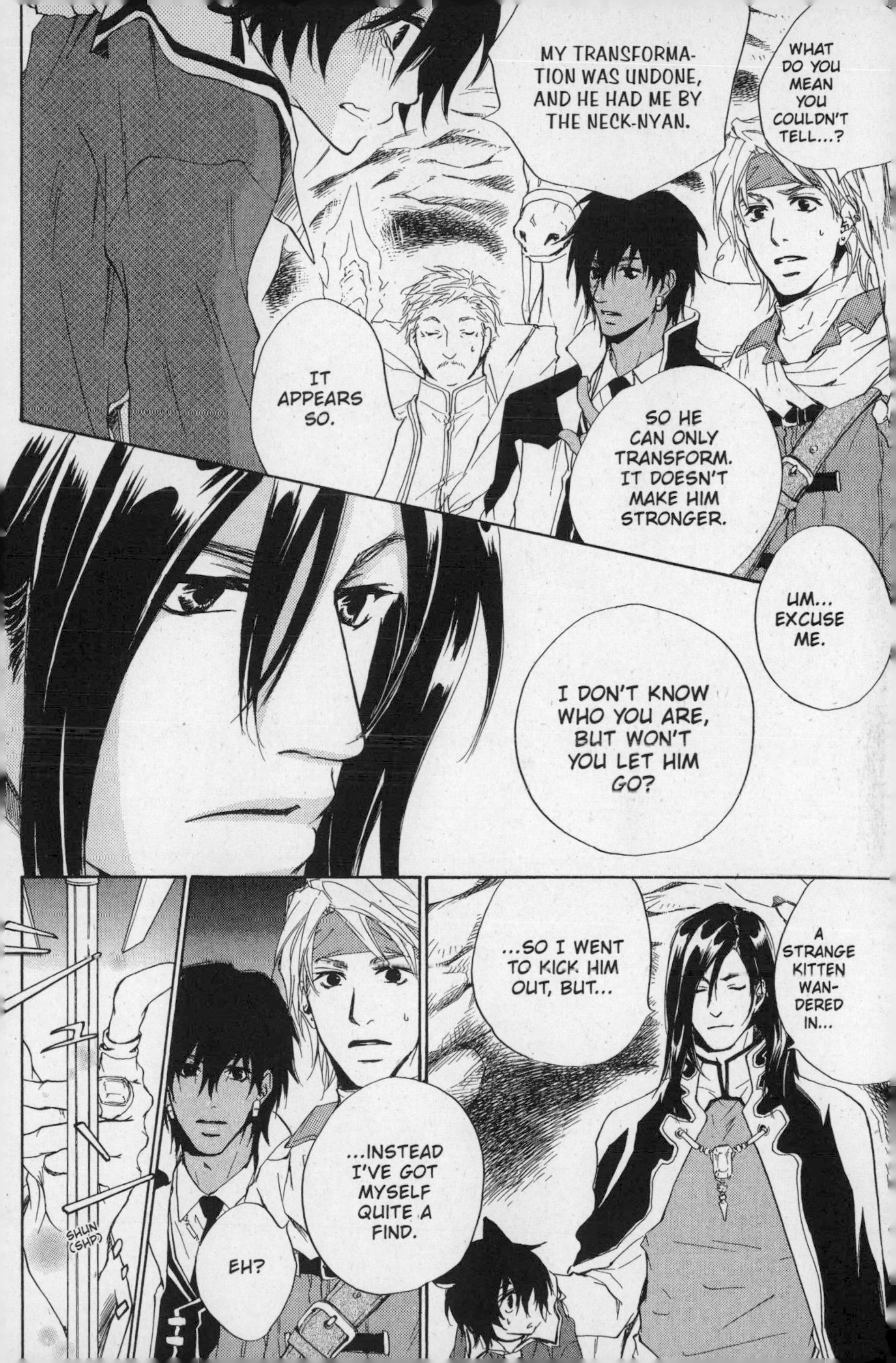

WHAT DO YOU MEAN YOU COULDN'T TELL...?
MY TRANSFORMATION WAS UNDONE, AND HE HAD ME BY THE NECK-NYAN.
SO HE CAN ONLY TRANSFORM. IT DOESN'T MAKE HIM STRONGER.
IT APPEARS SO.
UM... EXCUSE ME.
I DON'T KNOW WHO YOU ARE, BUT WON'T YOU LET HIM GO?
A STRANGE KITTEN WANDERED IN...
...SO I WENT TO KICK HIM OUT, BUT...
...INSTEAD I'VE GOT MYSELF QUITE A FIND.
SHUN (SHP)
EH?

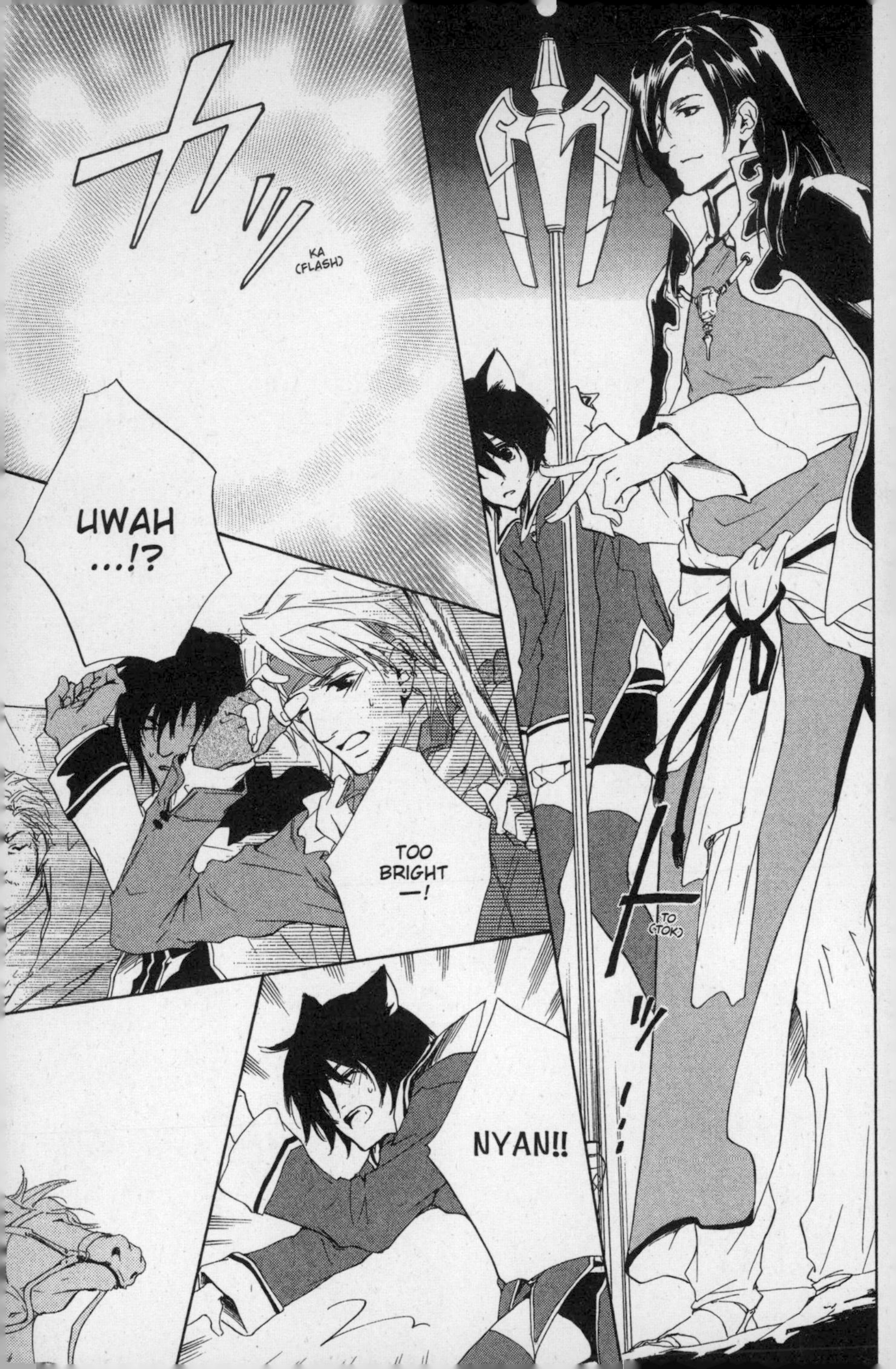
TO (TOK)
KA (FLASH)
UWAH ...!?
TOO BRIGHT—!
NYAN!!

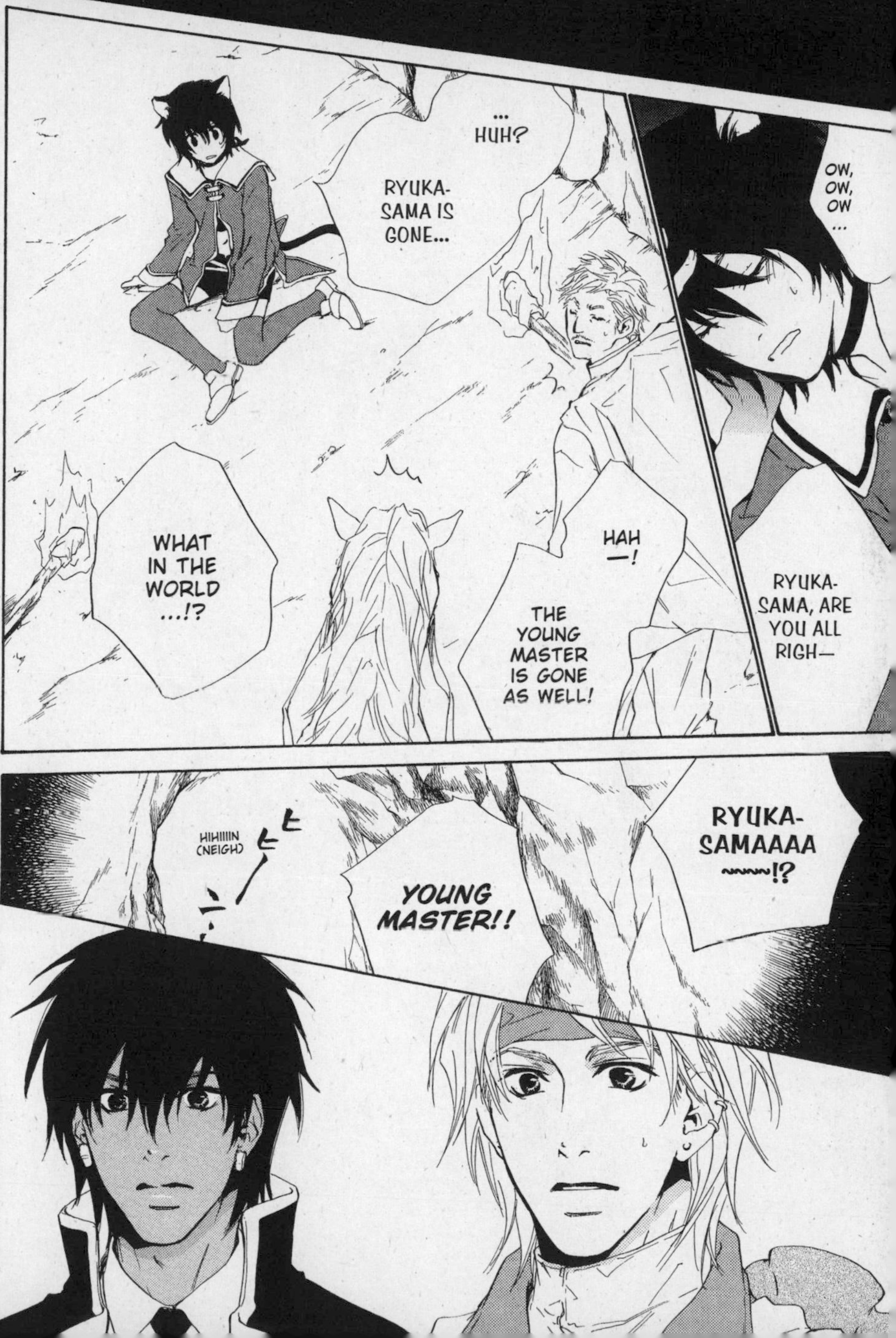
OW, OW, OW ...
RYUKA-SAMA, ARE YOU ALL RIGH—
... HUH?
RYUKA-SAMA IS GONE...
HAH—!
THE YOUNG MASTER IS GONE AS WELL!
WHAT IN THE WORLD ...!?
RYUKA-SAMAAAA ~~~~!?
YOUNG MASTER!!
HIHIIIIN (NEIGH)

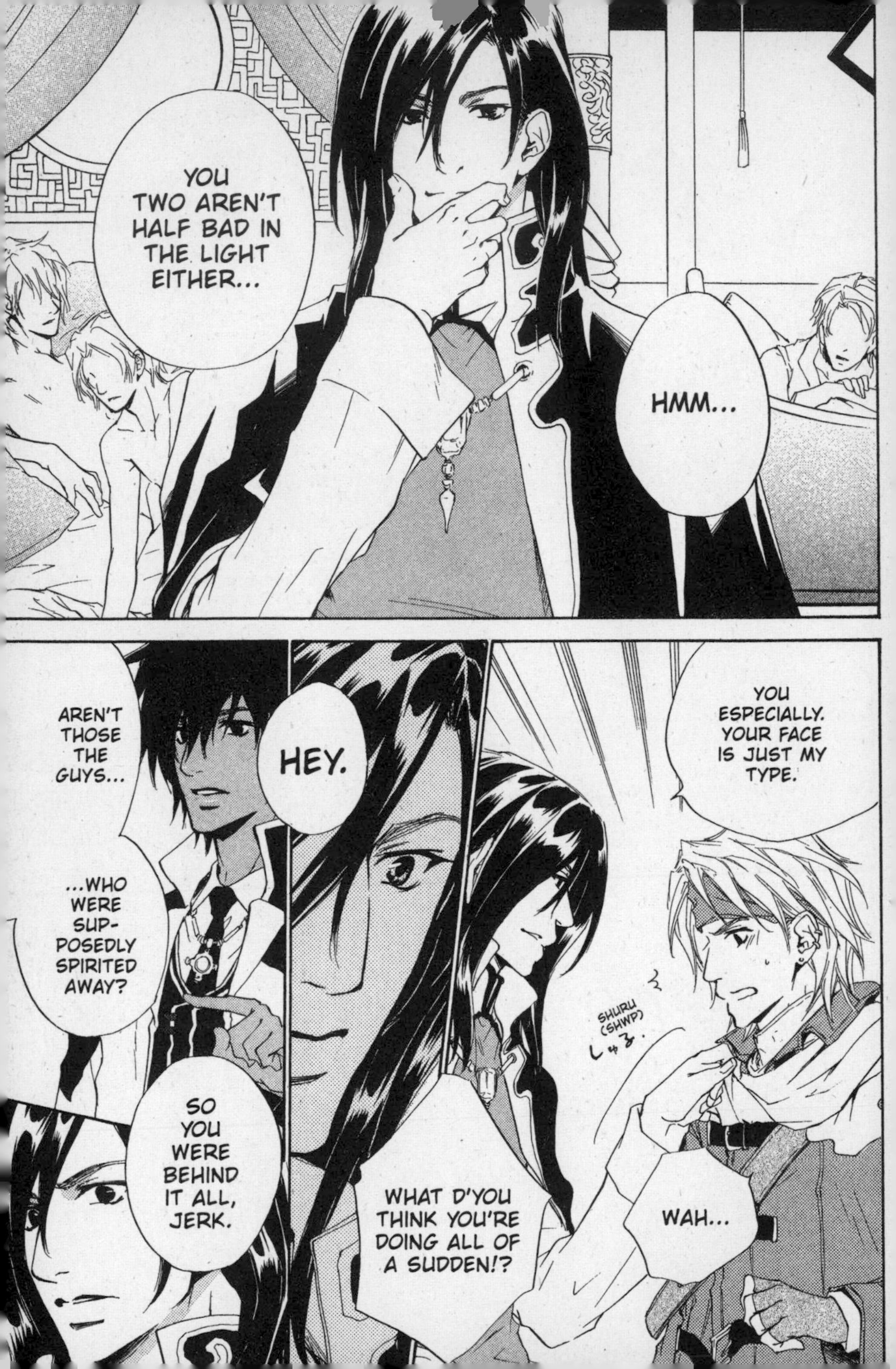
YOU TWO AREN'T HALF BAD IN THE LIGHT EITHER...
HMM...
YOU ESPECIALLY. YOUR FACE IS JUST MY TYPE.
SHURU (SHWP)
しゅる.
WAH...
WHAT D'YOU THINK YOU'RE DOING ALL OF A SUDDEN!?
HEY.
AREN'T THOSE THE GUYS...
...WHO WERE SUP-POSEDLY SPIRITED AWAY?
SO YOU WERE BEHIND IT ALL, JERK.

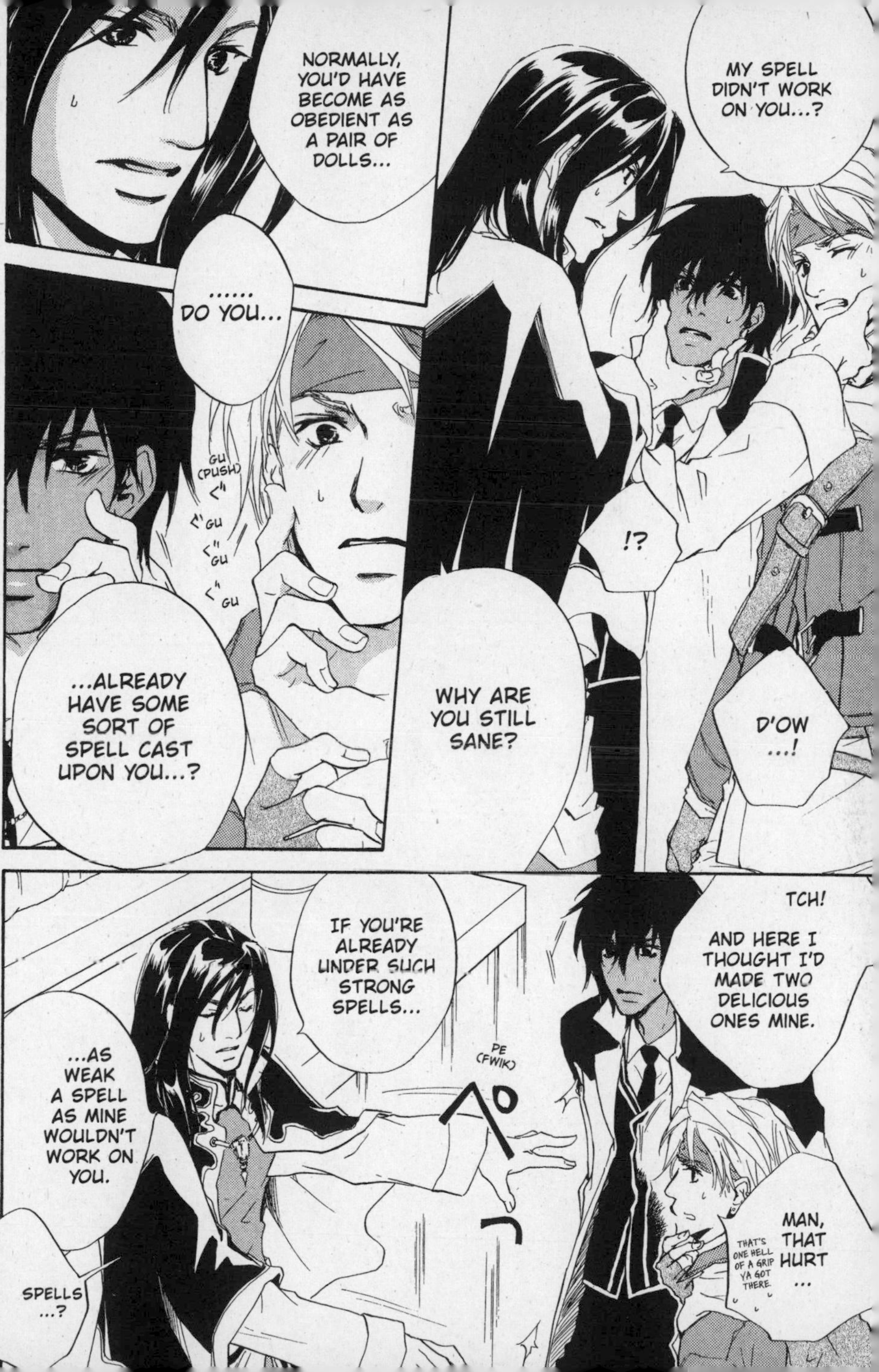
MY SPELL DIDN'T WORK ON YOU...?
!?
D'OW ...!
WHY ARE YOU STILL SANE?
NORMALLY, YOU'D HAVE BECOME AS OBEDIENT AS A PAIR OF DOLLS...
...... DO YOU...
GU (PUSH)
GU
GU
GU
...ALREADY HAVE SOME SORT OF SPELL CAST UPON YOU...?
TCH!
AND HERE I THOUGHT I'D MADE TWO DELICIOUS ONES MINE.
MAN, THAT HURT ...
THAT'S ONE HELL OF A GRIP YA GOT THERE.
IF YOU'RE ALREADY UNDER SUCH STRONG SPELLS...
PE (FWIK)
...AS WEAK A SPELL AS MINE WOULDN'T WORK ON YOU.
SPELLS ...?

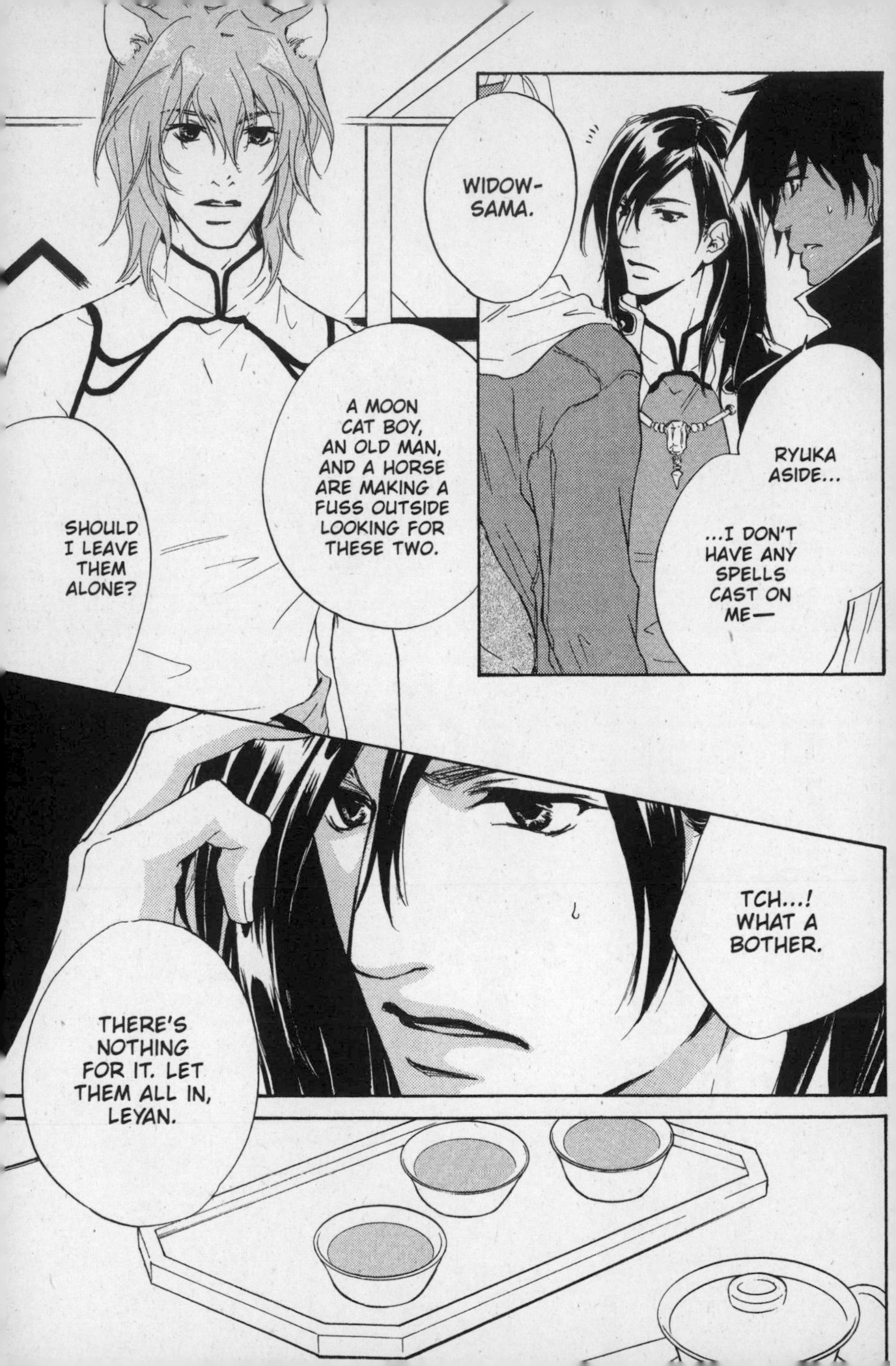
WIDOW-SAMA.
RYUKA ASIDE...
...I DON'T HAVE ANY SPELLS CAST ON ME—
A MOON CAT BOY, AN OLD MAN, AND A HORSE ARE MAKING A FUSS OUTSIDE LOOKING FOR THESE TWO.
SHOULD I LEAVE THEM ALONE?
TCH...! WHAT A BOTHER.
THERE'S NOTHING FOR IT. LET THEM ALL IN, LEYAN.

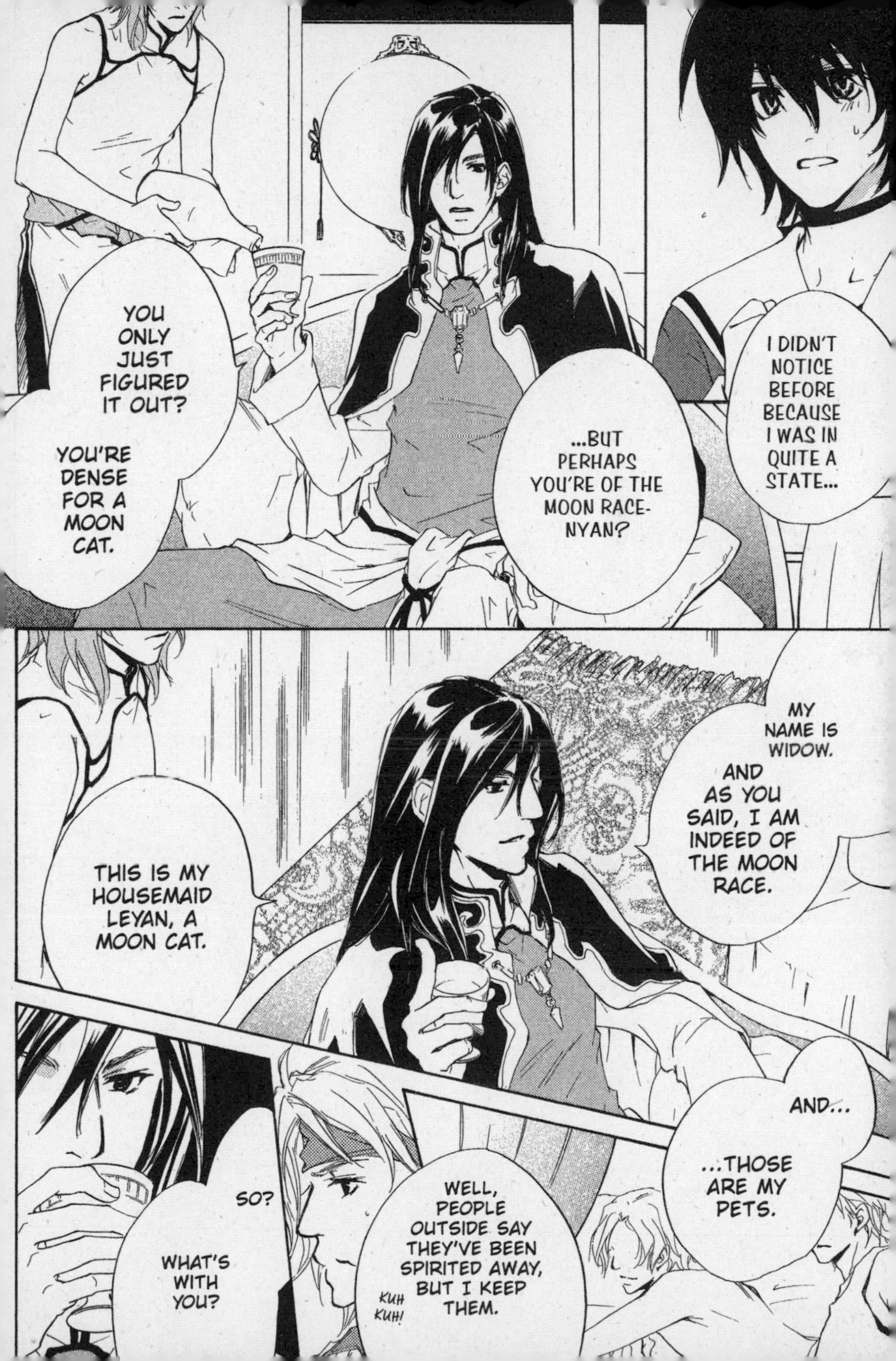
I DIDN'T NOTICE BEFORE BECAUSE I WAS IN QUITE A STATE...
...BUT PERHAPS YOU'RE OF THE MOON RACE-NYAN?
YOU ONLY JUST FIGURED IT OUT?
YOU'RE DENSE FOR A MOON CAT.
MY NAME IS WIDOW.
AND AS YOU SAID, I AM INDEED OF THE MOON RACE.
THIS IS MY HOUSEMAID LEYAN, A MOON CAT.
AND...
...THOSE ARE MY PETS.
WELL, PEOPLE OUTSIDE SAY THEY'VE BEEN SPIRITED AWAY, BUT I KEEP THEM.
KUH KUH!
SO?
WHAT'S WITH YOU?

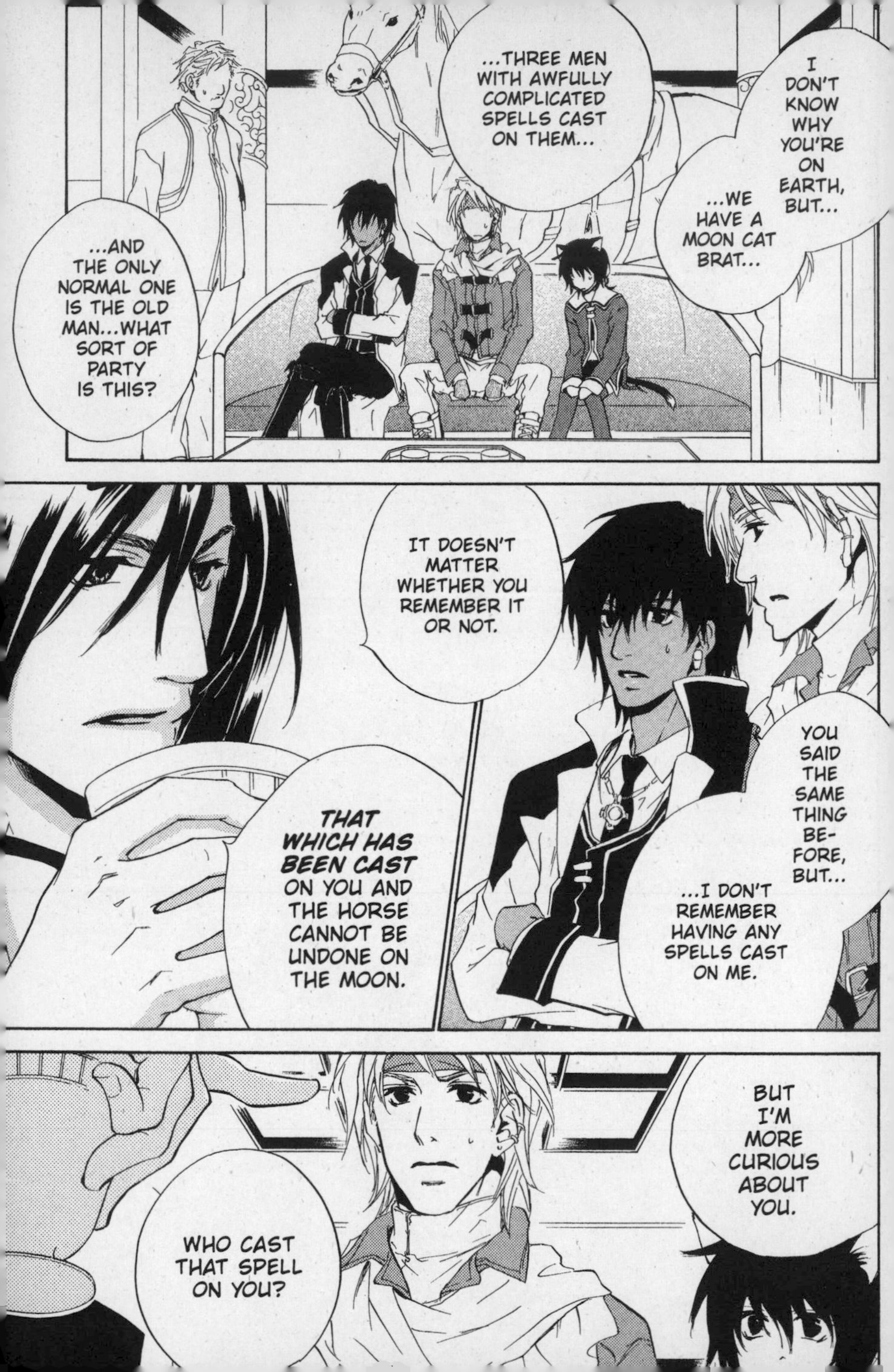
I DON'T KNOW WHY YOU'RE ON EARTH, BUT...
...WE HAVE A MOON CAT BRAT...
...THREE MEN WITH AWFULLY COMPLICATED SPELLS CAST ON THEM...
...AND THE ONLY NORMAL ONE IS THE OLD MAN...WHAT SORT OF PARTY IS THIS?
YOU SAID THE SAME THING BEFORE, BUT...
...I DON'T REMEMBER HAVING ANY SPELLS CAST ON ME.
IT DOESN'T MATTER WHETHER YOU REMEMBER IT OR NOT.
THAT WHICH HAS BEEN CAST ON YOU AND THE HORSE CANNOT BE UNDONE ON THE MOON.
BUT I'M MORE CURIOUS ABOUT YOU.
WHO CAST THAT SPELL ON YOU?

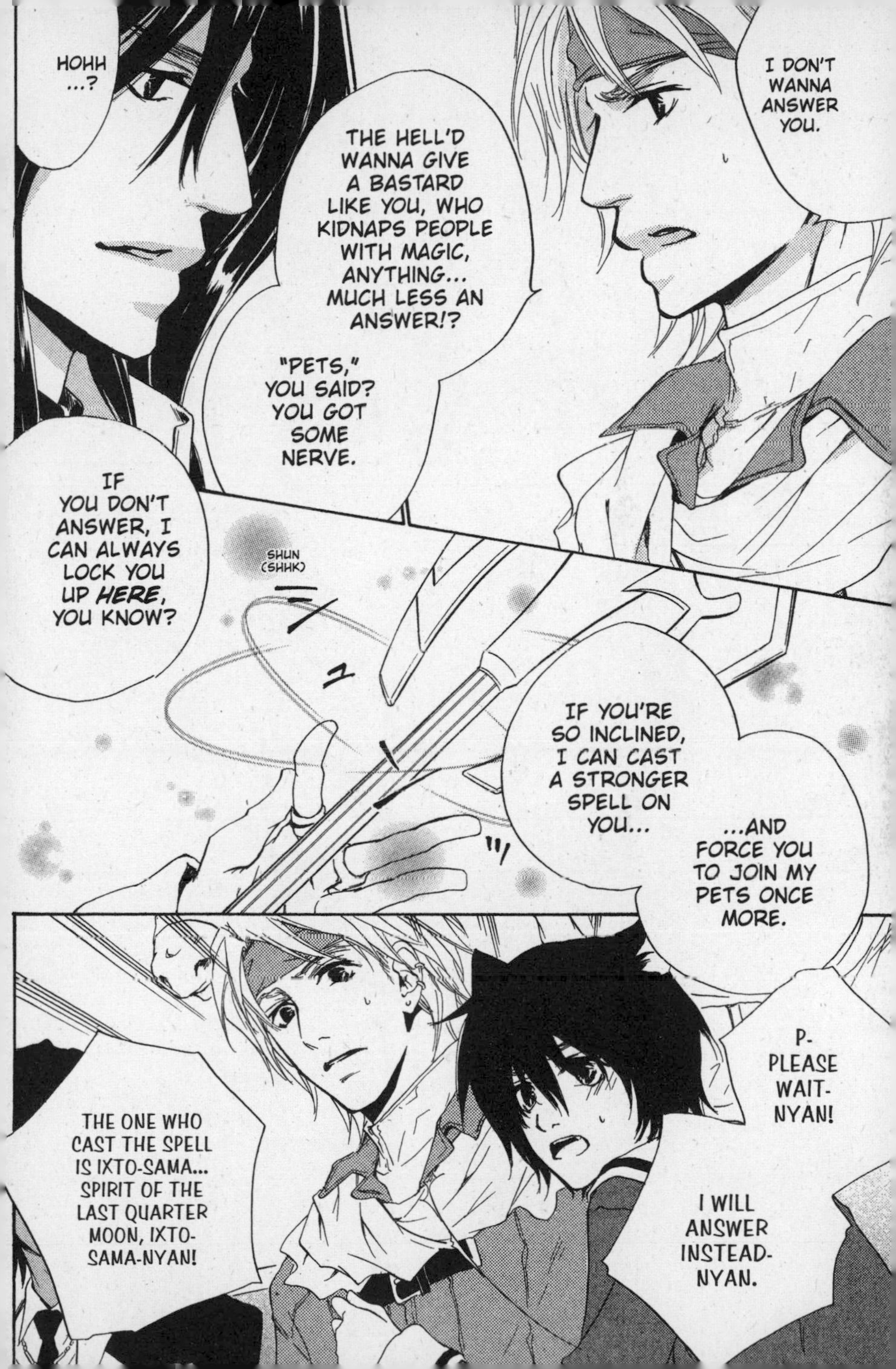
I DON'T WANNA ANSWER YOU.
HOHH ...?
THE HELL'D WANNA GIVE A BASTARD LIKE YOU, WHO KIDNAPS PEOPLE WITH MAGIC, ANYTHING... MUCH LESS AN ANSWER!?
"PETS," YOU SAID? YOU GOT SOME NERVE.
IF YOU DON'T ANSWER, I CAN ALWAYS LOCK YOU UP *HERE*, YOU KNOW?
SHUN (SHHK)
IF YOU'RE SO INCLINED, I CAN CAST A STRONGER SPELL ON YOU...
...AND FORCE YOU TO JOIN MY PETS ONCE MORE.
P- PLEASE WAIT-NYAN!
I WILL ANSWER INSTEAD-NYAN.
THE ONE WHO CAST THE SPELL IS IXTO-SAMA... SPIRIT OF THE LAST QUARTER MOON, IXTO-SAMA-NYAN!

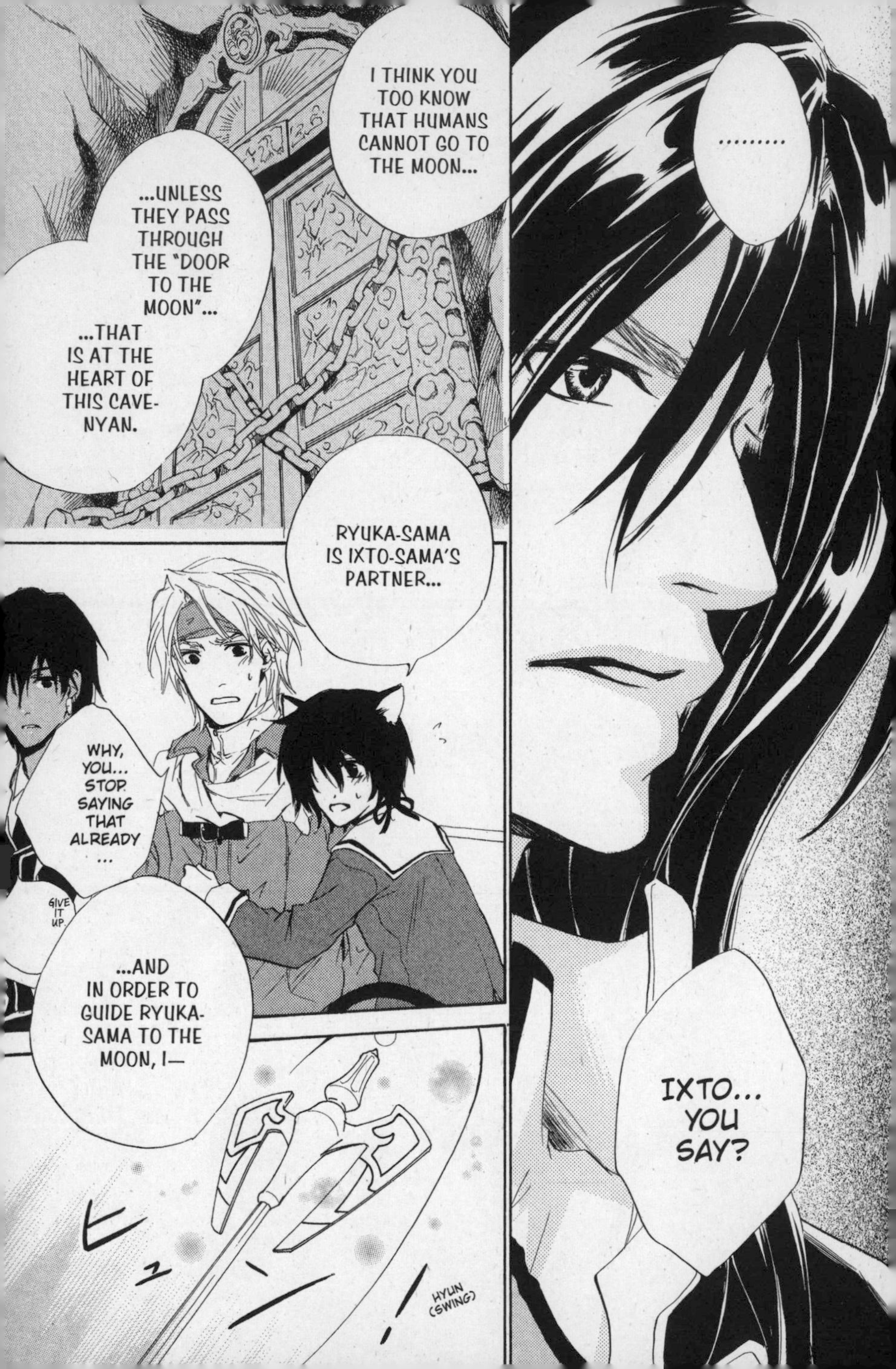
....
IXTO... YOU SAY?
I THINK YOU TOO KNOW THAT HUMANS CANNOT GO TO THE MOON...
...UNLESS THEY PASS THROUGH THE "DOOR TO THE MOON"...
...THAT IS AT THE HEART OF THIS CAVE-NYAN.
RYUKA-SAMA IS IXTO-SAMA'S PARTNER...
WHY, YOU... STOP SAYING THAT ALREADY...
GIVE IT UP.
...AND IN ORDER TO GUIDE RYUKA-SAMA TO THE MOON, I—
HYUN (SWING)

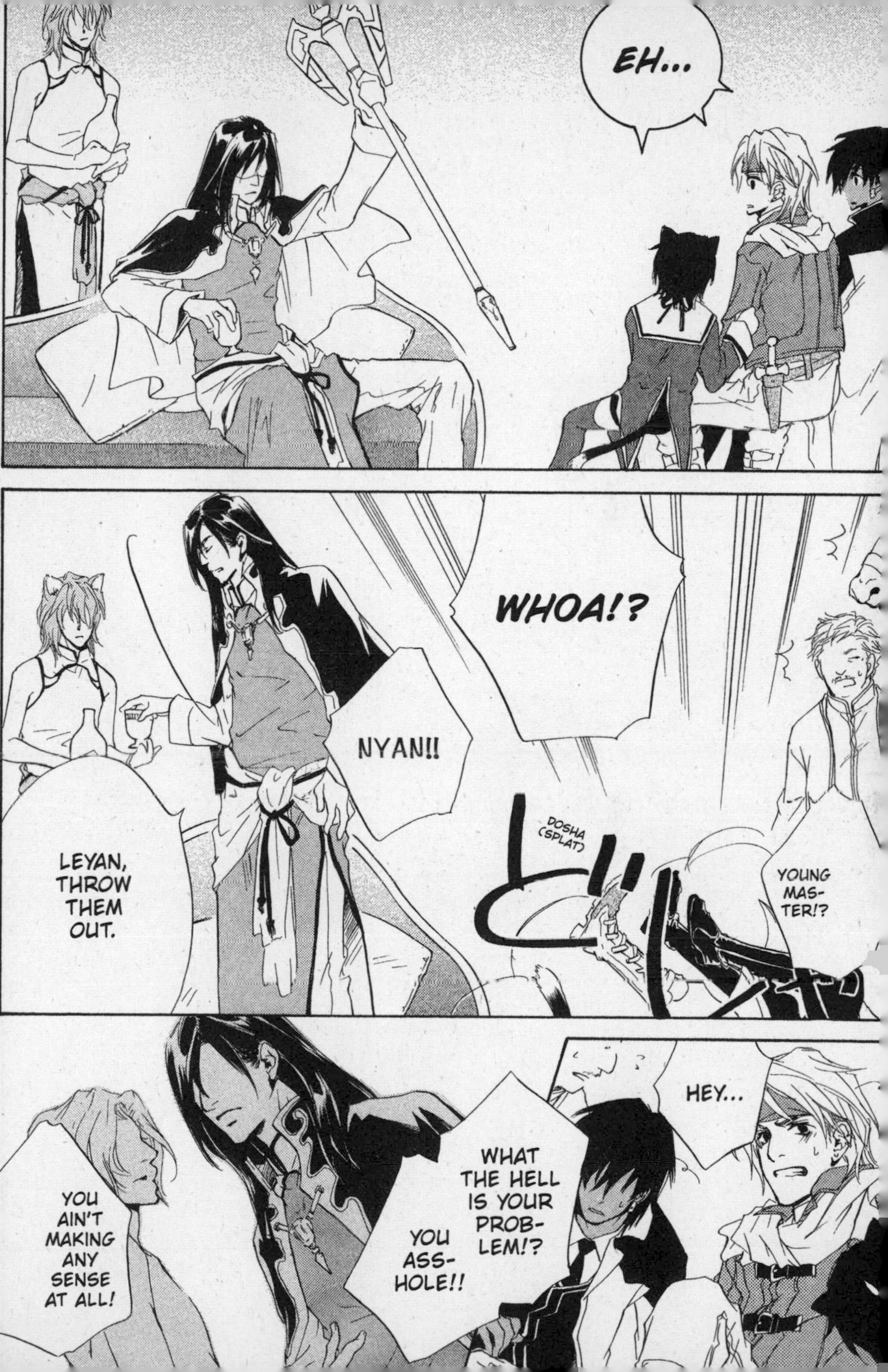
EH...
WHOA!?
YOUNG MASTER!?
DOSHA (SPLAT)
NYAN!!
LEYAN, THROW THEM OUT.
HEY...
WHAT THE HELL IS YOUR PROBLEM!?
YOU ASSHOLE!!
YOU AIN'T MAKING ANY SENSE AT ALL!

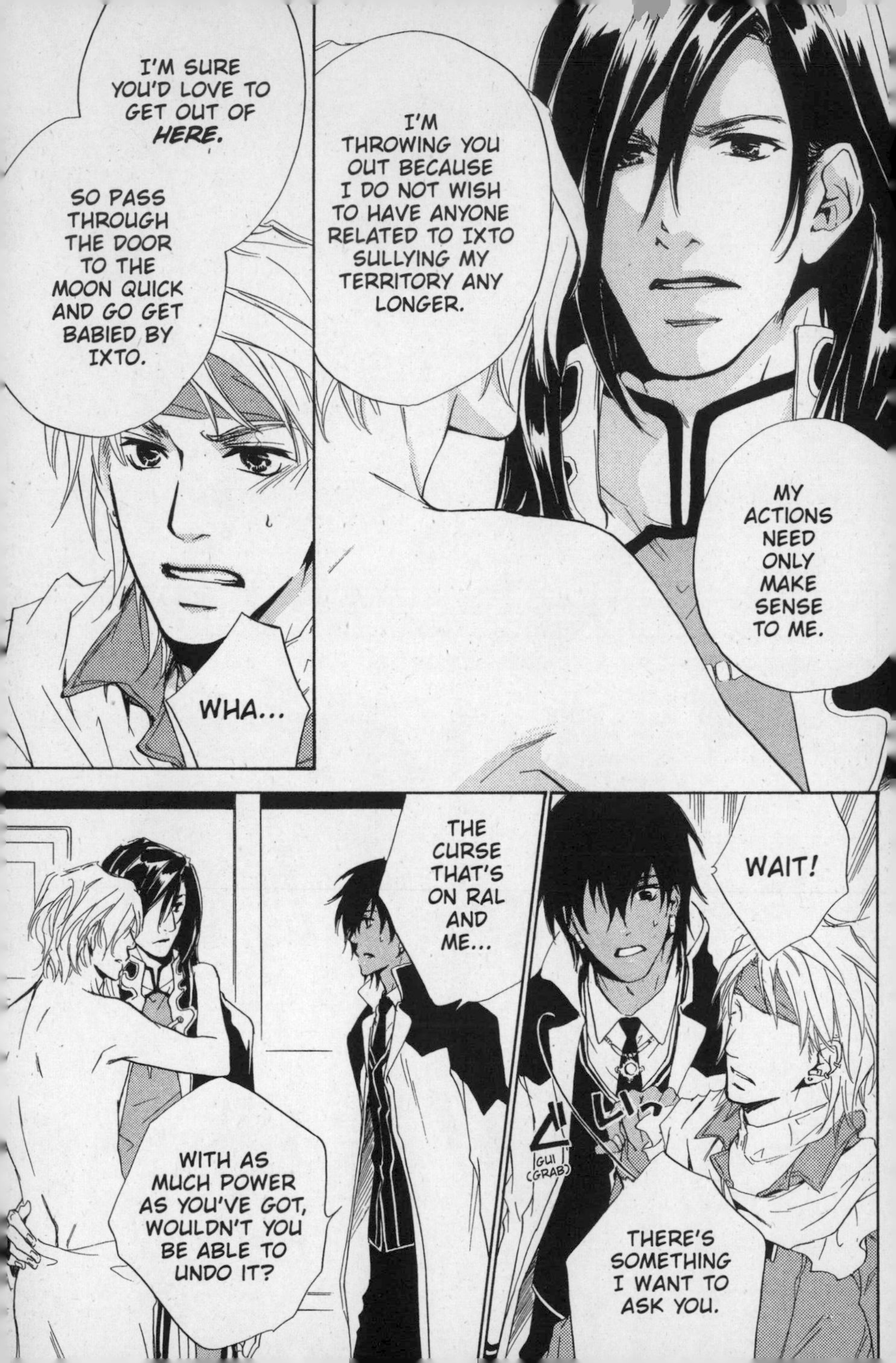
I'M THROWING YOU OUT BECAUSE I DO NOT WISH TO HAVE ANYONE RELATED TO IXTO SULLYING MY TERRITORY ANY LONGER.
MY ACTIONS NEED ONLY MAKE SENSE TO ME.
I'M SURE YOU'D LOVE TO GET OUT OF *HERE.*
SO PASS THROUGH THE DOOR TO THE MOON QUICK AND GO GET BABIED BY IXTO.
WHA...
WAIT!
GUI (GRAB)
THERE'S SOMETHING I WANT TO ASK YOU.
THE CURSE THAT'S ON RAL AND ME...
WITH AS MUCH POWER AS YOU'VE GOT, WOULDN'T YOU BE ABLE TO UNDO IT?

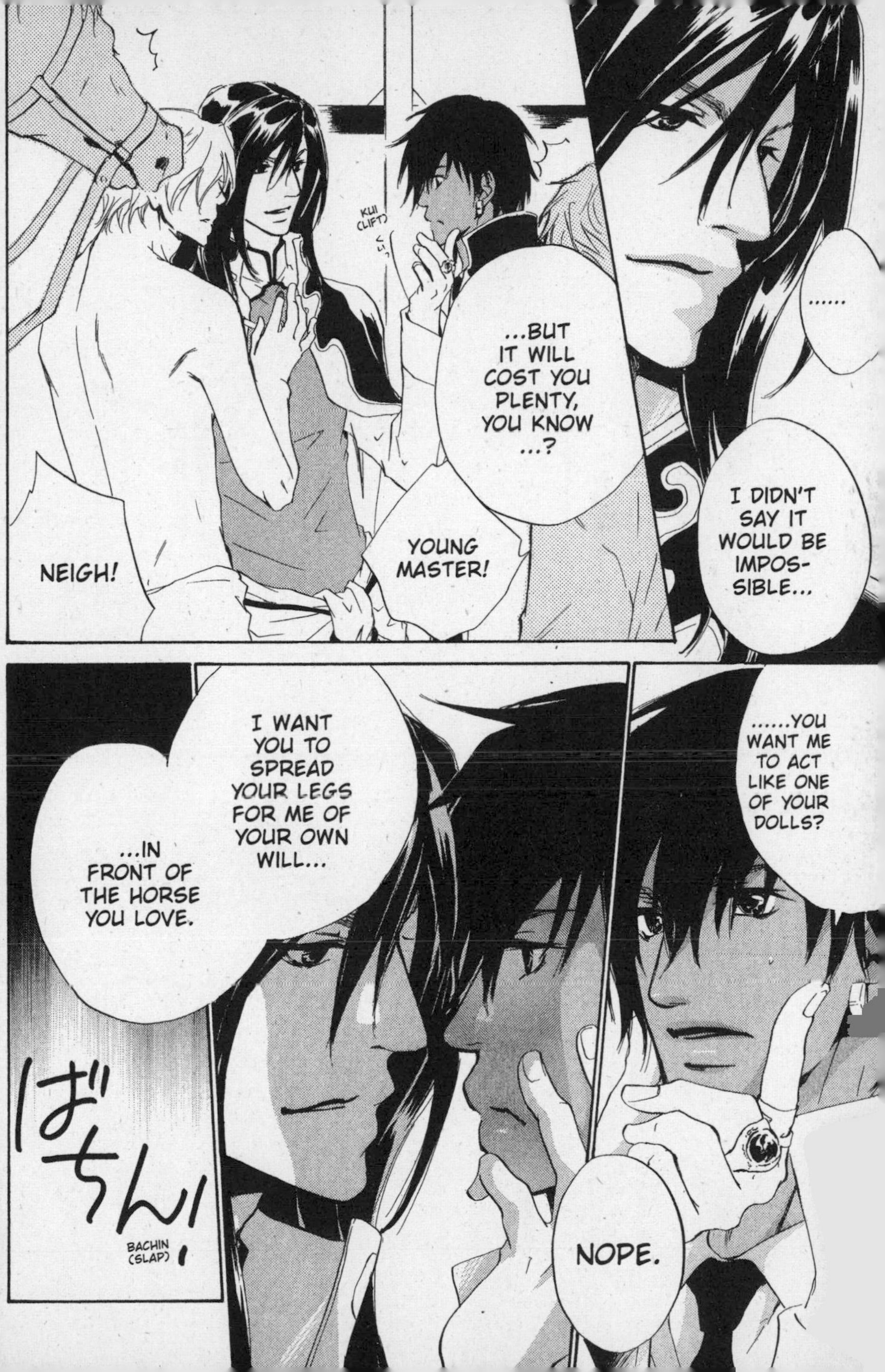
......
I DIDN'T SAY IT WOULD BE IMPOSSIBLE...
...BUT IT WILL COST YOU PLENTY, YOU KNOW...?
KUI (LIFT)
YOUNG MASTER!
NEIGH!
......YOU WANT ME TO ACT LIKE ONE OF YOUR DOLLS?
NOPE.
I WANT YOU TO SPREAD YOUR LEGS FOR ME OF YOUR OWN WILL...
...IN FRONT OF THE HORSE YOU LOVE.
ばちん!
BACHIN (SLAP)

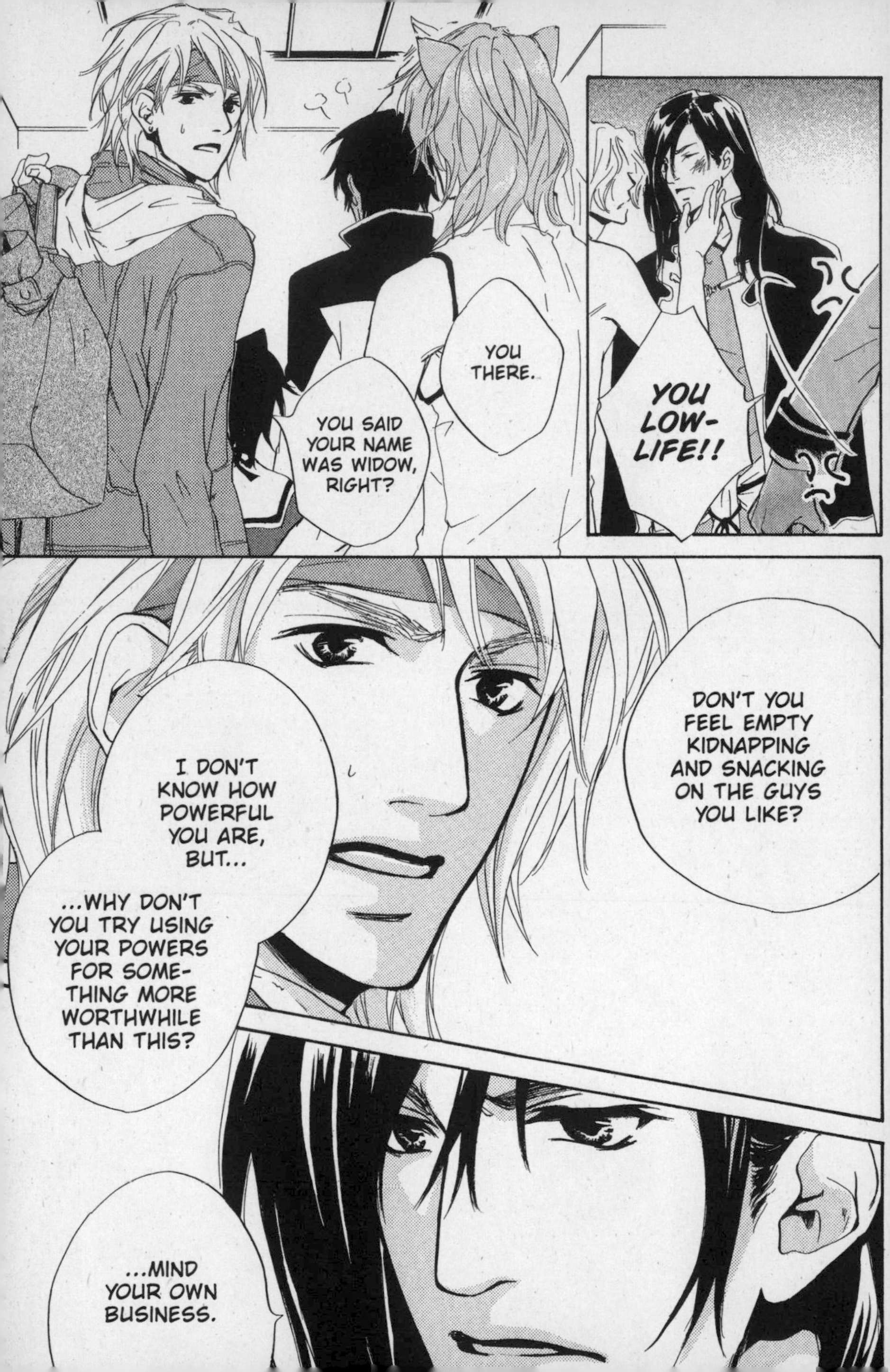
YOU LOW-LIFE!!
YOU THERE.
YOU SAID YOUR NAME WAS WIDOW, RIGHT?
DON'T YOU FEEL EMPTY KIDNAPPING AND SNACKING ON THE GUYS YOU LIKE?
I DON'T KNOW HOW POWERFUL YOU ARE, BUT...
...WHY DON'T YOU TRY USING YOUR POWERS FOR SOME-THING MORE WORTHWHILE THAN THIS?
...MIND YOUR OWN BUSINESS.

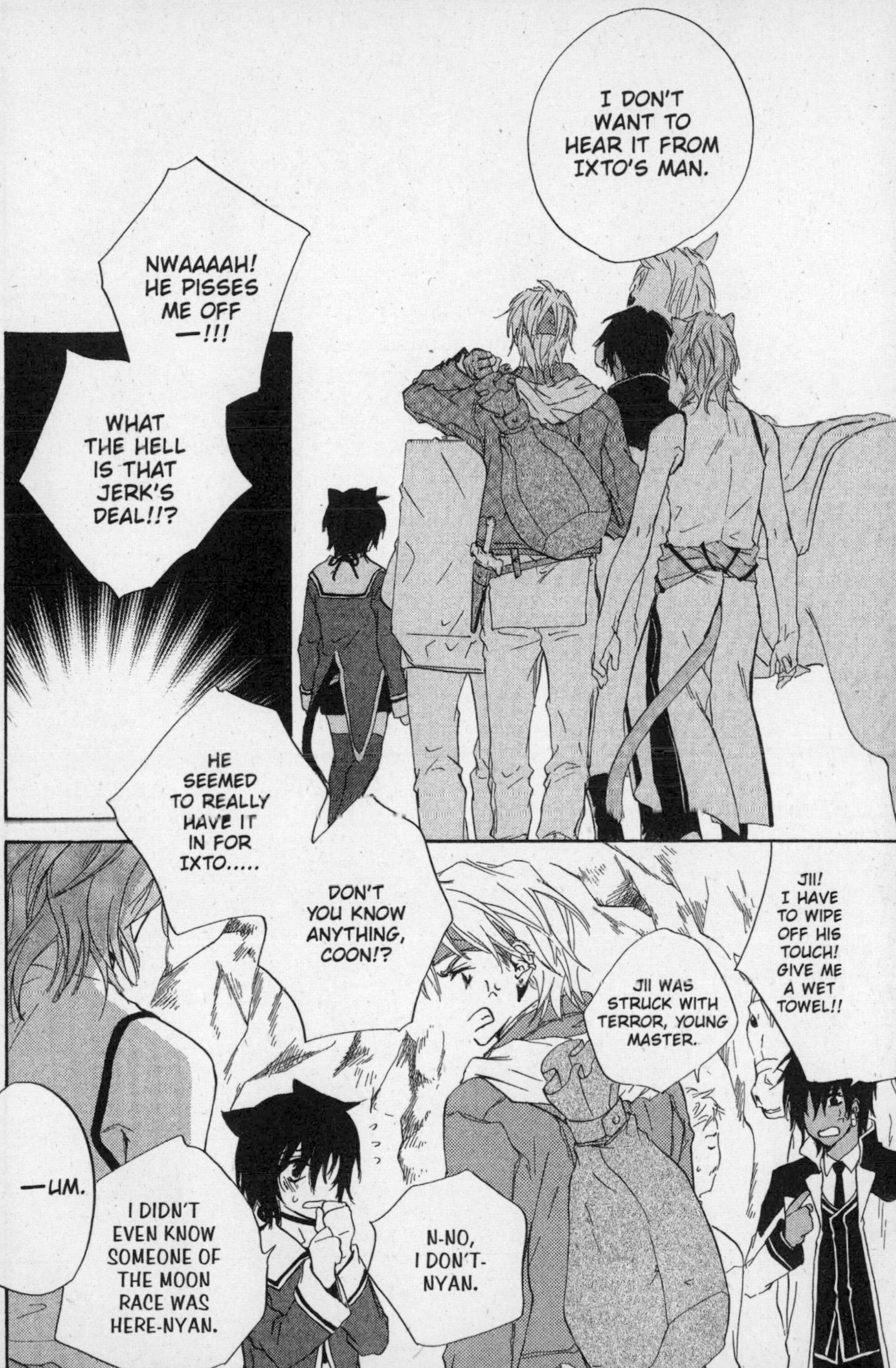
I DON'T WANT TO HEAR IT FROM IXTO'S MAN.
NWAAAAH! HE PISSES ME OFF—!!!
WHAT THE HELL IS THAT JERK'S DEAL!!?
JII! I HAVE TO WIPE OFF HIS TOUCH! GIVE ME A WET TOWEL!!
JII WAS STRUCK WITH TERROR, YOUNG MASTER.
HE SEEMED TO REALLY HAVE IT IN FOR IXTO.....
DON'T YOU KNOW ANYTHING, COON!?
N-NO, I DON'T-NYAN.
—UM.
I DIDN'T EVEN KNOW SOMEONE OF THE MOON RACE WAS HERE-NYAN.

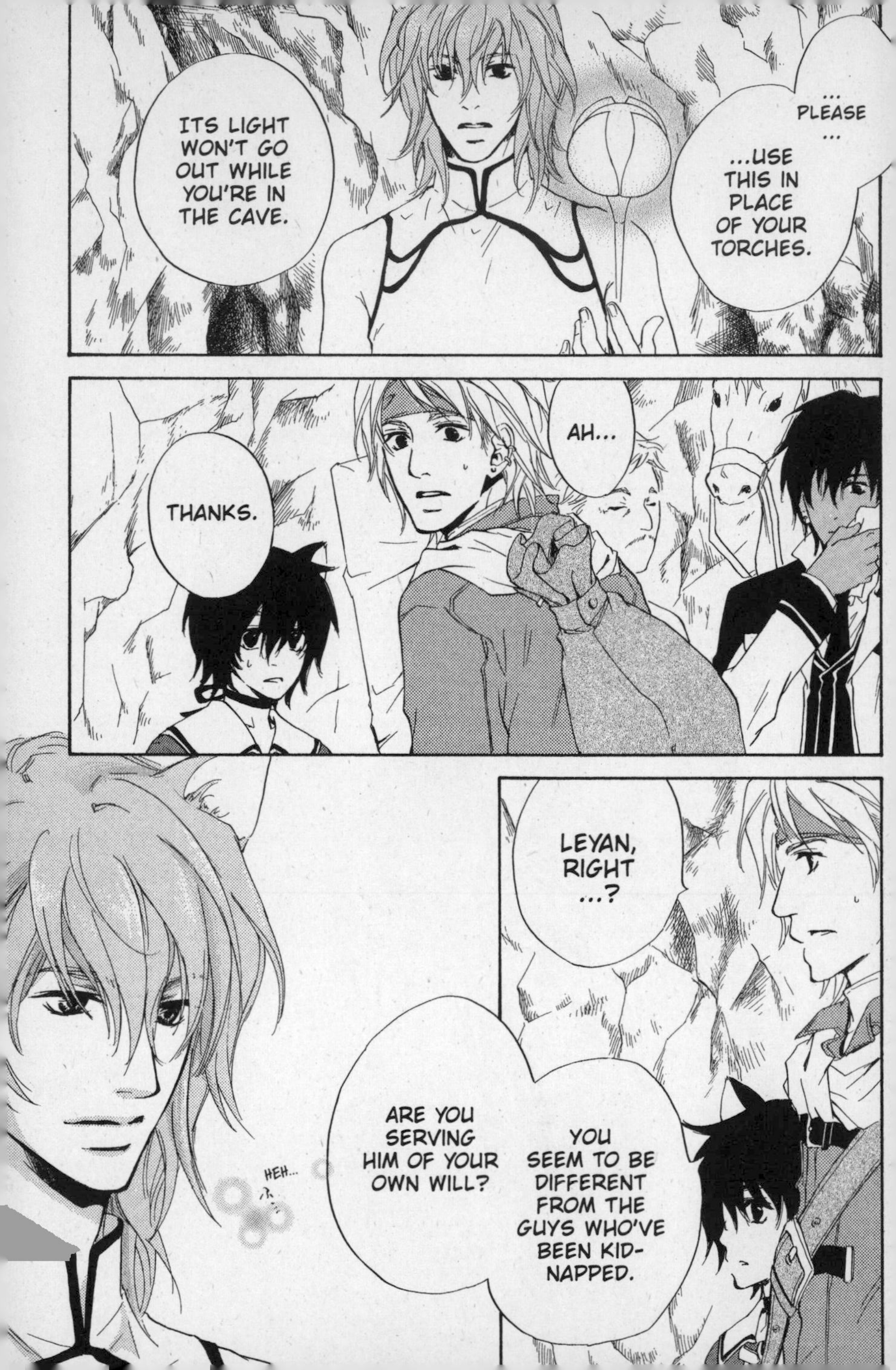
... PLEASE ...
...USE THIS IN PLACE OF YOUR TORCHES.
ITS LIGHT WON'T GO OUT WHILE YOU'RE IN THE CAVE.
AH...
THANKS.
LEYAN, RIGHT ...?
YOU SEEM TO BE DIFFERENT FROM THE GUYS WHO'VE BEEN KID-NAPPED.
ARE YOU SERVING HIM OF YOUR OWN WILL?
HEH...

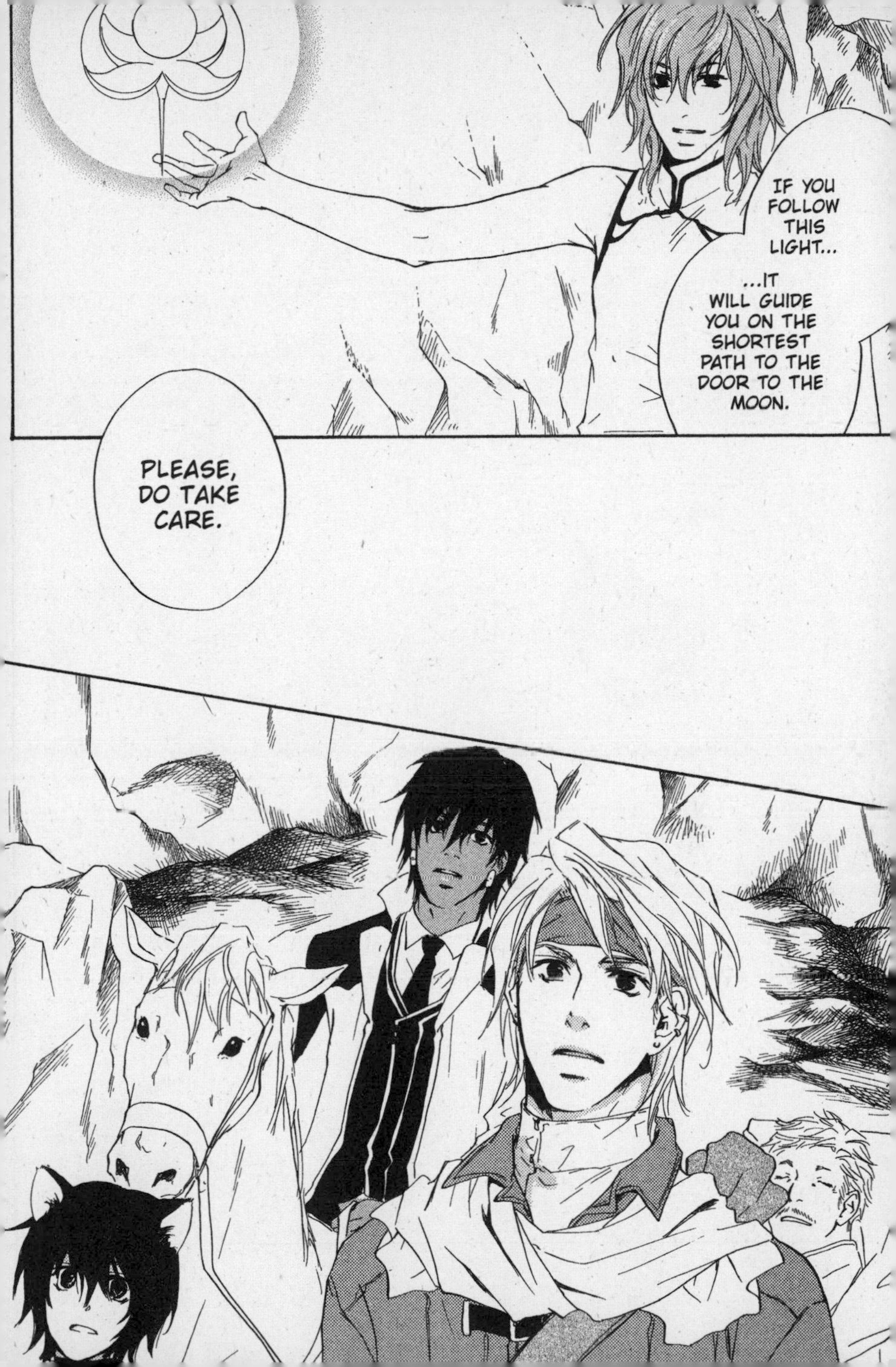
IF YOU FOLLOW THIS LIGHT...
...IT WILL GUIDE YOU ON THE SHORTEST PATH TO THE DOOR TO THE MOON.
PLEASE, DO TAKE CARE.

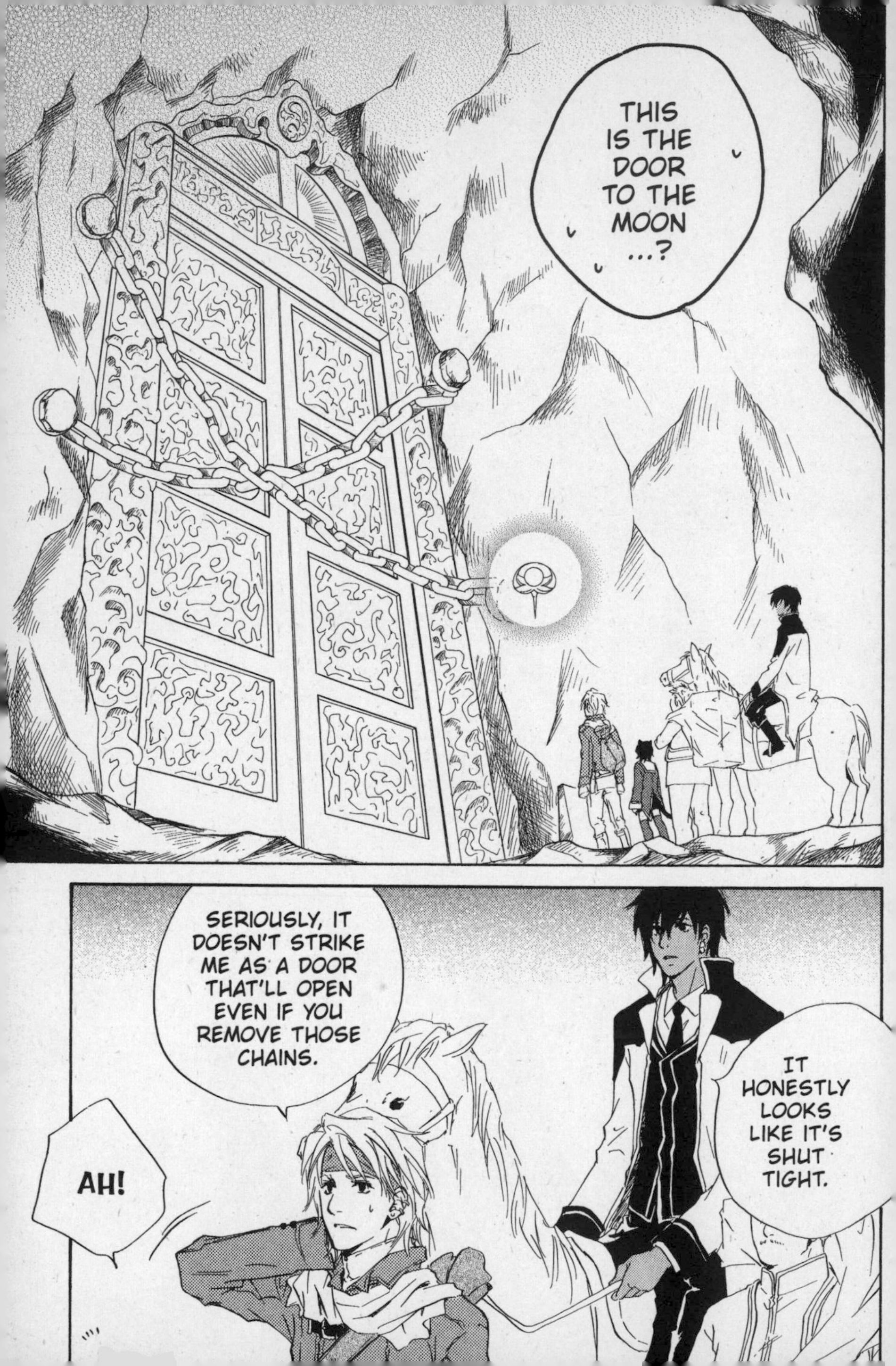
THIS IS THE DOOR TO THE MOON ...?
IT HONESTLY LOOKS LIKE IT'S SHUT TIGHT.
SERIOUSLY, IT DOESN'T STRIKE ME AS A DOOR THAT'LL OPEN EVEN IF YOU REMOVE THOSE CHAINS.
AH!

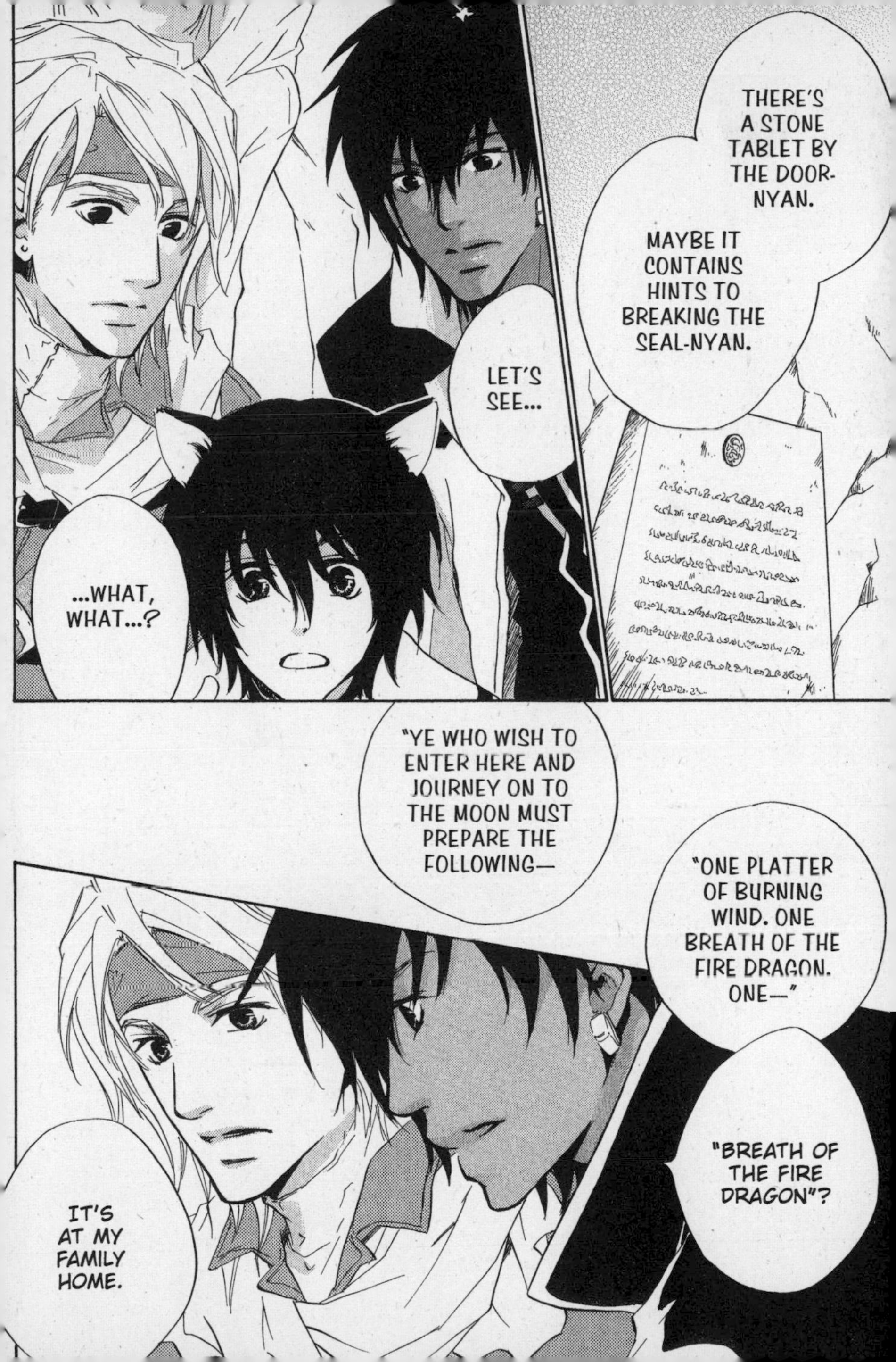
THERE'S A STONE TABLET BY THE DOOR-NYAN.
MAYBE IT CONTAINS HINTS TO BREAKING THE SEAL-NYAN.
LET'S SEE...
...WHAT, WHAT...?
"YE WHO WISH TO ENTER HERE AND JOURNEY ON TO THE MOON MUST PREPARE THE FOLLOWING—
"ONE PLATTER OF BURNING WIND. ONE BREATH OF THE FIRE DRAGON. ONE—"
"BREATH OF THE FIRE DRAGON"?
IT'S AT MY FAMILY HOME.

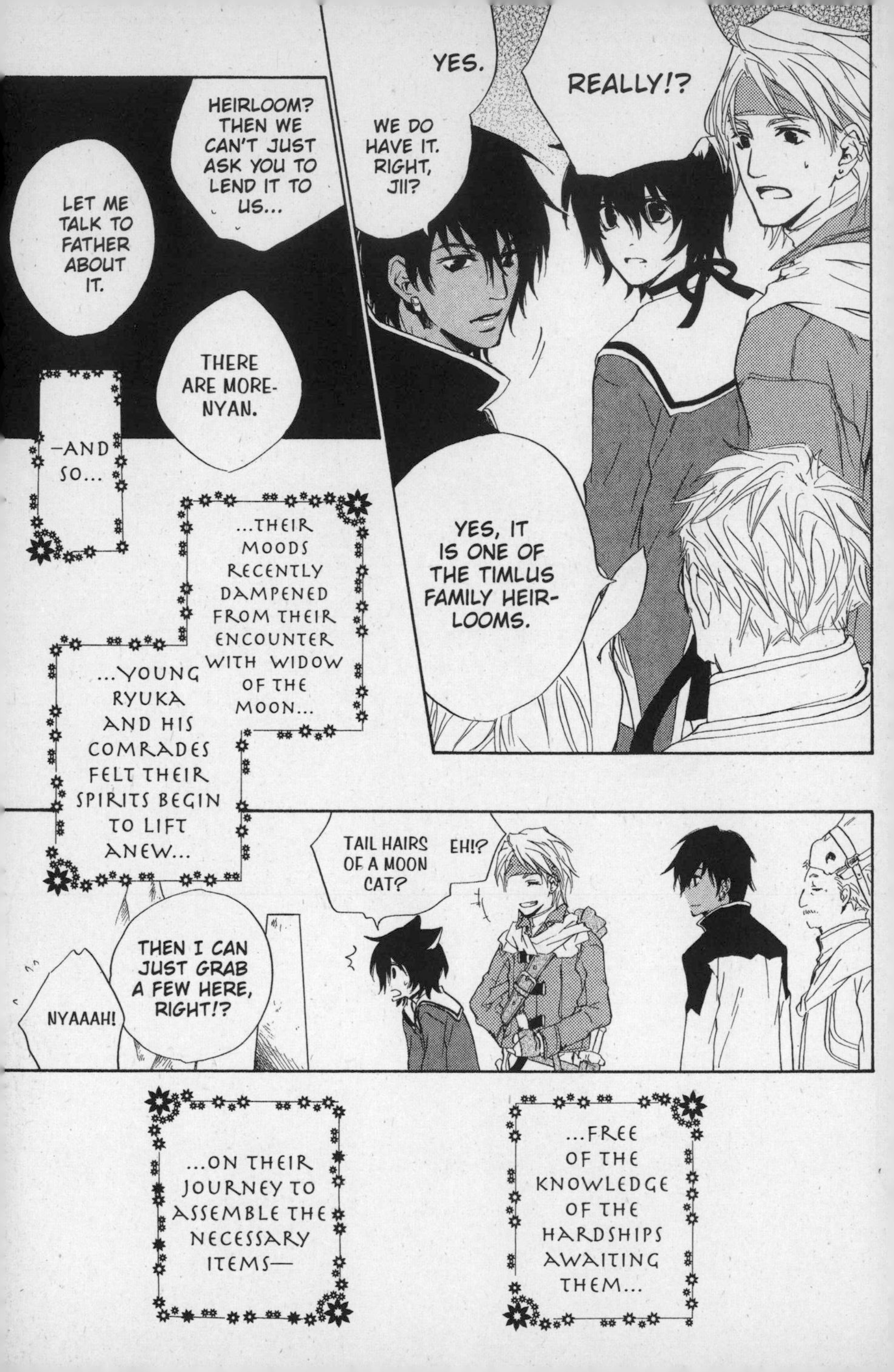
REALLY!?
YES.
WE DO HAVE IT. RIGHT, JII?
YES, IT IS ONE OF THE TIMLUS FAMILY HEIR-LOOMS.
HEIRLOOM? THEN WE CAN'T JUST ASK YOU TO LEND IT TO US...
LET ME TALK TO FATHER ABOUT IT.
THERE ARE MORE-NYAN.
—AND SO...
...THEIR MOODS RECENTLY DAMPENED FROM THEIR ENCOUNTER WITH WIDOW OF THE MOON...
...YOUNG RYUKA AND HIS COMRADES FELT THEIR SPIRITS BEGIN TO LIFT ANEW...
EH!?
TAIL HAIRS OF A MOON CAT?
THEN I CAN JUST GRAB A FEW HERE, RIGHT!?
NYAAAH!
...ON THEIR JOURNEY TO ASSEMBLE THE NECESSARY ITEMS—
...FREE OF THE KNOWLEDGE OF THE HARDSHIPS AWAITING THEM...

TALE OF THE WANING MOON

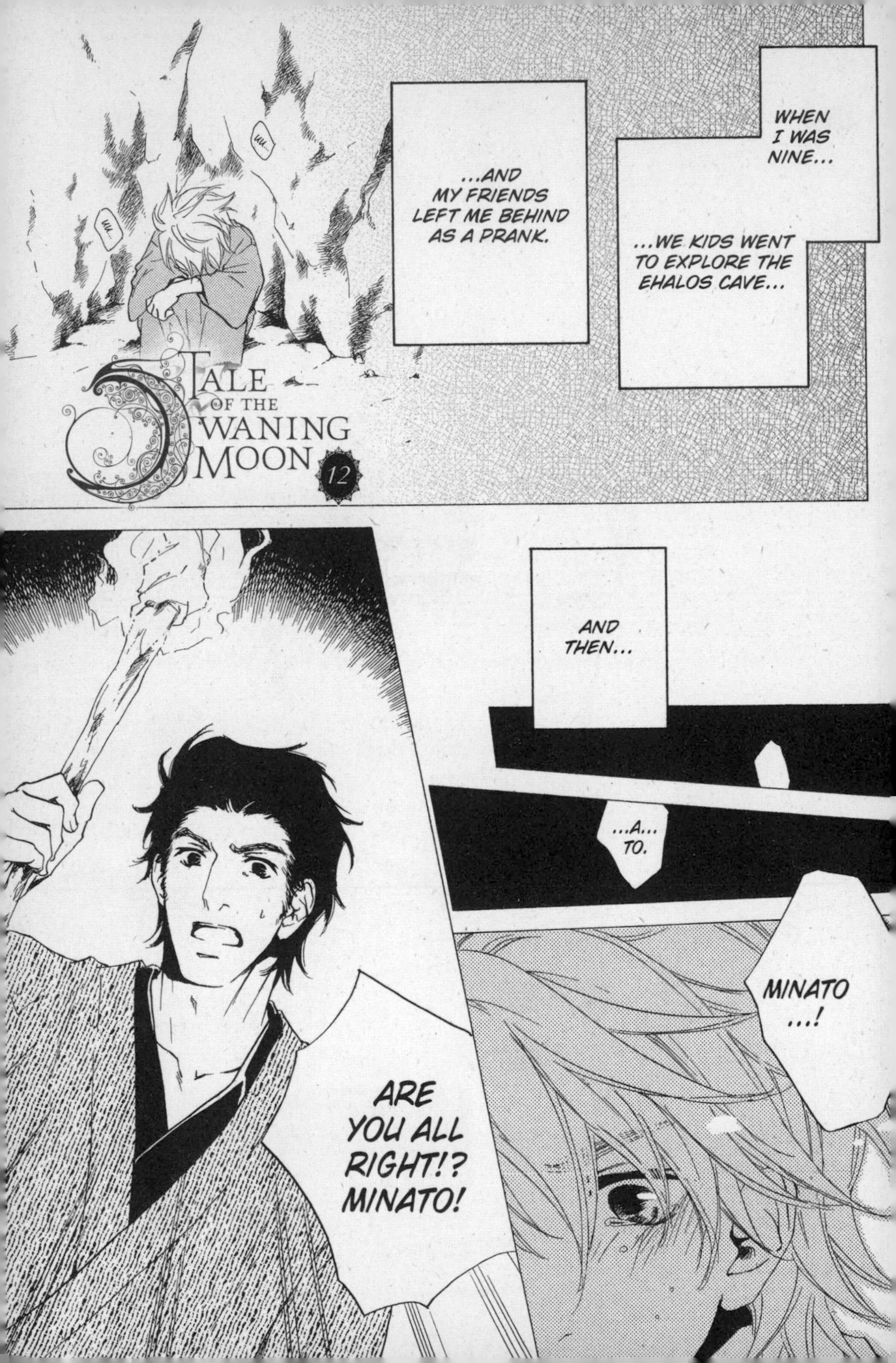
WHEN I WAS NINE...
...WE KIDS WENT TO EXPLORE THE EHALOS CAVE...
...AND MY FRIENDS LEFT ME BEHIND AS A PRANK.
TALE OF THE WANING MOON 12
AND THEN...
...A... TO.
MINATO ...!
ARE YOU ALL RIGHT!? MINATO!

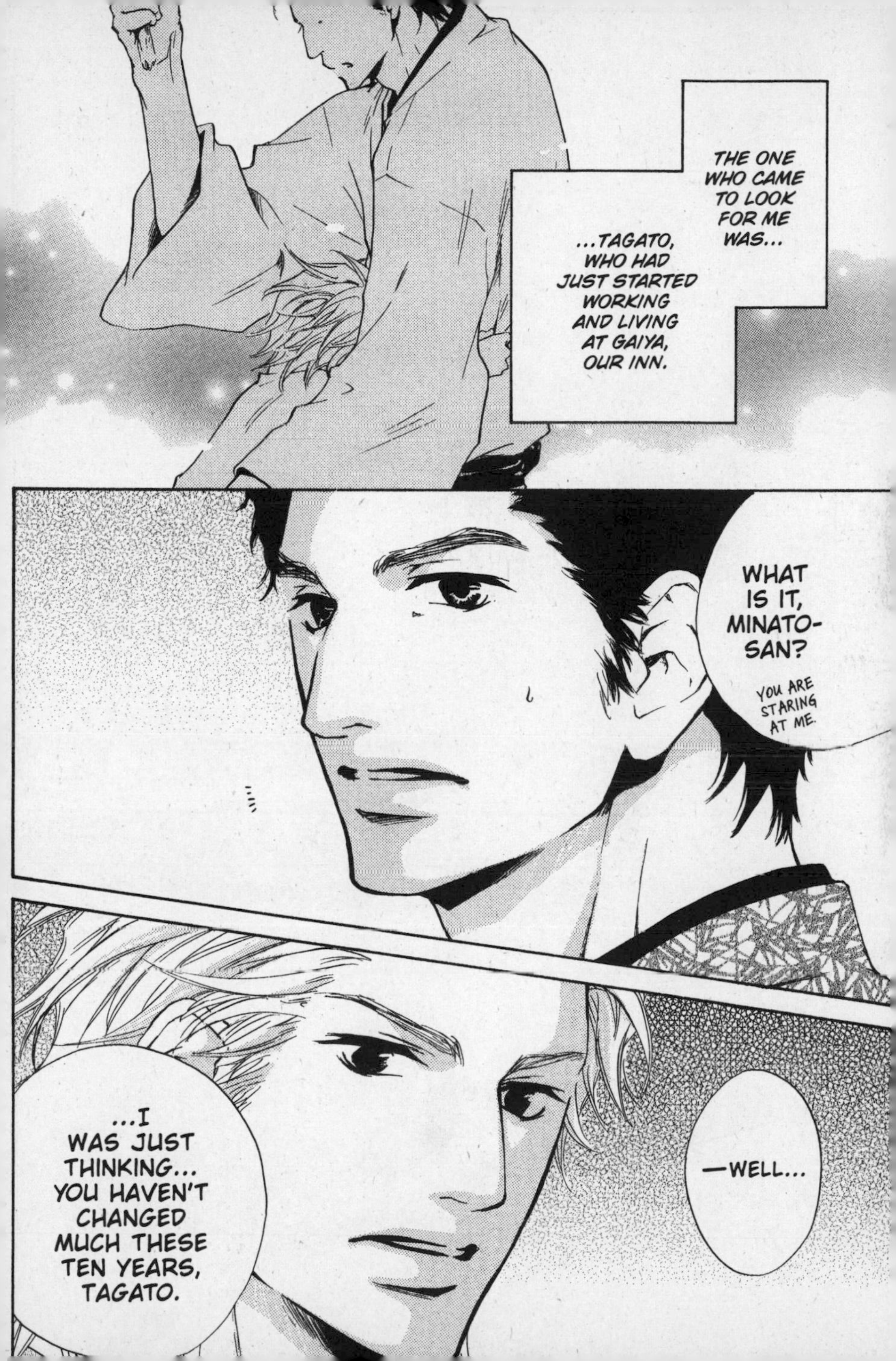
THE ONE WHO CAME TO LOOK FOR ME WAS...
...TAGATO, WHO HAD JUST STARTED WORKING AND LIVING AT GAIYA, OUR INN.
WHAT IS IT, MINATO-SAN?
YOU ARE STARING AT ME.
—WELL...
...I WAS JUST THINKING... YOU HAVEN'T CHANGED MUCH THESE TEN YEARS, TAGATO.

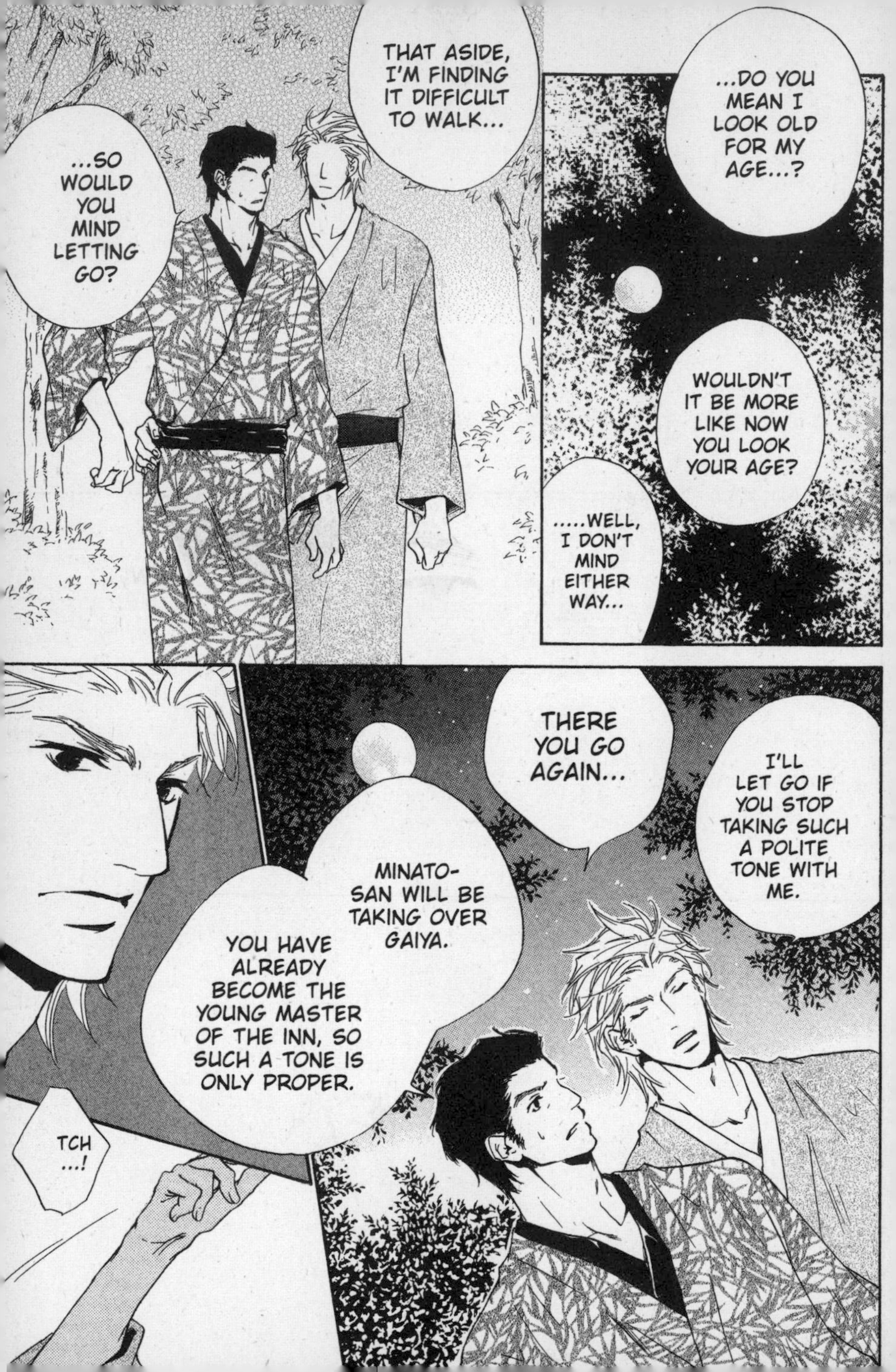
...DO YOU MEAN I LOOK OLD FOR MY AGE...?
WOULDN'T IT BE MORE LIKE NOW YOU LOOK YOUR AGE?
.....WELL, I DON'T MIND EITHER WAY...
THAT ASIDE, I'M FINDING IT DIFFICULT TO WALK...
...SO WOULD YOU MIND LETTING GO?
I'LL LET GO IF YOU STOP TAKING SUCH A POLITE TONE WITH ME.
THERE YOU GO AGAIN...
MINATO-SAN WILL BE TAKING OVER GAIYA.
YOU HAVE ALREADY BECOME THE YOUNG MASTER OF THE INN, SO SUCH A TONE IS ONLY PROPER.
TCH ...!

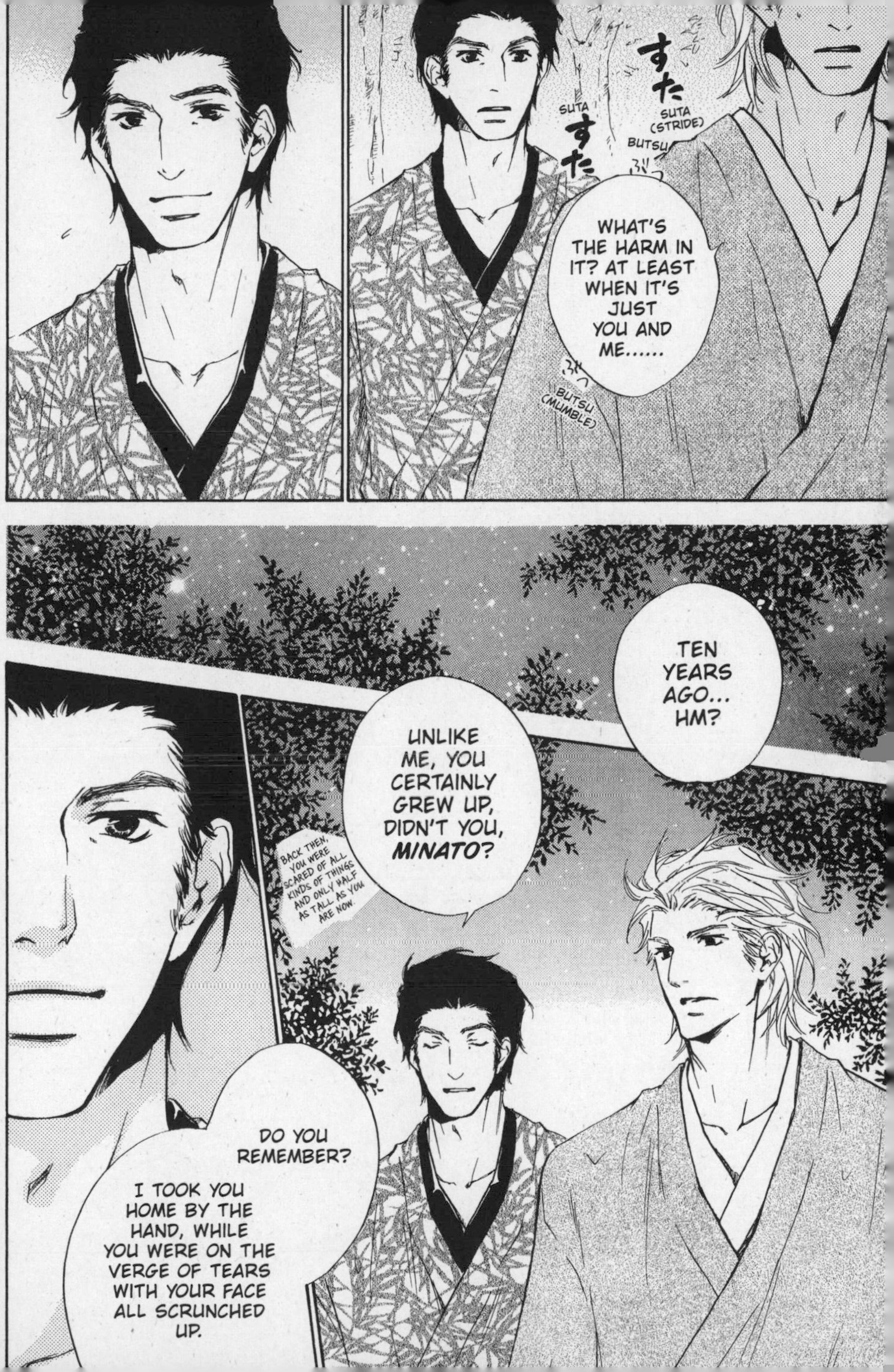
すた
SUTA (STRIDE)
すた
SUTA
ぶつ
BUTSU
WHAT'S THE HARM IN IT? AT LEAST WHEN IT'S JUST YOU AND ME......
ぶつ
BUTSU (MUMBLE)
TEN YEARS AGO... HM?
UNLIKE ME, YOU CERTAINLY GREW UP, DIDN'T YOU, MINATO?
BACK THEN, YOU WERE SCARED OF ALL KINDS OF THINGS AND ONLY HALF AS TALL AS YOU ARE NOW.
DO YOU REMEMBER?
I TOOK YOU HOME BY THE HAND, WHILE YOU WERE ON THE VERGE OF TEARS WITH YOUR FACE ALL SCRUNCHED UP.

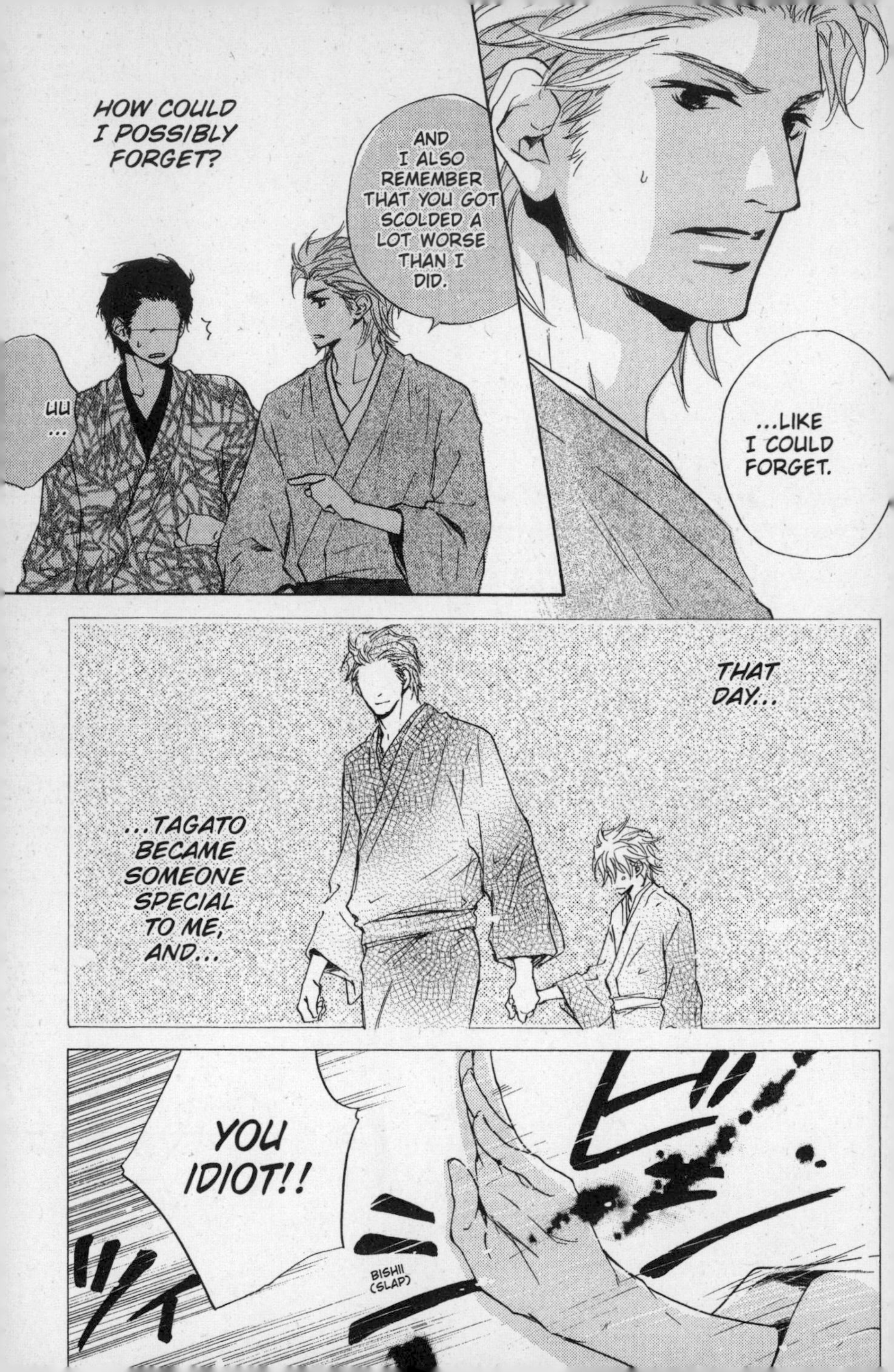
...LIKE I COULD FORGET.
AND I ALSO REMEMBER THAT YOU GOT SCOLDED A LOT WORSE THAN I DID.
HOW COULD I POSSIBLY FORGET?
UU ...
THAT DAY...
...TAGATO BECAME SOMEONE SPECIAL TO ME, AND...
YOU IDIOT!!
BISHII (SLAP)

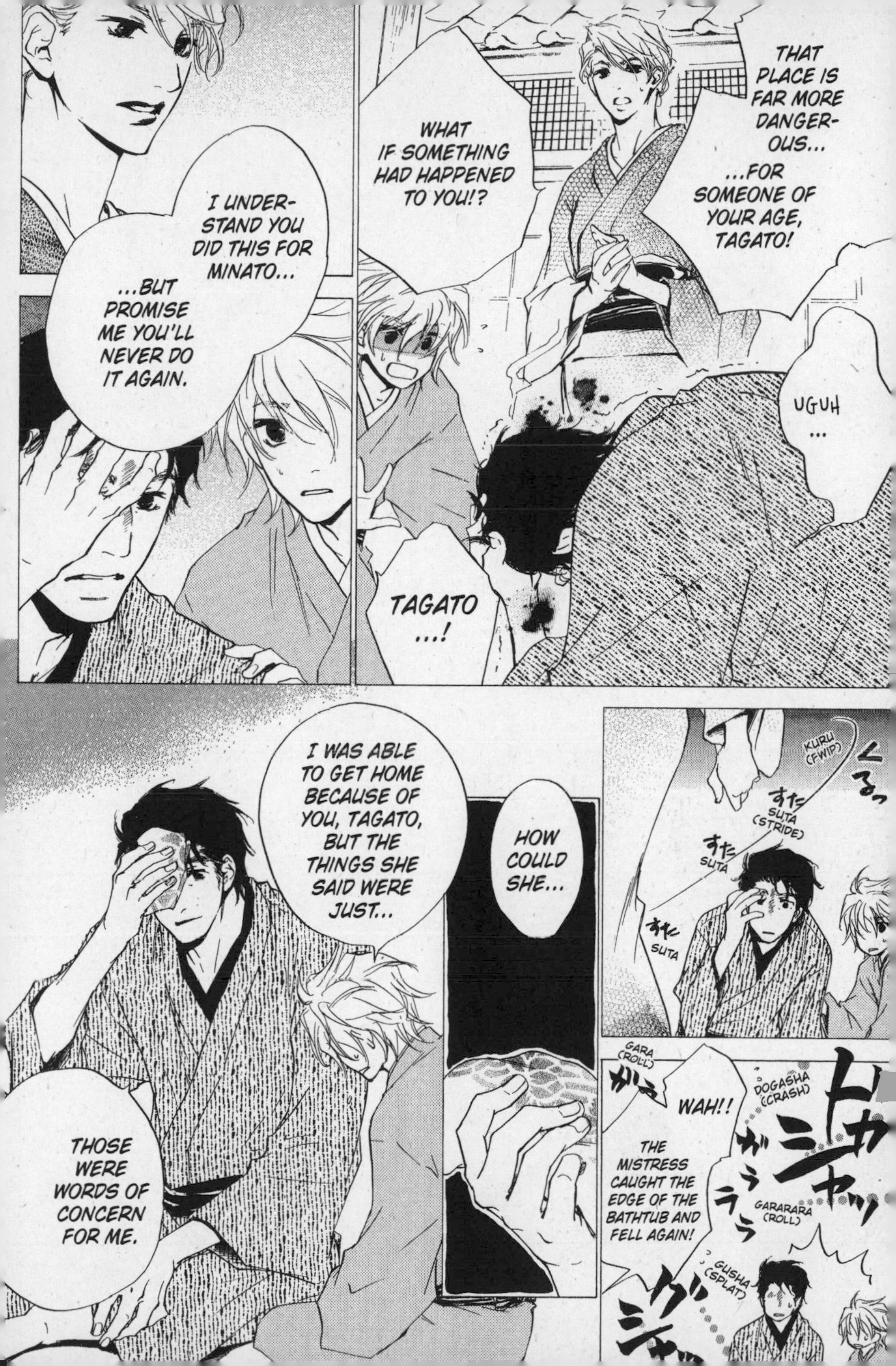
THAT PLACE IS FAR MORE DANGER-OUS...
...FOR SOMEONE OF YOUR AGE, TAGATO!
WHAT IF SOMETHING HAD HAPPENED TO YOU!?
UGUH ...
TAGATO ...!
I UNDER-STAND YOU DID THIS FOR MINATO...
...BUT PROMISE ME YOU'LL NEVER DO IT AGAIN.
KURU (FWIP)
SUTA (STRIDE)
SUTA
SUTA
DOGASHA (CRASH)
WAH!!
GARA (ROLL)
GARARARA (ROLL)
THE MISTRESS CAUGHT THE EDGE OF THE BATHTUB AND FELL AGAIN!
GUSHA (SPLAT)
HOW COULD SHE...
I WAS ABLE TO GET HOME BECAUSE OF YOU, TAGATO, BUT THE THINGS SHE SAID WERE JUST...
THOSE WERE WORDS OF CONCERN FOR ME.

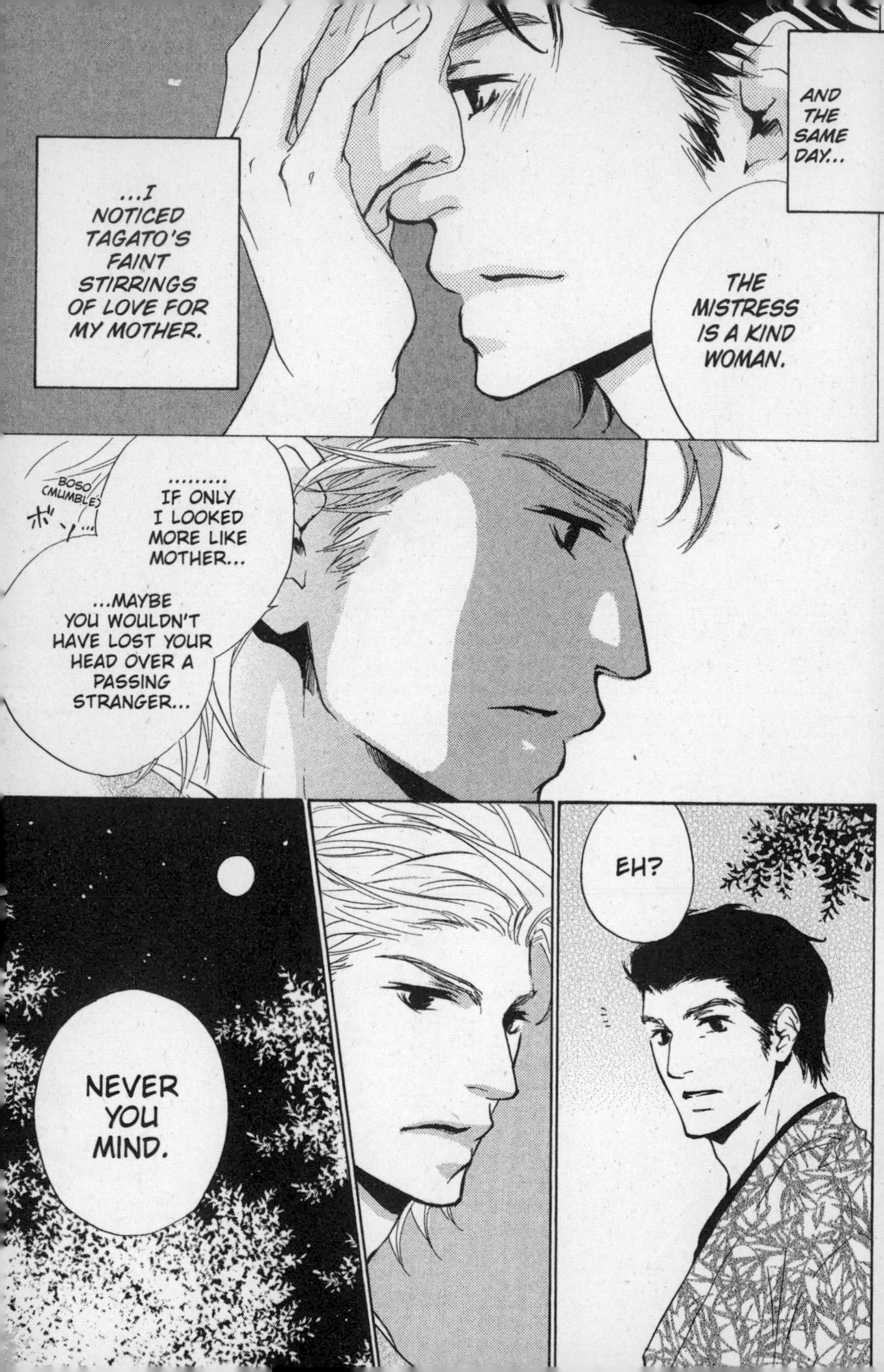
AND THE SAME DAY...
THE MISTRESS IS A KIND WOMAN.
...I NOTICED TAGATO'S FAINT STIRRINGS OF LOVE FOR MY MOTHER.
....
IF ONLY I LOOKED MORE LIKE MOTHER...
...MAYBE YOU WOULDN'T HAVE LOST YOUR HEAD OVER A PASSING STRANGER...
BOSO (MUMBLE)
ボソ…
EH?
NEVER YOU MIND.

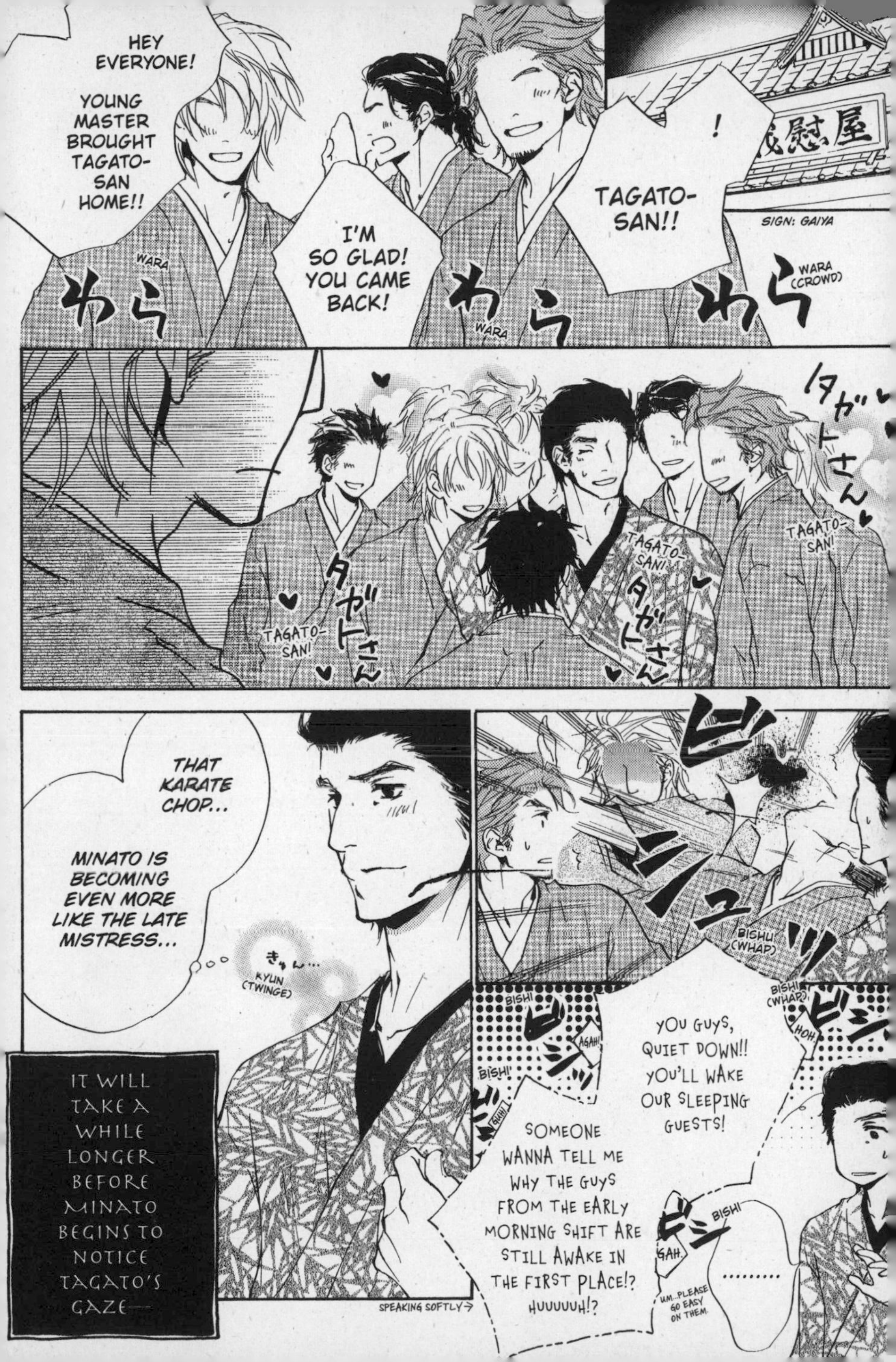

!
TAGATO-SAN!!
SIGN: GAIYA
わら
WARA (CROWD)
I'M SO GLAD! YOU CAME BACK!
わら
WARA
HEY EVERYONE!
YOUNG MASTER BROUGHT TAGATO-SAN HOME!!
わら
WARA
タガトさん
TAGATO-SAN!
タガトさん
TAGATO-SAN!
タガトさん
TAGATO-SAN!
BISHU (WHAP)
BISHI (WHAP)
HOH
YOU GUYS, QUIET DOWN!! YOU'LL WAKE OUR SLEEPING GUESTS!
BISHI
AGAH!
BISHI
SOMEONE WANNA TELL ME WHY THE GUYS FROM THE EARLY MORNING SHIFT ARE STILL AWAKE IN THE FIRST PLACE!? HUUUUUH!?
BISHI
GAH.
....
UM...PLEASE GO EASY ON THEM.
SPEAKING SOFTLY→
THAT KARATE CHOP...
MINATO IS BECOMING EVEN MORE LIKE THE LATE MISTRESS...
きゅん...
KYUN (TWINGE)
IT WILL TAKE A WHILE LONGER BEFORE MINATO BEGINS TO NOTICE TAGATO'S GAZE—

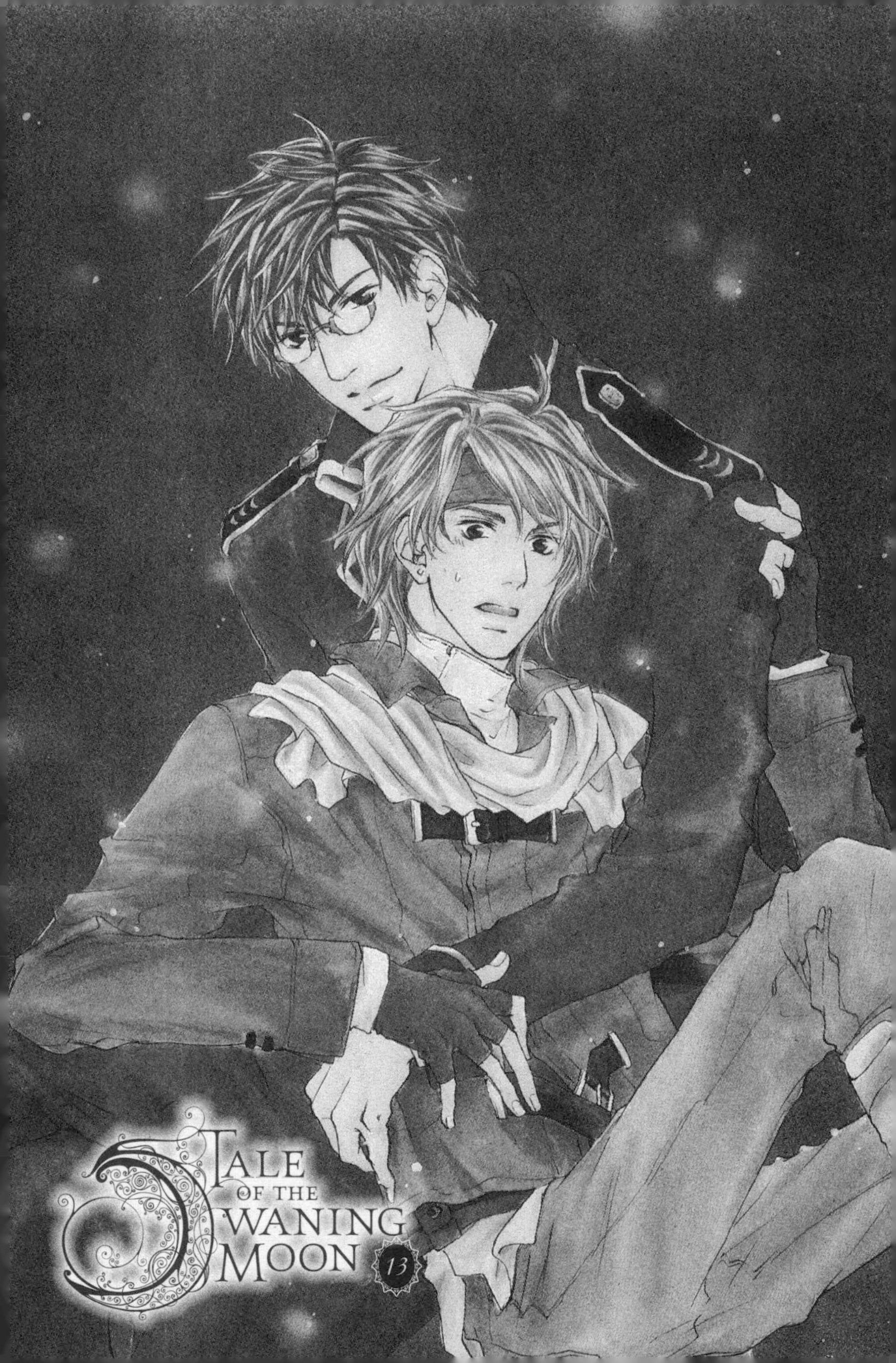
TALE OF THE WANING MOON
13

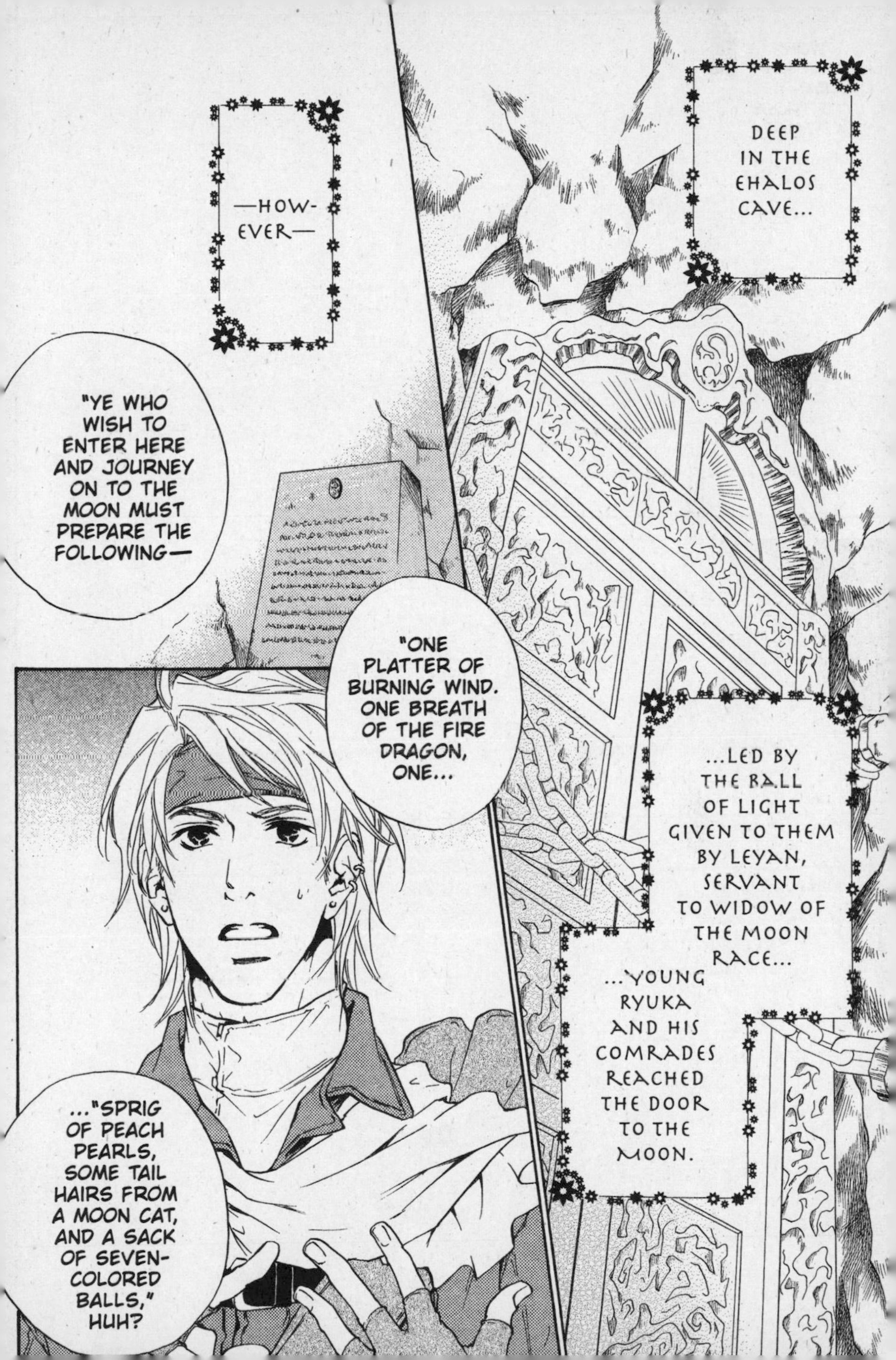
DEEP IN THE EHALOS CAVE...
...LED BY THE BALL OF LIGHT GIVEN TO THEM BY LEYAN, SERVANT TO WIDOW OF THE MOON RACE...
...YOUNG RYUKA AND HIS COMRADES REACHED THE DOOR TO THE MOON.
—HOW-EVER—
"YE WHO WISH TO ENTER HERE AND JOURNEY ON TO THE MOON MUST PREPARE THE FOLLOWING—
"ONE PLATTER OF BURNING WIND. ONE BREATH OF THE FIRE DRAGON, ONE...
..."SPRIG OF PEACH PEARLS, SOME TAIL HAIRS FROM A MOON CAT, AND A SACK OF SEVEN-COLORED BALLS," HUH?

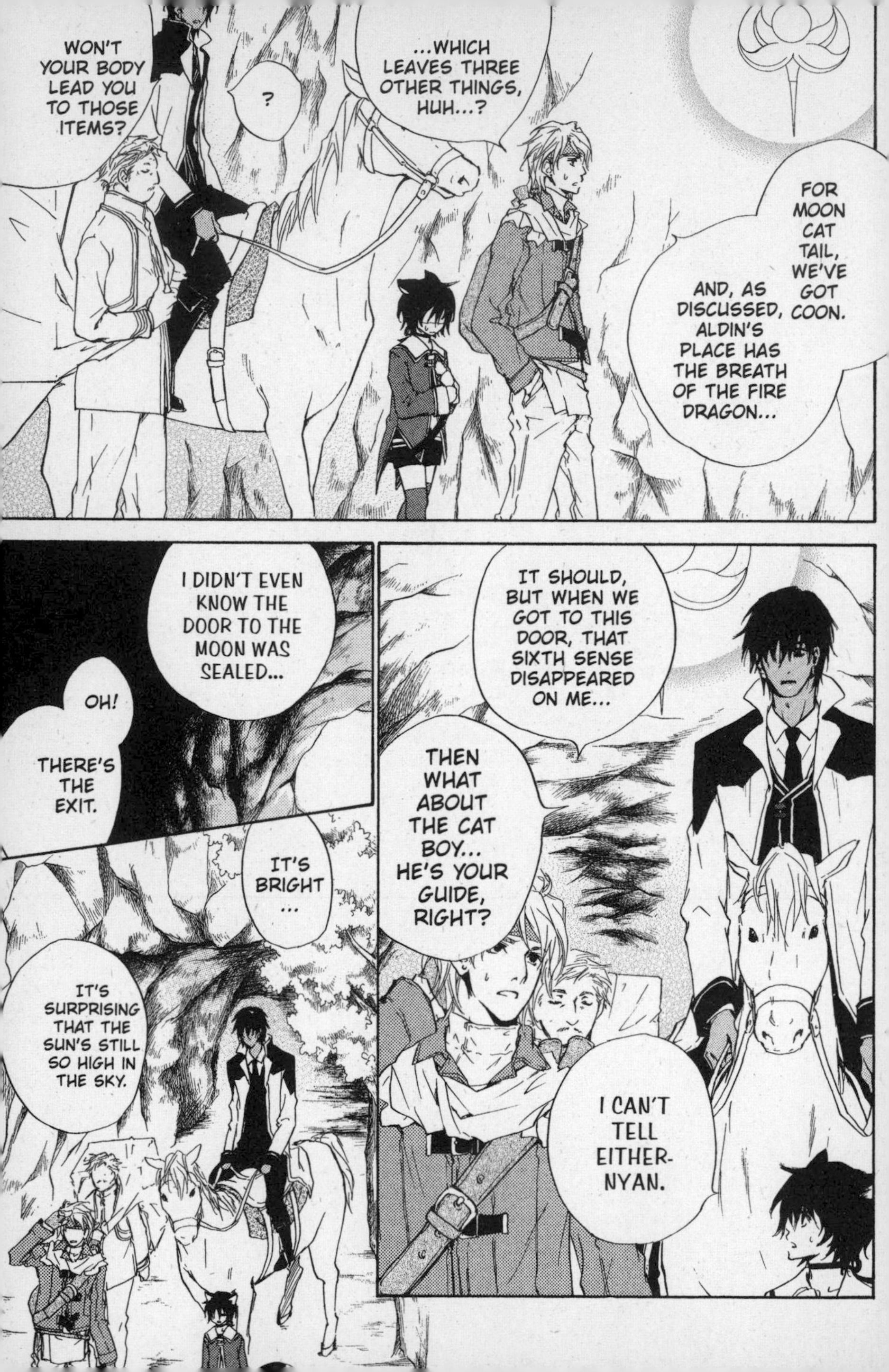
FOR MOON CAT TAIL, WE'VE GOT COON.
AND, AS DISCUSSED, ALDIN'S PLACE HAS THE BREATH OF THE FIRE DRAGON...
...WHICH LEAVES THREE OTHER THINGS, HUH...?
?
WON'T YOUR BODY LEAD YOU TO THOSE ITEMS?
IT SHOULD, BUT WHEN WE GOT TO THIS DOOR, THAT SIXTH SENSE DISAPPEARED ON ME...
THEN WHAT ABOUT THE CAT BOY... HE'S YOUR GUIDE, RIGHT?
I CAN'T TELL EITHER-NYAN.
I DIDN'T EVEN KNOW THE DOOR TO THE MOON WAS SEALED...
OH!
THERE'S THE EXIT.
IT'S BRIGHT...
IT'S SURPRISING THAT THE SUN'S STILL SO HIGH IN THE SKY.

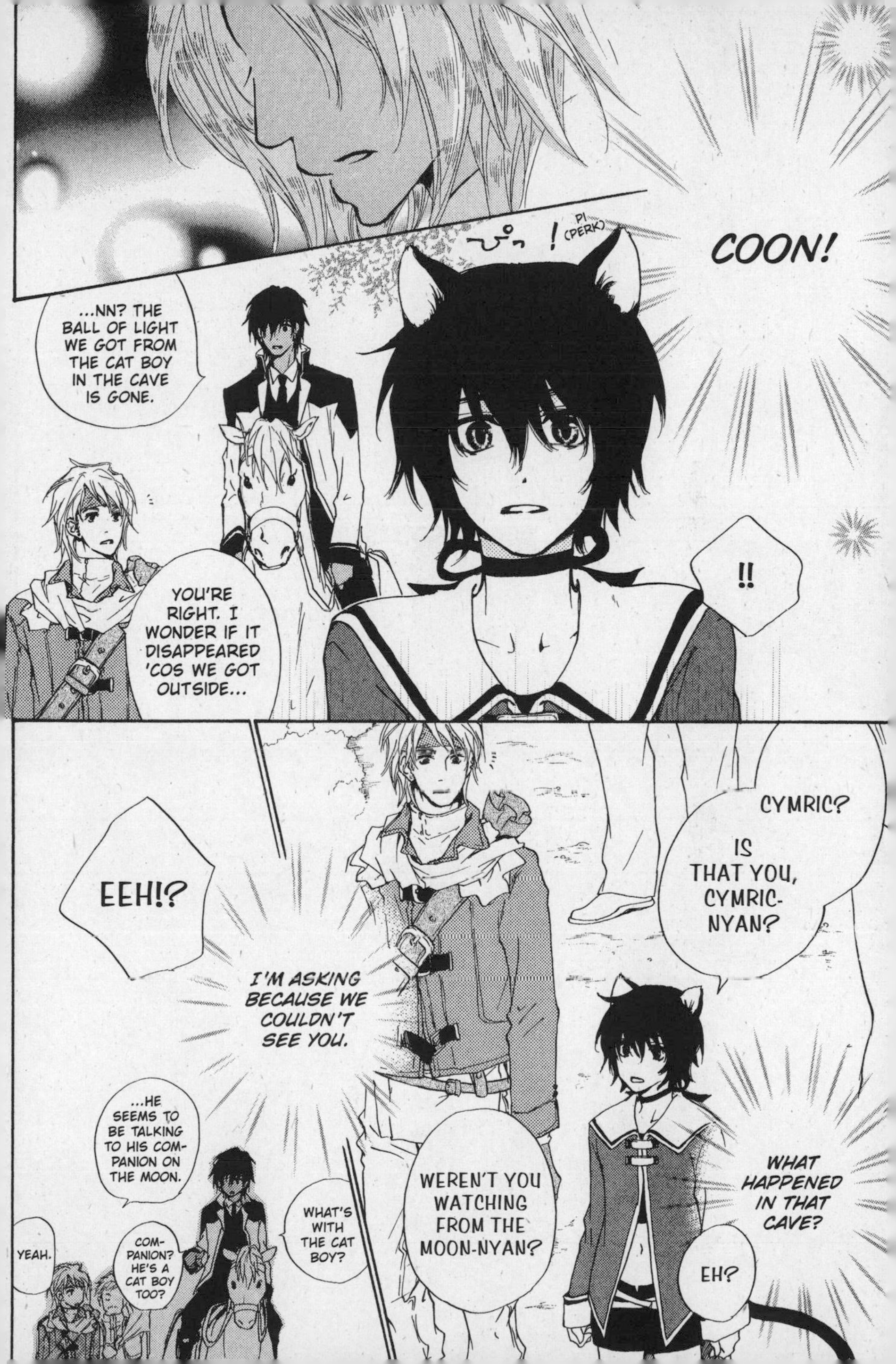
COON!
ぴっ !
PI (PERK)
!!
...NN? THE BALL OF LIGHT WE GOT FROM THE CAT BOY IN THE CAVE IS GONE.
YOU'RE RIGHT. I WONDER IF IT DISAPPEARED 'COS WE GOT OUTSIDE...
CYMRIC?
IS THAT YOU, CYMRIC-NYAN?
EEH!?
I'M ASKING BECAUSE WE COULDN'T SEE YOU.
WHAT HAPPENED IN THAT CAVE?
EH?
WEREN'T YOU WATCHING FROM THE MOON-NYAN?
...HE SEEMS TO BE TALKING TO HIS COM-PANION ON THE MOON.
WHAT'S WITH THE CAT BOY?
COM-PANION? HE'S A CAT BOY TOO?
YEAH.

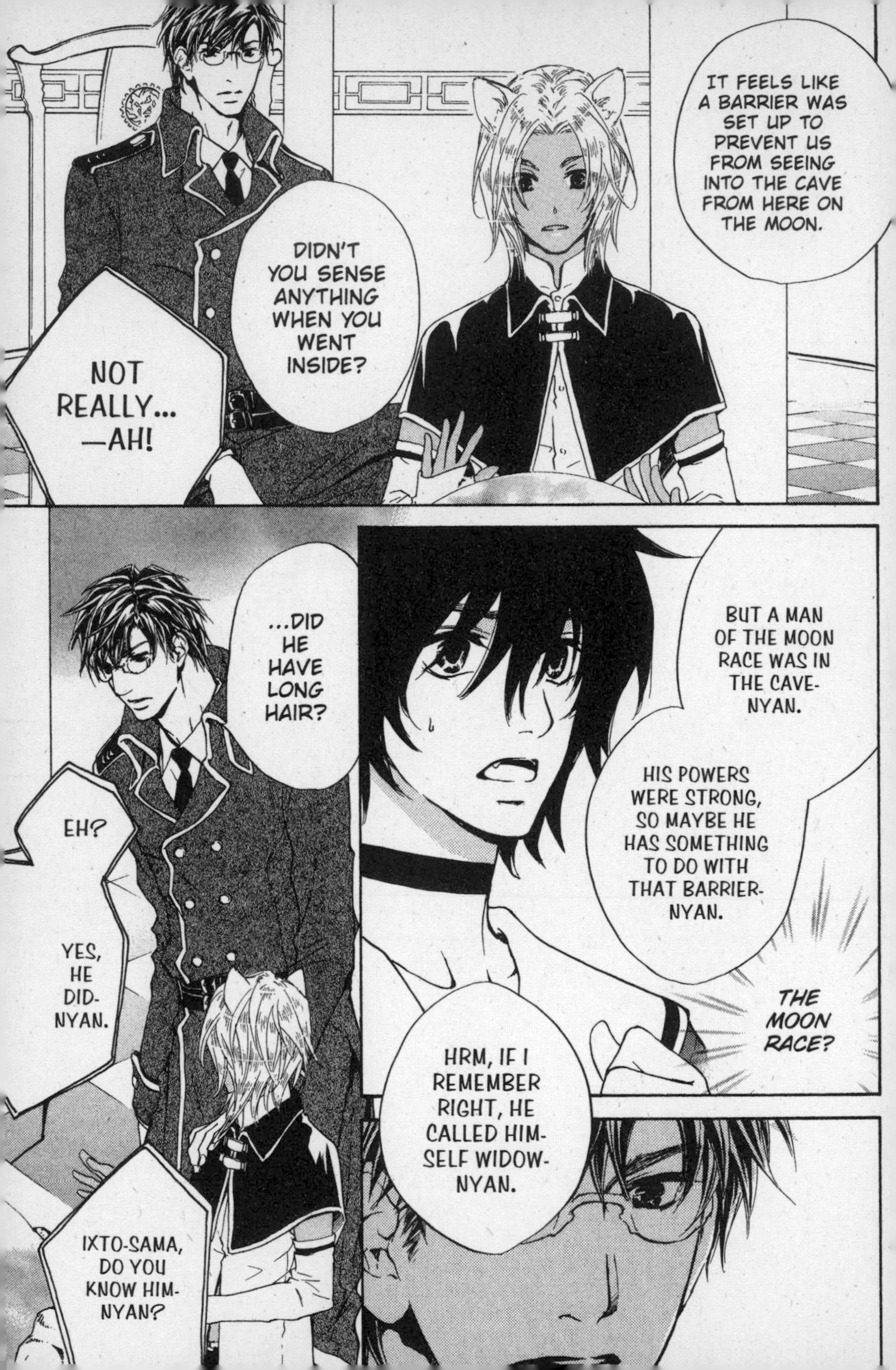
IT FEELS LIKE A BARRIER WAS SET UP TO PREVENT US FROM SEEING INTO THE CAVE FROM HERE ON THE MOON.
DIDN'T YOU SENSE ANYTHING WHEN YOU WENT INSIDE?
NOT REALLY... —AH!
BUT A MAN OF THE MOON RACE WAS IN THE CAVE-NYAN.
HIS POWERS WERE STRONG, SO MAYBE HE HAS SOMETHING TO DO WITH THAT BARRIER-NYAN.
THE MOON RACE?
HRM, IF I REMEMBER RIGHT, HE CALLED HIMSELF WIDOW-NYAN.
...DID HE HAVE LONG HAIR?
EH?
YES, HE DID-NYAN.
IXTO-SAMA, DO YOU KNOW HIM-NYAN?

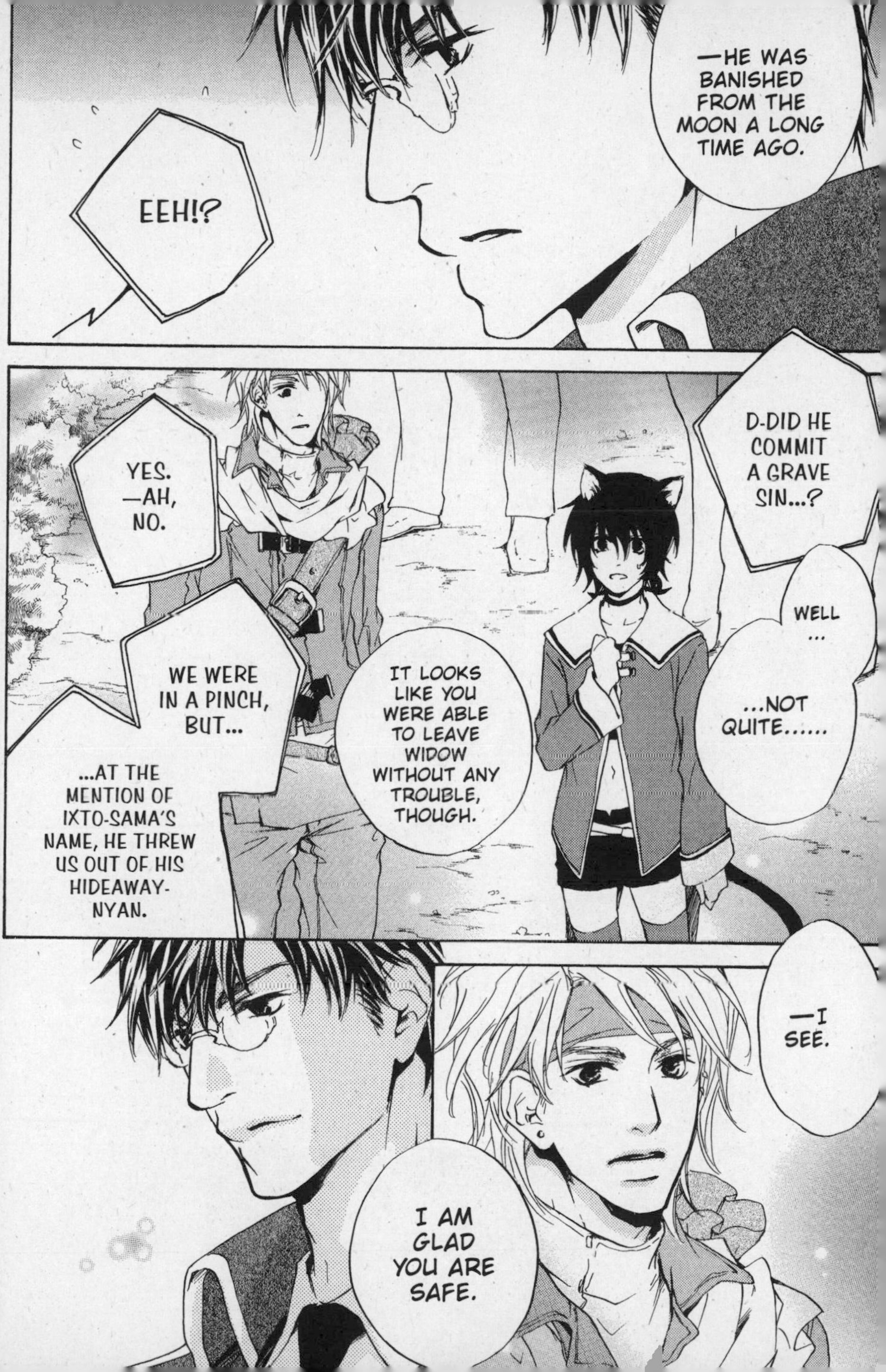
—HE WAS BANISHED FROM THE MOON A LONG TIME AGO.
EEH!?
D-DID HE COMMIT A GRAVE SIN...?
WELL ...
...NOT QUITE......
IT LOOKS LIKE YOU WERE ABLE TO LEAVE WIDOW WITHOUT ANY TROUBLE, THOUGH.
YES. —AH, NO.
WE WERE IN A PINCH, BUT...
...AT THE MENTION OF IXTO-SAMA'S NAME, HE THREW US OUT OF HIS HIDEAWAY-NYAN.
—I SEE.
I AM GLAD YOU ARE SAFE.

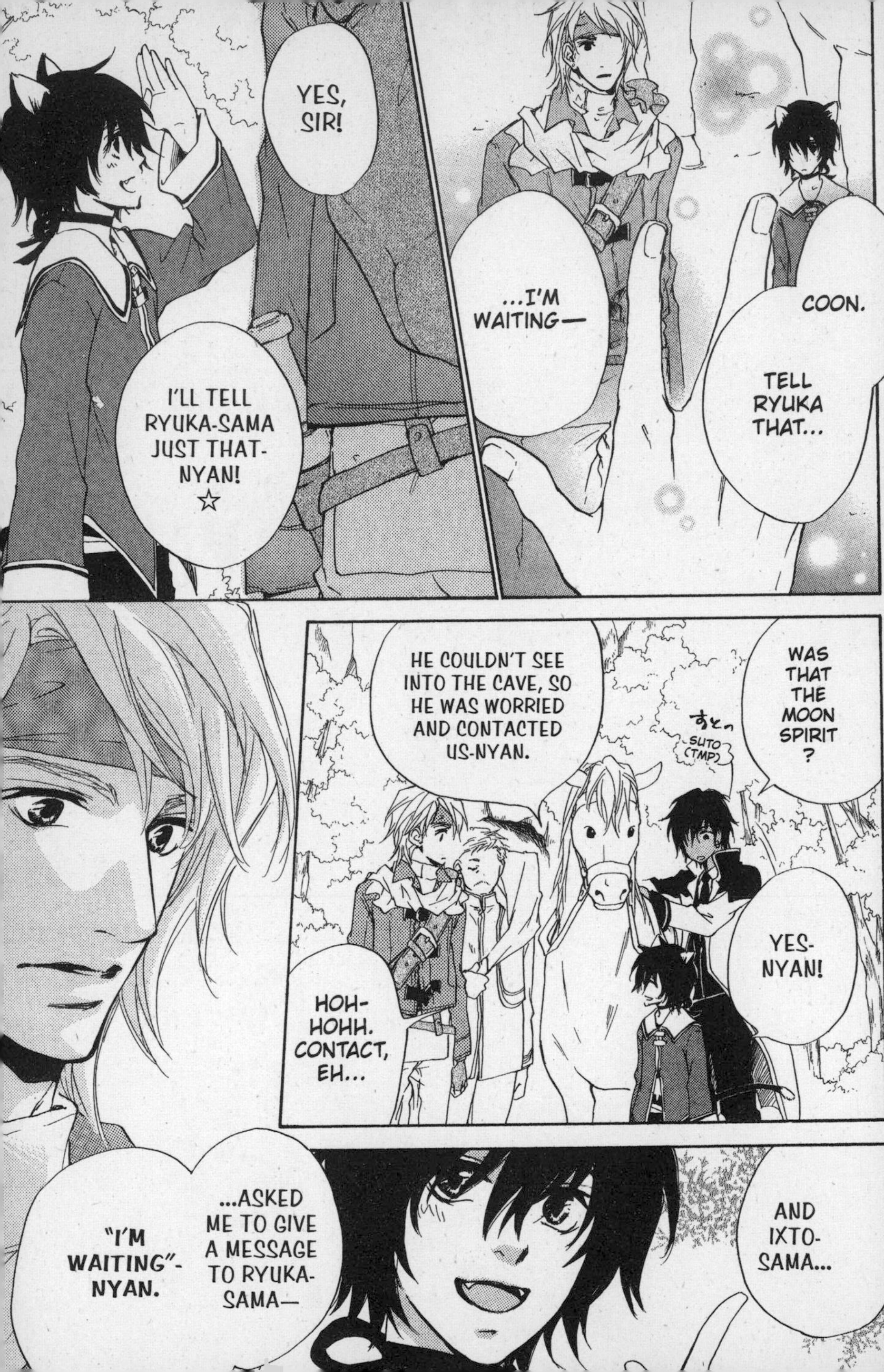
COON.
TELL RYUKA THAT...
...I'M WAITING—
YES, SIR!
I'LL TELL RYUKA-SAMA JUST THAT-NYAN! ☆
WAS THAT THE MOON SPIRIT?
YES-NYAN!
すとっ
SUTO (TMP)
HE COULDN'T SEE INTO THE CAVE, SO HE WAS WORRIED AND CONTACTED US-NYAN.
HOH-HOHH. CONTACT, EH...
AND IXTO-SAMA...
...ASKED ME TO GIVE A MESSAGE TO RYUKA-SAMA—
"I'M WAITING"-NYAN.

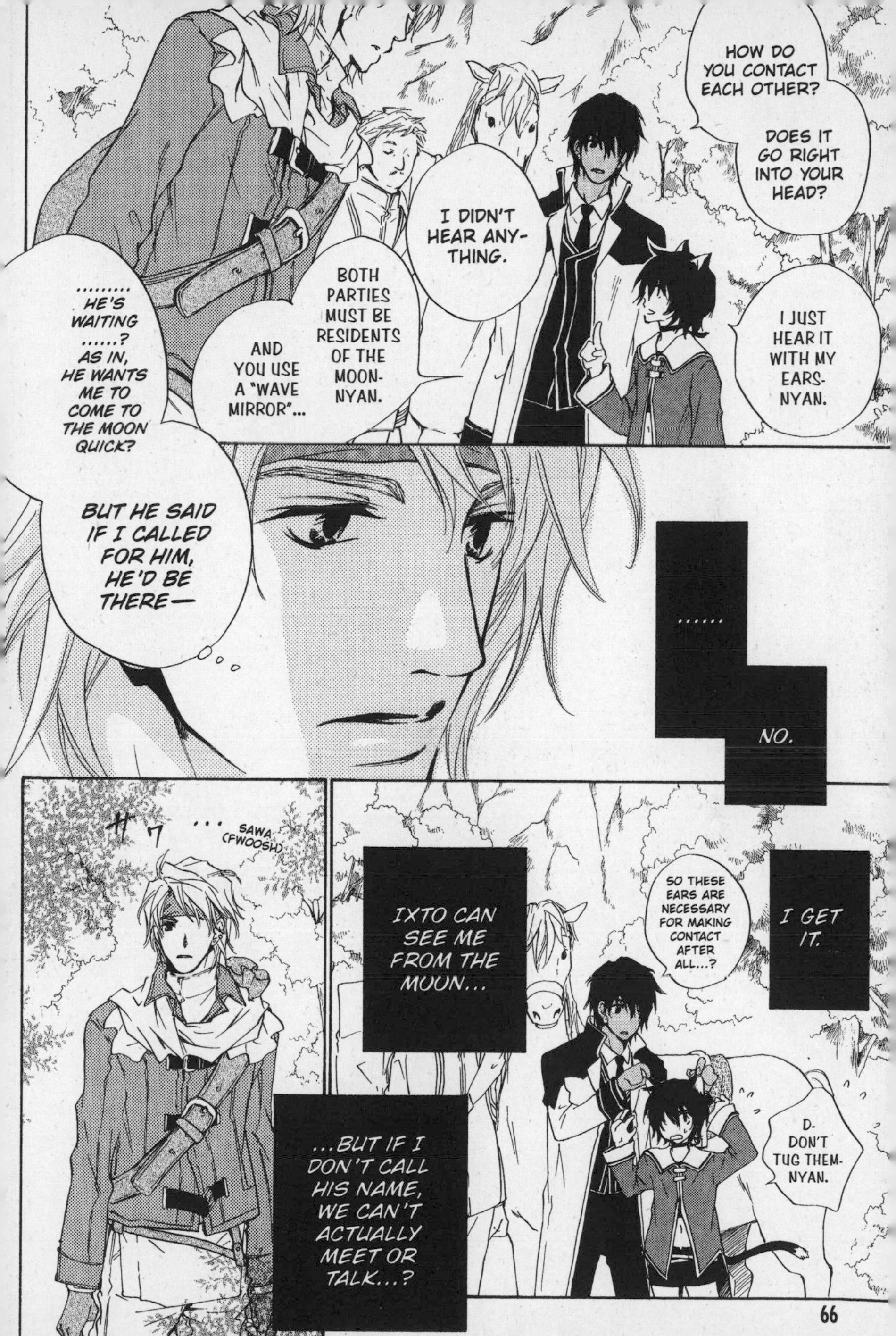
HOW DO YOU CONTACT EACH OTHER?
DOES IT GO RIGHT INTO YOUR HEAD?
I JUST HEAR IT WITH MY EARS-NYAN.
I DIDN'T HEAR ANY-THING.
BOTH PARTIES MUST BE RESIDENTS OF THE MOON-NYAN.
AND YOU USE A "WAVE MIRROR"...
.... HE'S WAITING ......? AS IN, HE WANTS ME TO COME TO THE MOON QUICK?
......
NO.
BUT HE SAID IF I CALLED FOR HIM, HE'D BE THERE—
I GET IT.
SO THESE EARS ARE NECESSARY FOR MAKING CONTACT AFTER ALL...?
IXTO CAN SEE ME FROM THE MOON...
D-DON'T TUG THEM-NYAN.
...BUT IF I DON'T CALL HIS NAME, WE CAN'T ACTUALLY MEET OR TALK...?
サワ...
SAWA (FWOOSH)

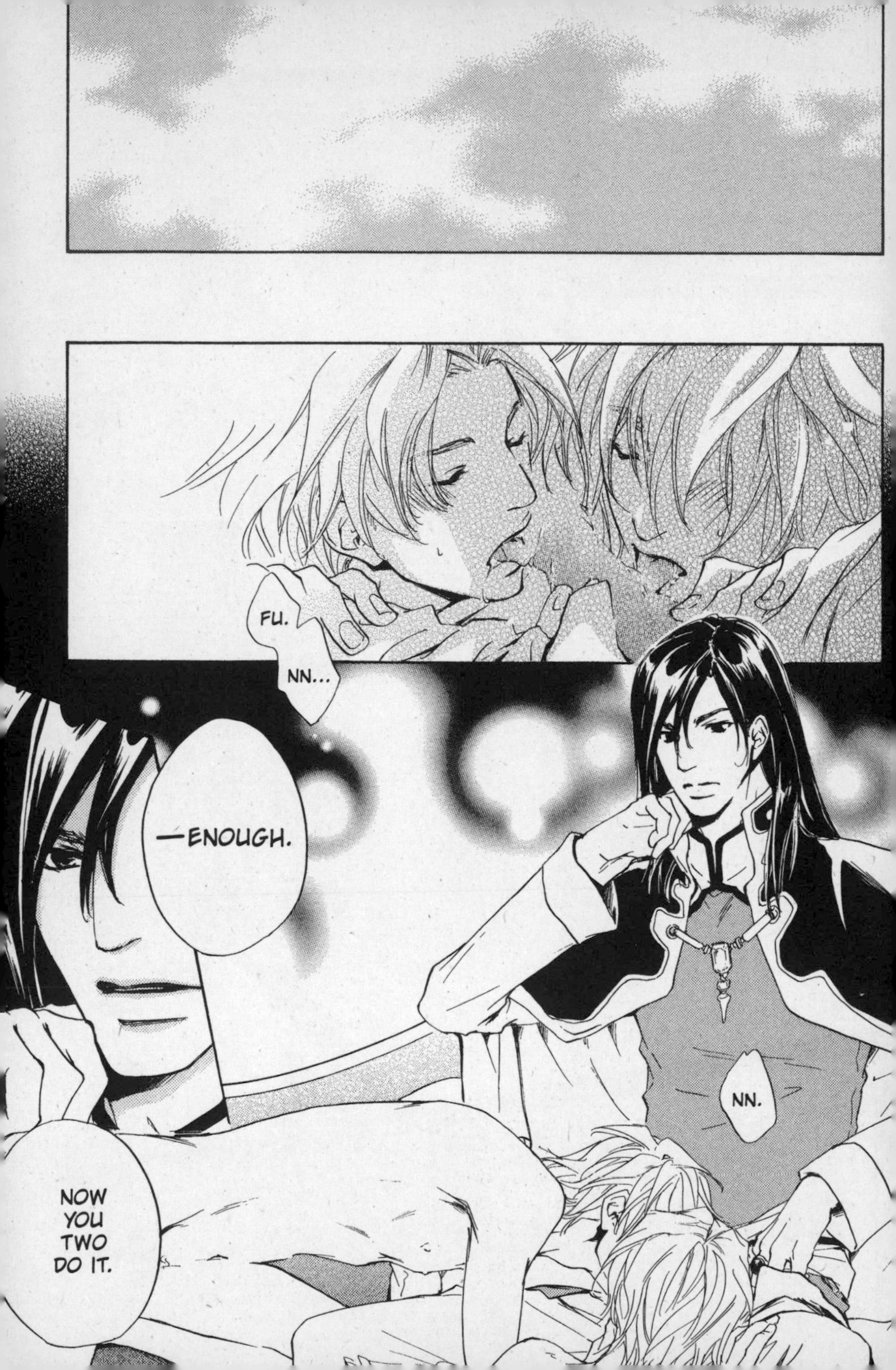
FU.
NN...
NN.
—ENOUGH.
NOW YOU TWO DO IT.

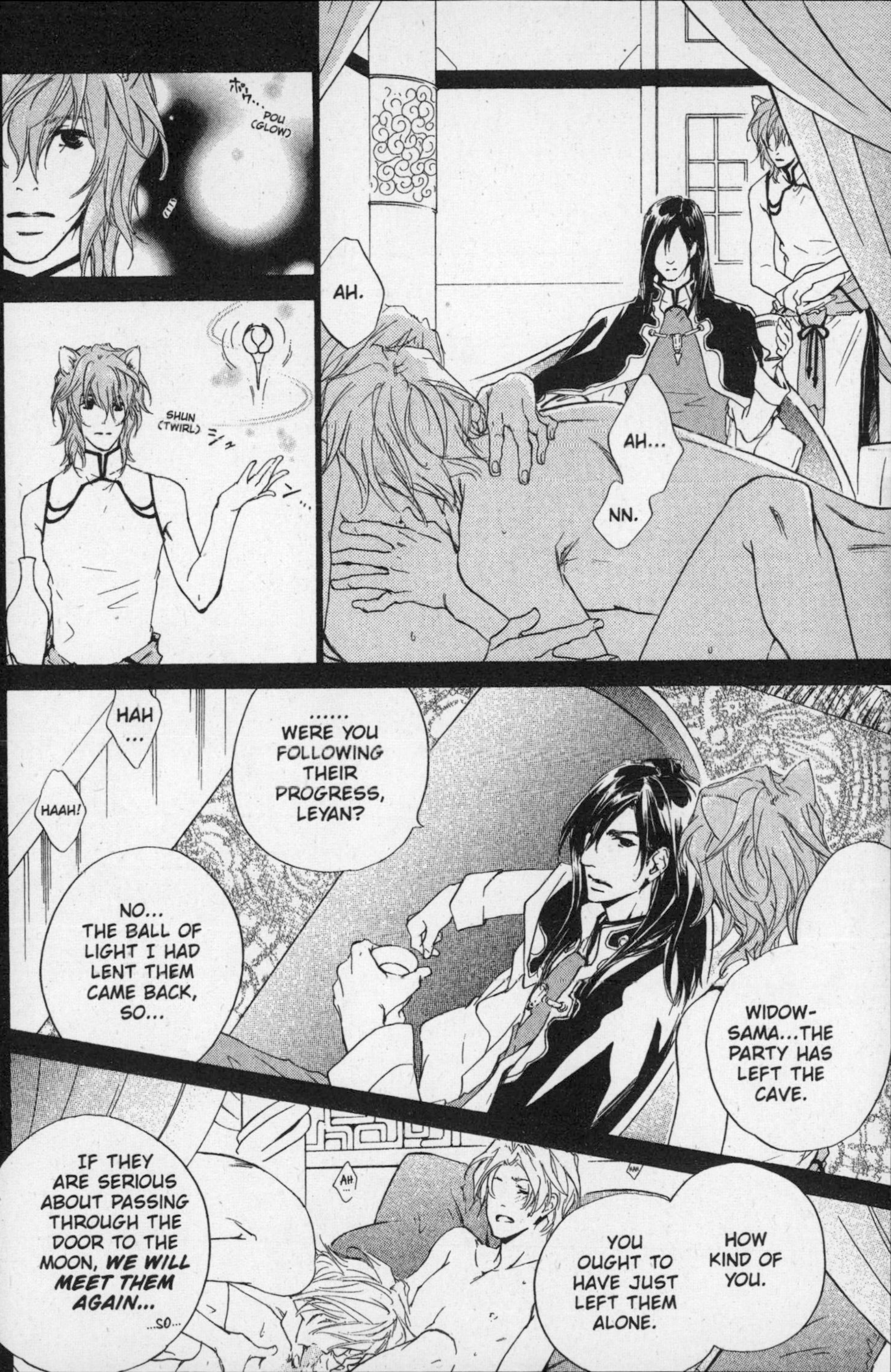
AH.
AH...
NN.
POU (GLOW)
SHUN (TWIRL)
WIDOW-SAMA...THE PARTY HAS LEFT THE CAVE.
......WERE YOU FOLLOWING THEIR PROGRESS, LEYAN?
HAH...
HAAH!
NO... THE BALL OF LIGHT I HAD LENT THEM CAME BACK, SO...
HOW KIND OF YOU.
YOU OUGHT TO HAVE JUST LEFT THEM ALONE.
AH...
IF THEY ARE SERIOUS ABOUT PASSING THROUGH THE DOOR TO THE MOON, ***WE WILL MEET THEM AGAIN...***
...SO...

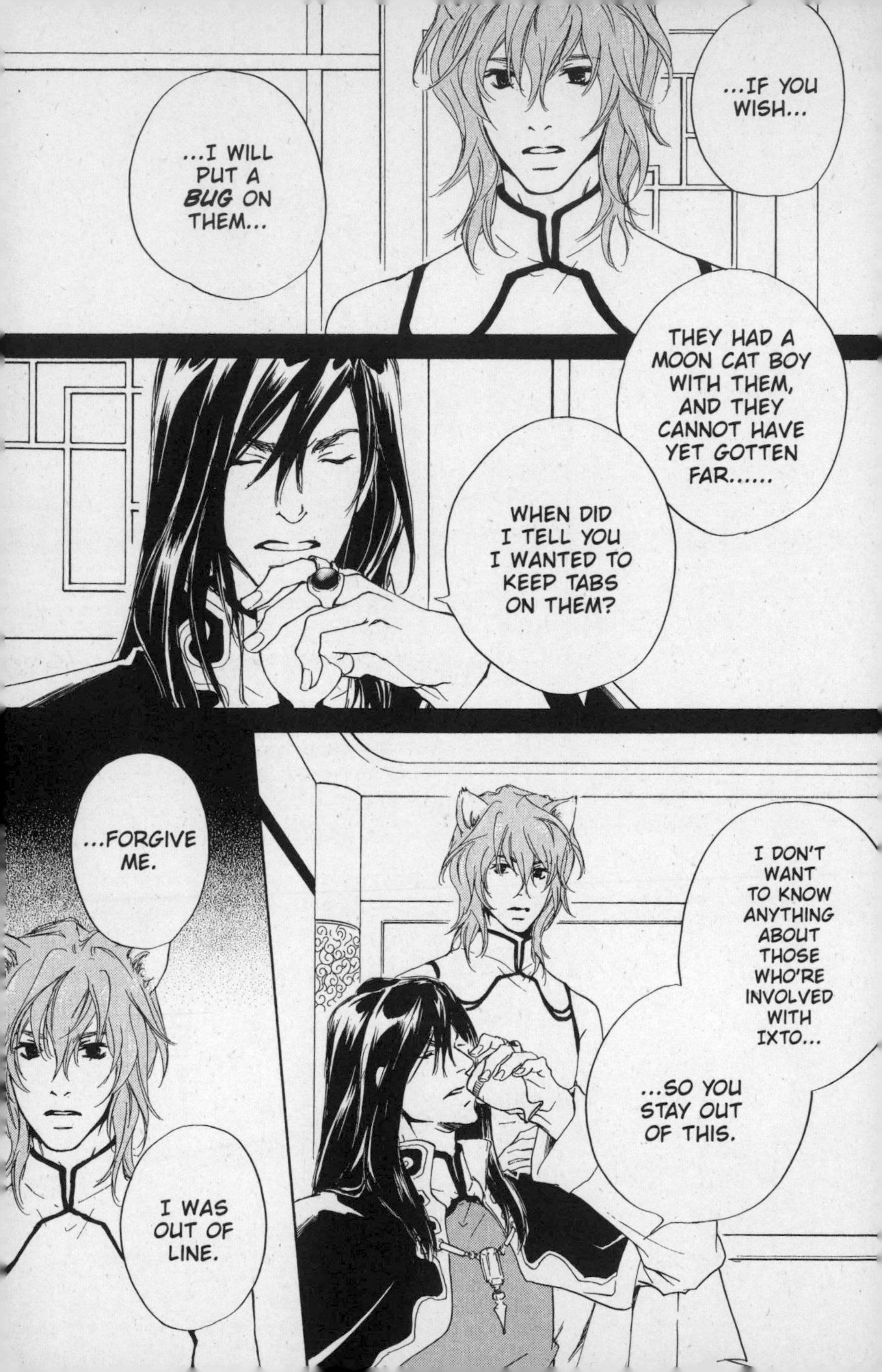

...IF YOU WISH...
...I WILL PUT A BUG ON THEM...
THEY HAD A MOON CAT BOY WITH THEM, AND THEY CANNOT HAVE YET GOTTEN FAR......
WHEN DID I TELL YOU I WANTED TO KEEP TABS ON THEM?
I DON'T WANT TO KNOW ANYTHING ABOUT THOSE WHO'RE INVOLVED WITH IXTO...
...SO YOU STAY OUT OF THIS.
...FORGIVE ME.
I WAS OUT OF LINE.

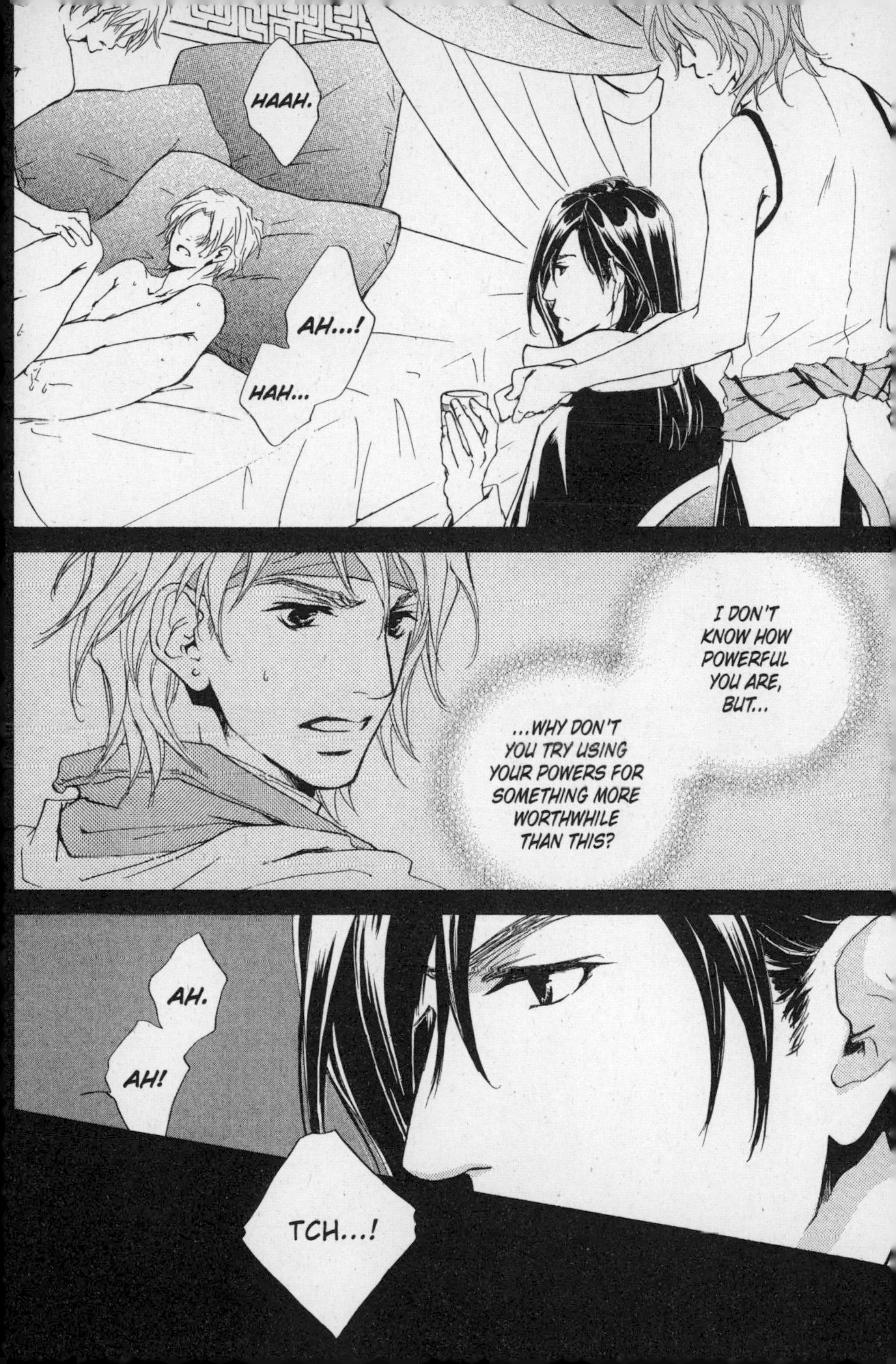
HAAH.
AH...!
HAH...
I DON'T KNOW HOW POWERFUL YOU ARE, BUT...
...WHY DON'T YOU TRY USING YOUR POWERS FOR SOMETHING MORE WORTHWHILE THAN THIS?
AH.
AH!
TCH...!

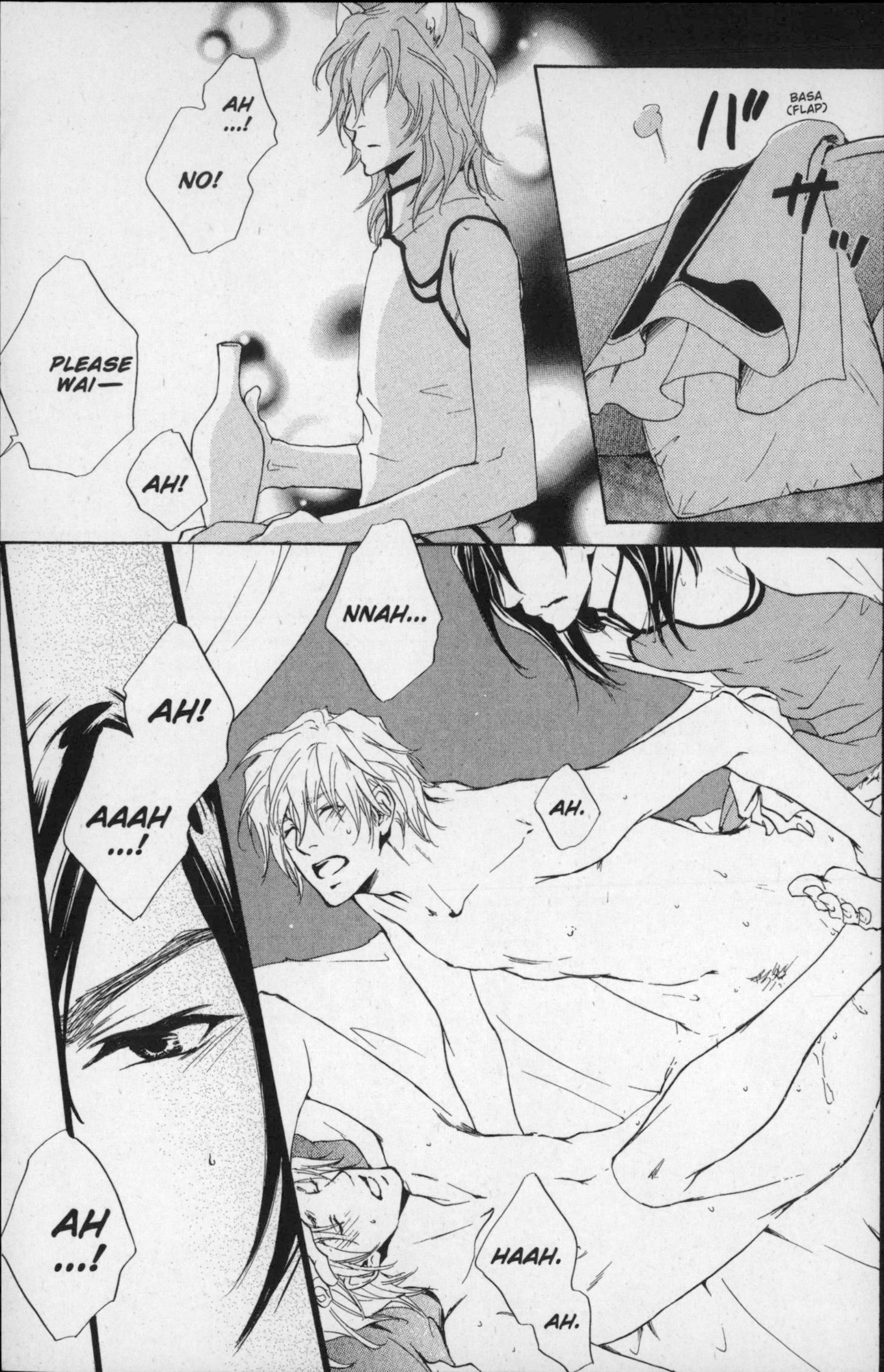
BASA (FLAP)
AH ...! NO!
PLEASE WAI—
AH!
NNAH...
AH.
AH!
AAAH ...!
HAAH.
AH.
AH ...!

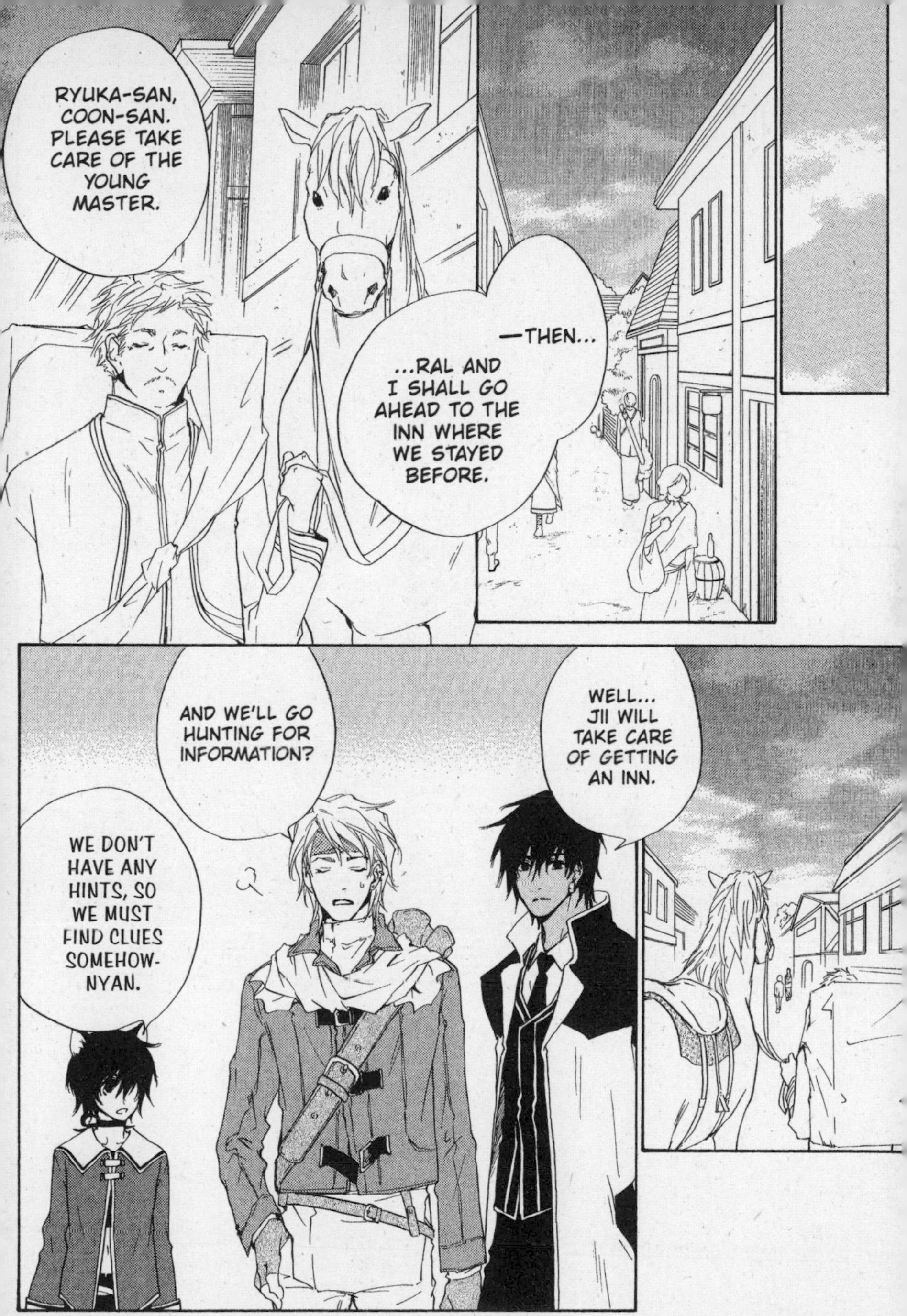
RYUKA-SAN, COON-SAN. PLEASE TAKE CARE OF THE YOUNG MASTER.
—THEN... ...RAL AND I SHALL GO AHEAD TO THE INN WHERE WE STAYED BEFORE.
WELL... JII WILL TAKE CARE OF GETTING AN INN.
AND WE'LL GO HUNTING FOR INFORMATION?
WE DON'T HAVE ANY HINTS, SO WE MUST FIND CLUES SOMEHOW-NYAN.

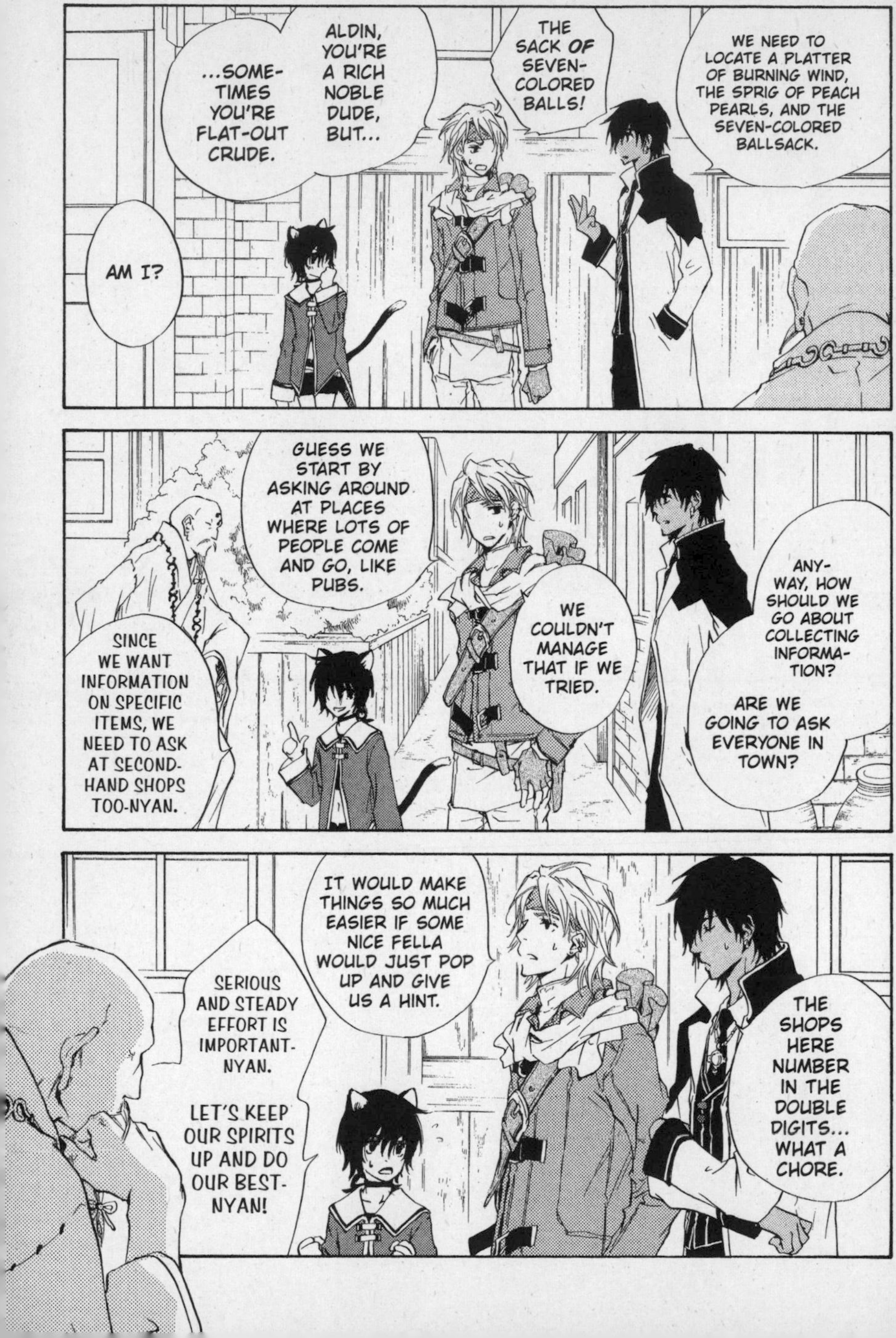
WE NEED TO LOCATE A PLATTER OF BURNING WIND, THE SPRIG OF PEACH PEARLS, AND THE SEVEN-COLORED BALLSACK.
THE SACK OF SEVEN-COLORED BALLS!
ALDIN, YOU'RE A RICH NOBLE DUDE, BUT...
...SOMETIMES YOU'RE FLAT-OUT CRUDE.
AM I?
ANYWAY, HOW SHOULD WE GO ABOUT COLLECTING INFORMATION?
ARE WE GOING TO ASK EVERYONE IN TOWN?
WE COULDN'T MANAGE THAT IF WE TRIED.
GUESS WE START BY ASKING AROUND AT PLACES WHERE LOTS OF PEOPLE COME AND GO, LIKE PUBS.
SINCE WE WANT INFORMATION ON SPECIFIC ITEMS, WE NEED TO ASK AT SECOND-HAND SHOPS TOO-NYAN.
THE SHOPS HERE NUMBER IN THE DOUBLE DIGITS... WHAT A CHORE.
IT WOULD MAKE THINGS SO MUCH EASIER IF SOME NICE FELLA WOULD JUST POP UP AND GIVE US A HINT.
SERIOUS AND STEADY EFFORT IS IMPORTANT-NYAN.
LET'S KEEP OUR SPIRITS UP AND DO OUR BEST-NYAN!

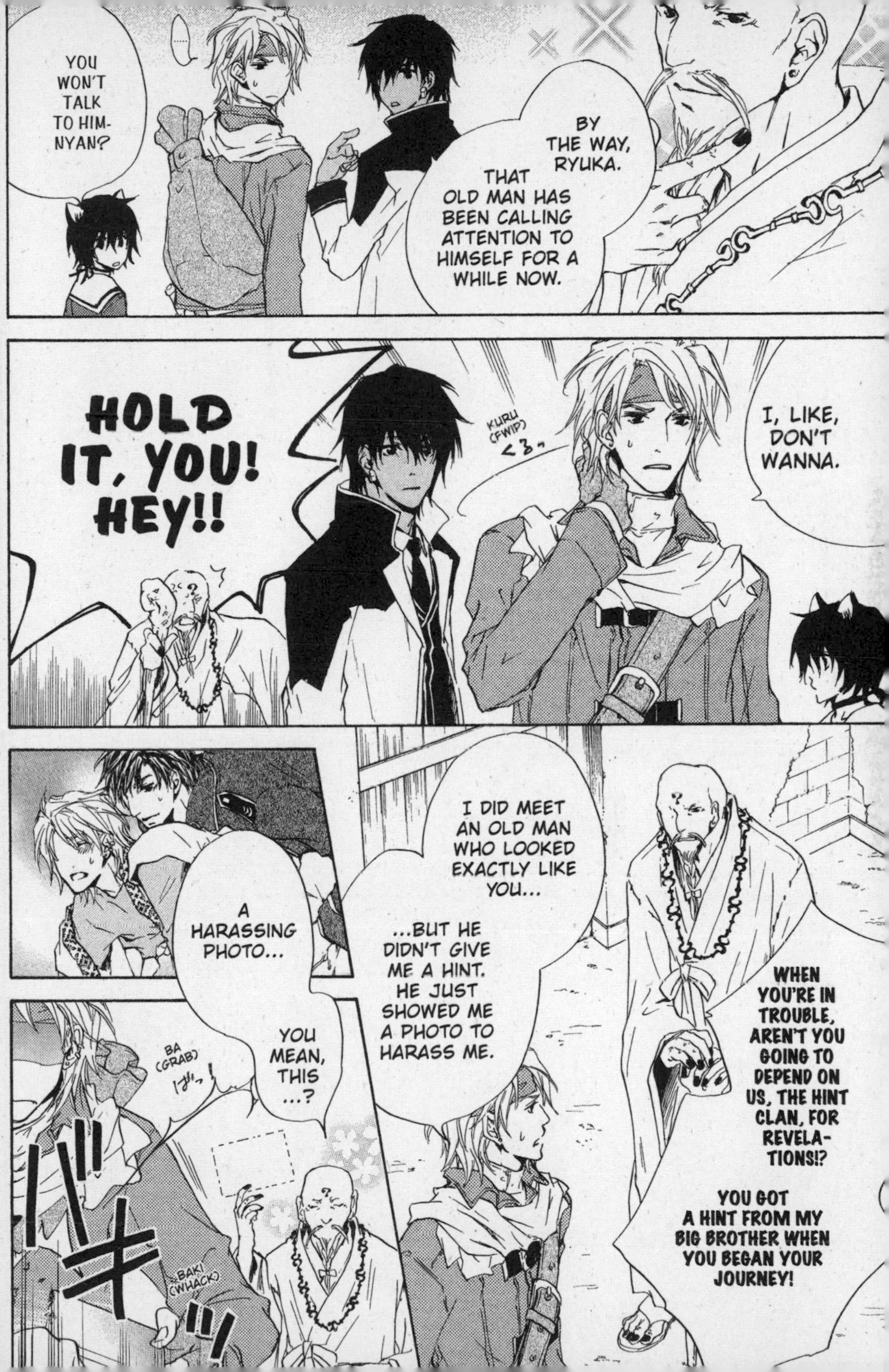

BY THE WAY, RYUKA.
THAT OLD MAN HAS BEEN CALLING ATTENTION TO HIMSELF FOR A WHILE NOW.
......
YOU WON'T TALK TO HIM-NYAN?
I, LIKE, DON'T WANNA.
KURU (FWIP)
HOLD IT, YOU! HEY!!
WHEN YOU'RE IN TROUBLE, AREN'T YOU GOING TO DEPEND ON US, THE HINT CLAN, FOR REVELATIONS!?
YOU GOT A HINT FROM MY BIG BROTHER WHEN YOU BEGAN YOUR JOURNEY!
I DID MEET AN OLD MAN WHO LOOKED EXACTLY LIKE YOU...
...BUT HE DIDN'T GIVE ME A HINT. HE JUST SHOWED ME A PHOTO TO HARASS ME.
YOU MEAN, THIS ...?
BA (GRAB)
A HARASSING PHOTO...
BAKI (WHACK)

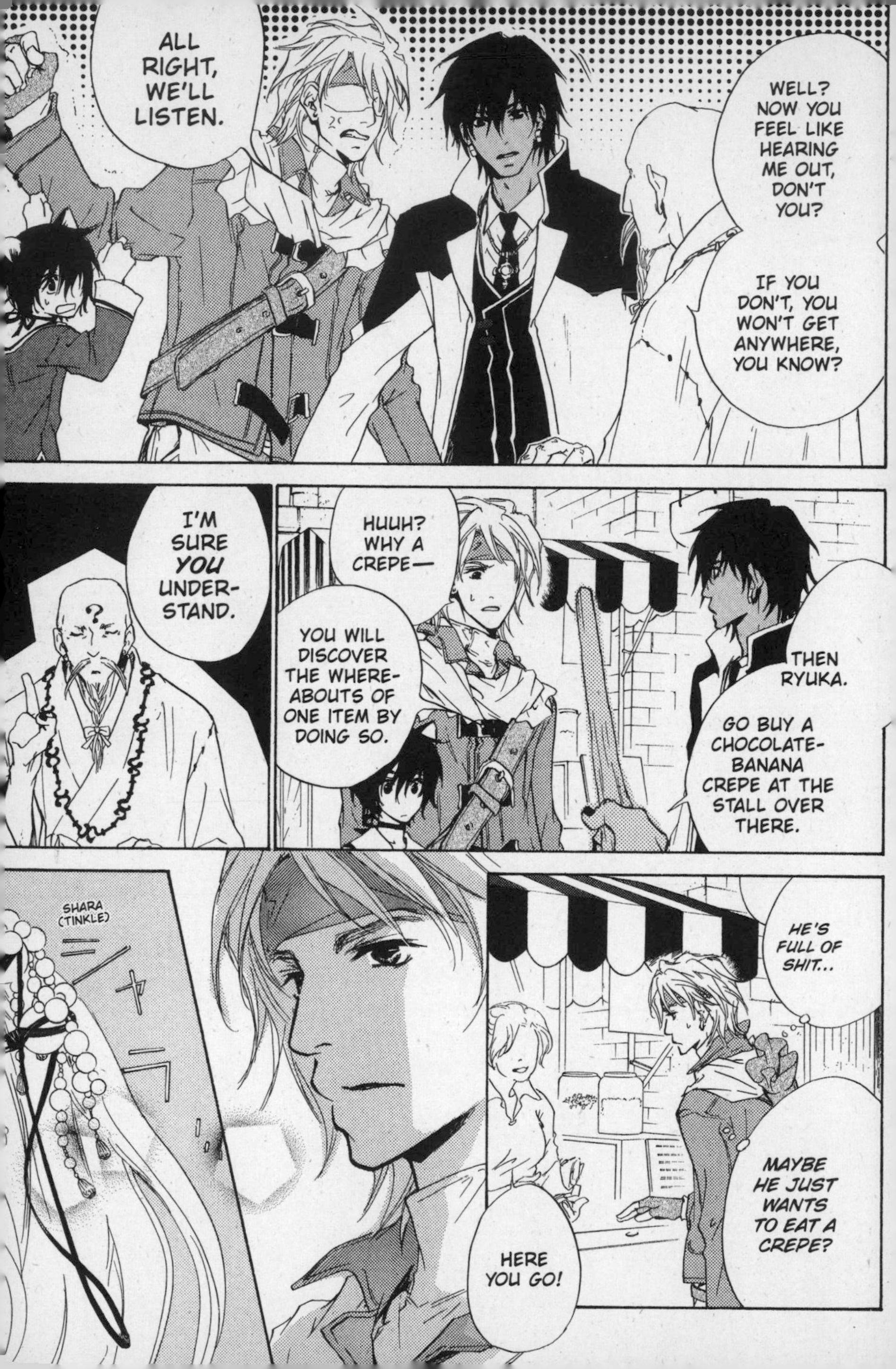
WELL? NOW YOU FEEL LIKE HEARING ME OUT, DON'T YOU?
IF YOU DON'T, YOU WON'T GET ANYWHERE, YOU KNOW?
ALL RIGHT, WE'LL LISTEN.
THEN RYUKA.
GO BUY A CHOCOLATE-BANANA CREPE AT THE STALL OVER THERE.
HUUH? WHY A CREPE—
YOU WILL DISCOVER THE WHERE-ABOUTS OF ONE ITEM BY DOING SO.
I'M SURE *YOU* UNDER-STAND.
HE'S FULL OF SHIT...
MAYBE HE JUST WANTS TO EAT A CREPE?
HERE YOU GO!
SHARA (TINKLE)

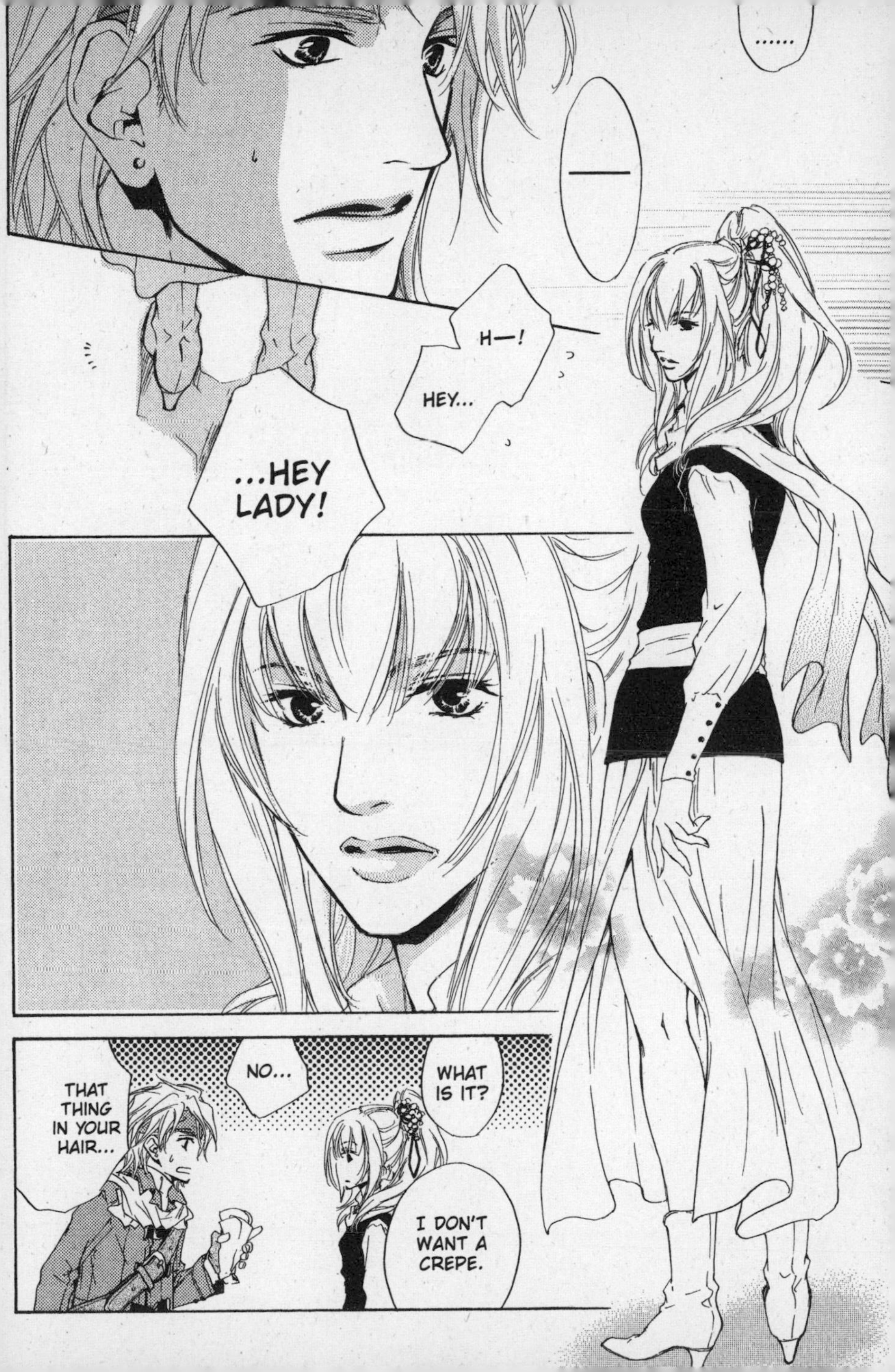

......
—
H—!
HEY...
...HEY LADY!
WHAT IS IT?
NO...
THAT THING IN YOUR HAIR...
I DON'T WANT A CREPE.

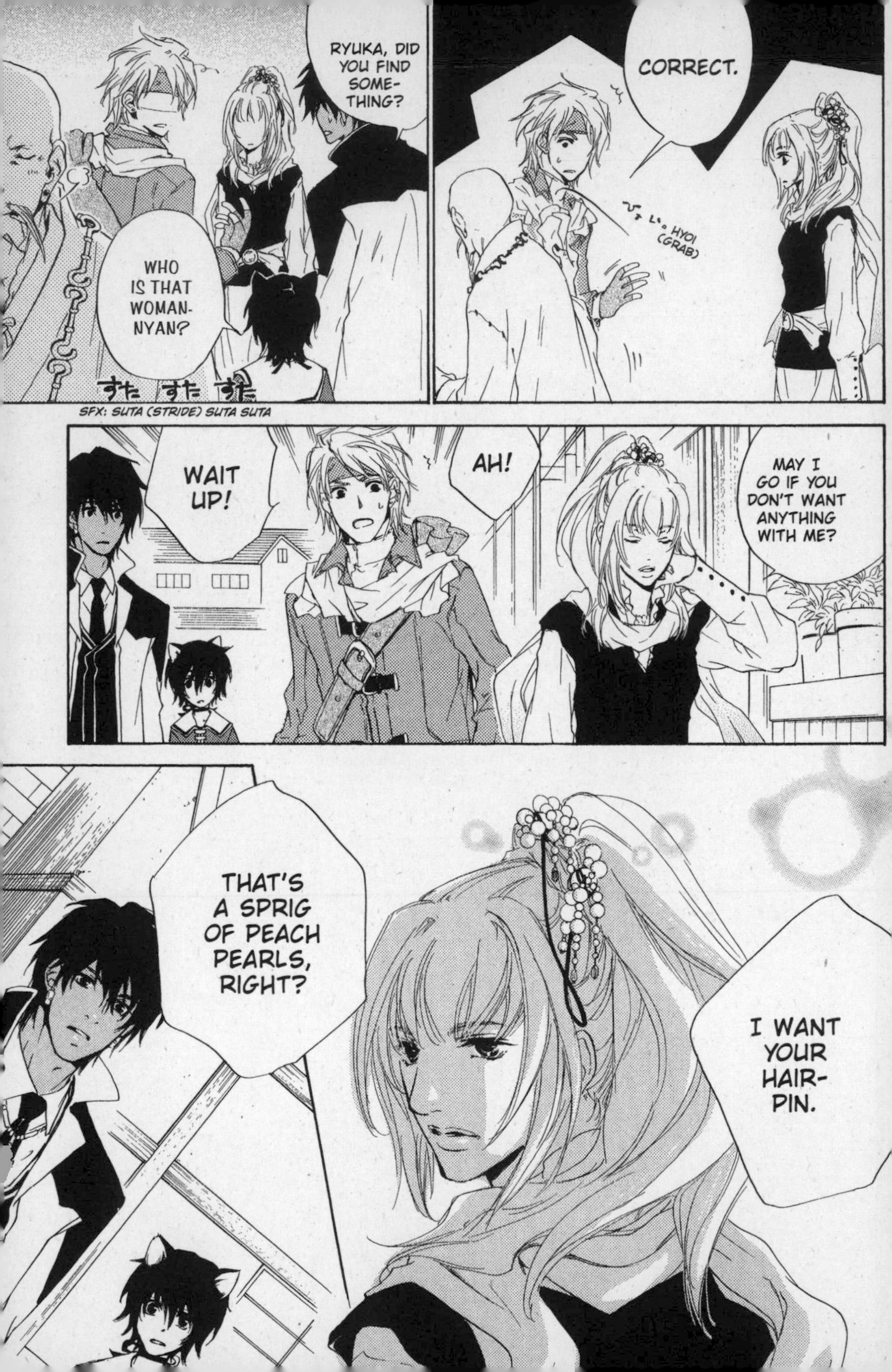
CORRECT.
ひょい。 HYOI (GRAB)
RYUKA, DID YOU FIND SOME-THING?
WHO IS THAT WOMAN-NYAN?
すた すた すた
SFX: SUTA (STRIDE) SUTA SUTA
MAY I GO IF YOU DON'T WANT ANYTHING WITH ME?
AH!
WAIT UP!
THAT'S A SPRIG OF PEACH PEARLS, RIGHT?
I WANT YOUR HAIR-PIN.

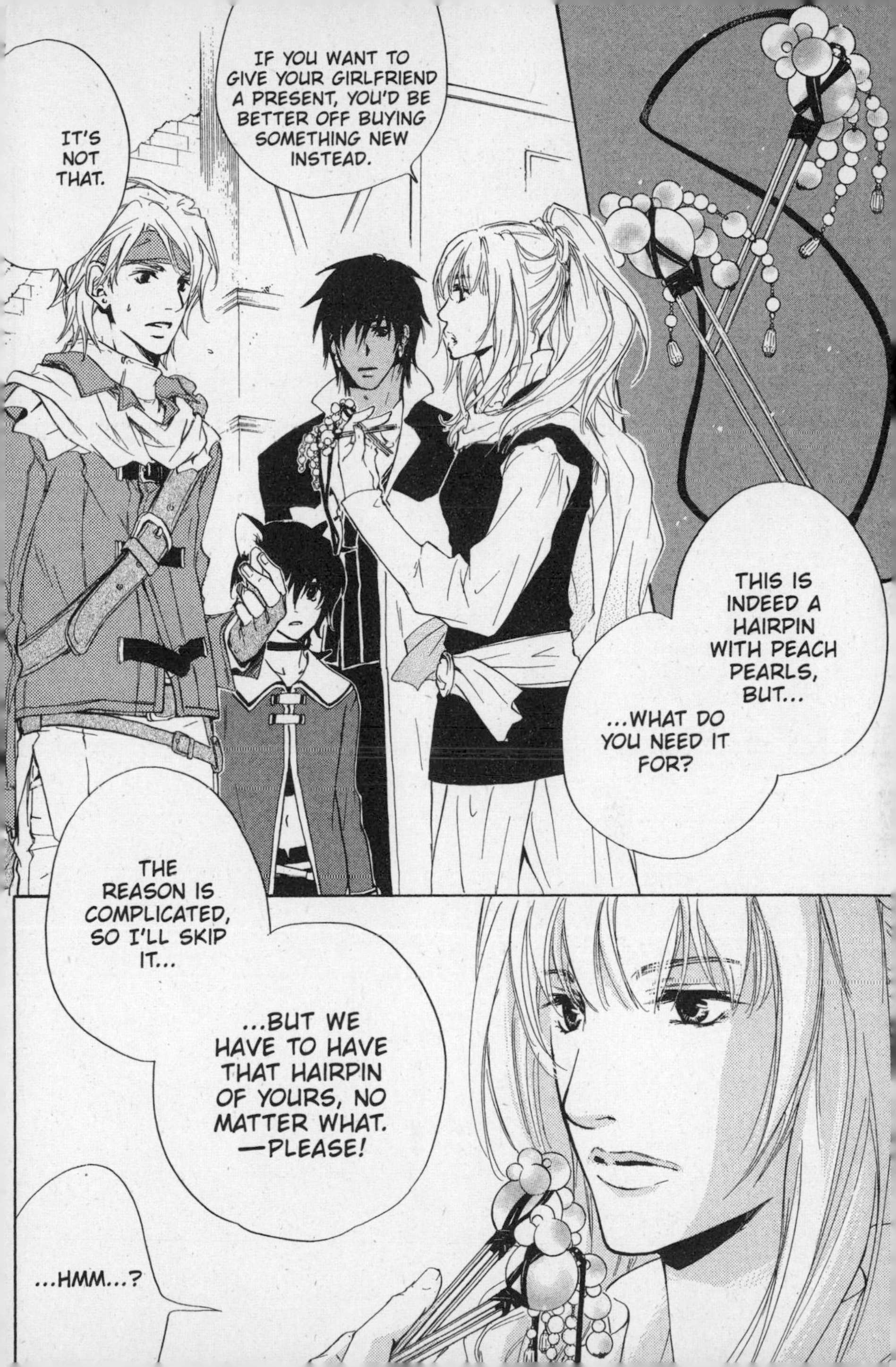
THIS IS INDEED A HAIRPIN WITH PEACH PEARLS, BUT...
...WHAT DO YOU NEED IT FOR?
IF YOU WANT TO GIVE YOUR GIRLFRIEND A PRESENT, YOU'D BE BETTER OFF BUYING SOMETHING NEW INSTEAD.
IT'S NOT THAT.
THE REASON IS COMPLICATED, SO I'LL SKIP IT...
...BUT WE HAVE TO HAVE THAT HAIRPIN OF YOURS, NO MATTER WHAT. —PLEASE!
...HMM...?

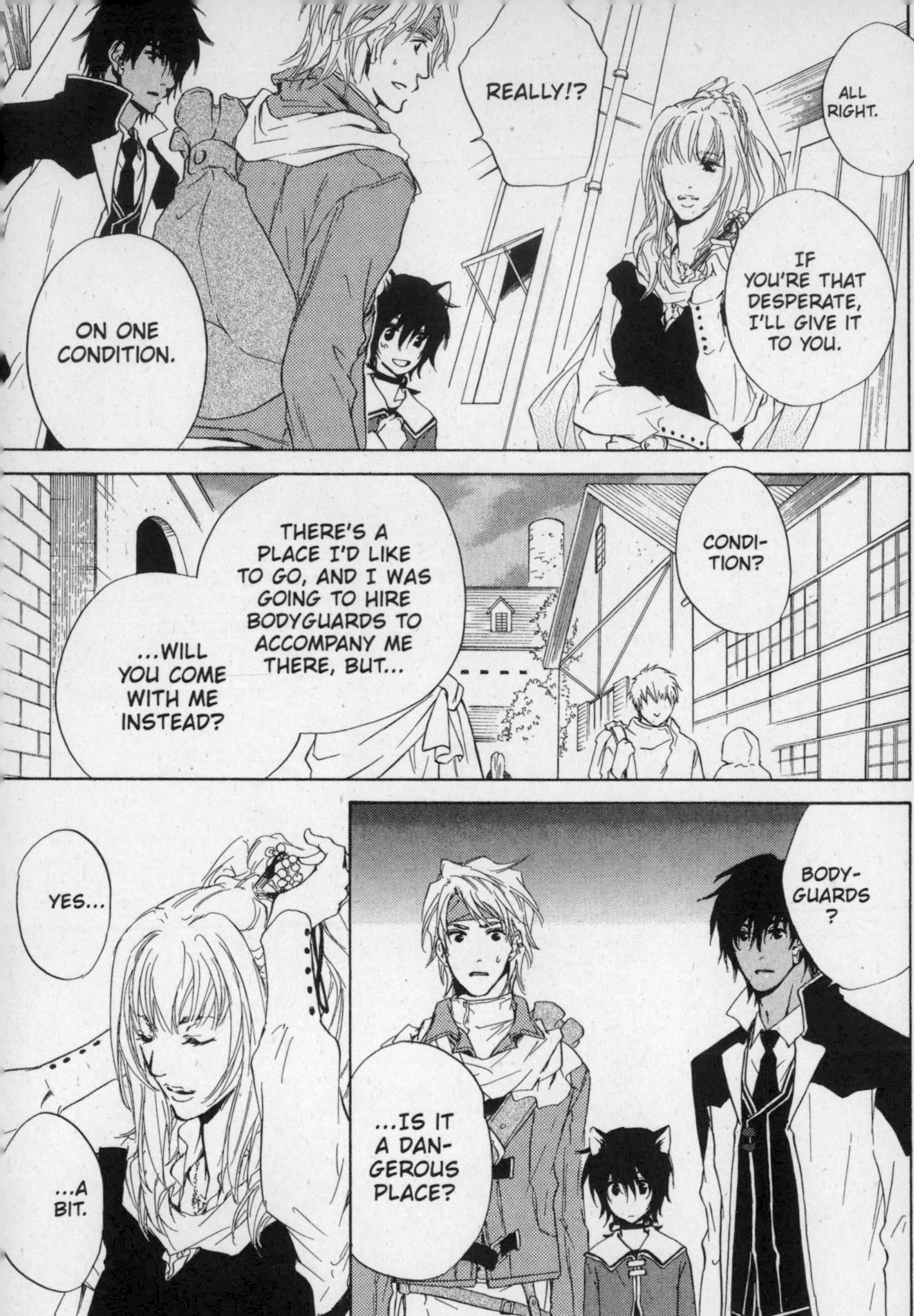
ALL RIGHT.
IF YOU'RE THAT DESPERATE, I'LL GIVE IT TO YOU.
REALLY!?
ON ONE CONDITION.
CONDI-TION?
THERE'S A PLACE I'D LIKE TO GO, AND I WAS GOING TO HIRE BODYGUARDS TO ACCOMPANY ME THERE, BUT...
...WILL YOU COME WITH ME INSTEAD?
BODY-GUARDS?
...IS IT A DAN-GEROUS PLACE?
YES...
...A BIT.

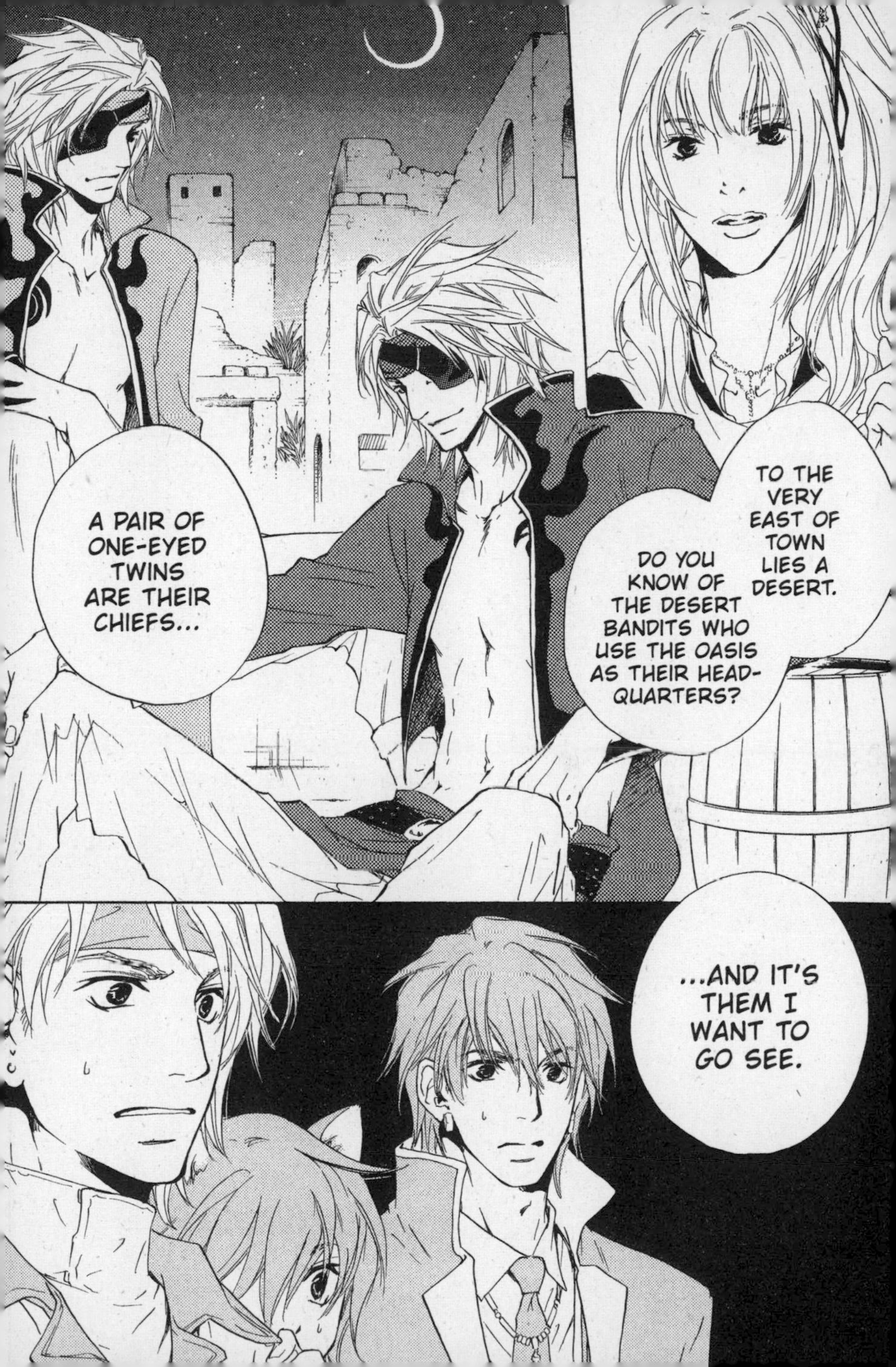
TO THE VERY EAST OF TOWN LIES A DESERT.
DO YOU KNOW OF THE DESERT BANDITS WHO USE THE OASIS AS THEIR HEAD-QUARTERS?
A PAIR OF ONE-EYED TWINS ARE THEIR CHIEFS...
...AND IT'S THEM I WANT TO GO SEE.

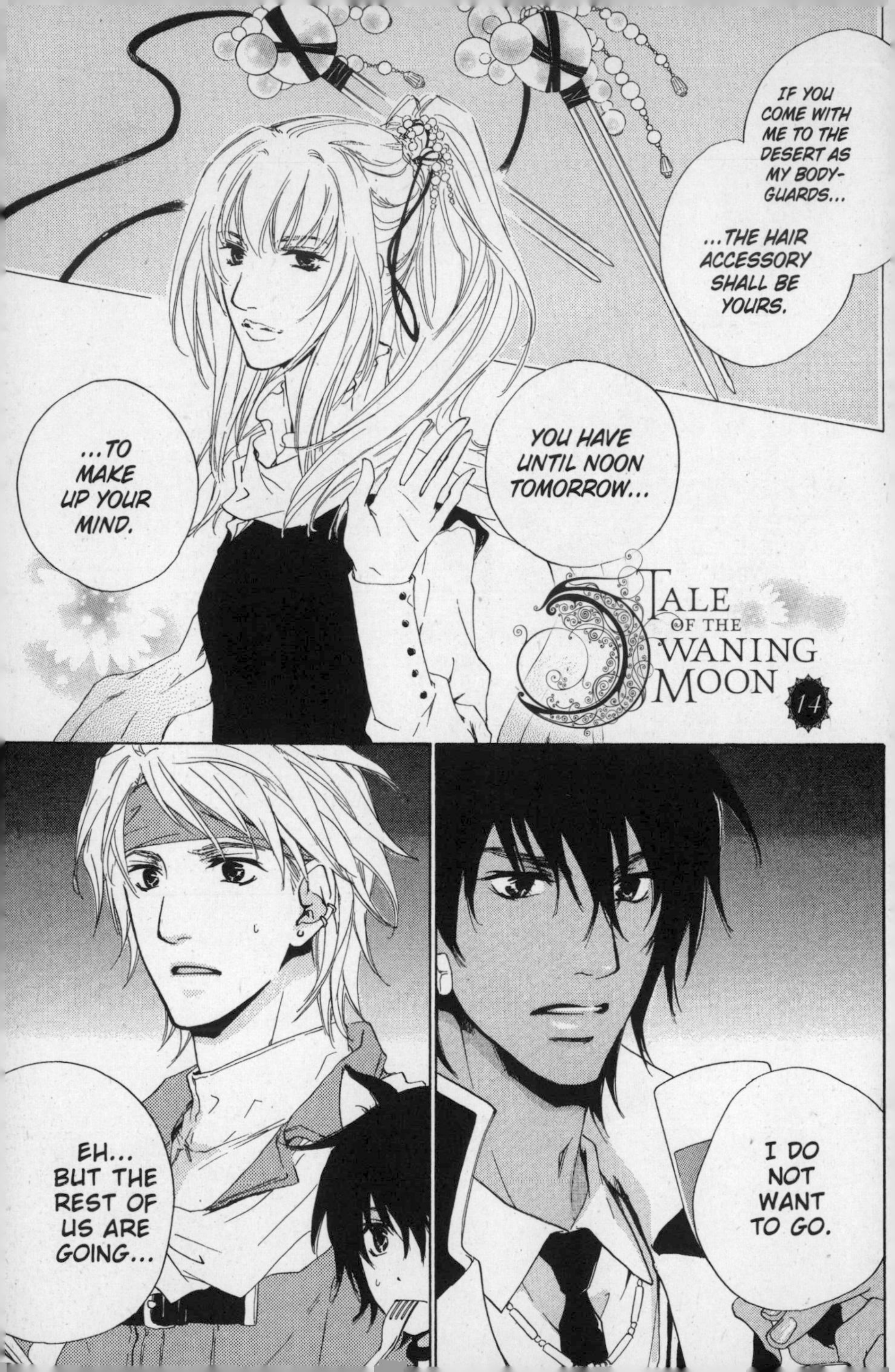
IF YOU COME WITH ME TO THE DESERT AS MY BODY-GUARDS...
...THE HAIR ACCESSORY SHALL BE YOURS.
YOU HAVE UNTIL NOON TOMORROW...
...TO MAKE UP YOUR MIND.
TALE OF THE WANING MOON
14
I DO NOT WANT TO GO.
EH... BUT THE REST OF US ARE GOING...

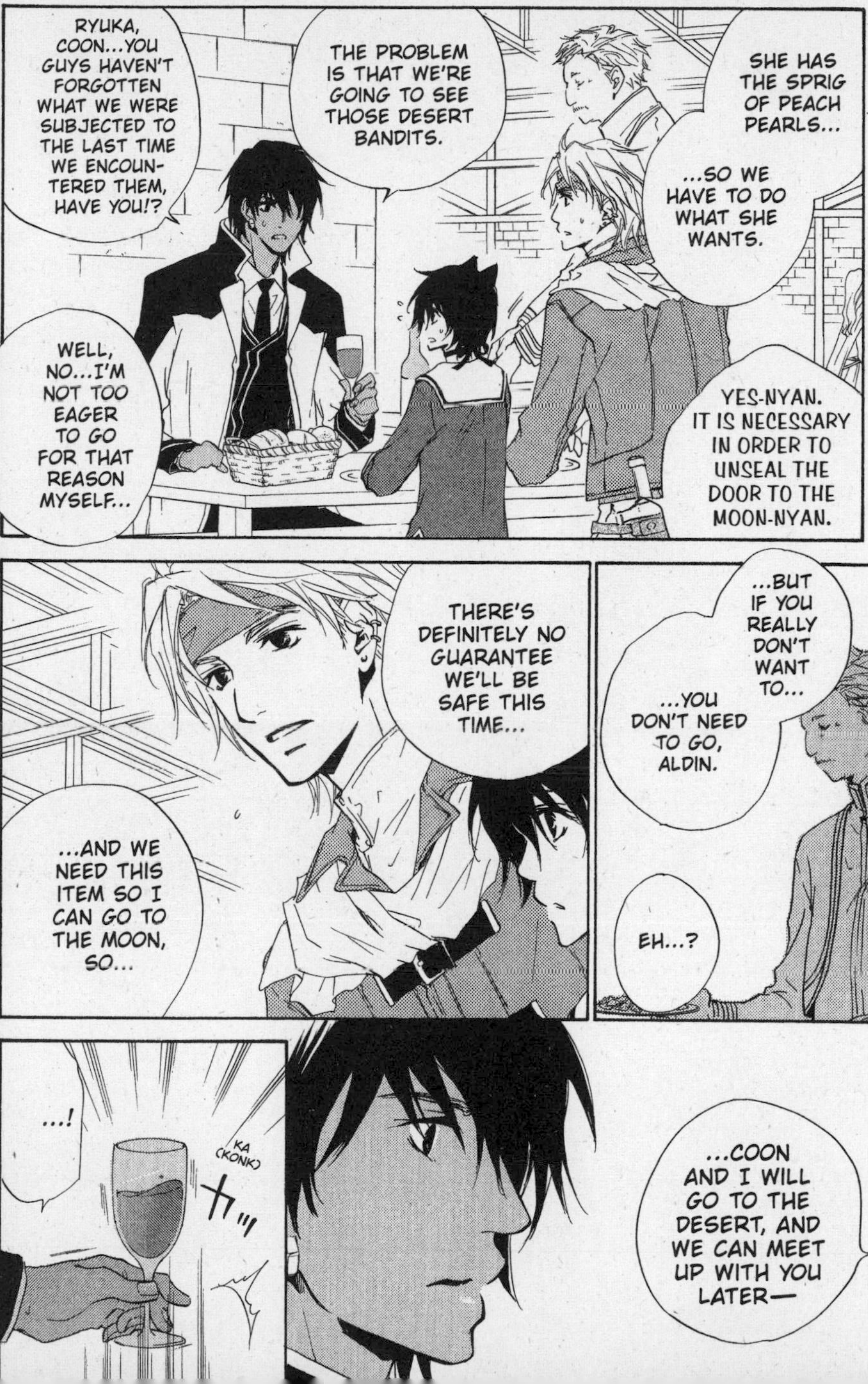
SHE HAS THE SPRIG OF PEACH PEARLS...
...SO WE HAVE TO DO WHAT SHE WANTS.
THE PROBLEM IS THAT WE'RE GOING TO SEE THOSE DESERT BANDITS.
RYUKA, COON...YOU GUYS HAVEN'T FORGOTTEN WHAT WE WERE SUBJECTED TO THE LAST TIME WE ENCOUNTERED THEM, HAVE YOU!?
YES-NYAN. IT IS NECESSARY IN ORDER TO UNSEAL THE DOOR TO THE MOON-NYAN.
WELL, NO...I'M NOT TOO EAGER TO GO FOR THAT REASON MYSELF...
...BUT IF YOU REALLY DON'T WANT TO...
...YOU DON'T NEED TO GO, ALDIN.
EH...?
THERE'S DEFINITELY NO GUARANTEE WE'LL BE SAFE THIS TIME...
...AND WE NEED THIS ITEM SO I CAN GO TO THE MOON, SO...
...COON AND I WILL GO TO THE DESERT, AND WE CAN MEET UP WITH YOU LATER—
KA (KONK)
...!

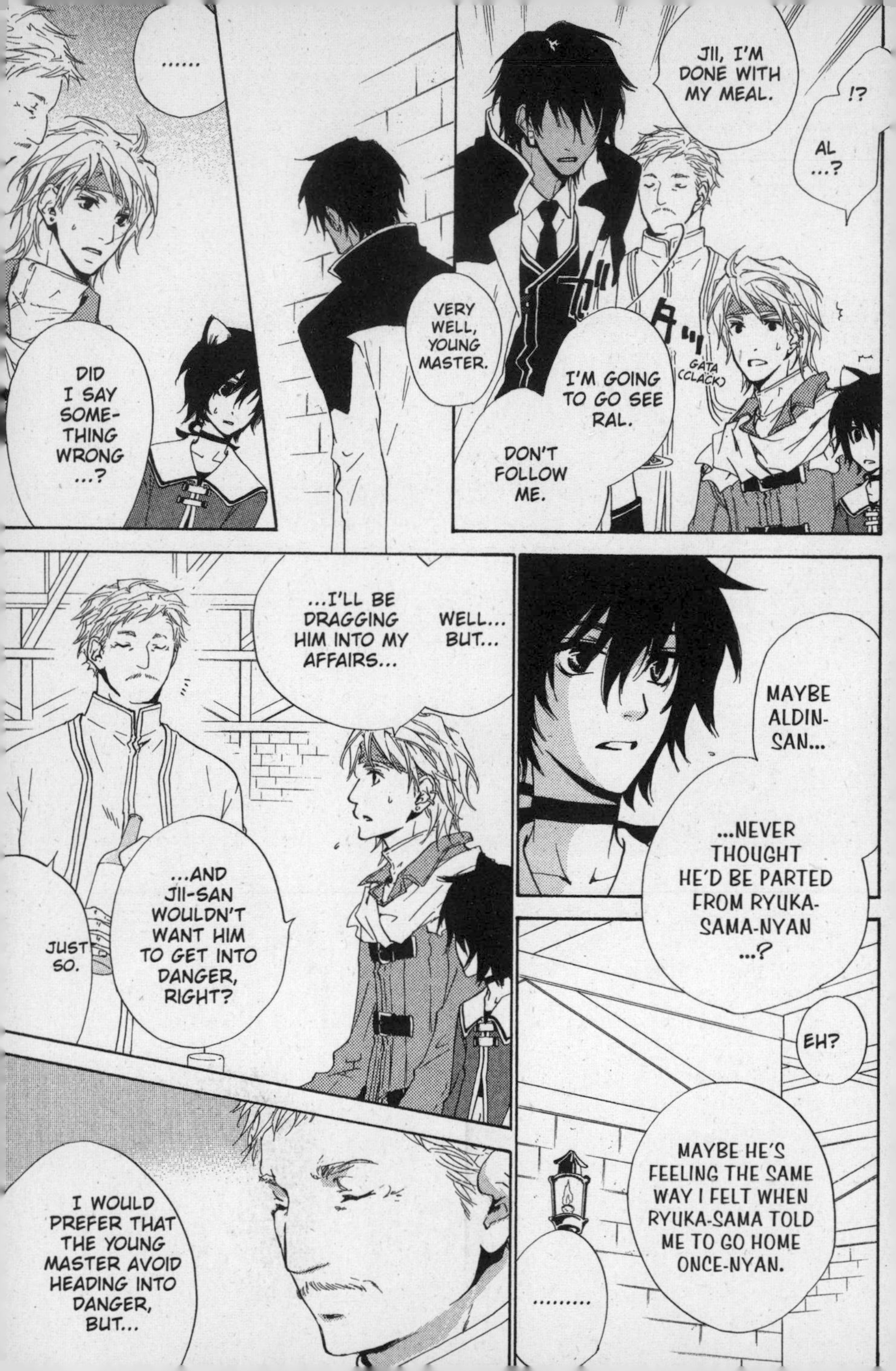
JII, I'M DONE WITH MY MEAL.
!?
AL ...?
GATA (CLACK)
I'M GOING TO GO SEE RAL.
DON'T FOLLOW ME.
VERY WELL, YOUNG MASTER.
......
DID I SAY SOME-THING WRONG ...?
MAYBE ALDIN-SAN...
...NEVER THOUGHT HE'D BE PARTED FROM RYUKA-SAMA-NYAN ...?
EH?
MAYBE HE'S FEELING THE SAME WAY I FELT WHEN RYUKA-SAMA TOLD ME TO GO HOME ONCE-NYAN.
....
WELL... BUT...
...I'LL BE DRAGGING HIM INTO MY AFFAIRS...
...AND JII-SAN WOULDN'T WANT HIM TO GET INTO DANGER, RIGHT?
JUST SO.
I WOULD PREFER THAT THE YOUNG MASTER AVOID HEADING INTO DANGER, BUT...

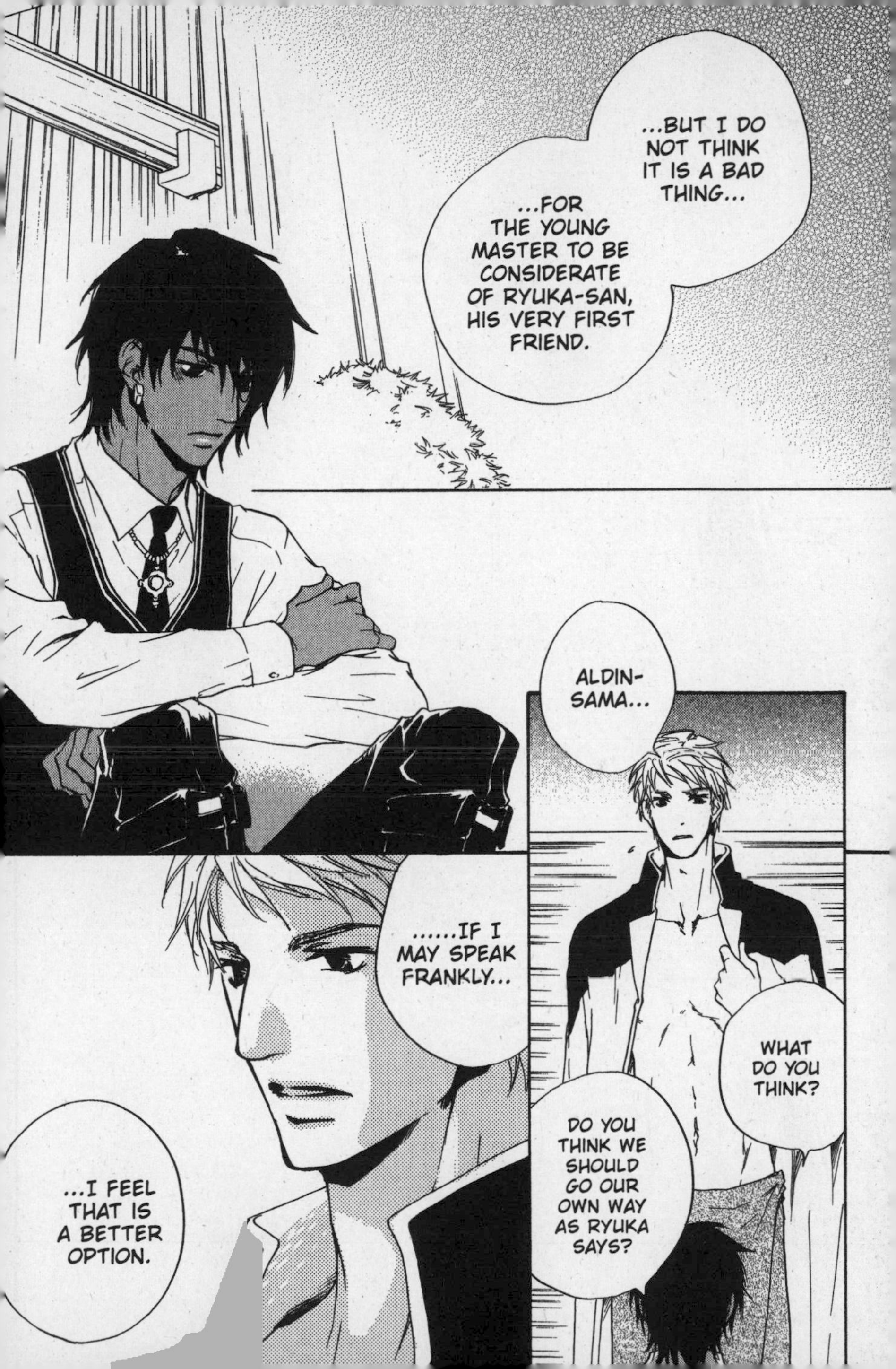
...BUT I DO NOT THINK IT IS A BAD THING...
...FOR THE YOUNG MASTER TO BE CONSIDERATE OF RYUKA-SAN, HIS VERY FIRST FRIEND.
ALDIN-SAMA...
WHAT DO YOU THINK?
DO YOU THINK WE SHOULD GO OUR OWN WAY AS RYUKA SAYS?
......IF I MAY SPEAK FRANKLY...
...I FEEL THAT IS A BETTER OPTION.

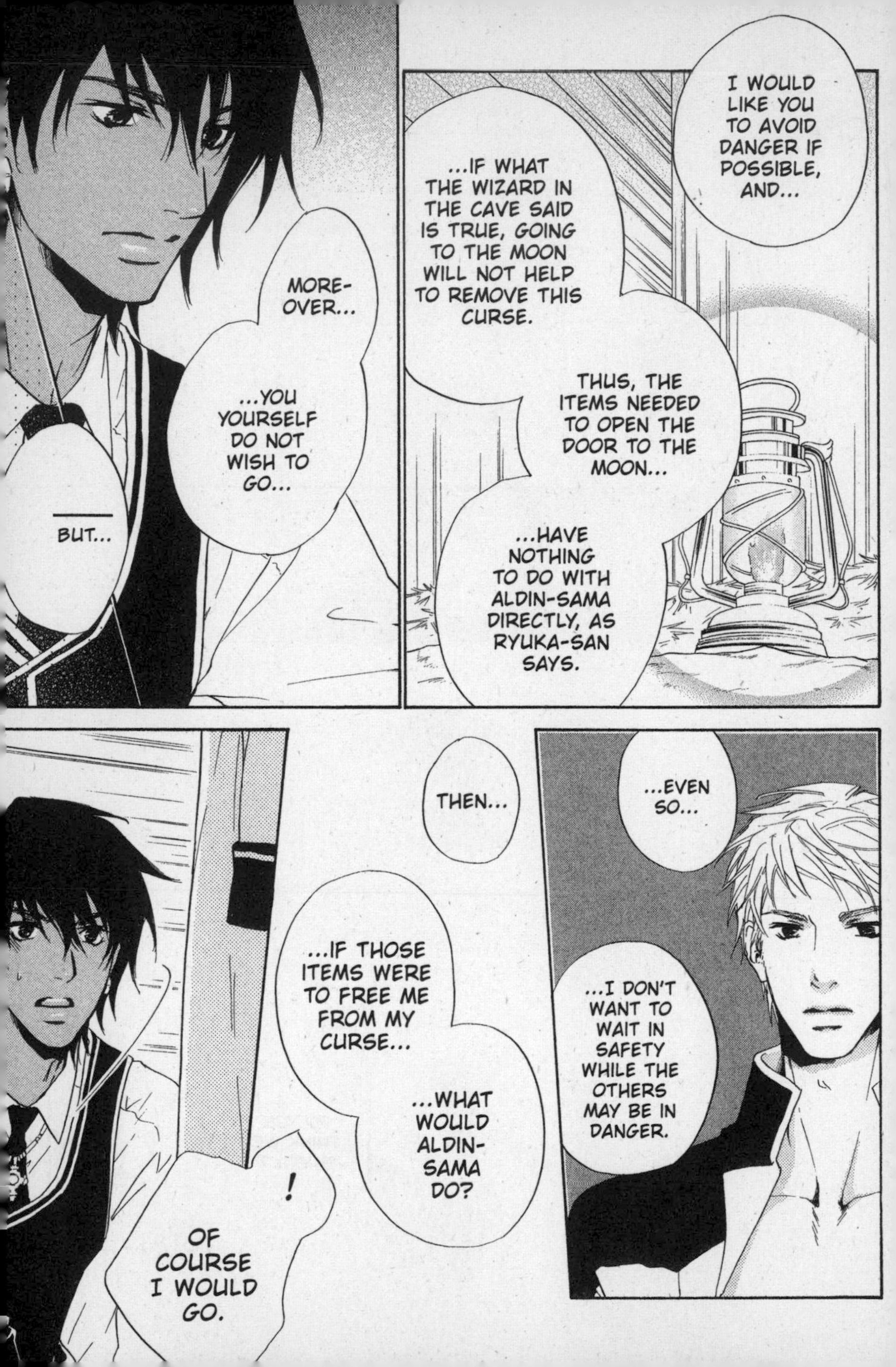
I WOULD LIKE YOU TO AVOID DANGER IF POSSIBLE, AND...
...IF WHAT THE WIZARD IN THE CAVE SAID IS TRUE, GOING TO THE MOON WILL NOT HELP TO REMOVE THIS CURSE.
THUS, THE ITEMS NEEDED TO OPEN THE DOOR TO THE MOON...
...HAVE NOTHING TO DO WITH ALDIN-SAMA DIRECTLY, AS RYUKA-SAN SAYS.
MORE-OVER...
...YOU YOURSELF DO NOT WISH TO GO...
BUT...
...EVEN SO...
...I DON'T WANT TO WAIT IN SAFETY WHILE THE OTHERS MAY BE IN DANGER.
THEN...
...IF THOSE ITEMS WERE TO FREE ME FROM MY CURSE...
...WHAT WOULD ALDIN-SAMA DO?
!
OF COURSE I WOULD GO.

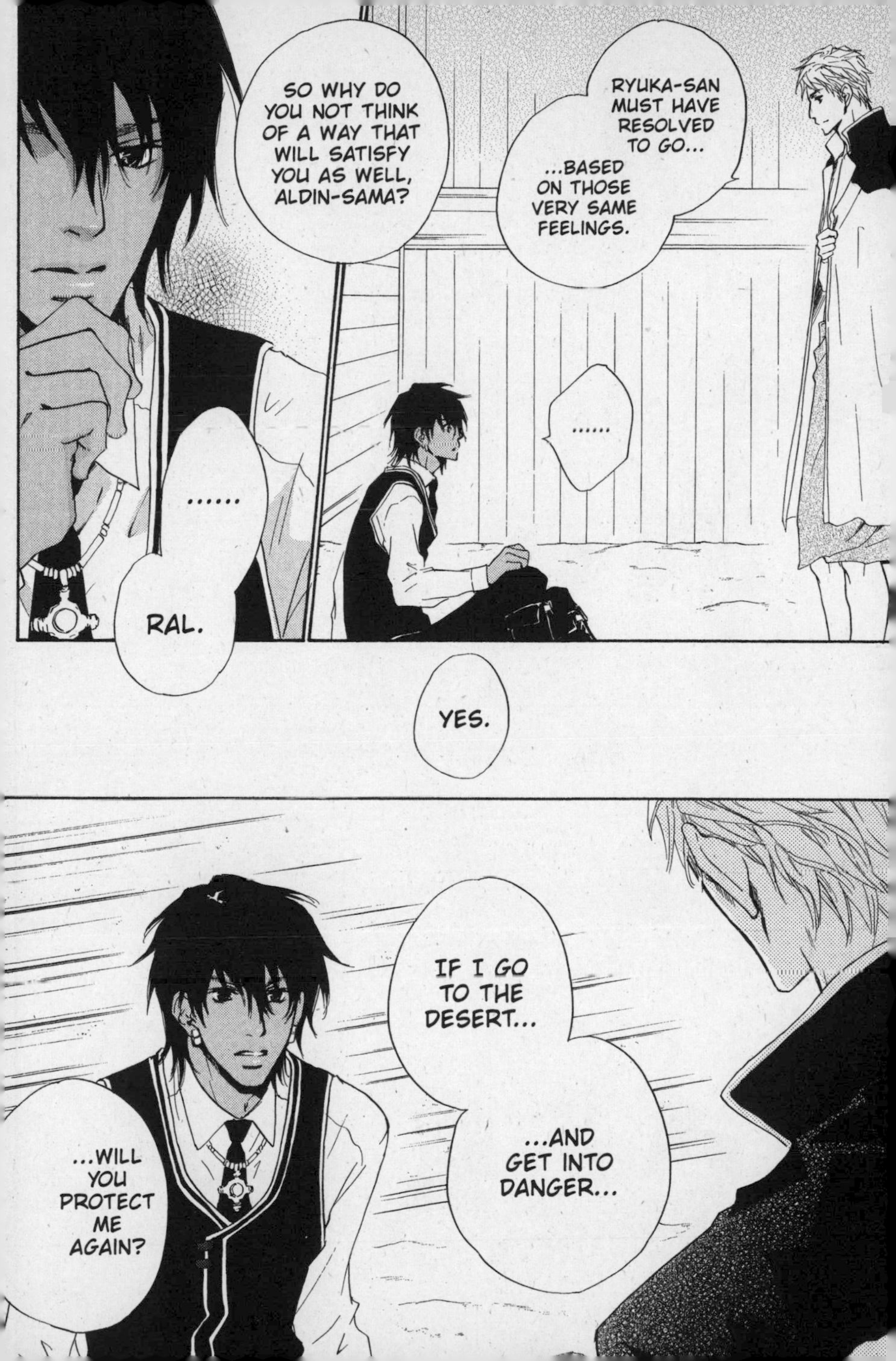

RYUKA-SAN MUST HAVE RESOLVED TO GO...
...BASED ON THOSE VERY SAME FEELINGS.
SO WHY DO YOU NOT THINK OF A WAY THAT WILL SATISFY YOU AS WELL, ALDIN-SAMA?
......
......
RAL.
YES.
IF I GO TO THE DESERT...
...AND GET INTO DANGER...
...WILL YOU PROTECT ME AGAIN?

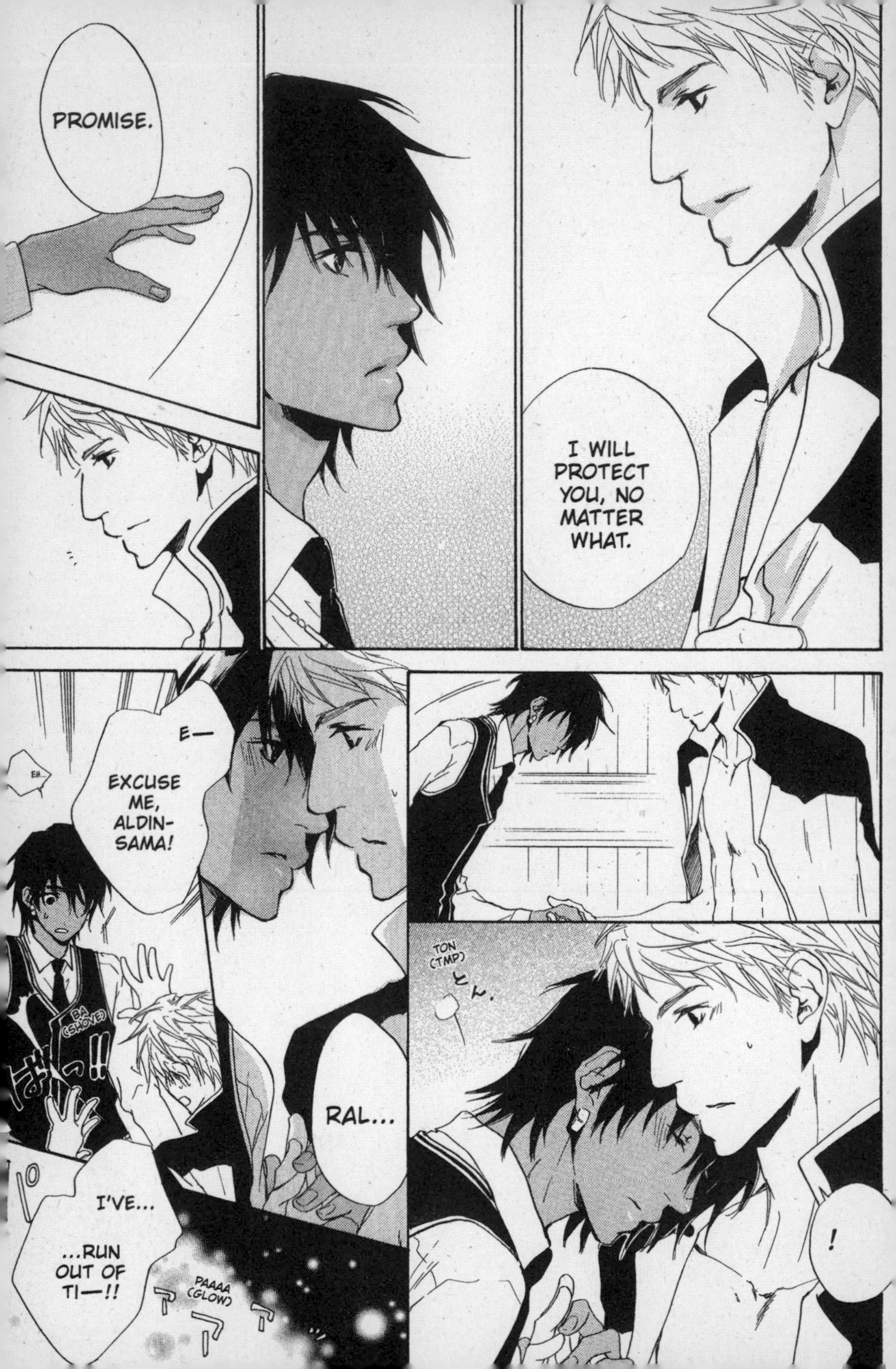
I WILL PROTECT YOU, NO MATTER WHAT.
PROMISE.
TON (TMP)
とん.
!
E—
EXCUSE ME, ALDIN-SAMA!
EH...
BA (SHOVE)
ばっ!!
RAL...
I'VE...
...RUN OUT OF TI—!!
PAAAA (GLOW)

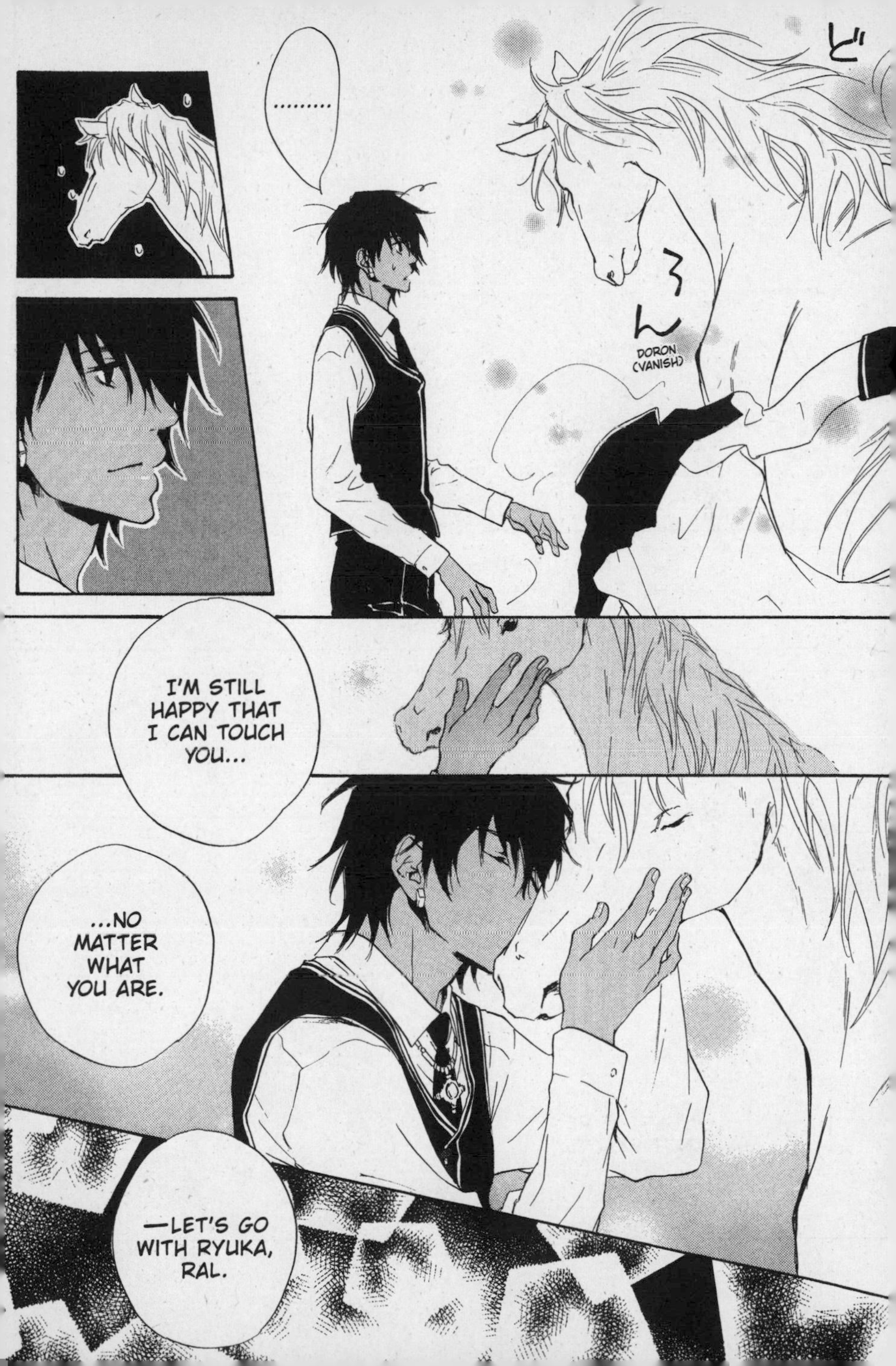

どろん
DORON (VANISH)
....
I'M STILL HAPPY THAT I CAN TOUCH YOU...
...NO MATTER WHAT YOU ARE.
—LET'S GO WITH RYUKA, RAL.

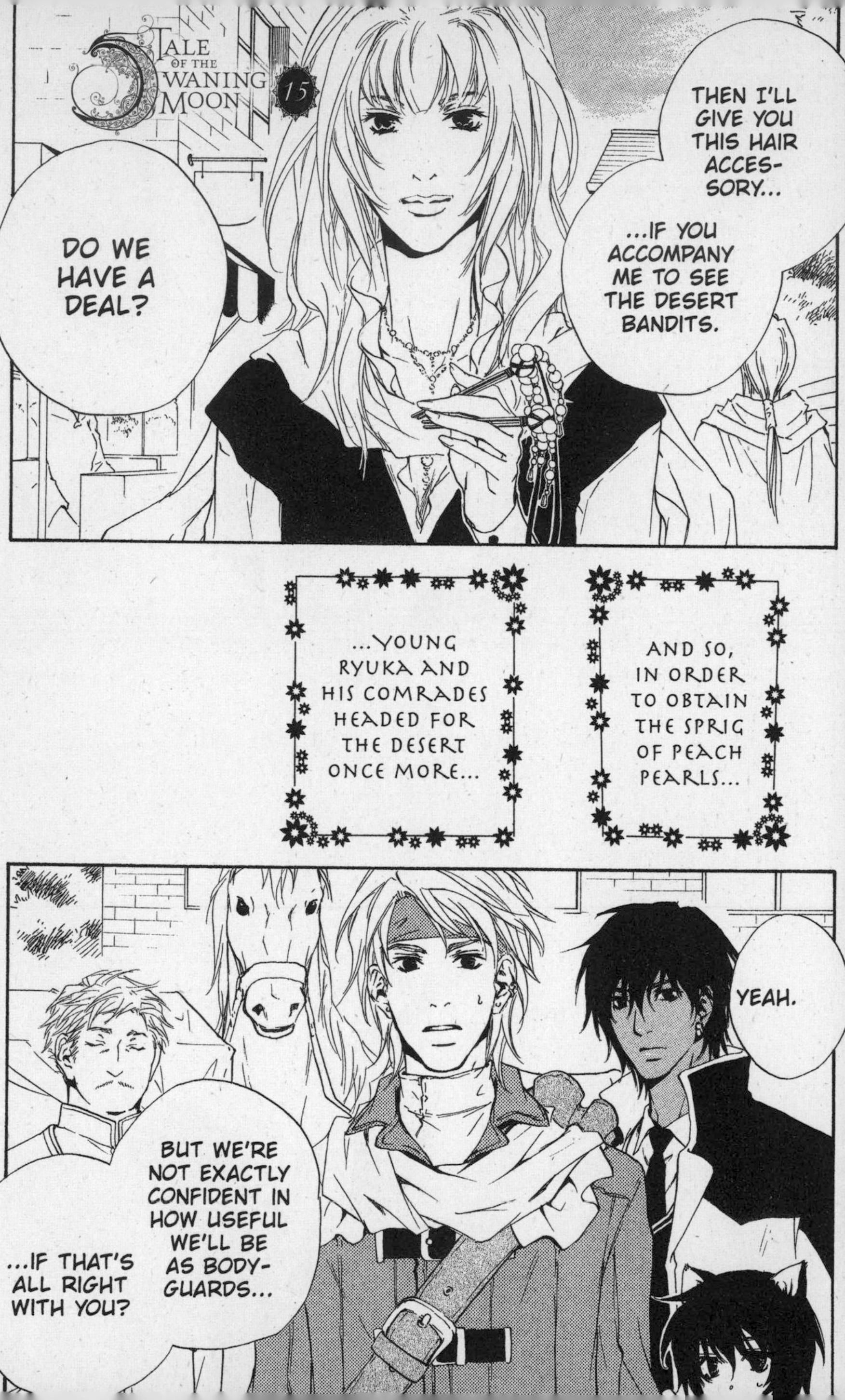
TALE OF THE WANING MOON 15
THEN I'LL GIVE YOU THIS HAIR ACCES-SORY...
...IF YOU ACCOMPANY ME TO SEE THE DESERT BANDITS.
DO WE HAVE A DEAL?
AND SO, IN ORDER TO OBTAIN THE SPRIG OF PEACH PEARLS...
...YOUNG RYUKA AND HIS COMRADES HEADED FOR THE DESERT ONCE MORE...
YEAH.
BUT WE'RE NOT EXACTLY CONFIDENT IN HOW USEFUL WE'LL BE AS BODY-GUARDS...
...IF THAT'S ALL RIGHT WITH YOU?

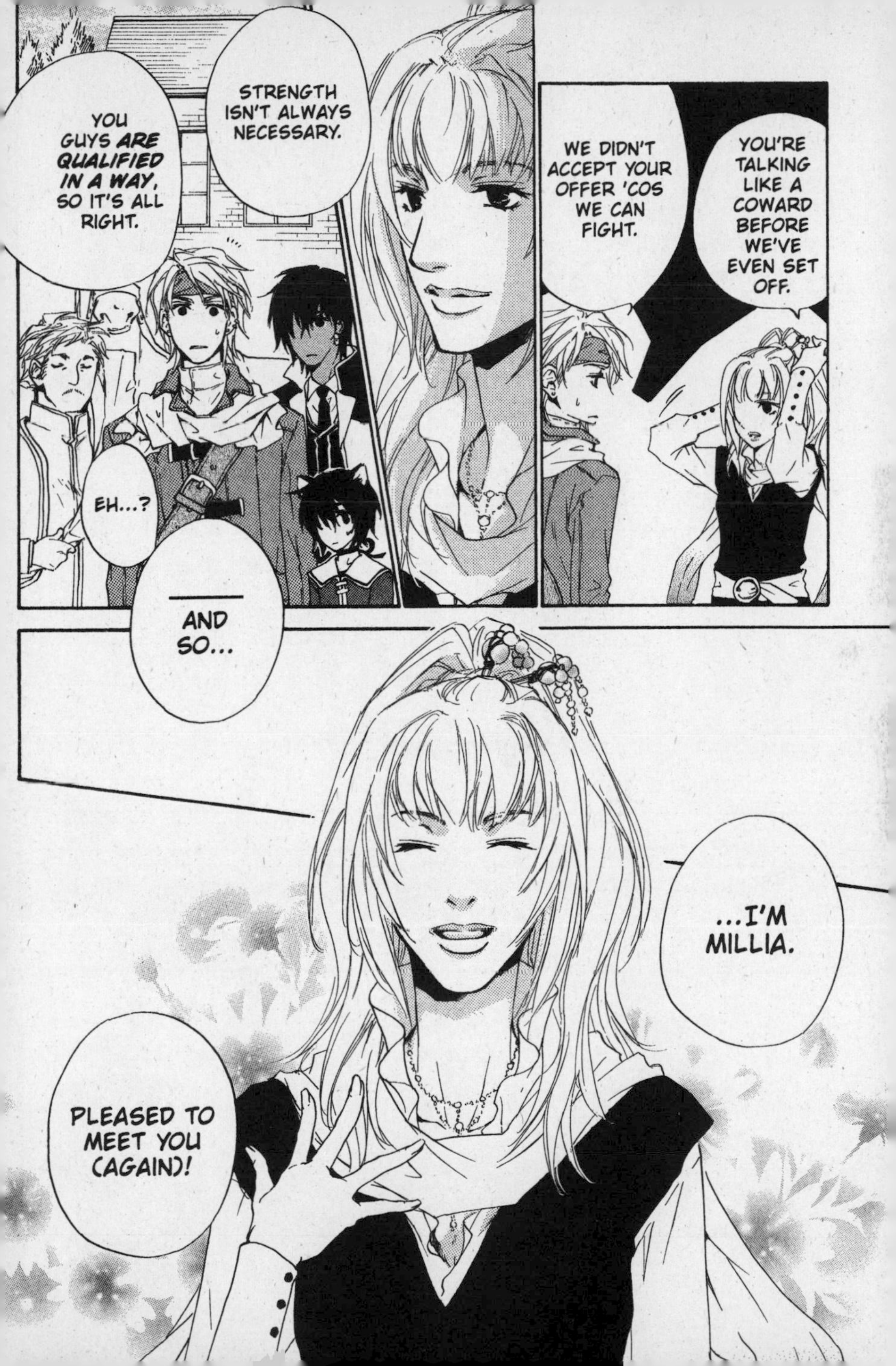
YOU'RE TALKING LIKE A COWARD BEFORE WE'VE EVEN SET OFF.
WE DIDN'T ACCEPT YOUR OFFER 'COS WE CAN FIGHT.
STRENGTH ISN'T ALWAYS NECESSARY.
YOU GUYS ***ARE QUALIFIED IN A WAY***, SO IT'S ALL RIGHT.
EH...?
AND SO...
...I'M MILLIA.
PLEASED TO MEET YOU (AGAIN)!

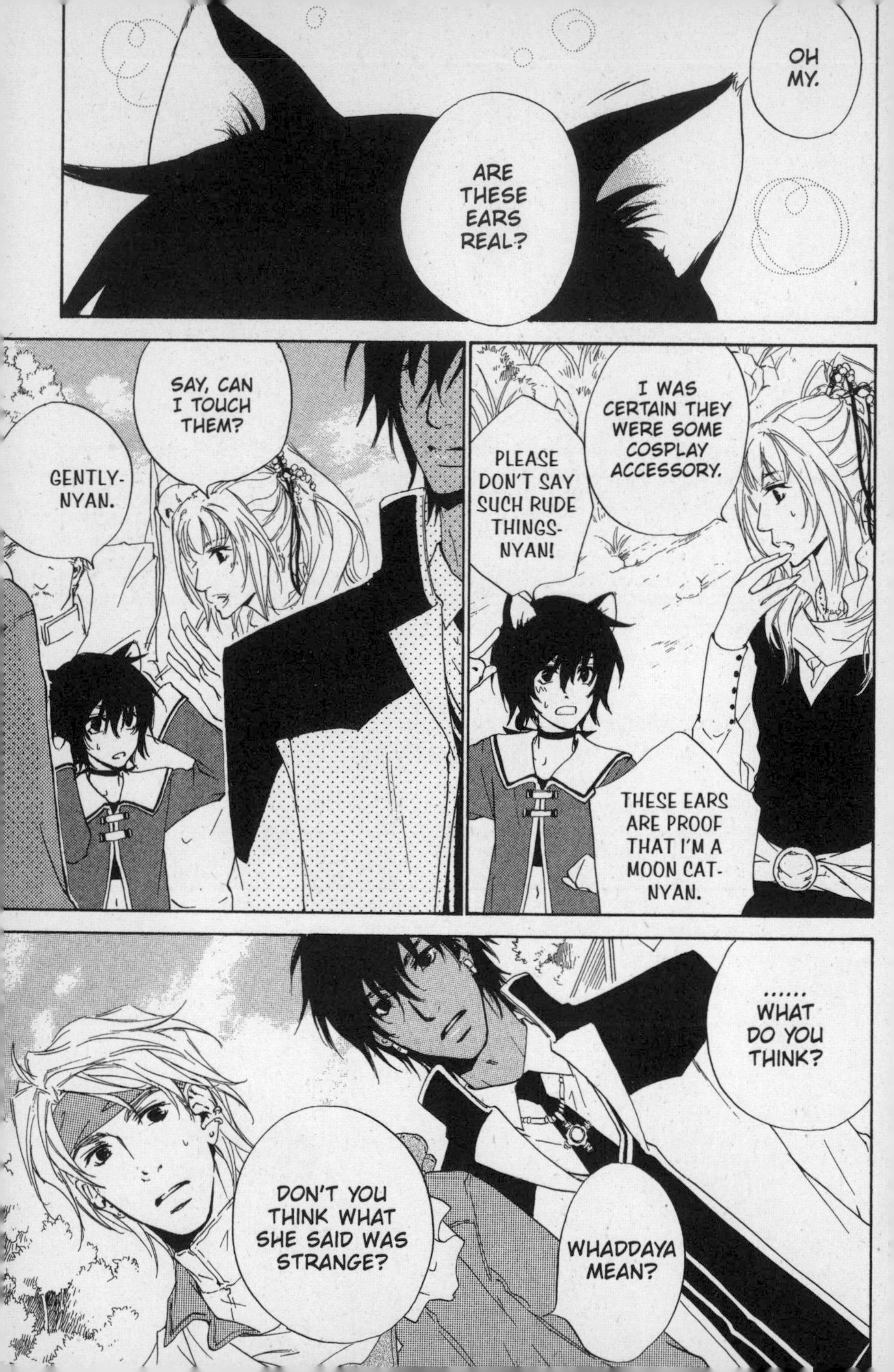
OH MY.
ARE THESE EARS REAL?
I WAS CERTAIN THEY WERE SOME COSPLAY ACCESSORY.
PLEASE DON'T SAY SUCH RUDE THINGS-NYAN!
THESE EARS ARE PROOF THAT I'M A MOON CAT-NYAN.
SAY, CAN I TOUCH THEM?
GENTLY-NYAN.
...... WHAT DO YOU THINK?
DON'T YOU THINK WHAT SHE SAID WAS STRANGE?
WHADDAYA MEAN?

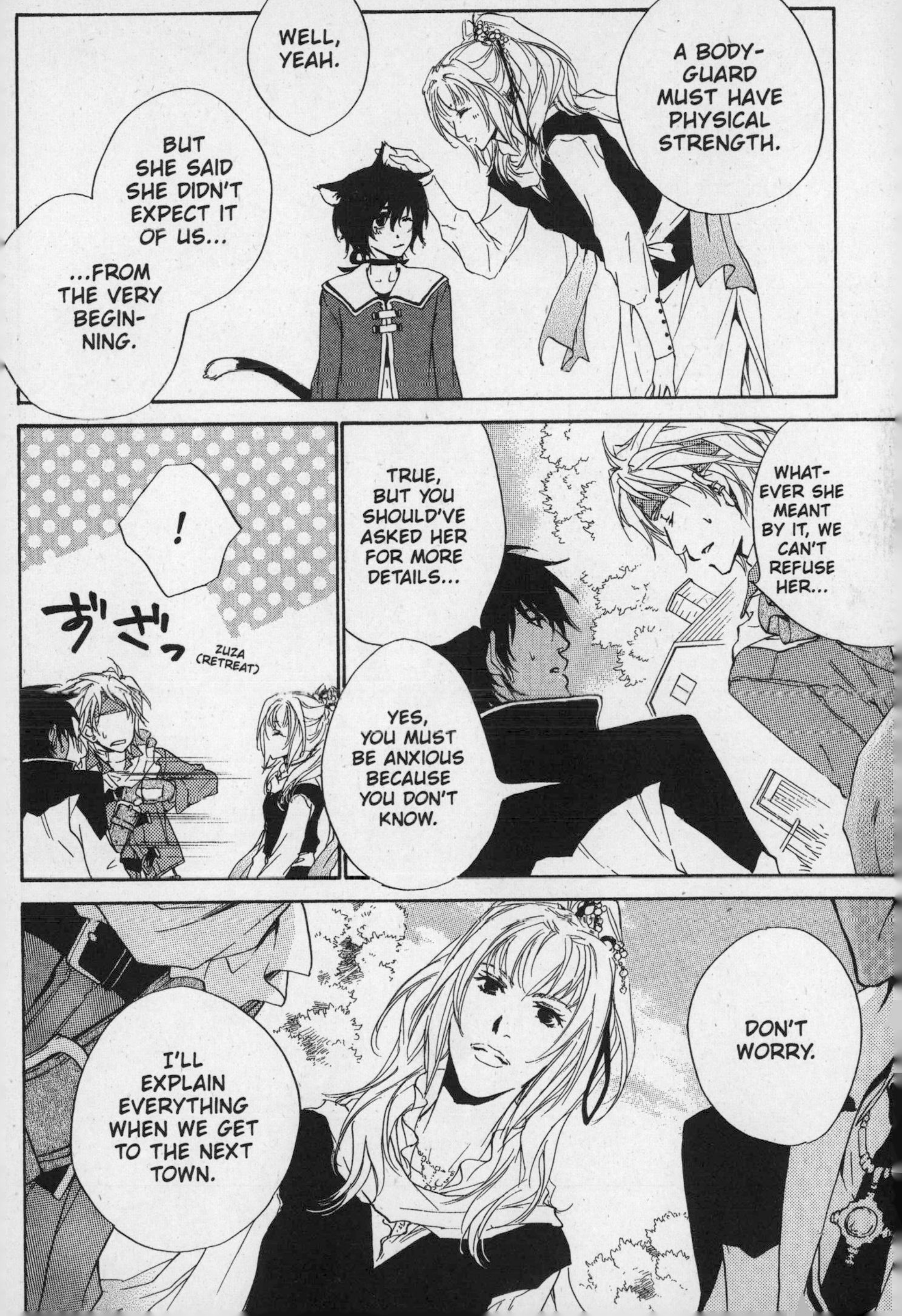
A BODY-GUARD MUST HAVE PHYSICAL STRENGTH.
WELL, YEAH.
BUT SHE SAID SHE DIDN'T EXPECT IT OF US...
...FROM THE VERY BEGINNING.
WHAT-EVER SHE MEANT BY IT, WE CAN'T REFUSE HER...
TRUE, BUT YOU SHOULD'VE ASKED HER FOR MORE DETAILS...
YES, YOU MUST BE ANXIOUS BECAUSE YOU DON'T KNOW.
!
ずざっ
ZUZA (RETREAT)
DON'T WORRY.
I'LL EXPLAIN EVERYTHING WHEN WE GET TO THE NEXT TOWN.

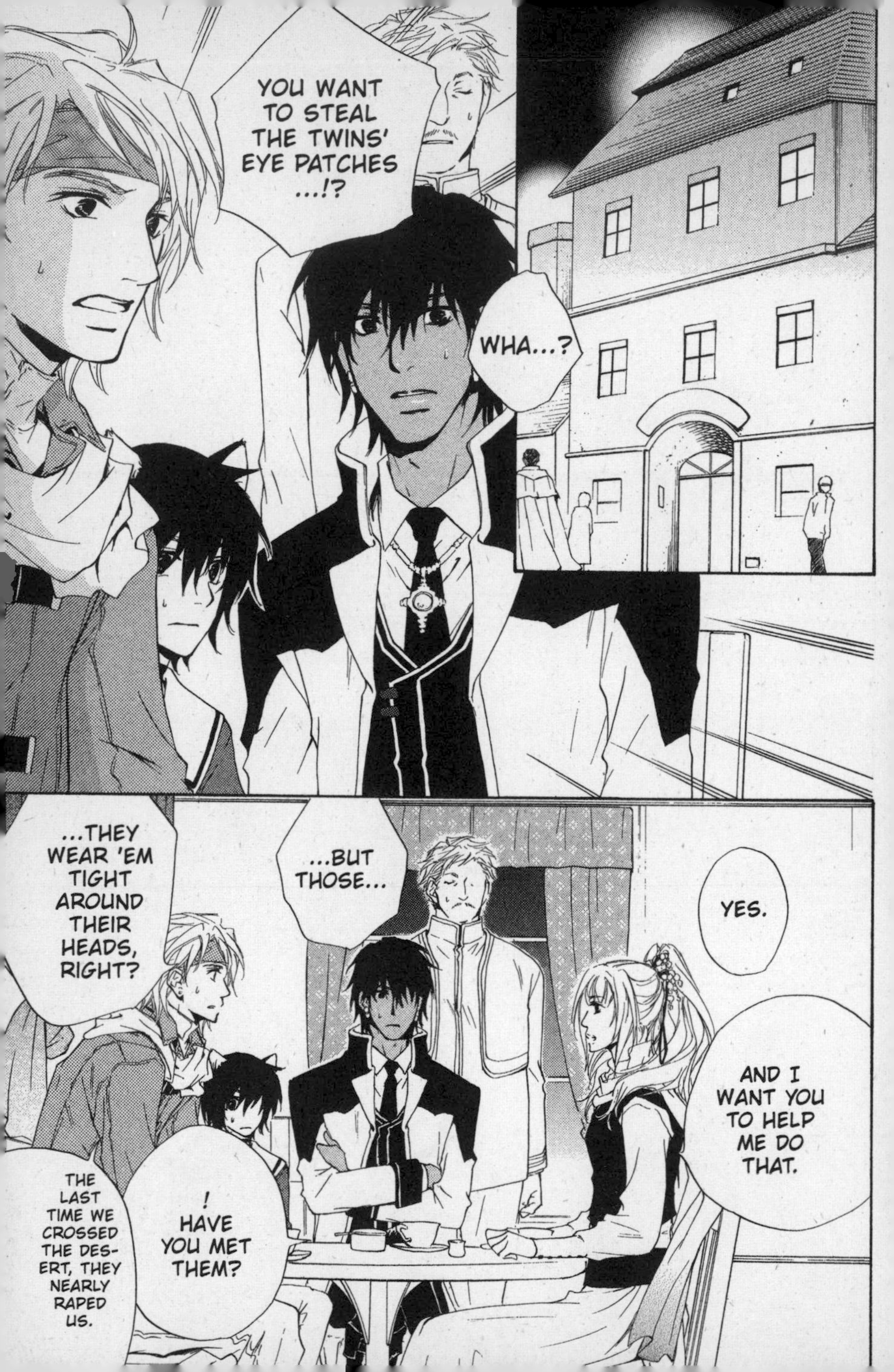
YOU WANT TO STEAL THE TWINS' EYE PATCHES ...!?
WHA...?
YES.
AND I WANT YOU TO HELP ME DO THAT.
...BUT THOSE...
...THEY WEAR 'EM TIGHT AROUND THEIR HEADS, RIGHT?
! HAVE YOU MET THEM?
THE LAST TIME WE CROSSED THE DES-ERT, THEY NEARLY RAPED US.

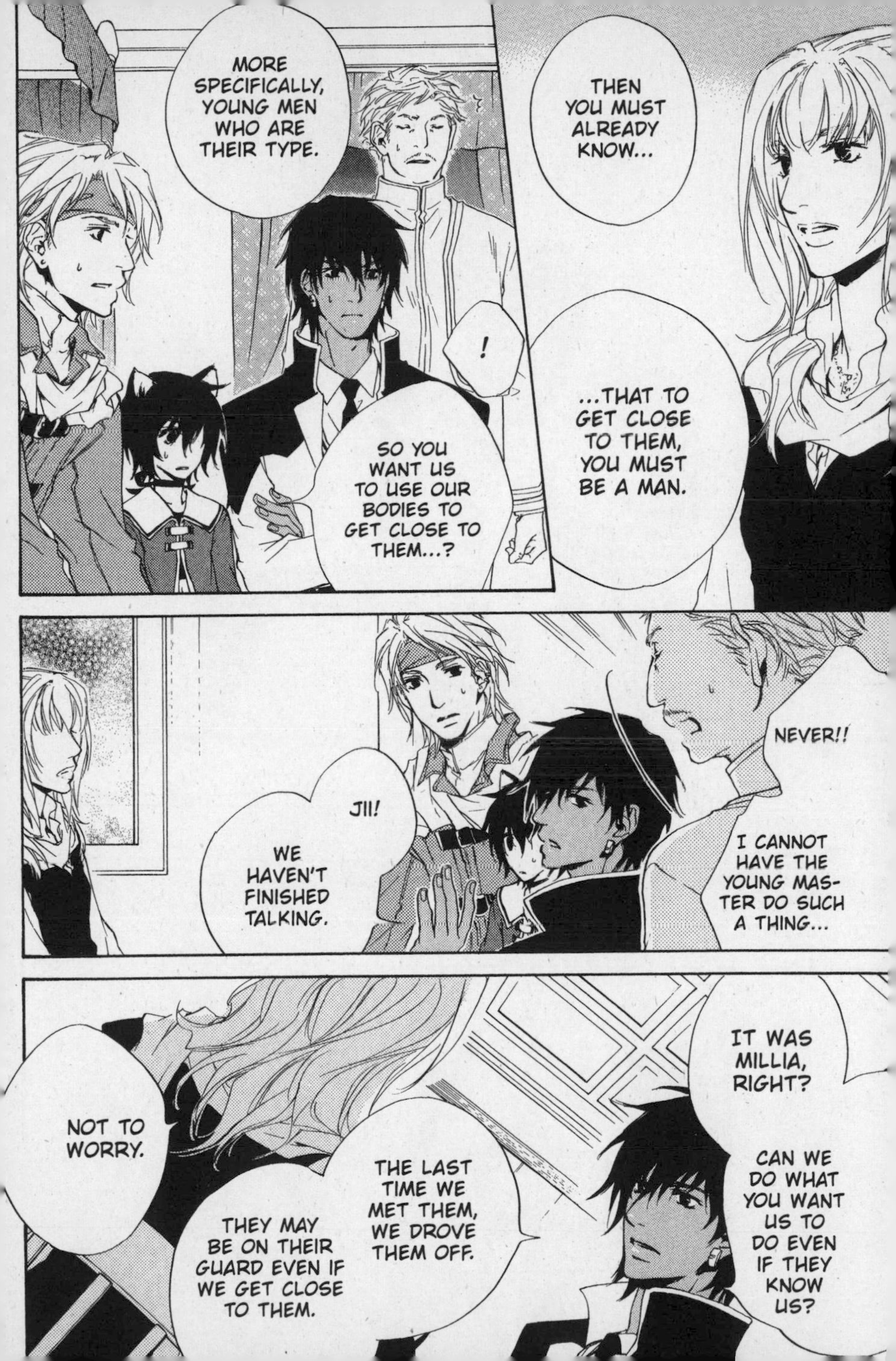
THEN YOU MUST ALREADY KNOW...
...THAT TO GET CLOSE TO THEM, YOU MUST BE A MAN.
MORE SPECIFICALLY, YOUNG MEN WHO ARE THEIR TYPE.
!
SO YOU WANT US TO USE OUR BODIES TO GET CLOSE TO THEM...?
NEVER!!
I CANNOT HAVE THE YOUNG MASTER DO SUCH A THING...
JII!
WE HAVEN'T FINISHED TALKING.
IT WAS MILLIA, RIGHT?
CAN WE DO WHAT YOU WANT US TO DO EVEN IF THEY KNOW US?
THE LAST TIME WE MET THEM, WE DROVE THEM OFF.
THEY MAY BE ON THEIR GUARD EVEN IF WE GET CLOSE TO THEM.
NOT TO WORRY.

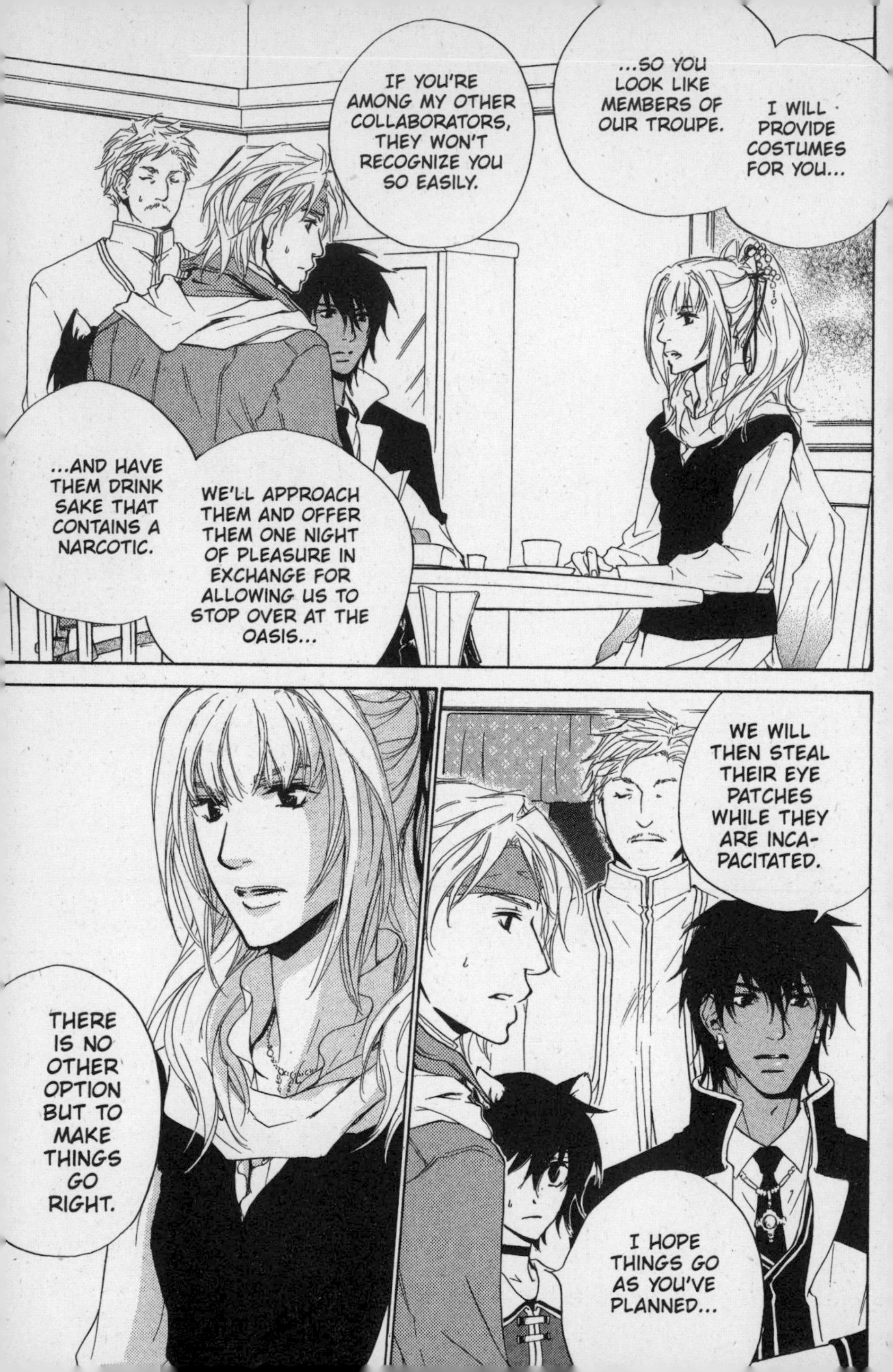
I WILL PROVIDE COSTUMES FOR YOU...
...SO YOU LOOK LIKE MEMBERS OF OUR TROUPE.
IF YOU'RE AMONG MY OTHER COLLABORATORS, THEY WON'T RECOGNIZE YOU SO EASILY.
WE'LL APPROACH THEM AND OFFER THEM ONE NIGHT OF PLEASURE IN EXCHANGE FOR ALLOWING US TO STOP OVER AT THE OASIS...
...AND HAVE THEM DRINK SAKE THAT CONTAINS A NARCOTIC.
WE WILL THEN STEAL THEIR EYE PATCHES WHILE THEY ARE INCA-PACITATED.
I HOPE THINGS GO AS YOU'VE PLANNED...
THERE IS NO OTHER OPTION BUT TO MAKE THINGS GO RIGHT.

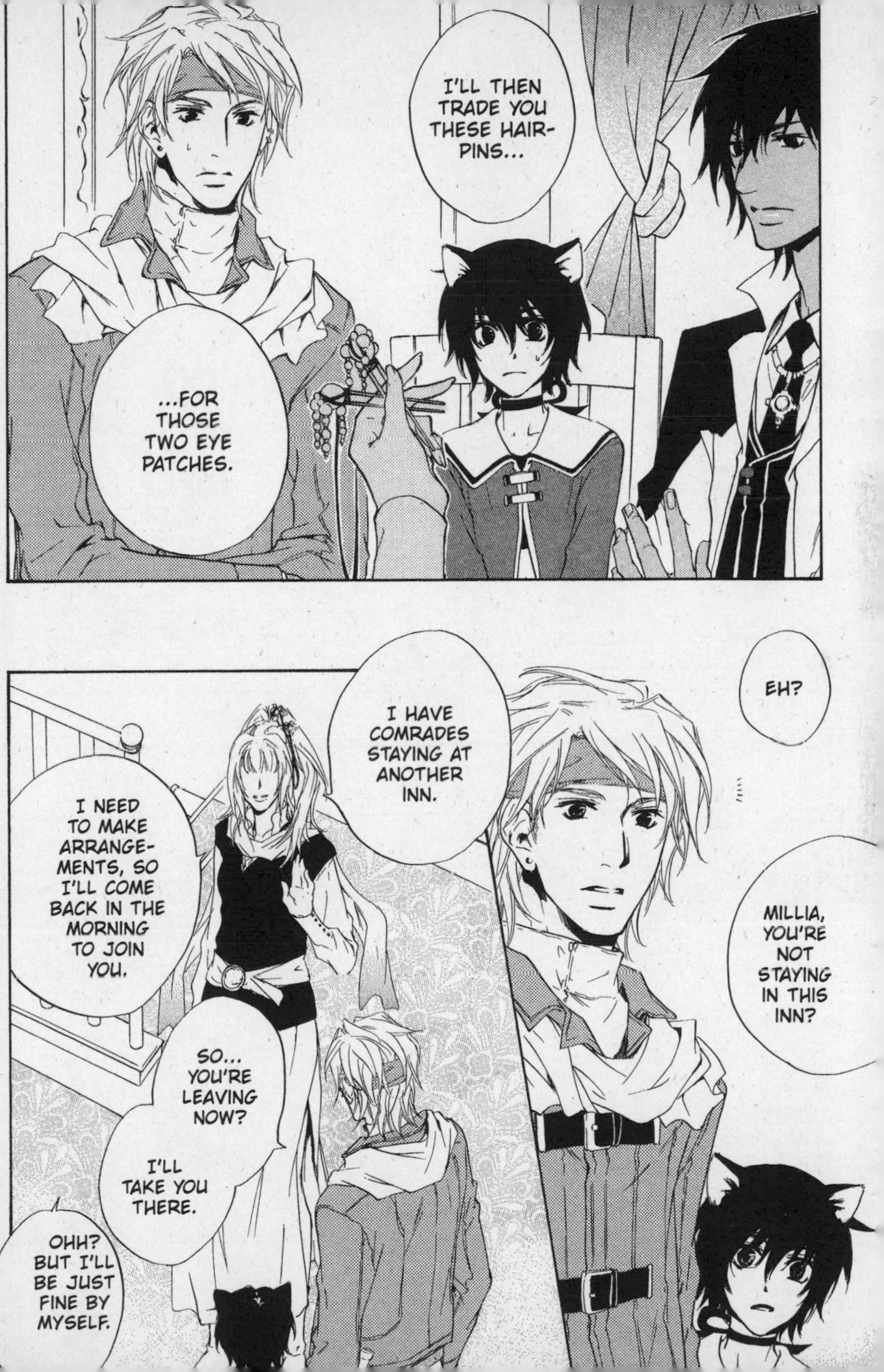
I'LL THEN TRADE YOU THESE HAIR-PINS...
...FOR THOSE TWO EYE PATCHES.
EH?
MILLIA, YOU'RE NOT STAYING IN THIS INN?
I HAVE COMRADES STAYING AT ANOTHER INN.
I NEED TO MAKE ARRANGE-MENTS, SO I'LL COME BACK IN THE MORNING TO JOIN YOU.
SO... YOU'RE LEAVING NOW?
I'LL TAKE YOU THERE.
OHH? BUT I'LL BE JUST FINE BY MYSELF.

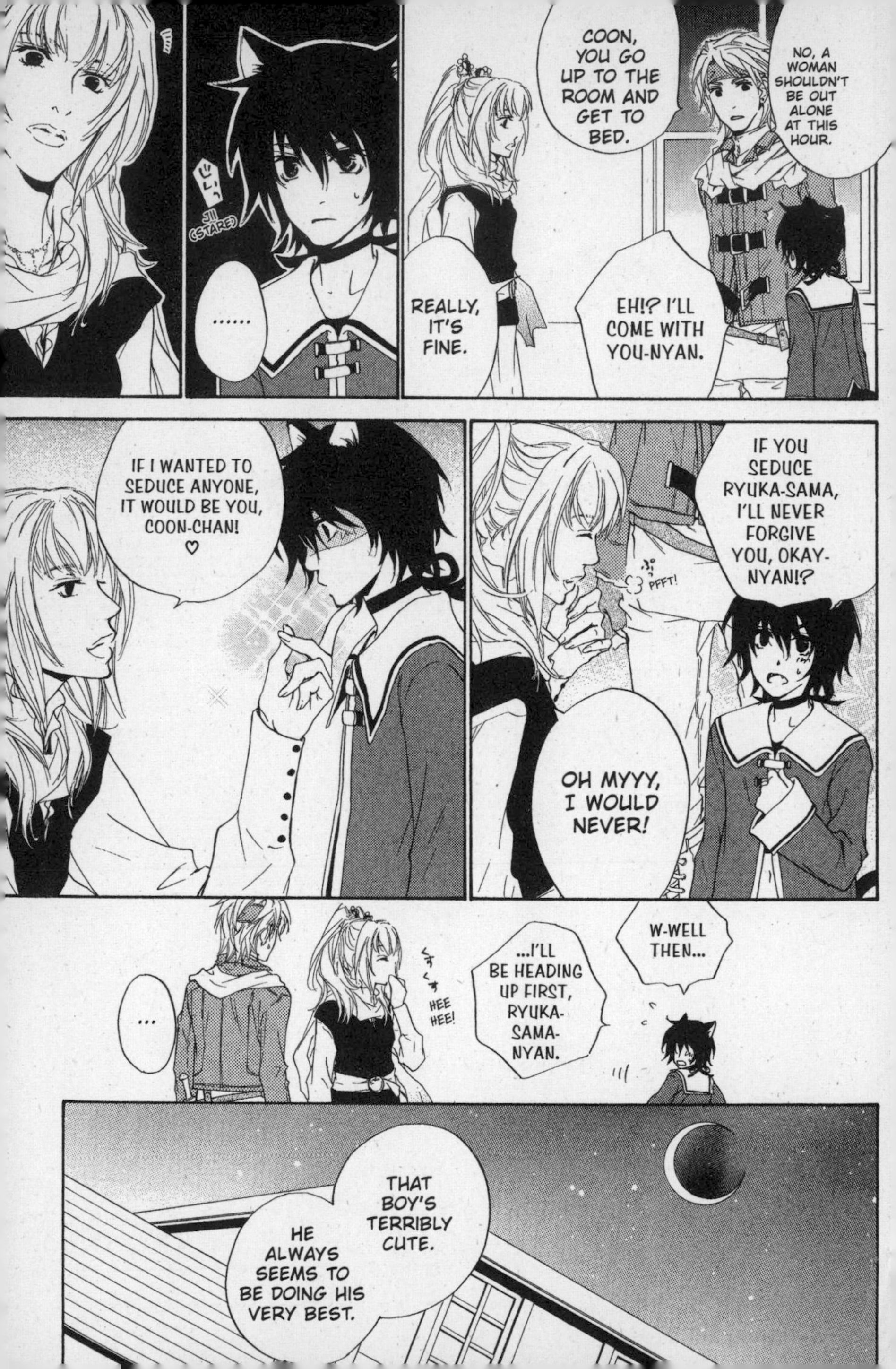
NO, A WOMAN SHOULDN'T BE OUT ALONE AT THIS HOUR.
COON, YOU GO UP TO THE ROOM AND GET TO BED.
EH!? I'LL COME WITH YOU-NYAN.
REALLY, IT'S FINE.
JII (STARE)
......
IF YOU SEDUCE RYUKA-SAMA, I'LL NEVER FORGIVE YOU, OKAY-NYAN!?
PFFT!
OH MYYY, I WOULD NEVER!
IF I WANTED TO SEDUCE ANYONE, IT WOULD BE YOU, COON-CHAN! ♡
W-WELL THEN...
...I'LL BE HEADING UP FIRST, RYUKA-SAMA-NYAN.
HEE HEE!
...
THAT BOY'S TERRIBLY CUTE.
HE ALWAYS SEEMS TO BE DOING HIS VERY BEST.

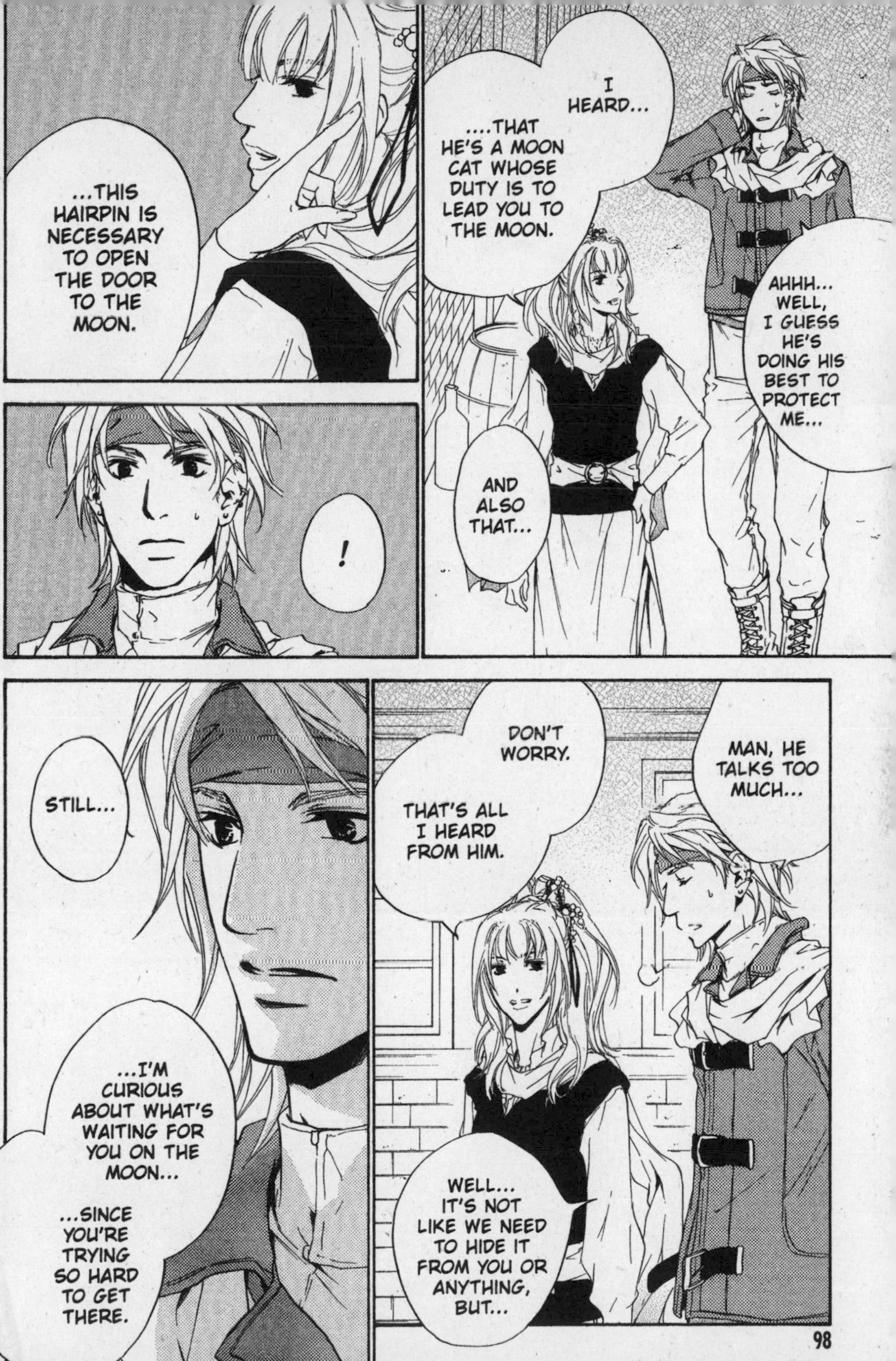
I HEARD...
....THAT HE'S A MOON CAT WHOSE DUTY IS TO LEAD YOU TO THE MOON.
AHHH... WELL, I GUESS HE'S DOING HIS BEST TO PROTECT ME...
AND ALSO THAT...
...THIS HAIRPIN IS NECESSARY TO OPEN THE DOOR TO THE MOON.
!
MAN, HE TALKS TOO MUCH...
DON'T WORRY.
THAT'S ALL I HEARD FROM HIM.
WELL... IT'S NOT LIKE WE NEED TO HIDE IT FROM YOU OR ANYTHING, BUT...
STILL...
...I'M CURIOUS ABOUT WHAT'S WAITING FOR YOU ON THE MOON...
...SINCE YOU'RE TRYING SO HARD TO GET THERE.

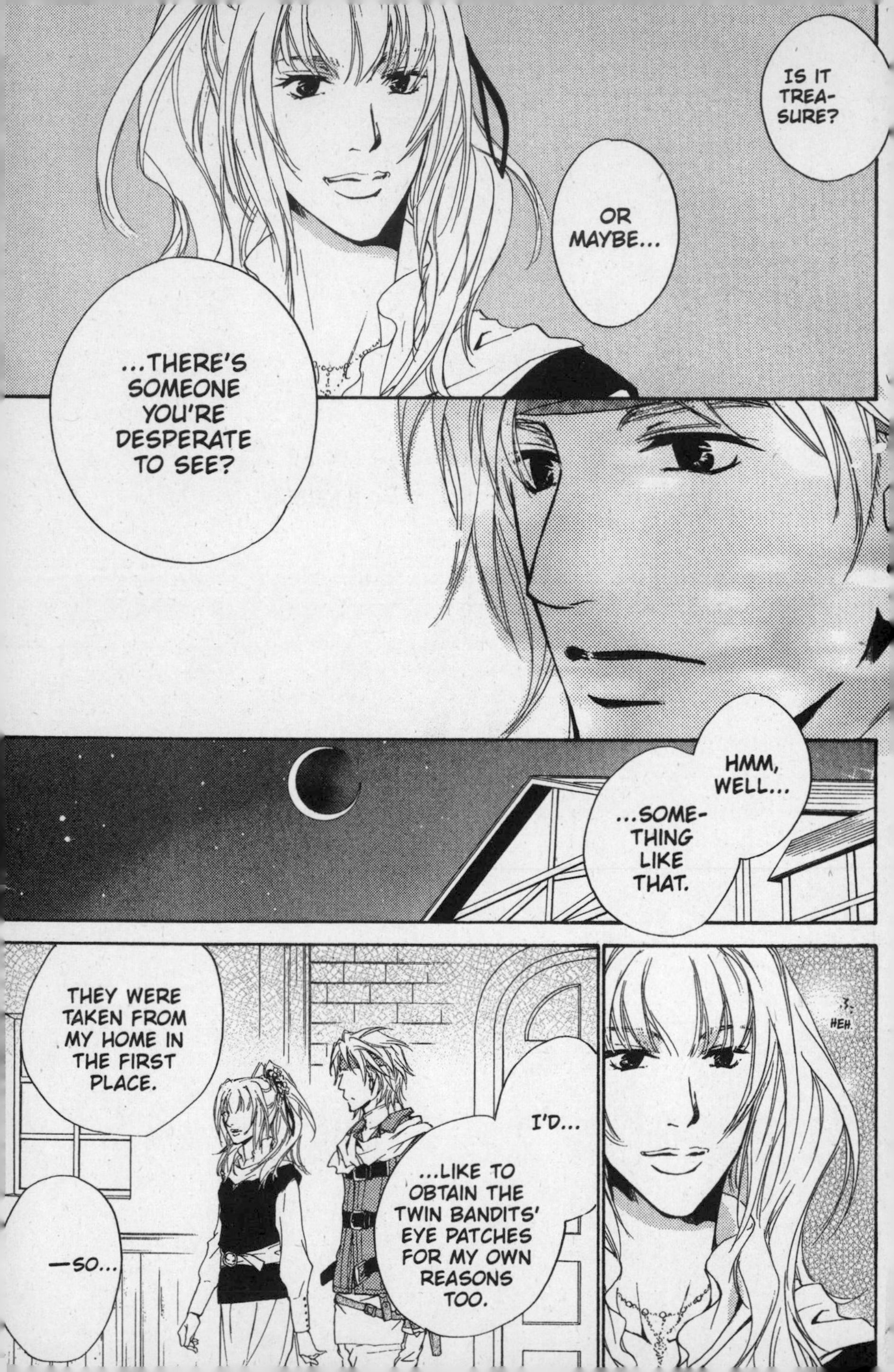
IS IT TREA-SURE?
OR MAYBE...
...THERE'S SOMEONE YOU'RE DESPERATE TO SEE?
HMM, WELL...
...SOME-THING LIKE THAT.
HEH.
I'D...
...LIKE TO OBTAIN THE TWIN BANDITS' EYE PATCHES FOR MY OWN REASONS TOO.
THEY WERE TAKEN FROM MY HOME IN THE FIRST PLACE.
—SO...

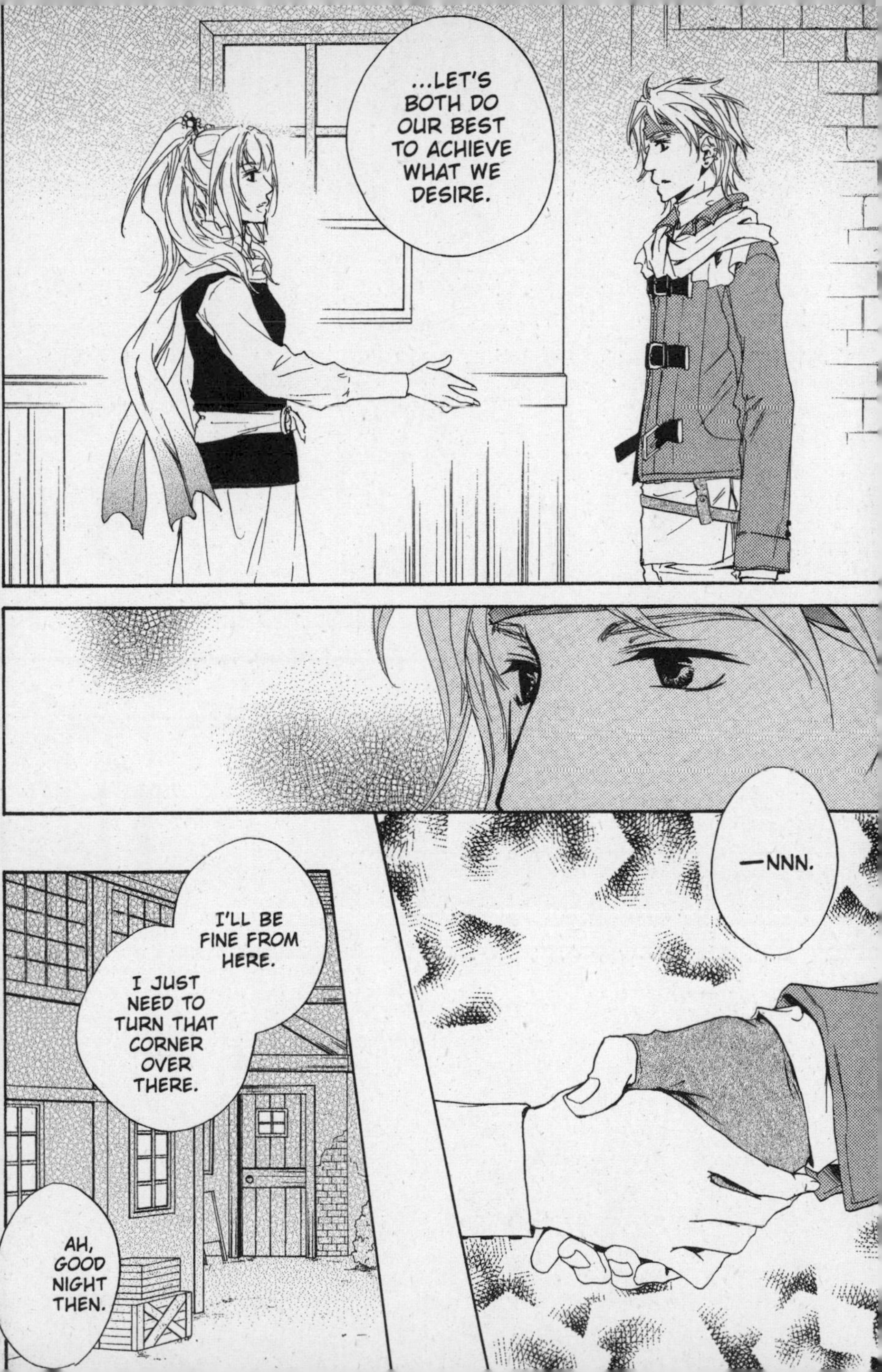
...LET'S BOTH DO OUR BEST TO ACHIEVE WHAT WE DESIRE.
—NNN.
I'LL BE FINE FROM HERE.
I JUST NEED TO TURN THAT CORNER OVER THERE.
AH, GOOD NIGHT THEN.

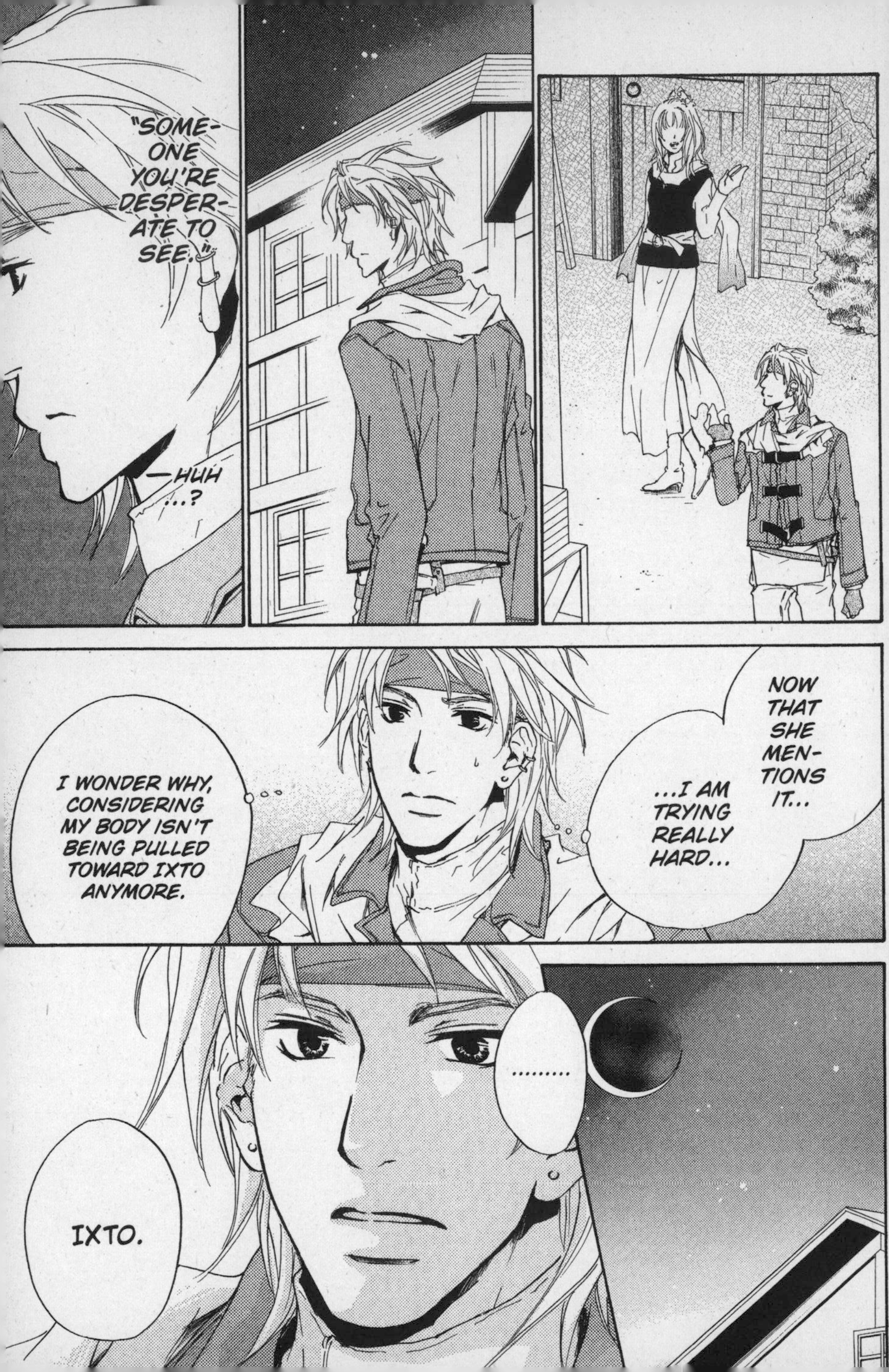
"SOME-ONE YOU'RE DESPER-ATE TO SEE."
—HUH ...?
NOW THAT SHE MEN-TIONS IT...
...I AM TRYING REALLY HARD...
I WONDER WHY, CONSIDERING MY BODY ISN'T BEING PULLED TOWARD IXTO ANYMORE.
....
IXTO.

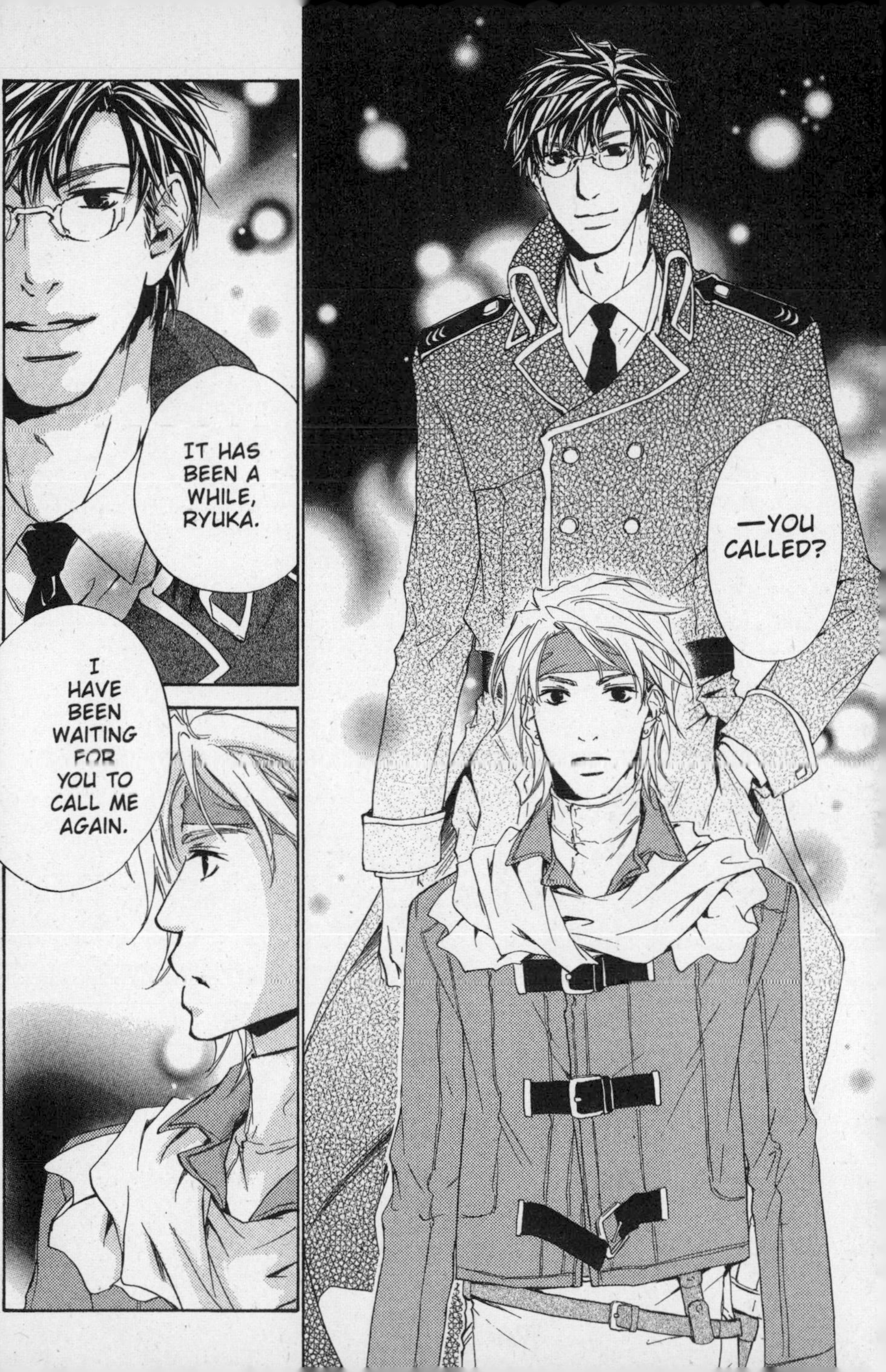
—YOU CALLED?
IT HAS BEEN A WHILE, RYUKA.
I HAVE BEEN WAITING FOR YOU TO CALL ME AGAIN.

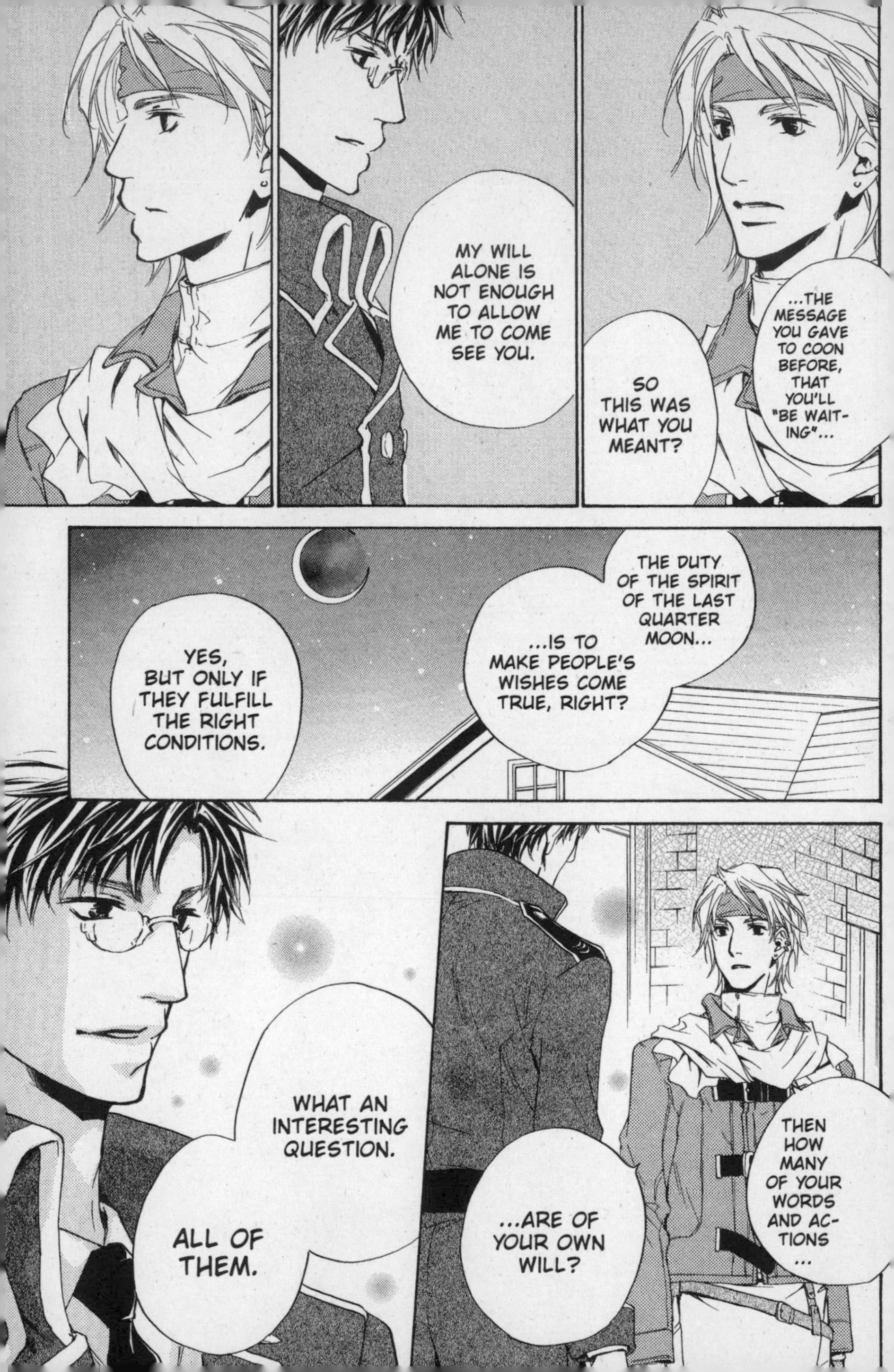

...THE MESSAGE YOU GAVE TO COON BEFORE, THAT YOU'LL "BE WAITING"...
SO THIS WAS WHAT YOU MEANT?
MY WILL ALONE IS NOT ENOUGH TO ALLOW ME TO COME SEE YOU.
THE DUTY OF THE SPIRIT OF THE LAST QUARTER MOON...
...IS TO MAKE PEOPLE'S WISHES COME TRUE, RIGHT?
YES, BUT ONLY IF THEY FULFILL THE RIGHT CONDITIONS.
THEN HOW MANY OF YOUR WORDS AND ACTIONS ...
...ARE OF YOUR OWN WILL?
WHAT AN INTERESTING QUESTION.
ALL OF THEM.

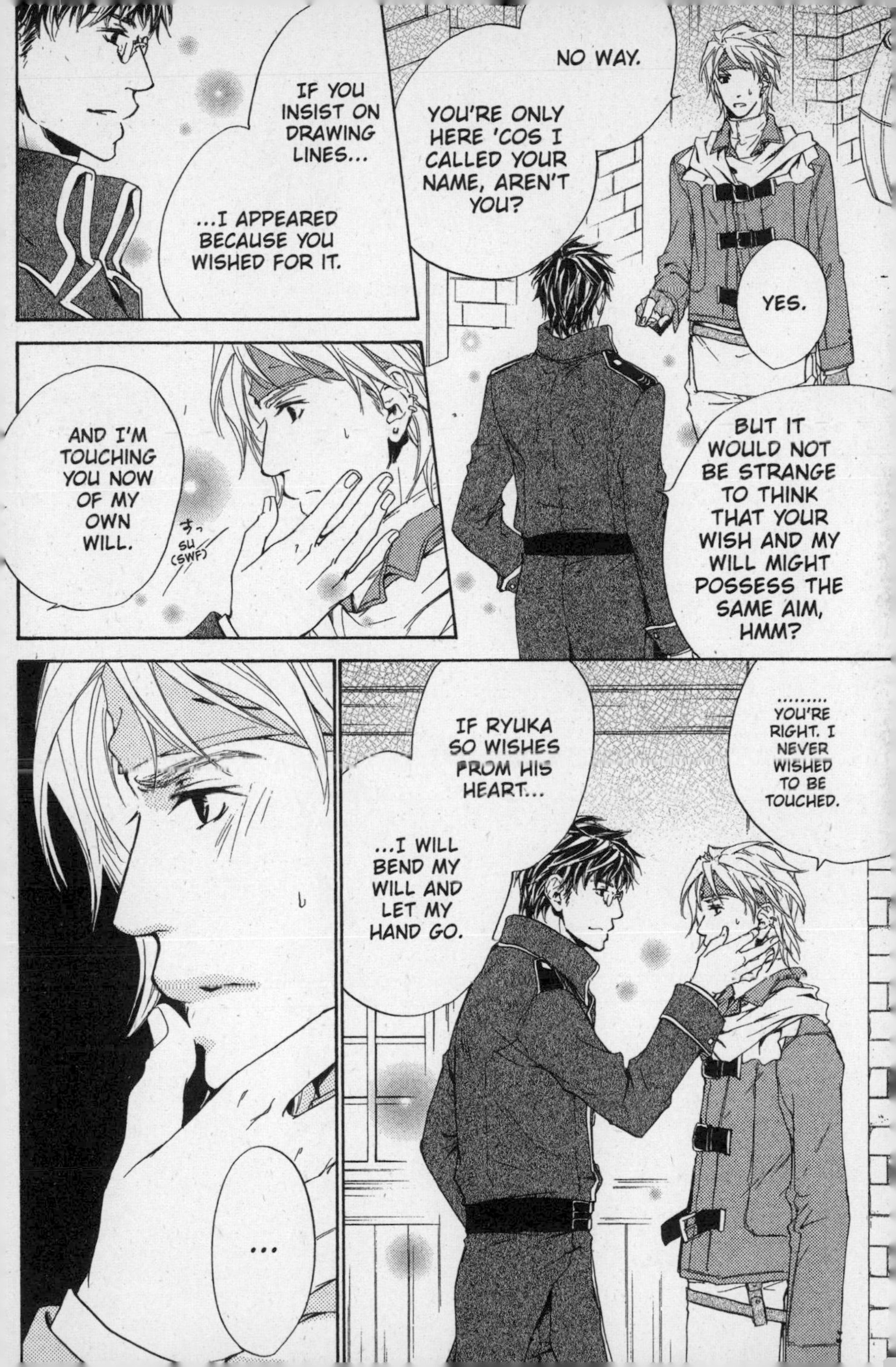
NO WAY.
YOU'RE ONLY HERE 'COS I CALLED YOUR NAME, AREN'T YOU?
YES.
BUT IT WOULD NOT BE STRANGE TO THINK THAT YOUR WISH AND MY WILL MIGHT POSSESS THE SAME AIM, HMM?
IF YOU INSIST ON DRAWING LINES...
...I APPEARED BECAUSE YOU WISHED FOR IT.
AND I'M TOUCHING YOU NOW OF MY OWN WILL.
すっ SU (SWF)
....
YOU'RE RIGHT. I NEVER WISHED TO BE TOUCHED.
IF RYUKA SO WISHES FROM HIS HEART...
...I WILL BEND MY WILL AND LET MY HAND GO.
...

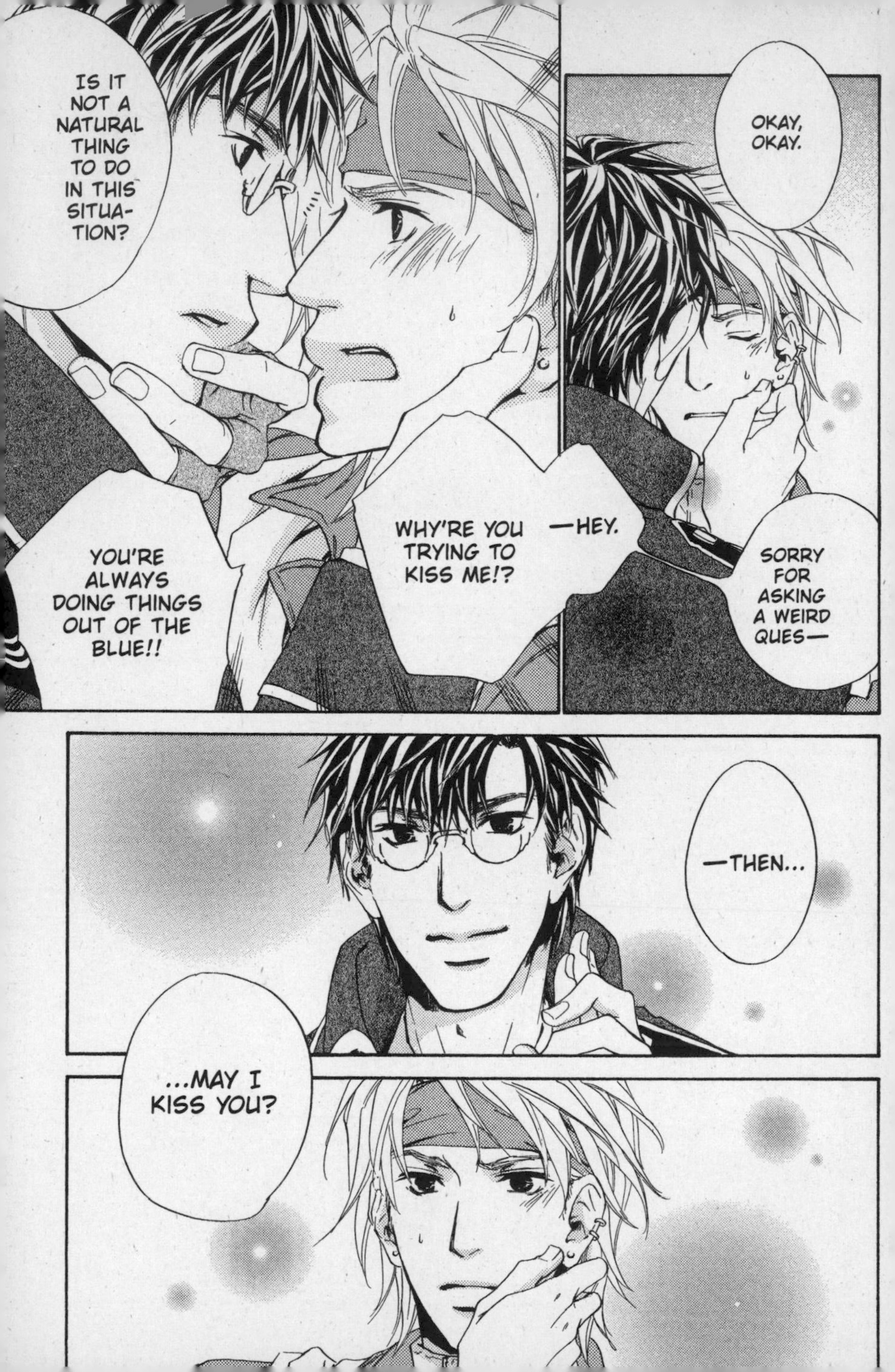
OKAY, OKAY.
SORRY FOR ASKING A WEIRD QUES—
—HEY. WHY'RE YOU TRYING TO KISS ME!?
YOU'RE ALWAYS DOING THINGS OUT OF THE BLUE!!
IS IT NOT A NATURAL THING TO DO IN THIS SITUATION?
—THEN...
...MAY I KISS YOU?

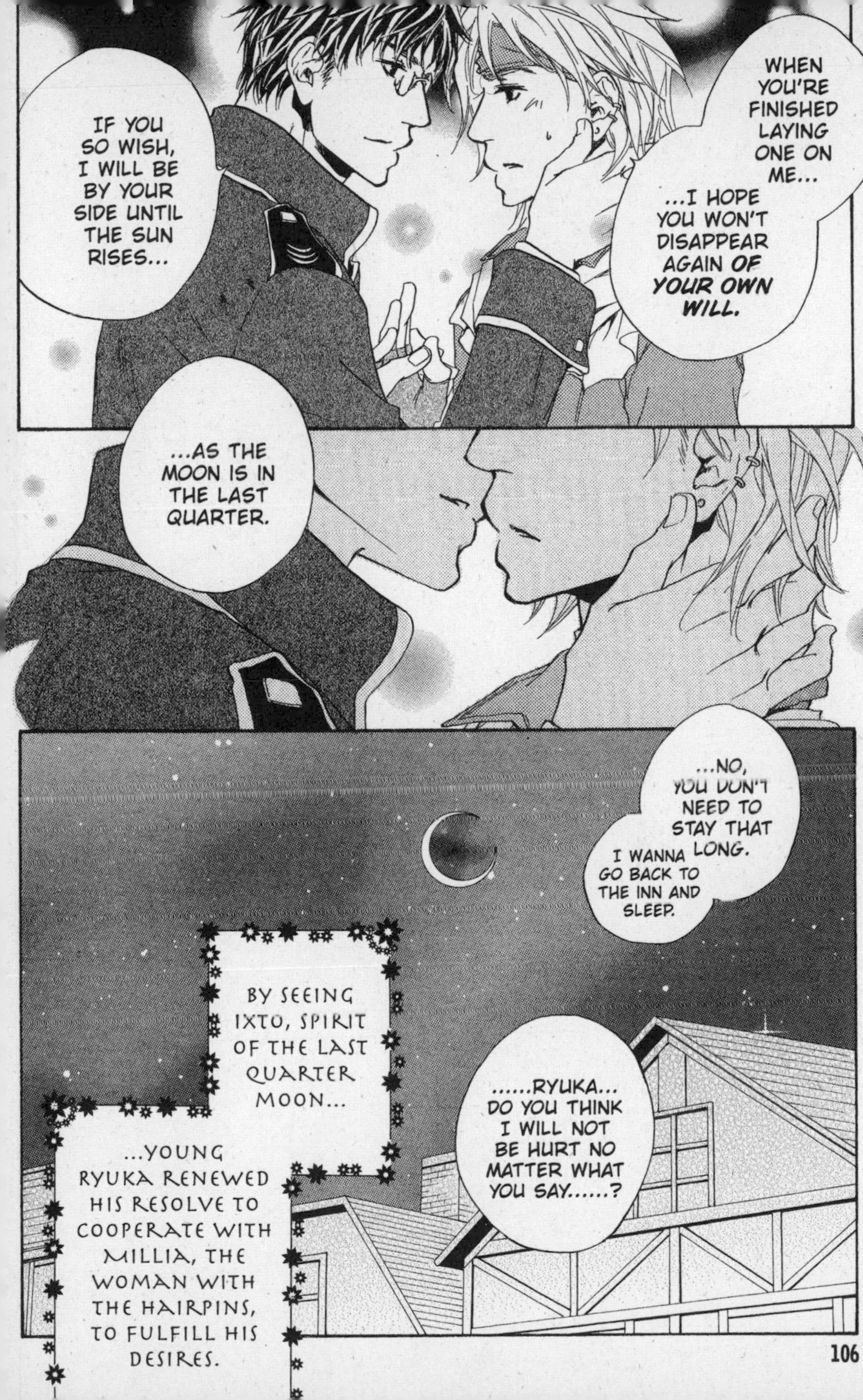
WHEN YOU'RE FINISHED LAYING ONE ON ME...
...I HOPE YOU WON'T DISAPPEAR AGAIN *OF YOUR OWN WILL.*
IF YOU SO WISH, I WILL BE BY YOUR SIDE UNTIL THE SUN RISES...
...AS THE MOON IS IN THE LAST QUARTER.
...NO, YOU DON'T NEED TO STAY THAT LONG.
I WANNA GO BACK TO THE INN AND SLEEP.
......RYUKA... DO YOU THINK I WILL NOT BE HURT NO MATTER WHAT YOU SAY......?
BY SEEING IXTO, SPIRIT OF THE LAST QUARTER MOON...
...YOUNG RYUKA RENEWED HIS RESOLVE TO COOPERATE WITH MILLIA, THE WOMAN WITH THE HAIRPINS, TO FULFILL HIS DESIRES.

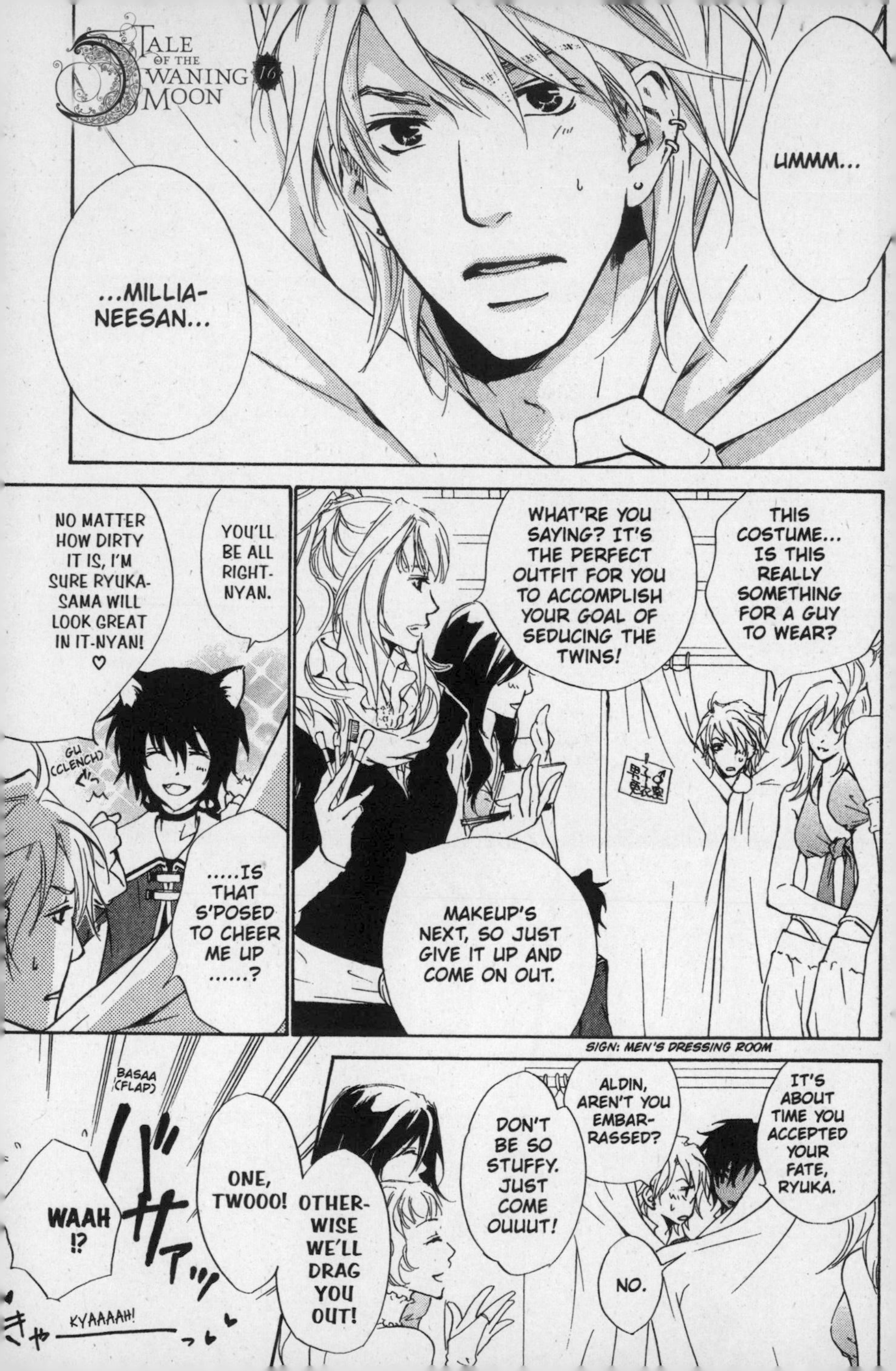
UMMM...
...MILLIA-NEESAN...
THIS COSTUME... IS THIS REALLY SOMETHING FOR A GUY TO WEAR?
WHAT'RE YOU SAYING? IT'S THE PERFECT OUTFIT FOR YOU TO ACCOMPLISH YOUR GOAL OF SEDUCING THE TWINS!
MAKEUP'S NEXT, SO JUST GIVE IT UP AND COME ON OUT.
YOU'LL BE ALL RIGHT-NYAN.
NO MATTER HOW DIRTY IT IS, I'M SURE RYUKA-SAMA WILL LOOK GREAT IN IT-NYAN! ♡
GU (CLENCH)
.....IS THAT S'POSED TO CHEER ME UP ......?
SIGN: MEN'S DRESSING ROOM
IT'S ABOUT TIME YOU ACCEPTED YOUR FATE, RYUKA.
ALDIN, AREN'T YOU EMBARRASSED?
NO.
DON'T BE SO STUFFY. JUST COME OUUUT!
ONE, TWOOO!
OTHERWISE WE'LL DRAG YOU OUT!
BASAA (FLAP)
WAAH !?
KYAAAAH!

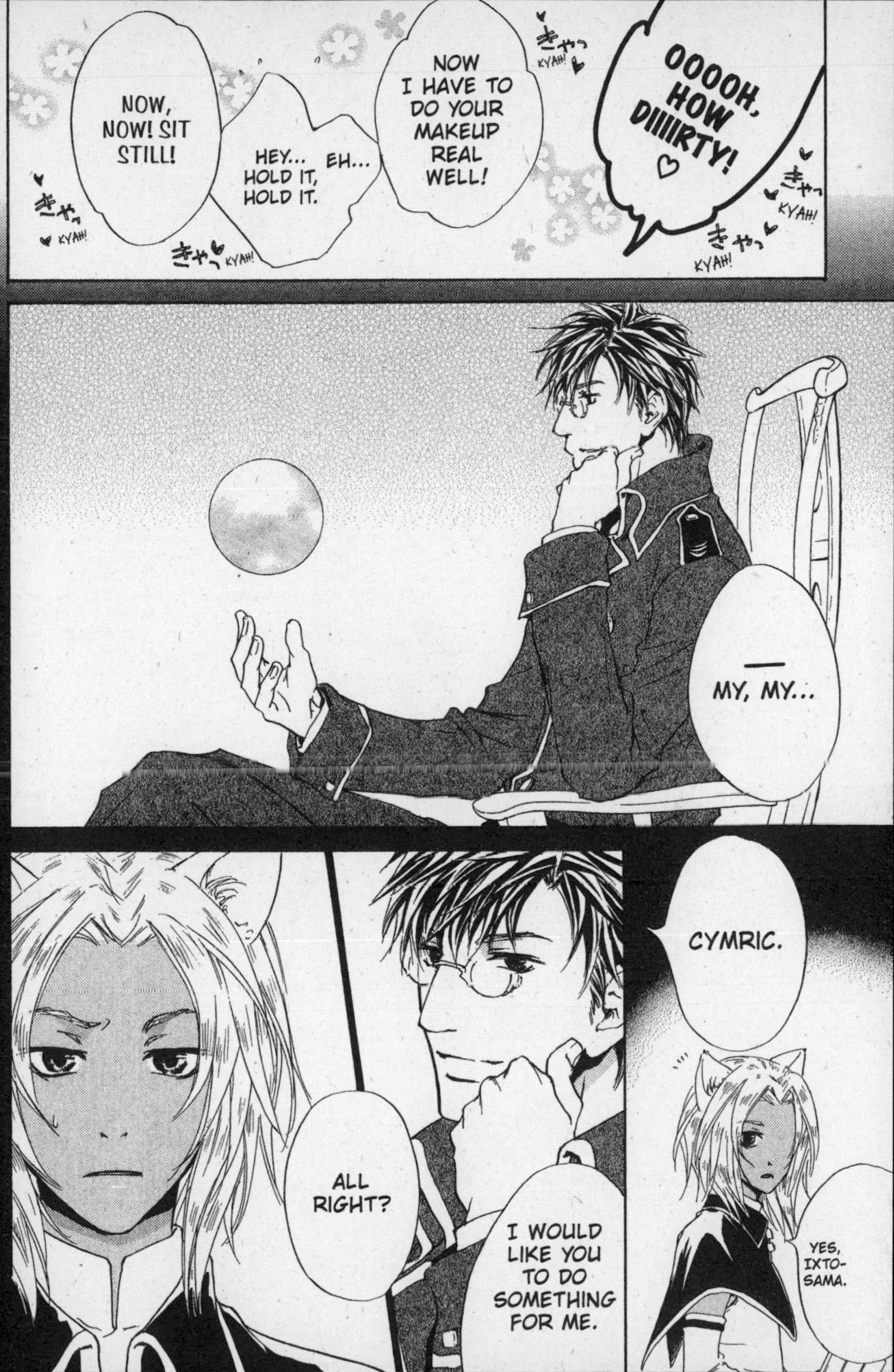
OOOOH, HOW DIIIIRTY! ♡
きゃっ KYAH!
きゃっ KYAH!
きゃっ KYAH!
NOW I HAVE TO DO YOUR MAKEUP REAL WELL!
HEY... EH... HOLD IT, HOLD IT.
きゃっ KYAH!
NOW, NOW! SIT STILL!
きゃっ KYAH!
—MY, MY...
CYMRIC.
YES, IXTO-SAMA.
I WOULD LIKE YOU TO DO SOMETHING FOR ME.
ALL RIGHT?

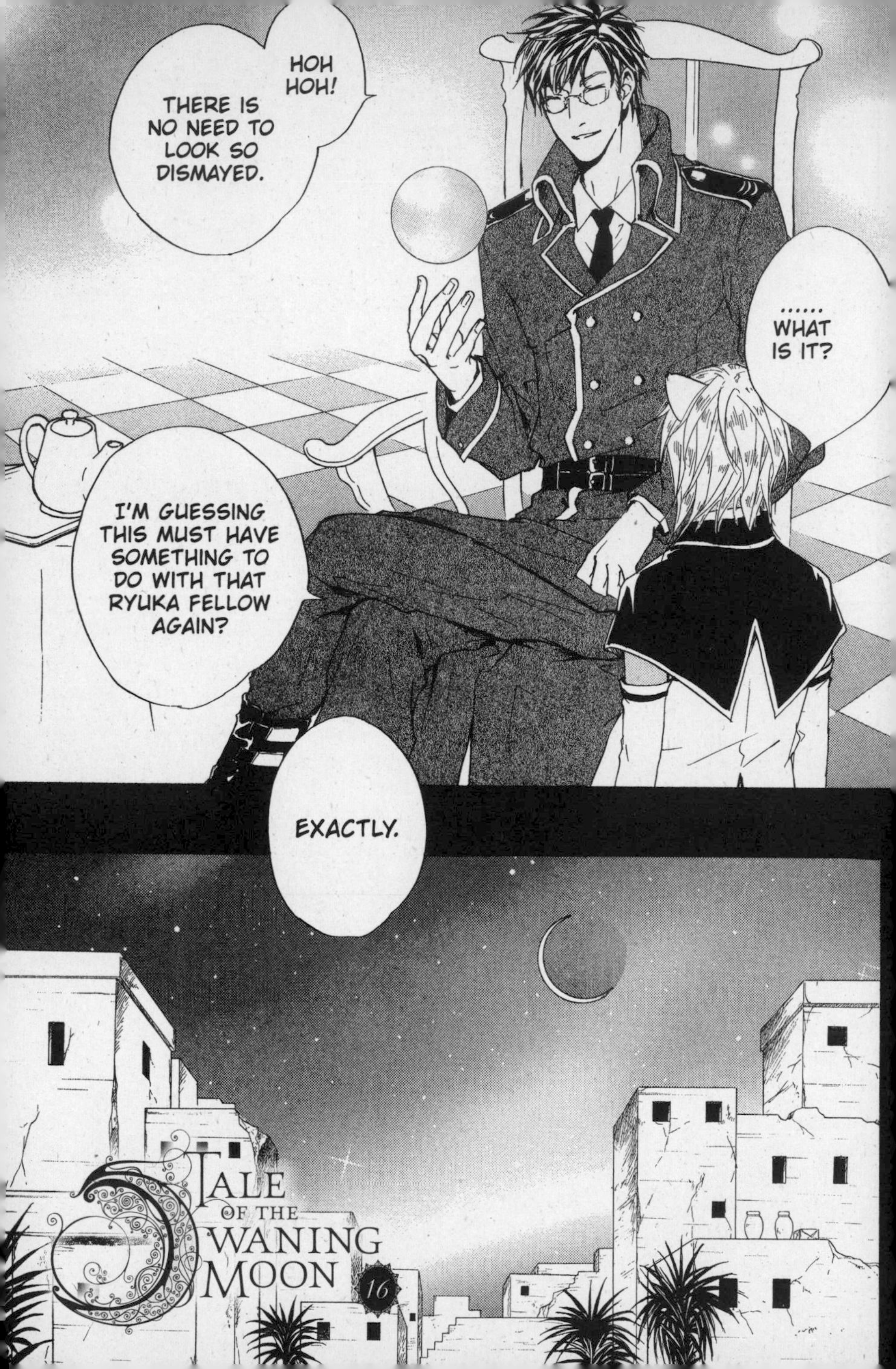
HOH HOH! THERE IS NO NEED TO LOOK SO DISMAYED.
...... WHAT IS IT?
I'M GUESSING THIS MUST HAVE SOMETHING TO DO WITH THAT RYUKA FELLOW AGAIN?
EXACTLY.
TALE OF THE WANING MOON
16

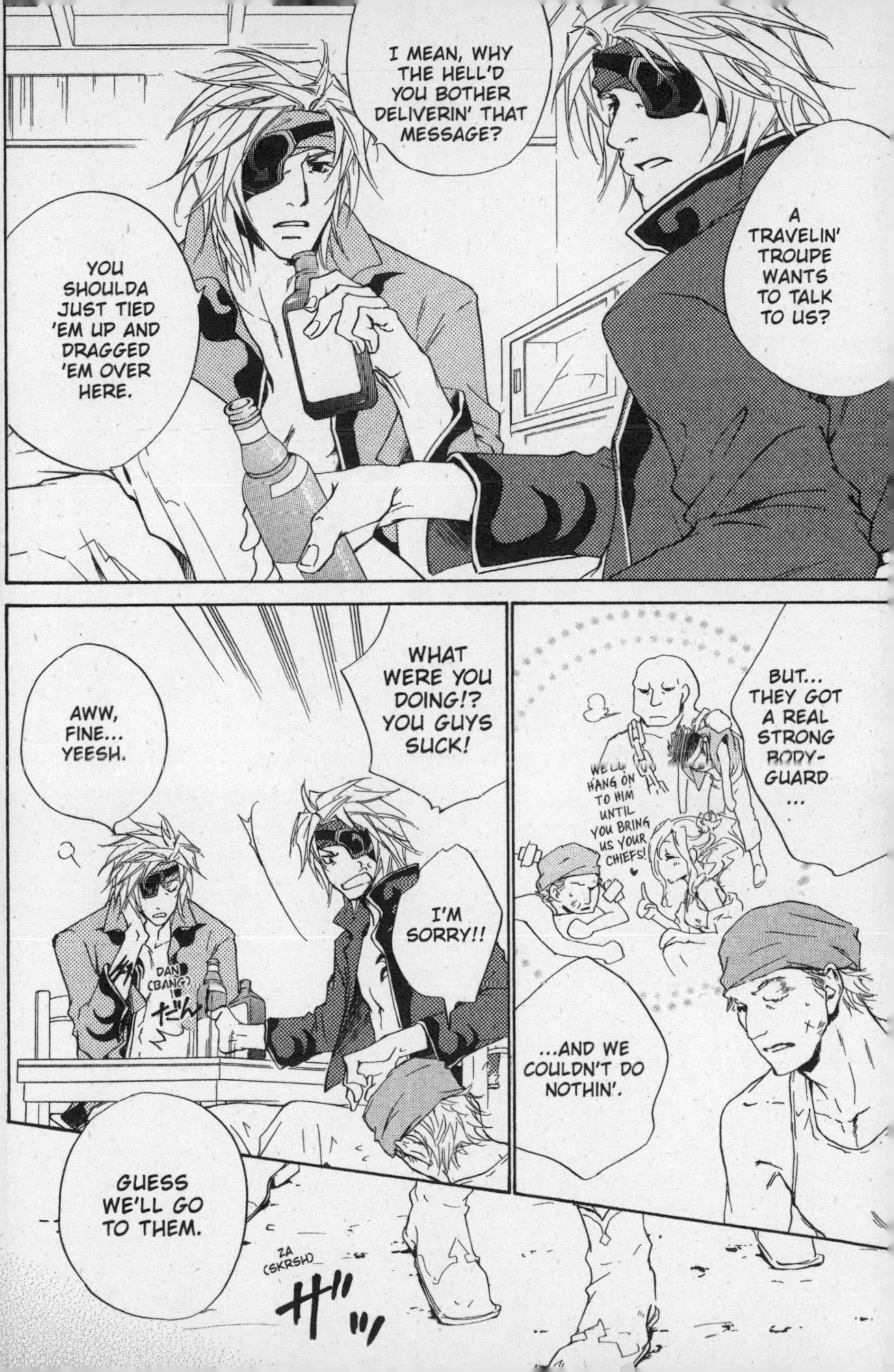
A TRAVELIN' TROUPE WANTS TO TALK TO US?
I MEAN, WHY THE HELL'D YOU BOTHER DELIVERIN' THAT MESSAGE?
YOU SHOULDA JUST TIED 'EM UP AND DRAGGED 'EM OVER HERE.
BUT... THEY GOT A REAL STRONG BODY-GUARD...
WE'LL HANG ON TO HIM UNTIL YOU BRING US YOUR CHIEFS!
...AND WE COULDN'T DO NOTHIN'.
WHAT WERE YOU DOING!? YOU GUYS SUCK!
I'M SORRY!!
AWW, FINE... YEESH.
DAN (BANG)
だん
GUESS WE'LL GO TO THEM.
ZA (SKRSH)
ザッ

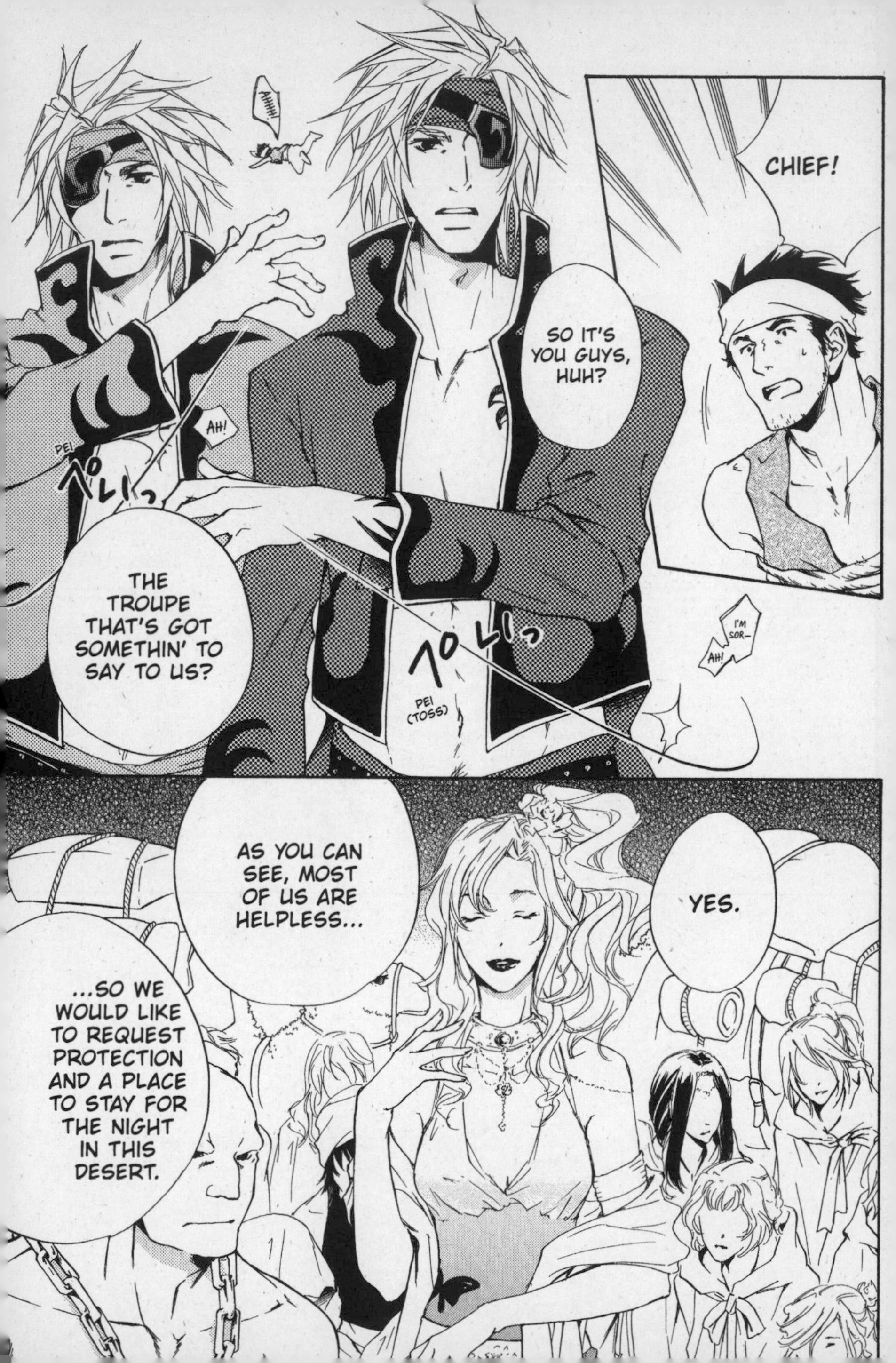
CHIEF!
I'M SOR— AH!
SO IT'S YOU GUYS, HUH?
AHHH!
AH!
PEI
PEI (TOSS)
THE TROUPE THAT'S GOT SOMETHIN' TO SAY TO US?
YES.
AS YOU CAN SEE, MOST OF US ARE HELPLESS...
...SO WE WOULD LIKE TO REQUEST PROTECTION AND A PLACE TO STAY FOR THE NIGHT IN THIS DESERT.

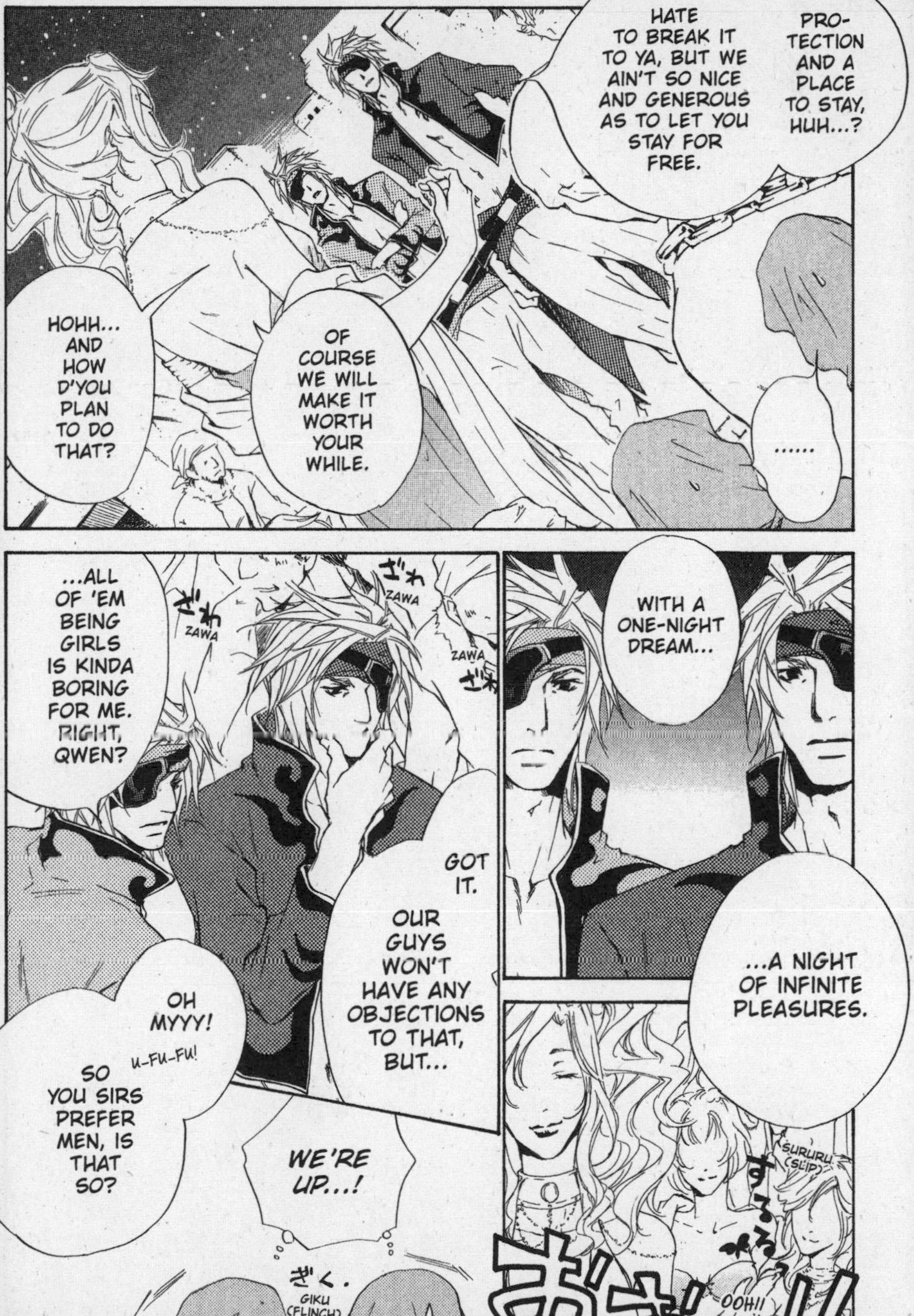
PRO-TECTION AND A PLACE TO STAY, HUH...?
HATE TO BREAK IT TO YA, BUT WE AIN'T SO NICE AND GENEROUS AS TO LET YOU STAY FOR FREE.
......
OF COURSE WE WILL MAKE IT WORTH YOUR WHILE.
HOHH... AND HOW D'YOU PLAN TO DO THAT?
WITH A ONE-NIGHT DREAM...
...A NIGHT OF INFINITE PLEASURES.
するる
SURURU (SLIP)
おおっ!!
OOH!!
ざわ
ZAWA
ざわ
ZAWA
ざわ
ZAWA
...ALL OF 'EM BEING GIRLS IS KINDA BORING FOR ME. RIGHT, QWEN?
GOT IT.
OUR GUYS WON'T HAVE ANY OBJECTIONS TO THAT, BUT...
OH MYYY!
U-FU-FU!
SO YOU SIRS PREFER MEN, IS THAT SO?
WE'RE UP...!
ぎく.
GIKU (FLINCH)

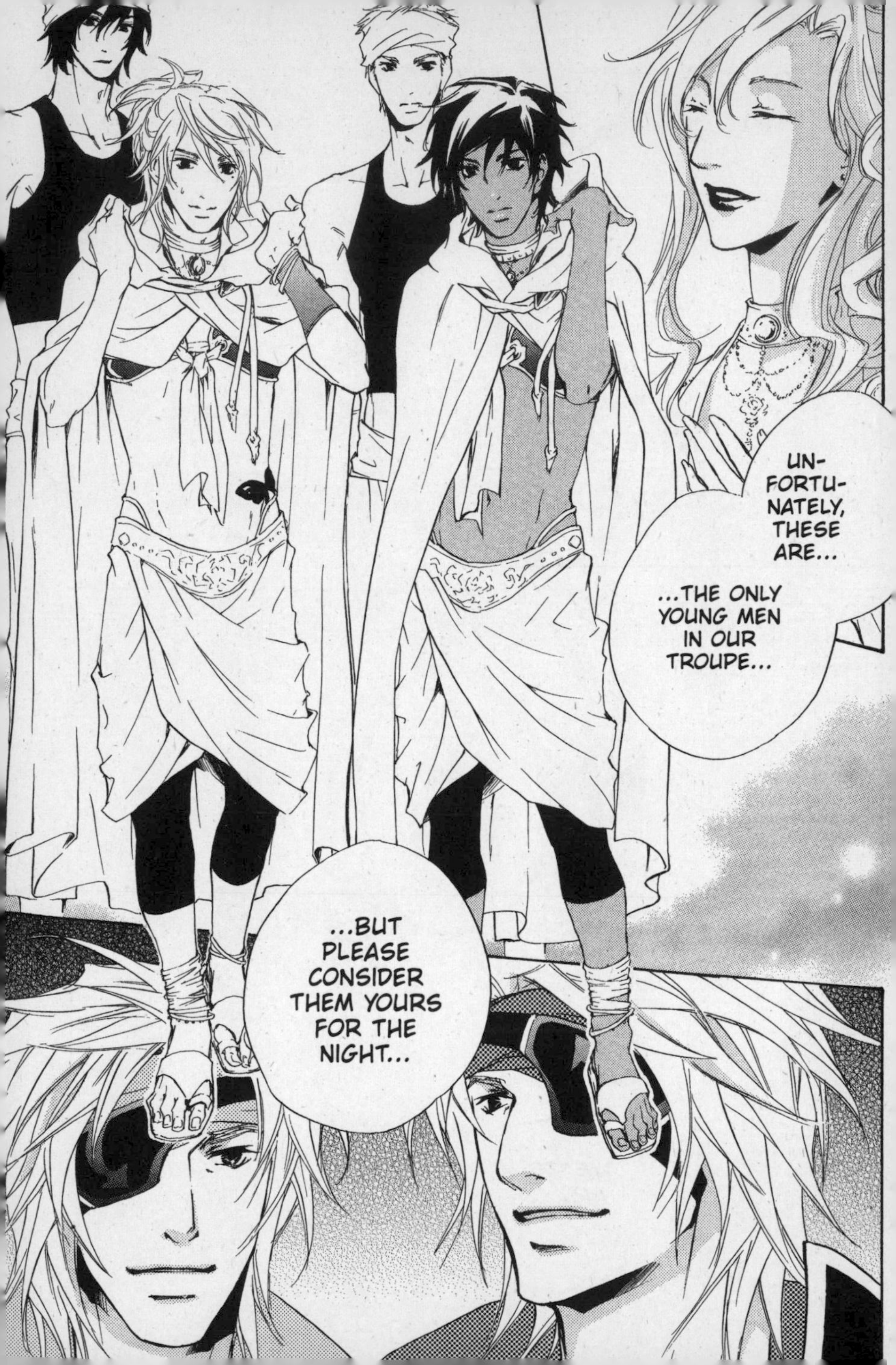
UN-FORTU-NATELY, THESE ARE...
...THE ONLY YOUNG MEN IN OUR TROUPE...
...BUT PLEASE CONSIDER THEM YOURS FOR THE NIGHT...

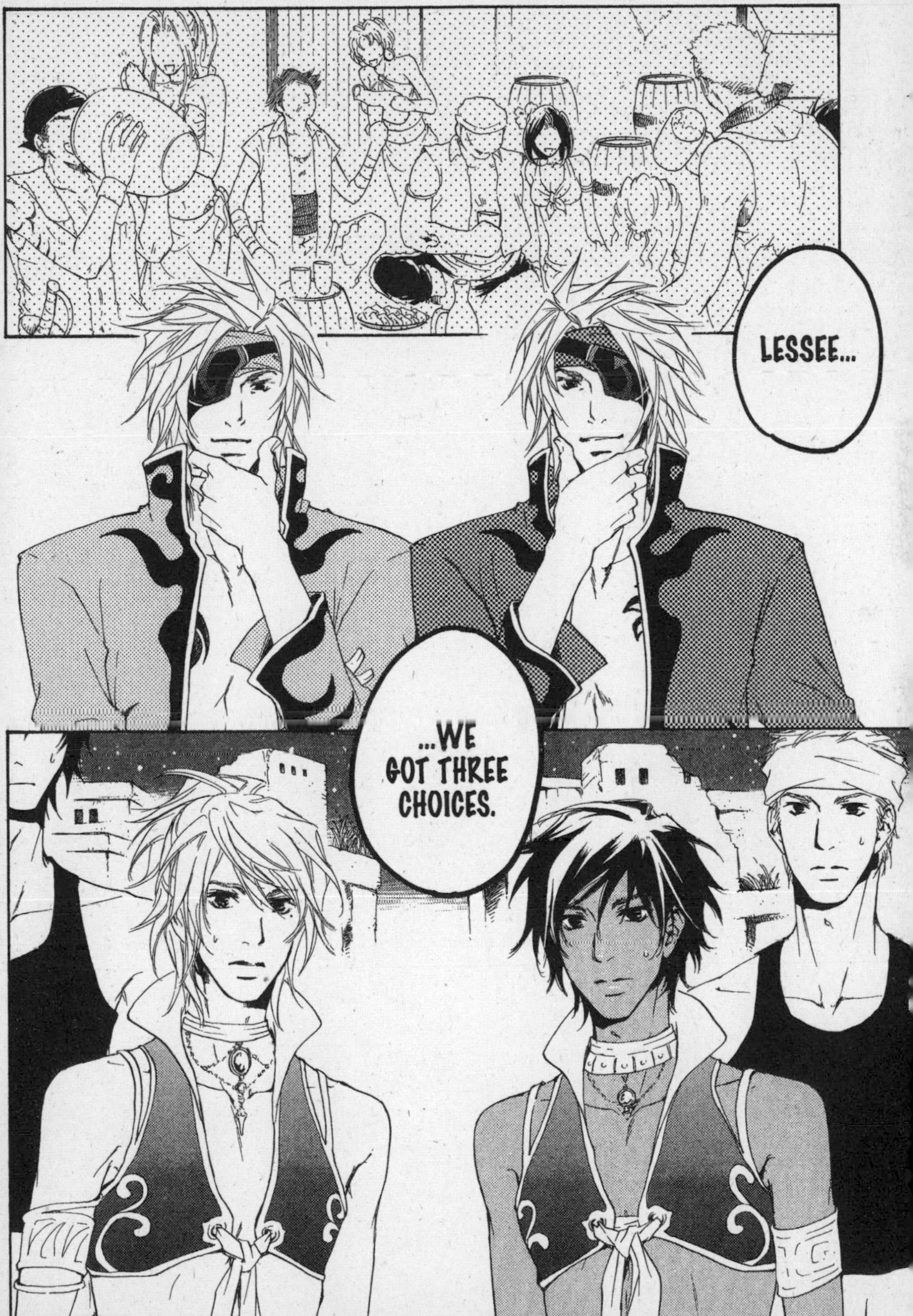
LESSEE...
...WE GOT THREE CHOICES.

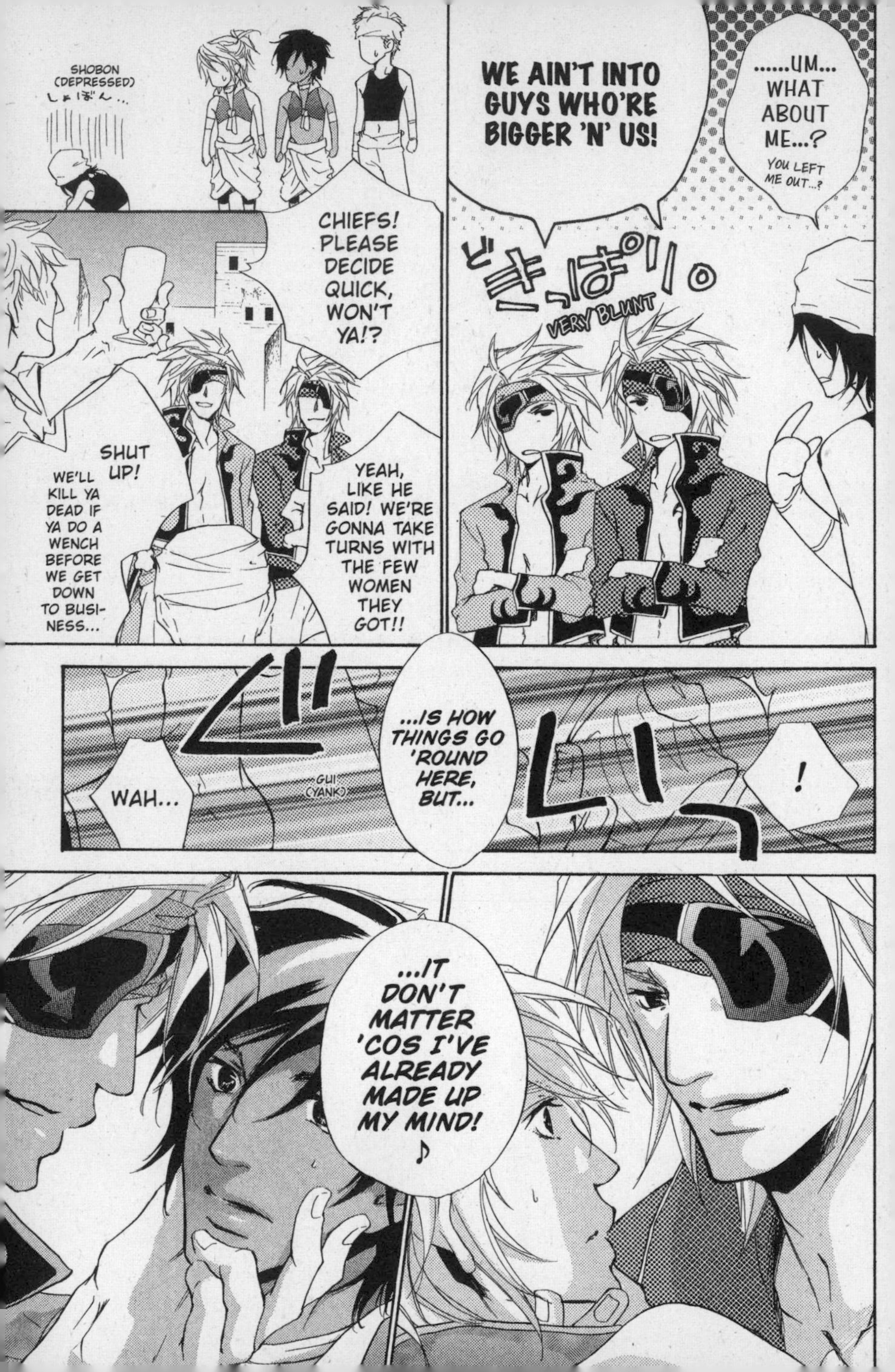
WE AIN'T INTO GUYS WHO'RE BIGGER 'N' US!
......UM... WHAT ABOUT ME...?
YOU LEFT ME OUT...?
どきっぱり。
VERY BLUNT
SHOBON (DEPRESSED)
しょぼん...
CHIEFS! PLEASE DECIDE QUICK, WON'T YA!?
YEAH, LIKE HE SAID! WE'RE GONNA TAKE TURNS WITH THE FEW WOMEN THEY GOT!!
SHUT UP!
WE'LL KILL YA DEAD IF YA DO A WENCH BEFORE WE GET DOWN TO BUSI-NESS...
!
ぐいっ
...IS HOW THINGS GO 'ROUND HERE, BUT...
GUI (YANK)
WAH...
...IT DON'T MATTER 'COS I'VE ALREADY MADE UP MY MIND! ♪

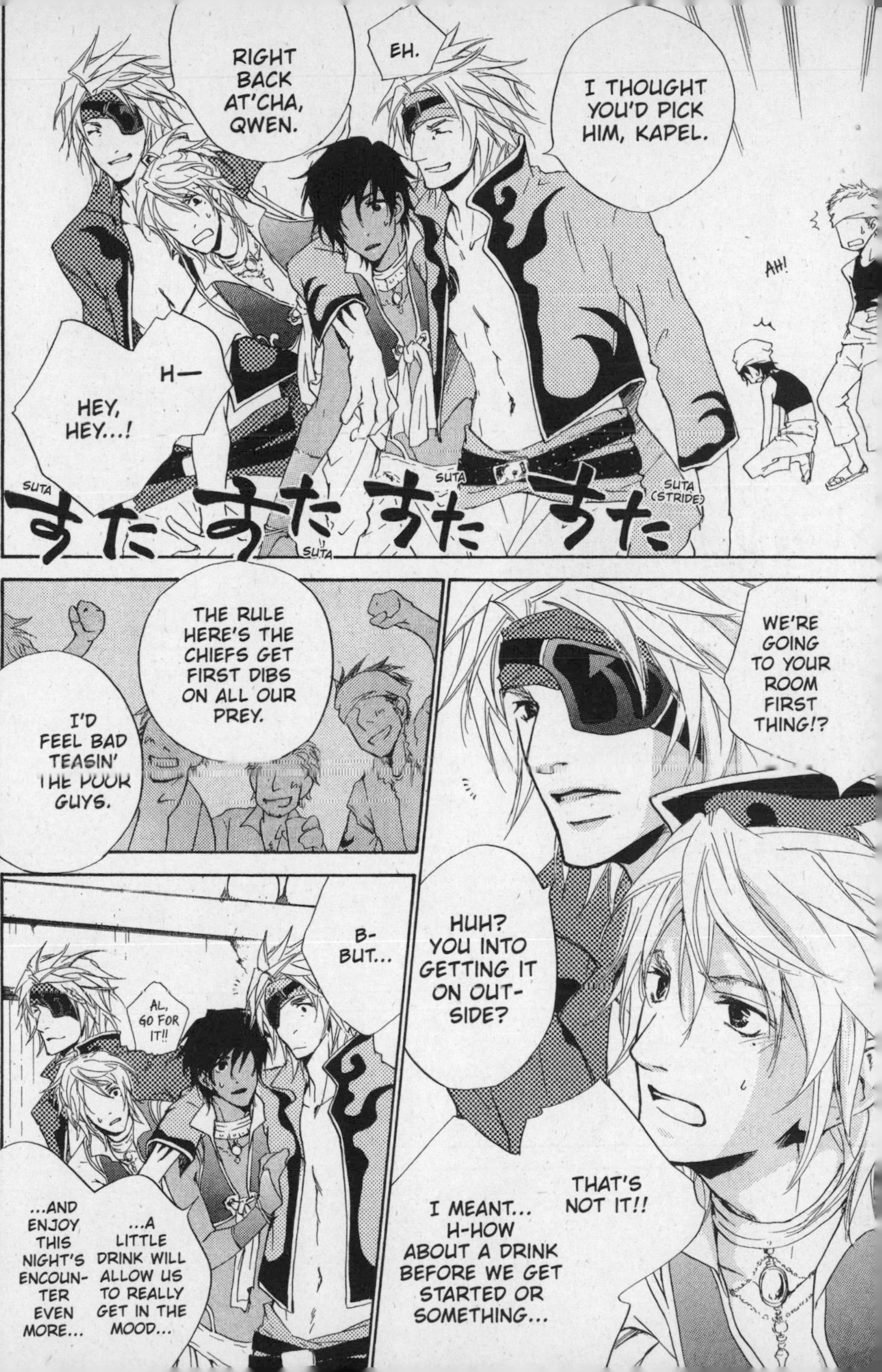

I THOUGHT YOU'D PICK HIM, KAPEL.
EH.
RIGHT BACK AT'CHA, QWEN.
AH!
H—
HEY, HEY...!
SUTA (STRIDE)
SUTA
SUTA
SUTA
すたすたすたすた
WE'RE GOING TO YOUR ROOM FIRST THING!?
HUH? YOU INTO GETTING IT ON OUT-SIDE?
THAT'S NOT IT!!
I MEANT... H-HOW ABOUT A DRINK BEFORE WE GET STARTED OR SOMETHING...
THE RULE HERE'S THE CHIEFS GET FIRST DIBS ON ALL OUR PREY.
I'D FEEL BAD TEASIN' THE POOR GUYS.
B-BUT...
AL, GO FOR IT!!
...A LITTLE DRINK WILL ALLOW US TO REALLY GET IN THE MOOD...
...AND ENJOY THIS NIGHT'S ENCOUN-TER EVEN MORE...

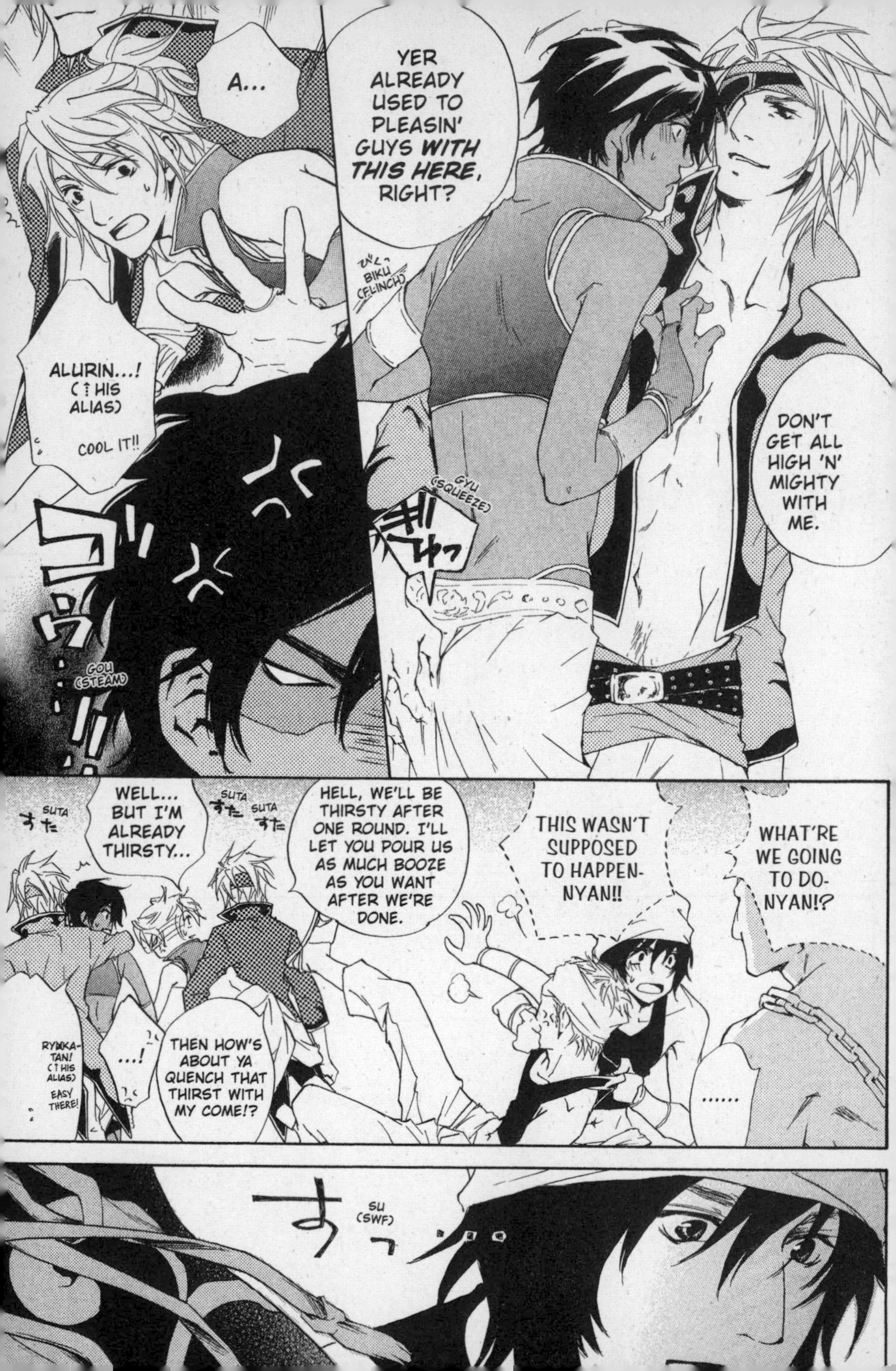
YER ALREADY USED TO PLEASIN' GUYS *WITH THIS HERE*, RIGHT?
BIKU (FLINCH)
GYU (SQUEEZE)
DON'T GET ALL HIGH 'N' MIGHTY WITH ME.
A...
ALURIN...! (↑ HIS ALIAS)
COOL IT!!
GOU (STEAM)
WHAT'RE WE GOING TO DO-NYAN!?
......
THIS WASN'T SUPPOSED TO HAPPEN-NYAN!!
HELL, WE'LL BE THIRSTY AFTER ONE ROUND. I'LL LET YOU POUR US AS MUCH BOOZE AS YOU WANT AFTER WE'RE DONE.
SUTA SUTA SUTA
WELL... BUT I'M ALREADY THIRSTY...
THEN HOW'S ABOUT YA QUENCH THAT THIRST WITH MY COME!?
...!
RYOKATAN! (↑ HIS ALIAS) EASY THERE!
SU (SWF)

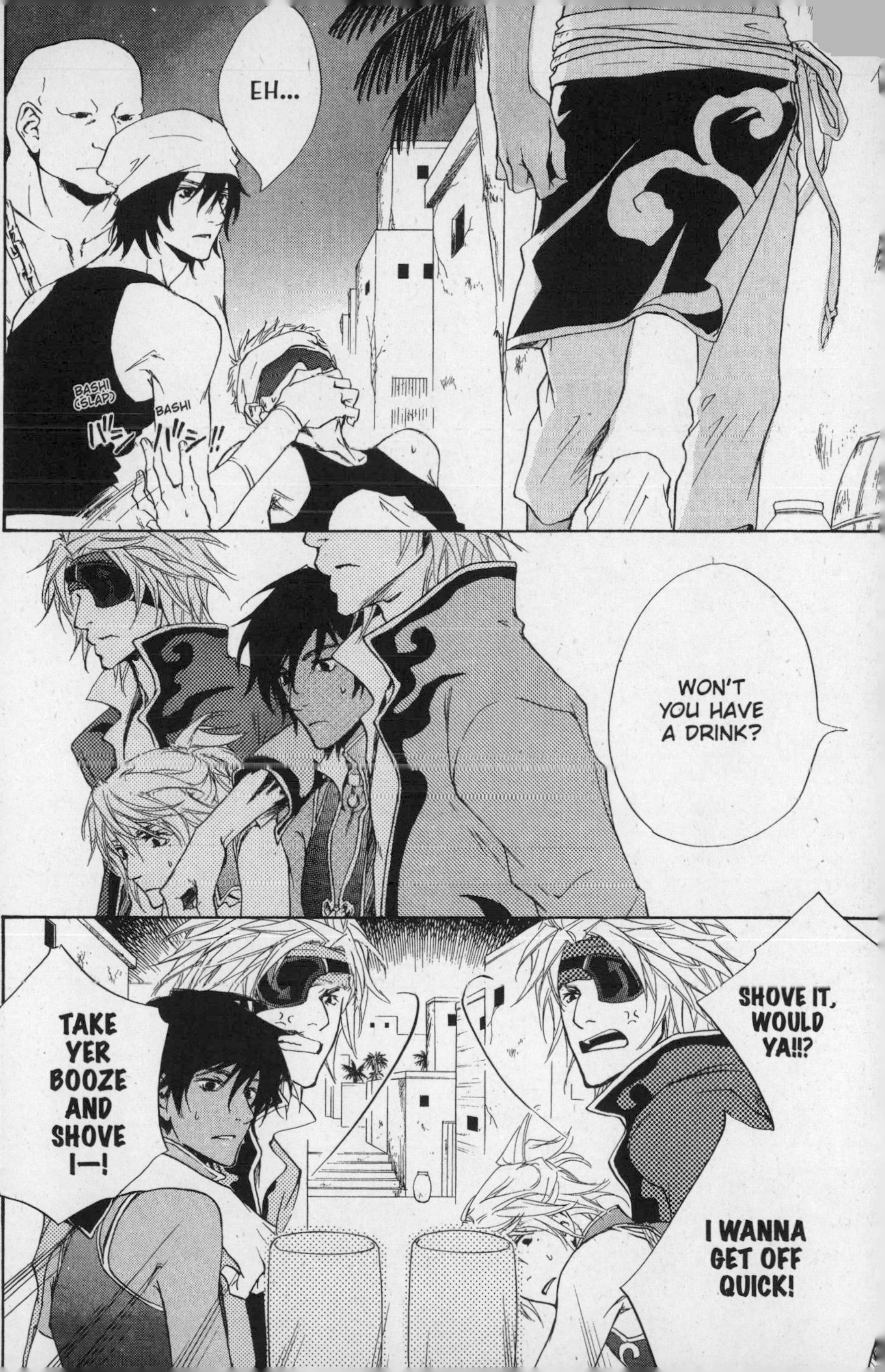

EH...
BASHI (SLAP)
BASHI
WON'T YOU HAVE A DRINK?
SHOVE IT, WOULD YA!!?
I WANNA GET OFF QUICK!
TAKE YER BOOZE AND SHOVE I—!

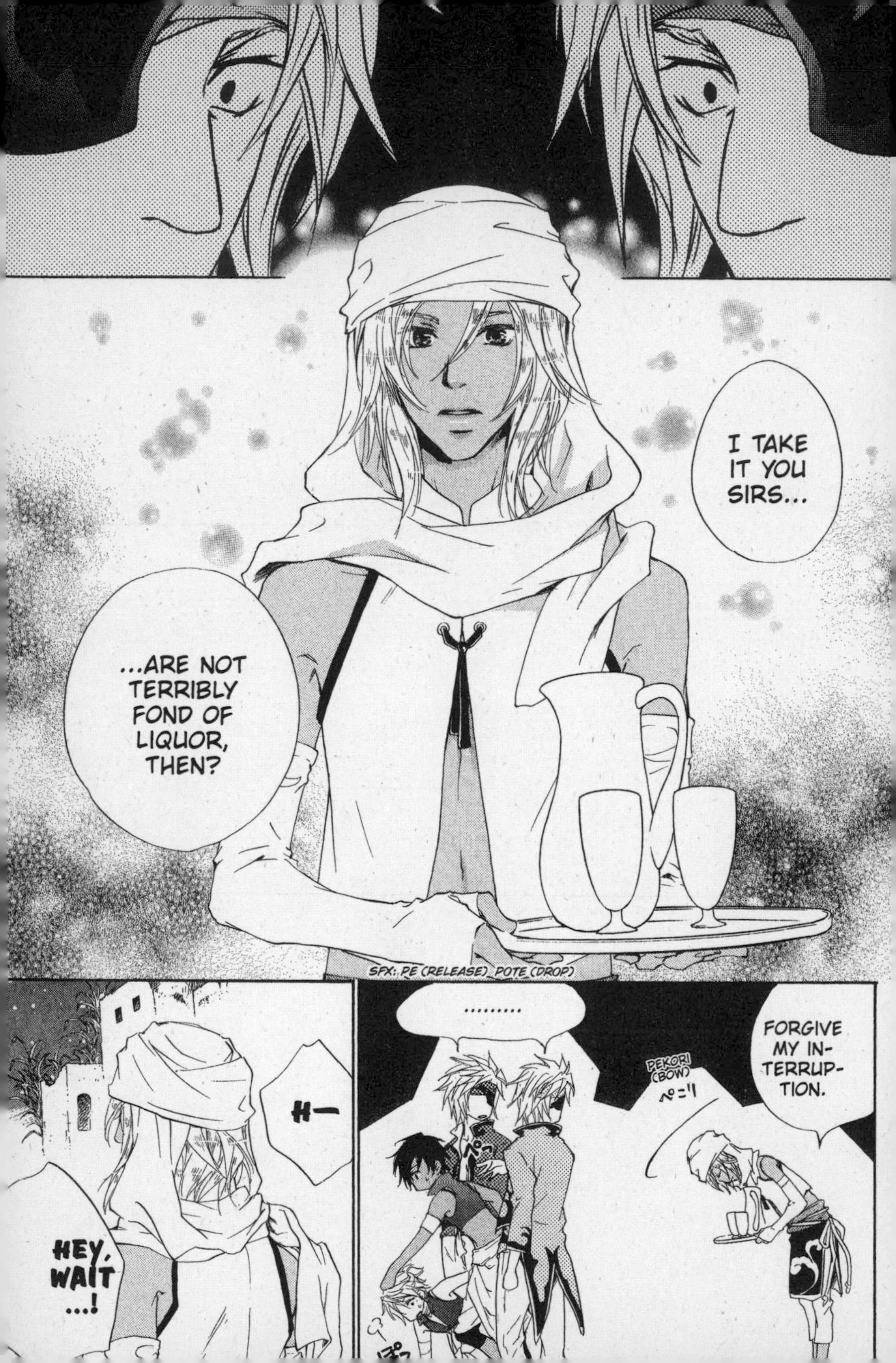
I TAKE IT YOU SIRS...
...ARE NOT TERRIBLY FOND OF LIQUOR, THEN?
SFX: PE (RELEASE) POTE (DROP)
FORGIVE MY IN-TERRUP-TION.
PEKORI (BOW)
ぺこり
....
H—
HEY, WAIT ...!

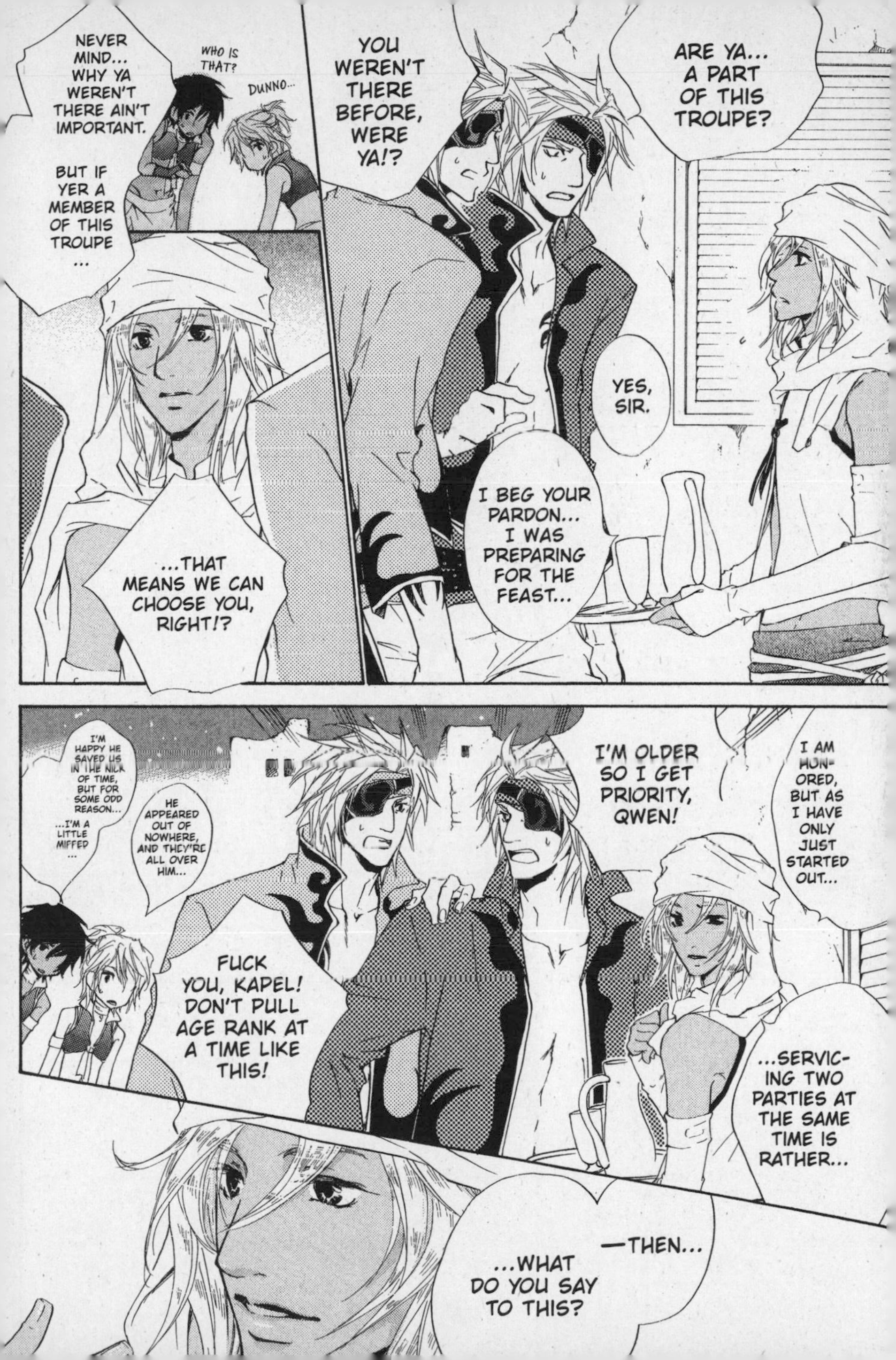
ARE YA... A PART OF THIS TROUPE?
YOU WEREN'T THERE BEFORE, WERE YA!?
YES, SIR.
I BEG YOUR PARDON... I WAS PREPARING FOR THE FEAST...
NEVER MIND... WHY YA WEREN'T THERE AIN'T IMPORTANT.
WHO IS THAT?
DUNNO...
BUT IF YER A MEMBER OF THIS TROUPE...
...THAT MEANS WE CAN CHOOSE YOU, RIGHT!?
I AM HONORED, BUT AS I HAVE ONLY JUST STARTED OUT...
I'M OLDER SO I GET PRIORITY, QWEN!
HE APPEARED OUT OF NOWHERE, AND THEY'RE ALL OVER HIM...
I'M HAPPY HE SAVED US IN THE NICK OF TIME, BUT FOR SOME ODD REASON...
...I'M A LITTLE MIFFED...
FUCK YOU, KAPEL! DON'T PULL AGE RANK AT A TIME LIKE THIS!
...SERVICING TWO PARTIES AT THE SAME TIME IS RATHER...
—THEN...
...WHAT DO YOU SAY TO THIS?

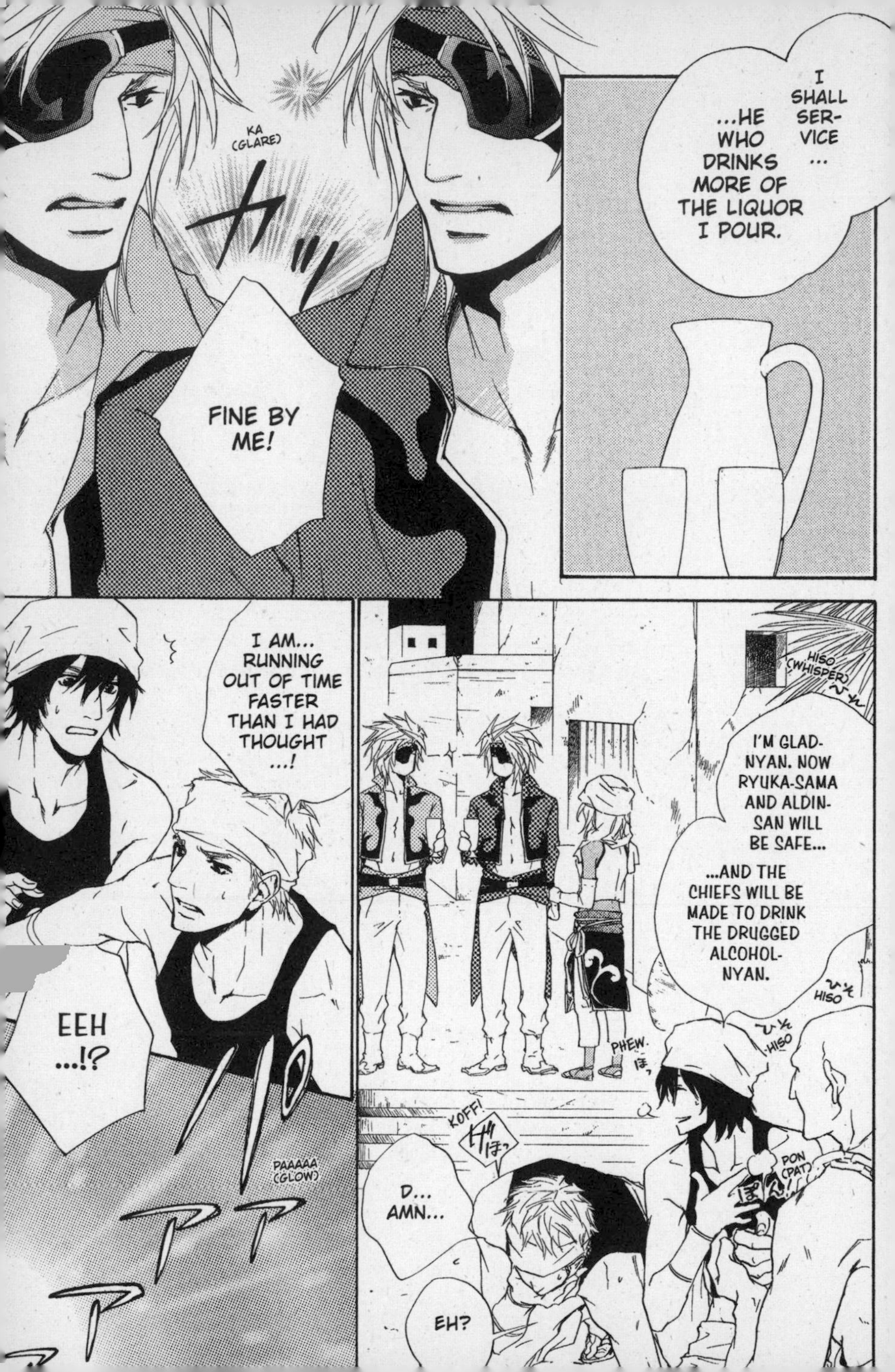
I SHALL SERVICE...
...HE WHO DRINKS MORE OF THE LIQUOR I POUR.
KA (GLARE)
FINE BY ME!
HISO (WHISPER)
I'M GLADNYAN. NOW RYUKA-SAMA AND ALDIN-SAN WILL BE SAFE...
...AND THE CHIEFS WILL BE MADE TO DRINK THE DRUGGED ALCOHOL-NYAN.
HISO
HISO
PHEW.
KOFF!
D... AMN...
PON (PAT)!
EH?
I AM... RUNNING OUT OF TIME FASTER THAN I HAD THOUGHT ...!
EEH ...!?
PAAAAA (GLOW)

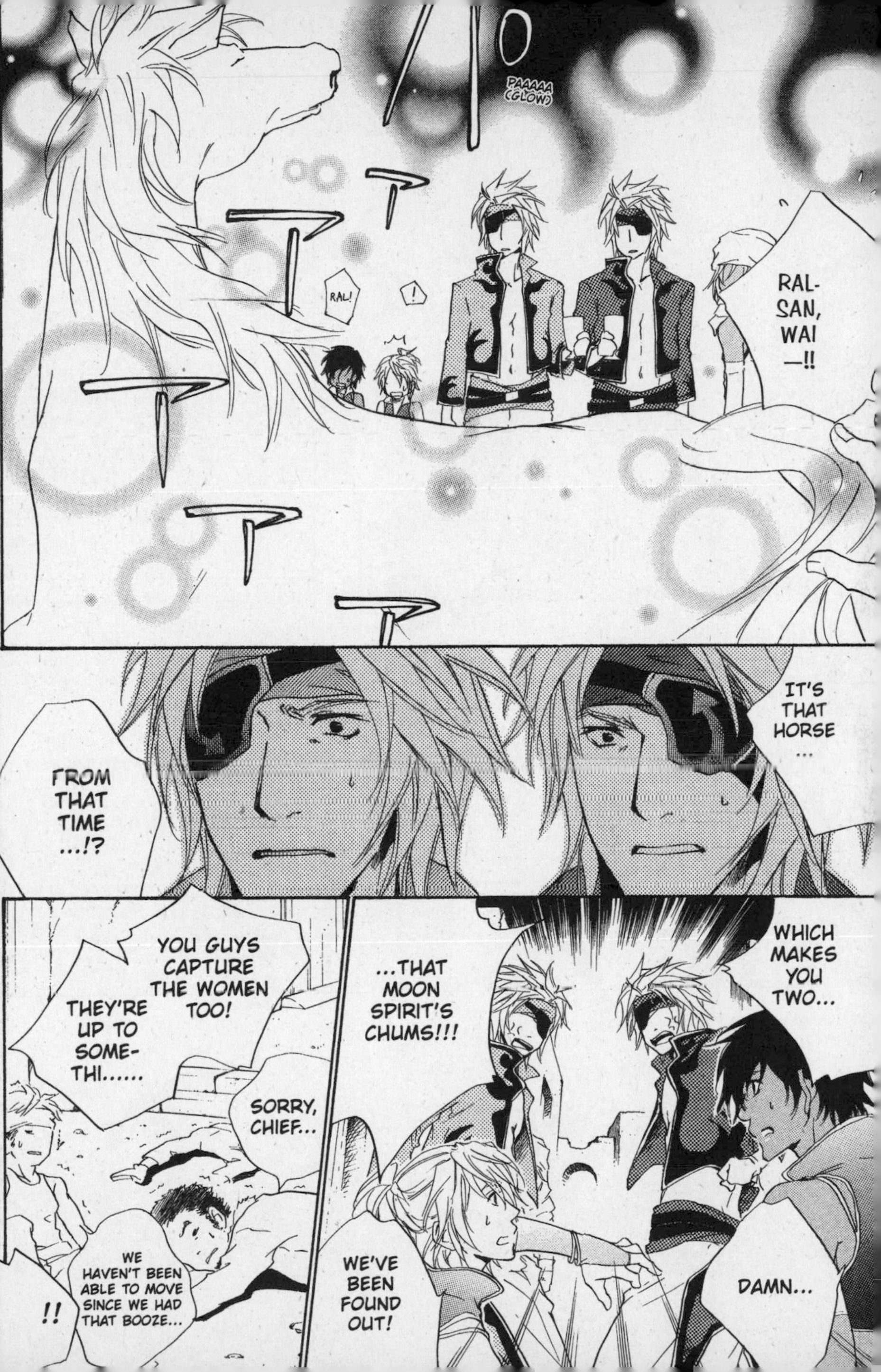
PAAAAA (GLOW)
RAL-SAN, WAI—!!
!
RAL!
IT'S THAT HORSE...
FROM THAT TIME...!?
WHICH MAKES YOU TWO...
...THAT MOON SPIRIT'S CHUMS!!!
DAMN...
WE'VE BEEN FOUND OUT!
YOU GUYS CAPTURE THE WOMEN TOO!
THEY'RE UP TO SOME-THI......
SORRY, CHIEF...
WE HAVEN'T BEEN ABLE TO MOVE SINCE WE HAD THAT BOOZE...
!!

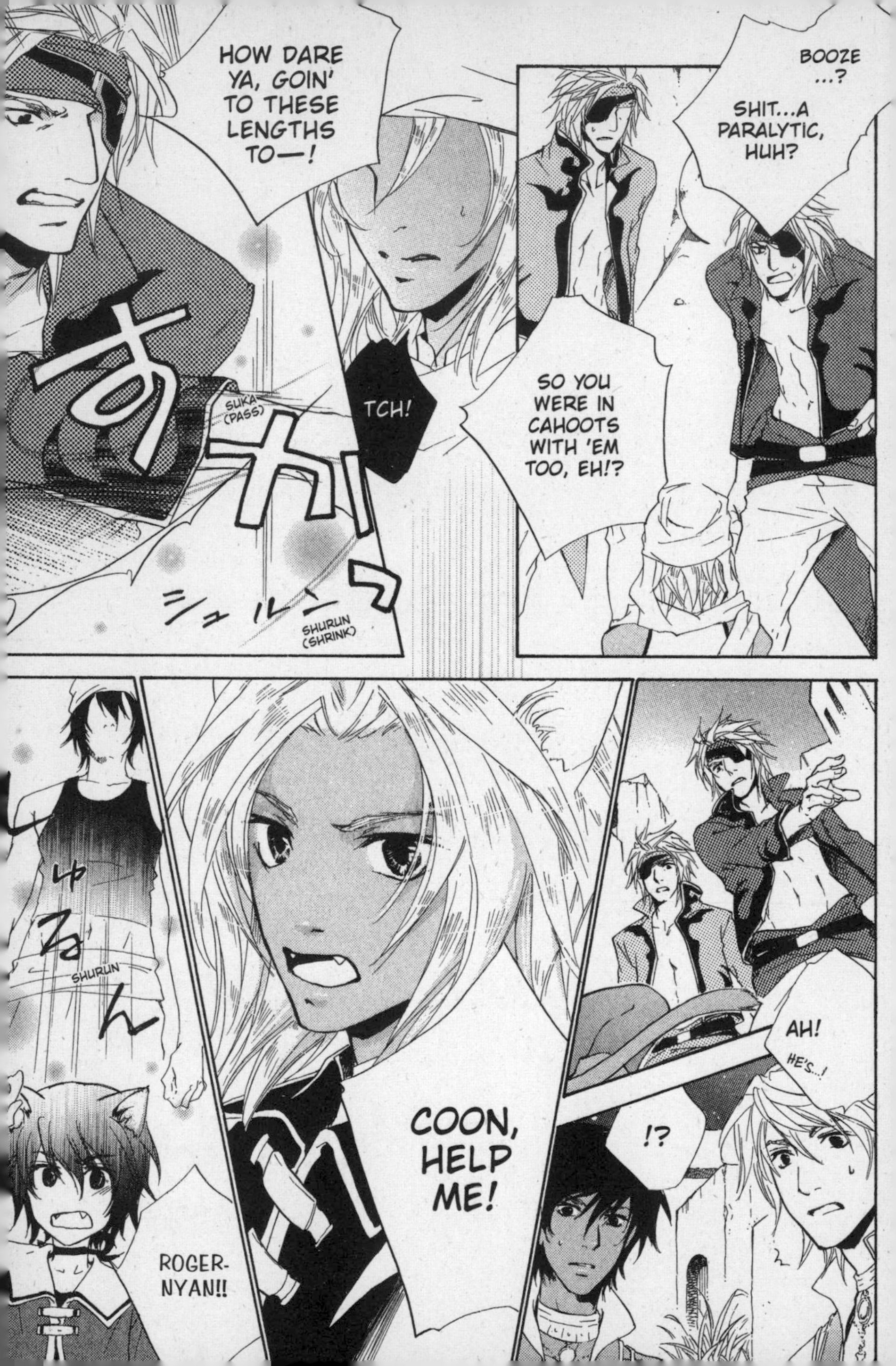

BOOZE ...?
SHIT...A PARALYTIC, HUH?
SO YOU WERE IN CAHOOTS WITH 'EM TOO, EH!?
TCH!
HOW DARE YA, GOIN' TO THESE LENGTHS TO—!
SUKA (PASS)
SHURUN (SHRINK)
AH!
HE'S...!
!?
COON, HELP ME!
SHURUN
ROGER-NYAN!!

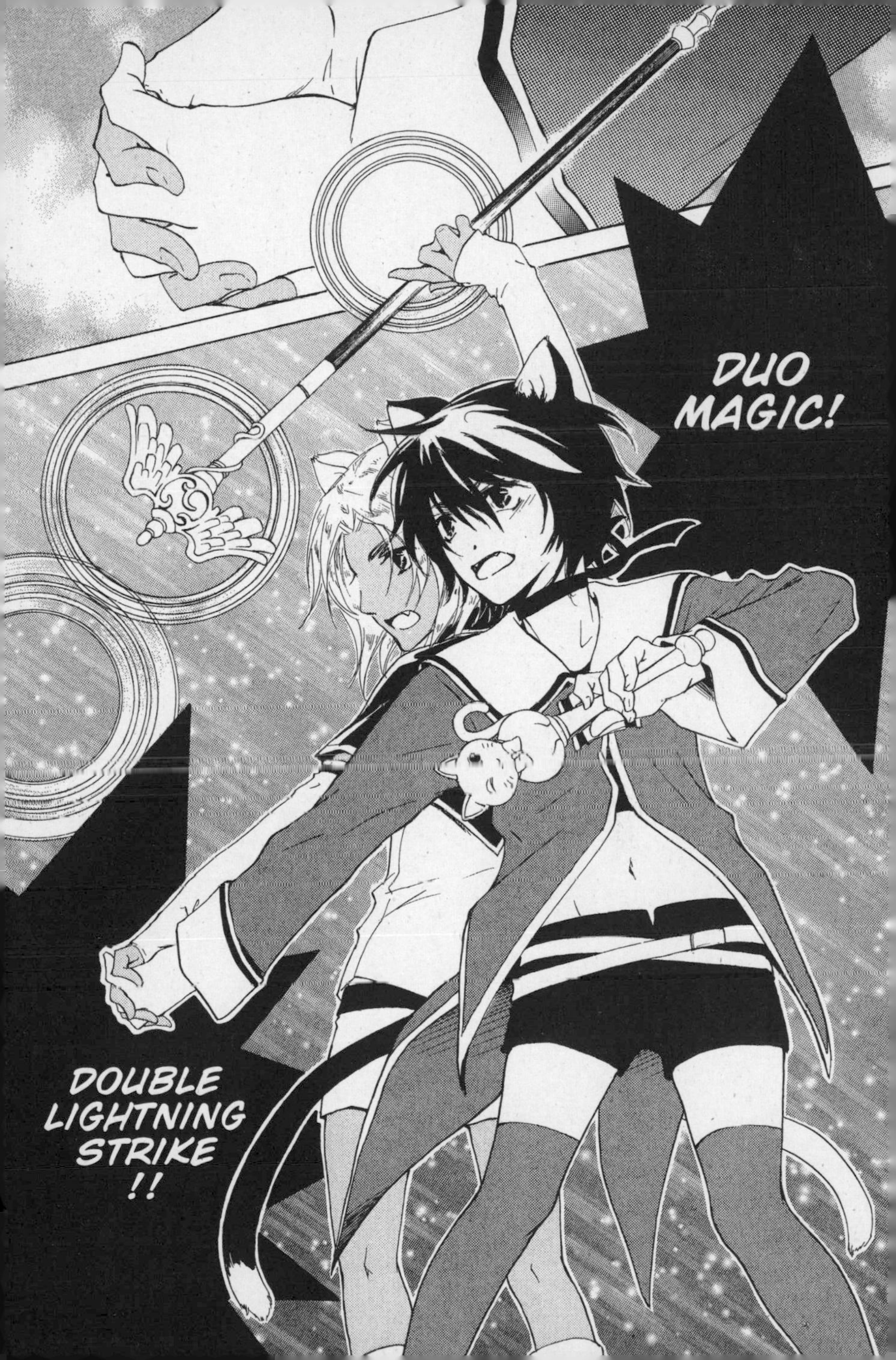
DUO MAGIC!
DOUBLE LIGHTNING STRIKE!!

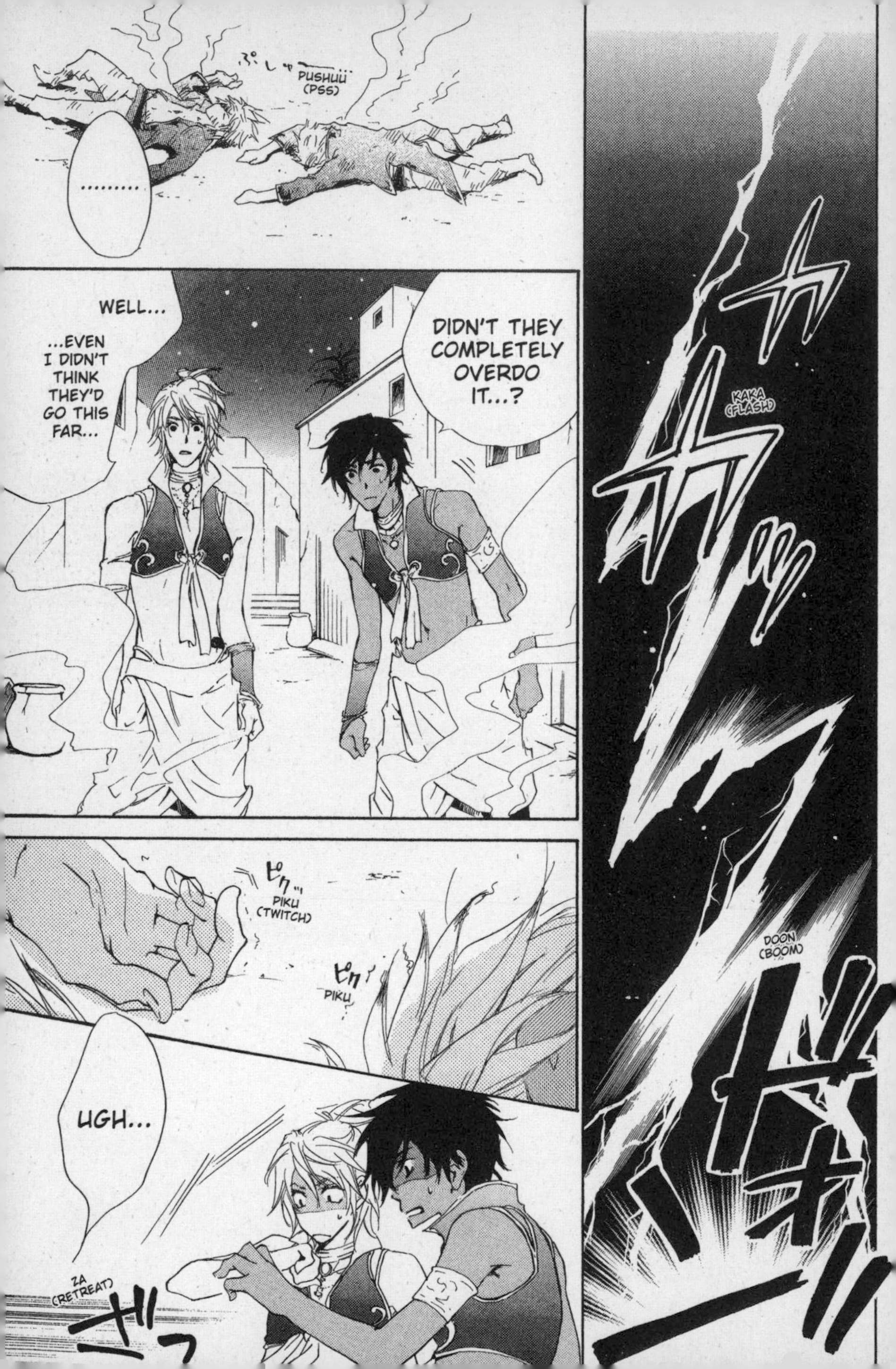
KAKA (FLASH)
DOON (BOOM)
PUSHUU (PSS)
....
DIDN'T THEY COMPLETELY OVERDO IT...?
WELL...
...EVEN I DIDN'T THINK THEY'D GO THIS FAR...
PIKU (TWITCH)
PIKU
UGH...
ZA (RETREAT)

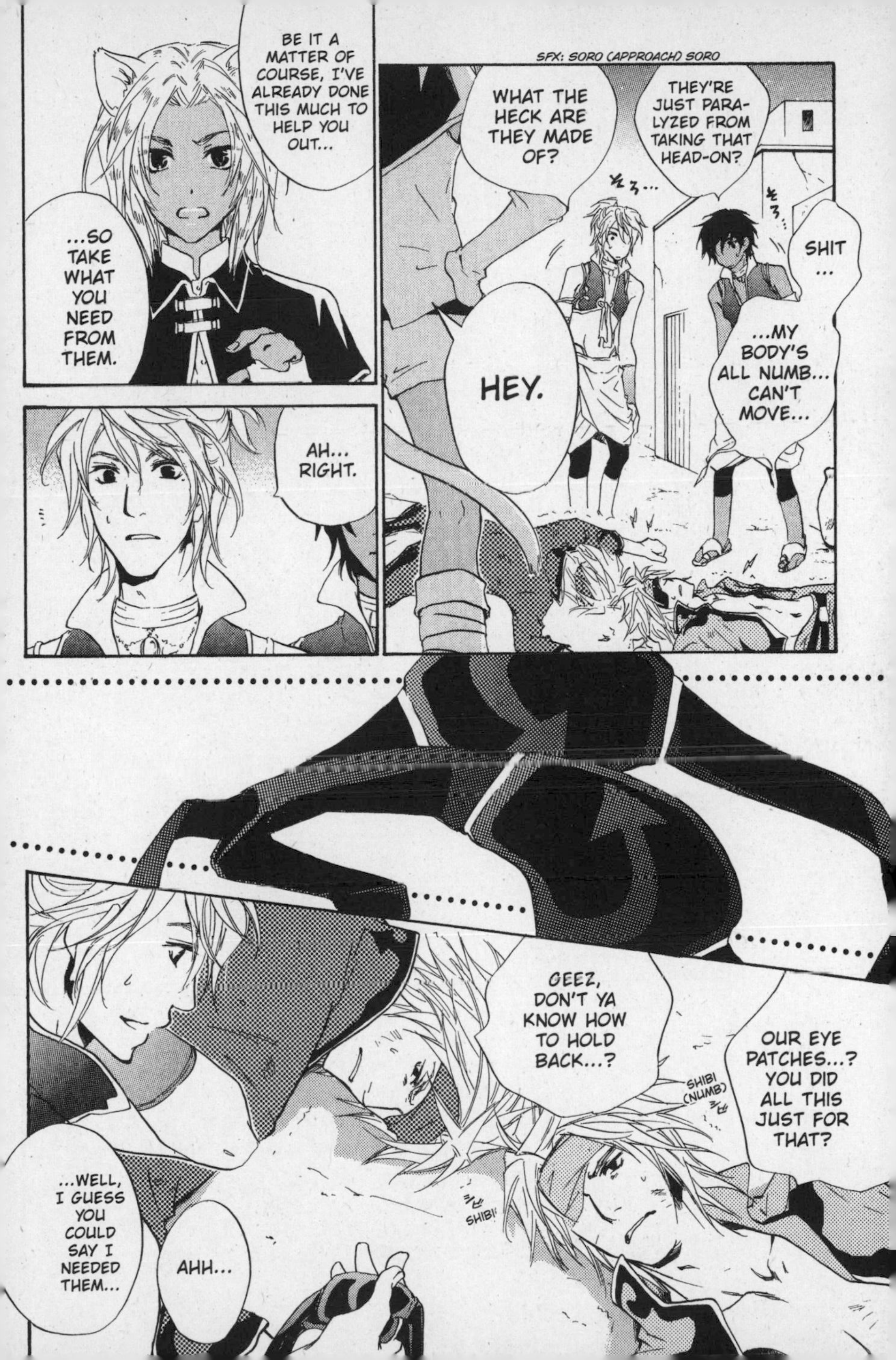
SFX: SORO (APPROACH) SORO
THEY'RE JUST PARA-LYZED FROM TAKING THAT HEAD-ON?
WHAT THE HECK ARE THEY MADE OF?
SHIT ...
...MY BODY'S ALL NUMB... CAN'T MOVE...
HEY.
BE IT A MATTER OF COURSE, I'VE ALREADY DONE THIS MUCH TO HELP YOU OUT...
...SO TAKE WHAT YOU NEED FROM THEM.
AH... RIGHT.
OUR EYE PATCHES...? YOU DID ALL THIS JUST FOR THAT?
GEEZ, DON'T YA KNOW HOW TO HOLD BACK...?
SHIBI (NUMB)
SHIBI
...WELL, I GUESS YOU COULD SAY I NEEDED THEM...
AHH...

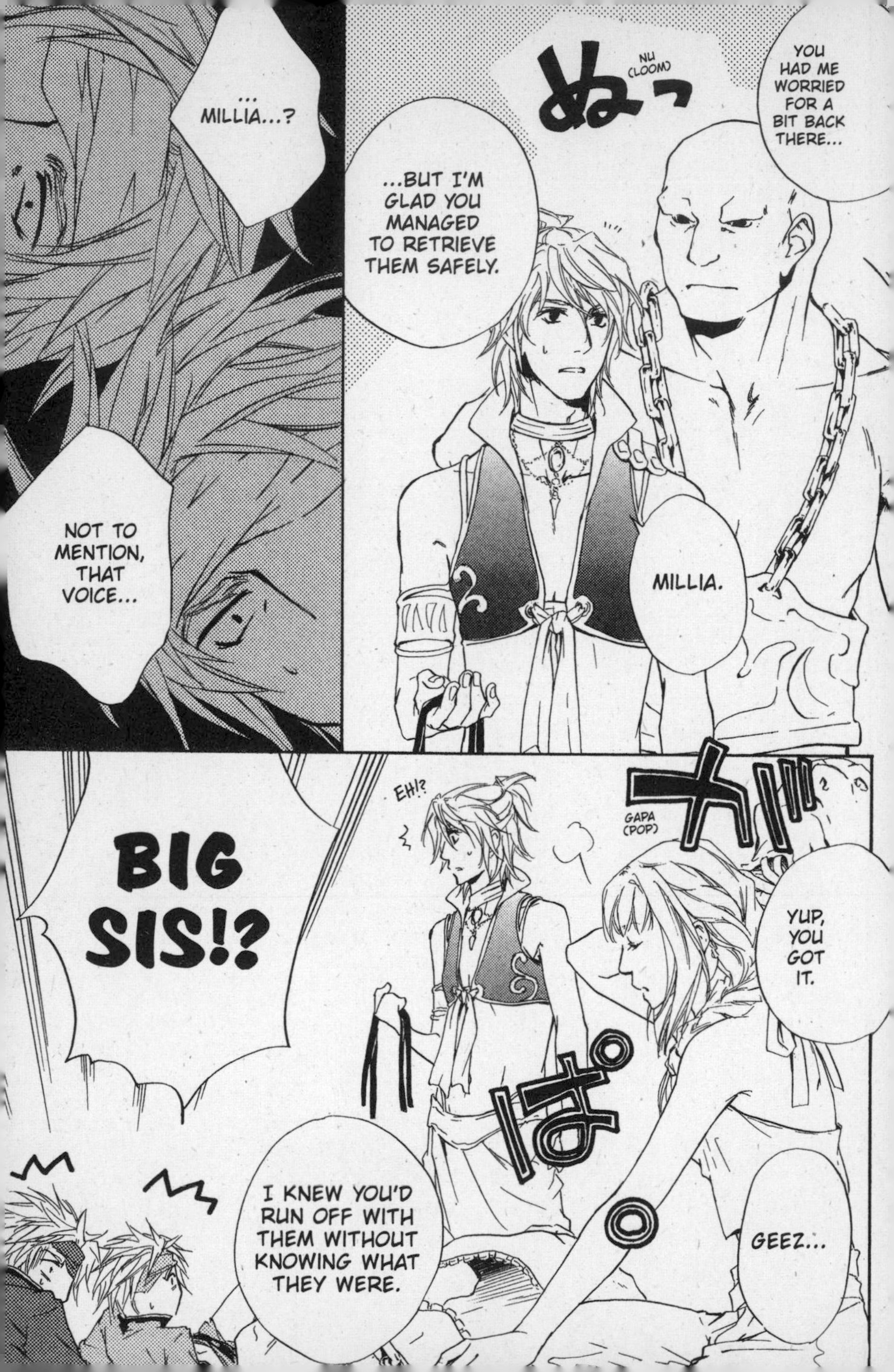

YOU HAD ME WORRIED FOR A BIT BACK THERE...
ぬっ
NU (LOOM)
...BUT I'M GLAD YOU MANAGED TO RETRIEVE THEM SAFELY.
MILLIA.
... MILLIA...?
NOT TO MENTION, THAT VOICE...
ガバ
GAPA (POP)
YUP, YOU GOT IT.
EH!?
ぱ
GEEZ...
I KNEW YOU'D RUN OFF WITH THEM WITHOUT KNOWING WHAT THEY WERE.
BIG SIS!?

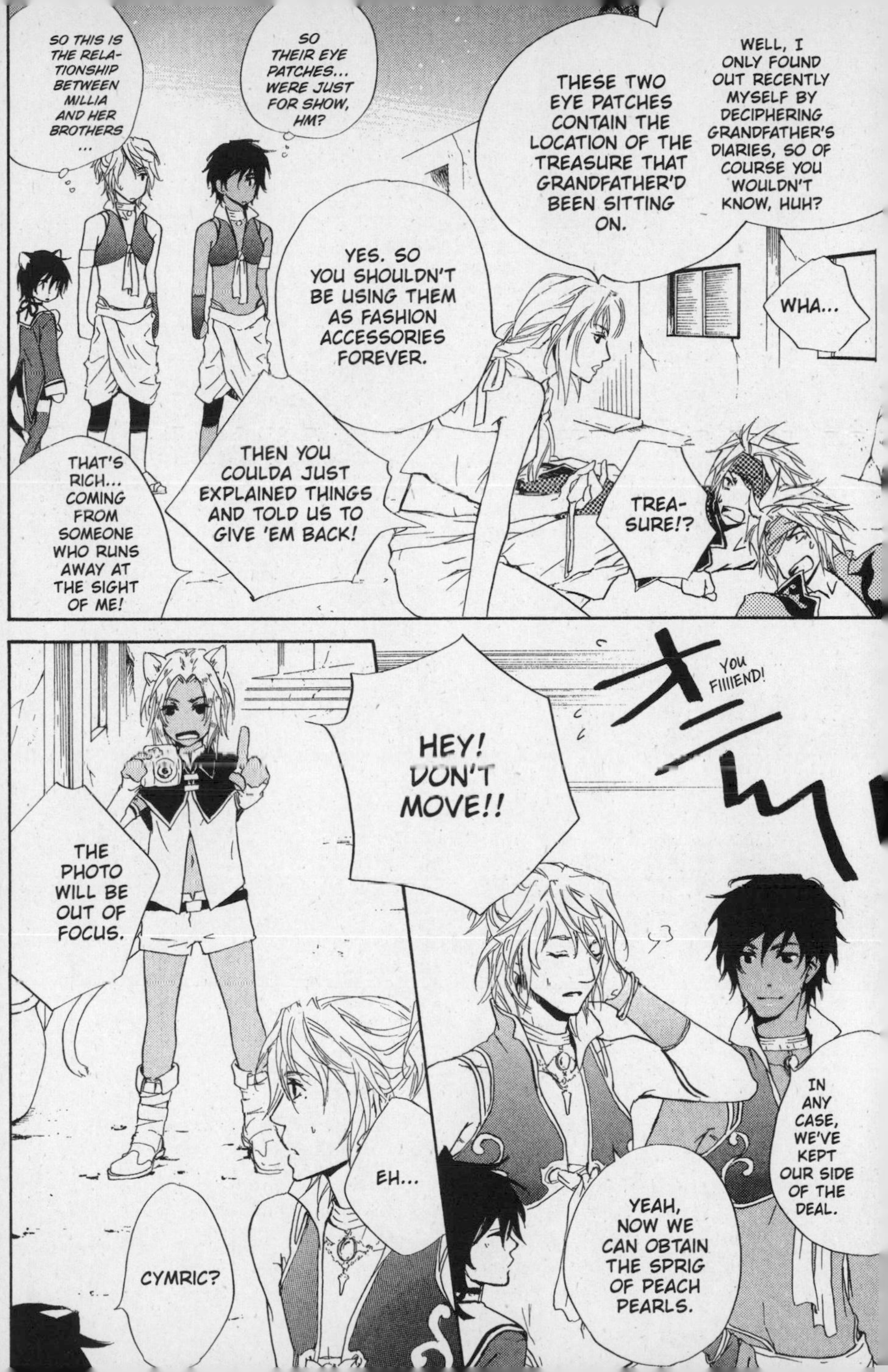
WELL, I ONLY FOUND OUT RECENTLY MYSELF BY DECIPHERING GRANDFATHER'S DIARIES, SO OF COURSE YOU WOULDN'T KNOW, HUH?
THESE TWO EYE PATCHES CONTAIN THE LOCATION OF THE TREASURE THAT GRANDFATHER'D BEEN SITTING ON.
WHA...
YES. SO YOU SHOULDN'T BE USING THEM AS FASHION ACCESSORIES FOREVER.
TREA-SURE!?
SO THEIR EYE PATCHES... WERE JUST FOR SHOW, HM?
SO THIS IS THE RELA-TIONSHIP BETWEEN MILLIA AND HER BROTHERS ...
THEN YOU COULDA JUST EXPLAINED THINGS AND TOLD US TO GIVE 'EM BACK!
THAT'S RICH... COMING FROM SOMEONE WHO RUNS AWAY AT THE SIGHT OF ME!
YOU FIIIIEND!
HEY! DON'T MOVE!!
THE PHOTO WILL BE OUT OF FOCUS.
IN ANY CASE, WE'VE KEPT OUR SIDE OF THE DEAL.
YEAH, NOW WE CAN OBTAIN THE SPRIG OF PEACH PEARLS.
EH...
CYMRIC?

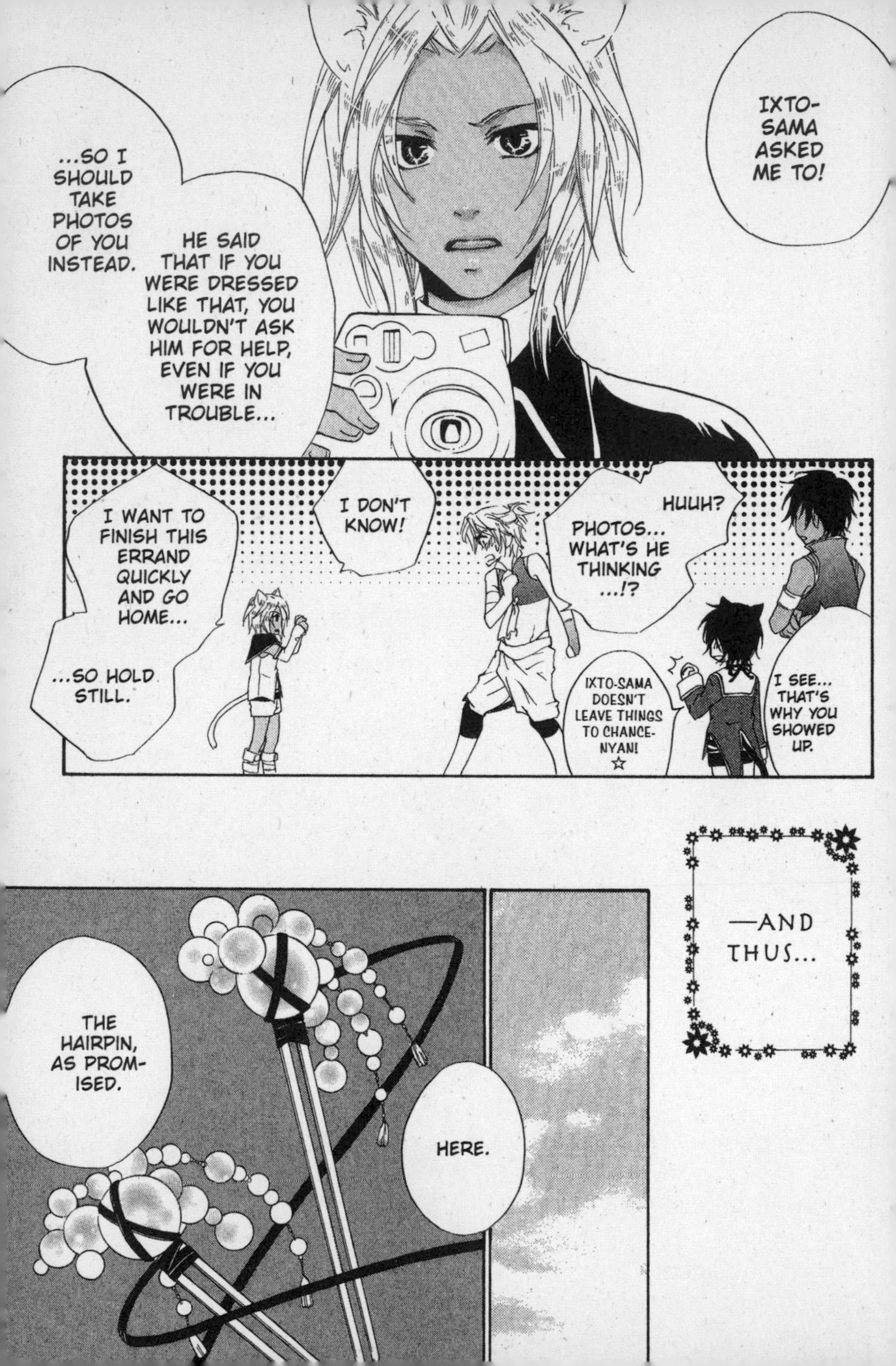
IXTO-SAMA ASKED ME TO!
HE SAID THAT IF YOU WERE DRESSED LIKE THAT, YOU WOULDN'T ASK HIM FOR HELP, EVEN IF YOU WERE IN TROUBLE...
...SO I SHOULD TAKE PHOTOS OF YOU INSTEAD.
I SEE... THAT'S WHY YOU SHOWED UP.
IXTO-SAMA DOESN'T LEAVE THINGS TO CHANCE-NYAN! ☆
HUUH?
PHOTOS... WHAT'S HE THINKING ...!?
I DON'T KNOW!
I WANT TO FINISH THIS ERRAND QUICKLY AND GO HOME...
...SO HOLD STILL.
—AND THUS...
HERE.
THE HAIRPIN, AS PROM-ISED.

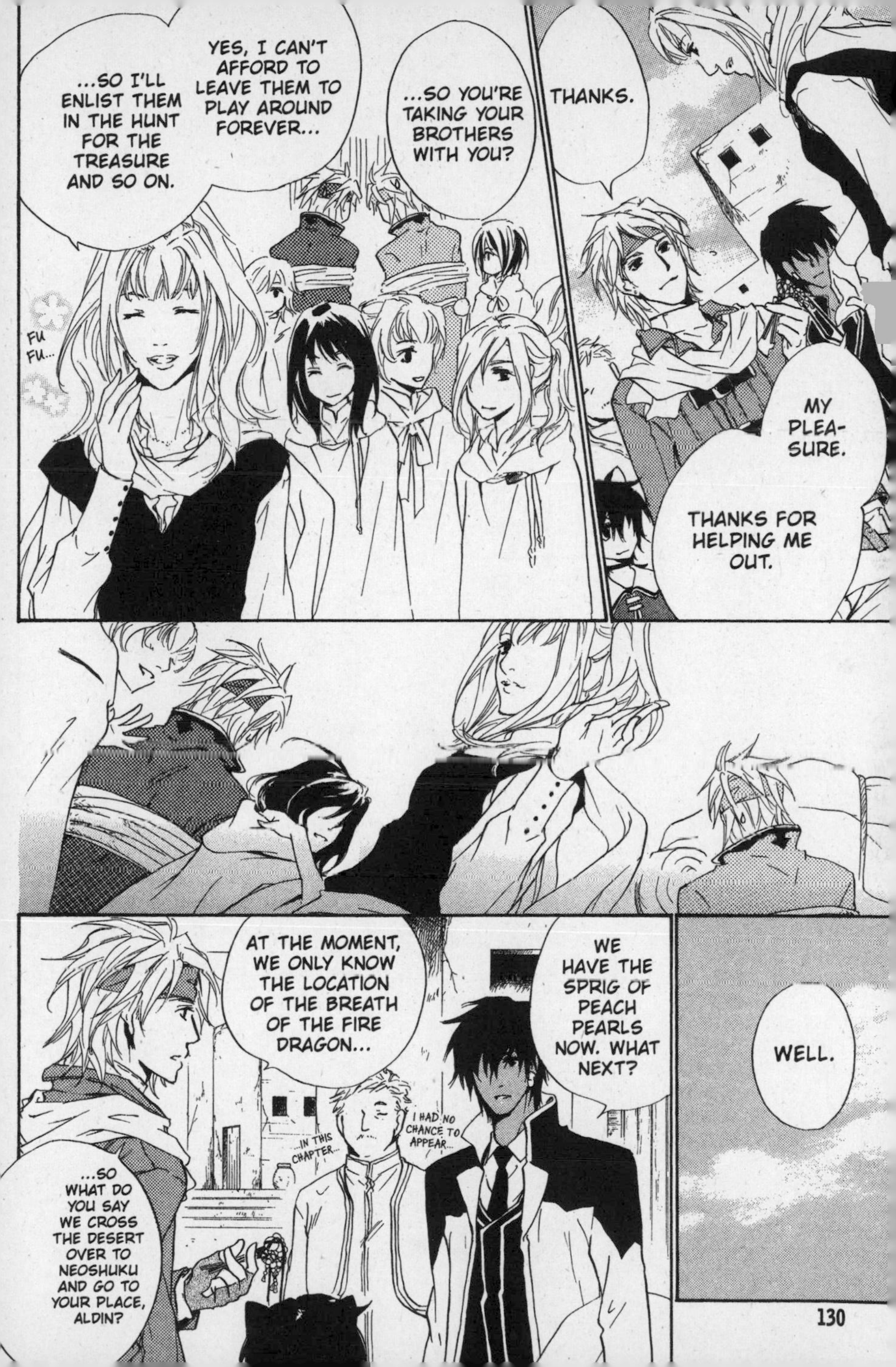
THANKS.
MY PLEASURE.
THANKS FOR HELPING ME OUT.
...SO YOU'RE TAKING YOUR BROTHERS WITH YOU?
YES, I CAN'T AFFORD TO LEAVE THEM TO PLAY AROUND FOREVER...
...SO I'LL ENLIST THEM IN THE HUNT FOR THE TREASURE AND SO ON.
FU FU...
WELL.
WE HAVE THE SPRIG OF PEACH PEARLS NOW. WHAT NEXT?
AT THE MOMENT, WE ONLY KNOW THE LOCATION OF THE BREATH OF THE FIRE DRAGON...
I HAD NO CHANCE TO APPEAR...
...IN THIS CHAPTER...
...SO WHAT DO YOU SAY WE CROSS THE DESERT OVER TO NEOSHUKU AND GO TO YOUR PLACE, ALDIN?

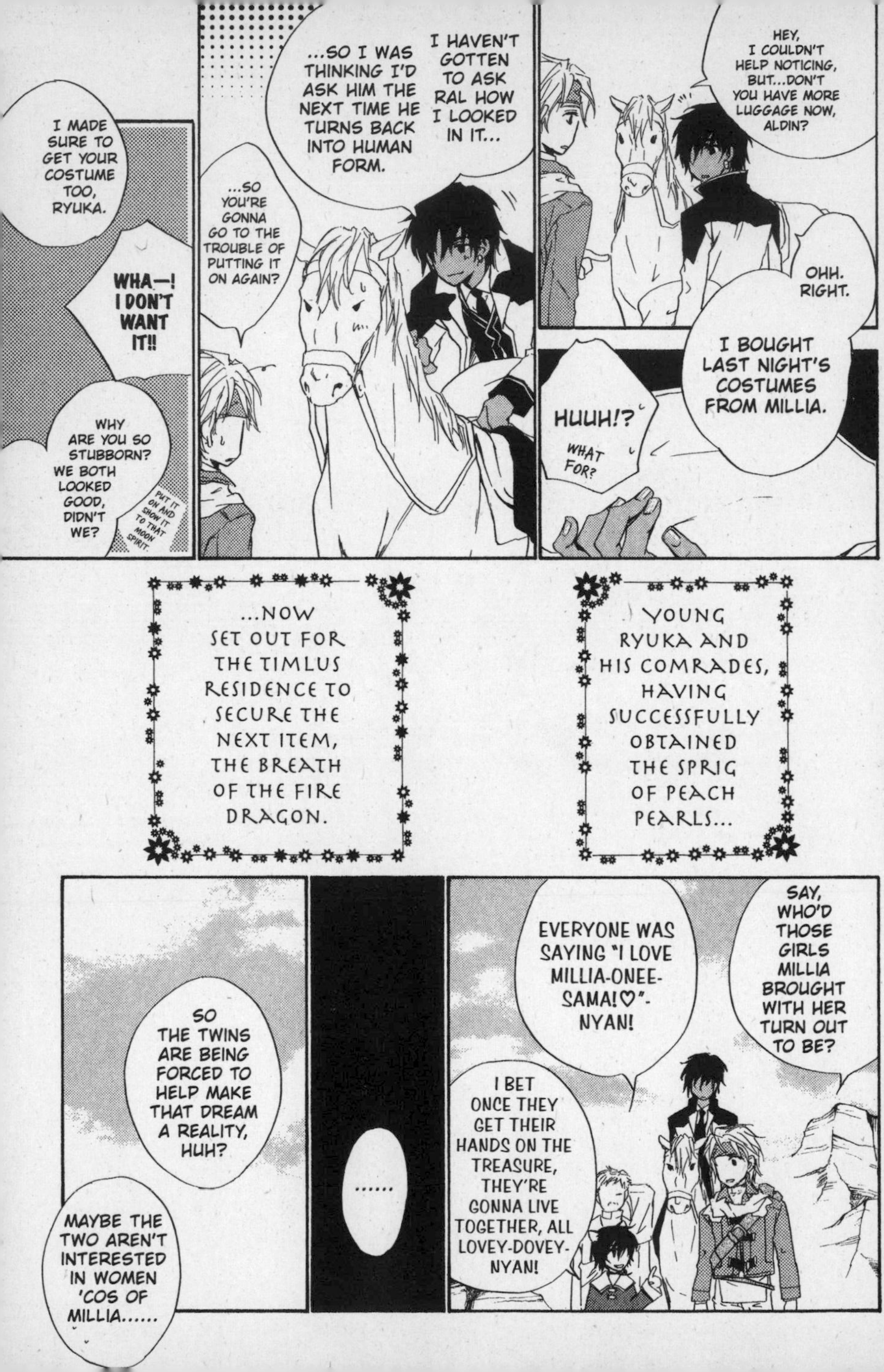
HEY, I COULDN'T HELP NOTICING, BUT...DON'T YOU HAVE MORE LUGGAGE NOW, ALDIN?
OHH. RIGHT.
I BOUGHT LAST NIGHT'S COSTUMES FROM MILLIA.
HUUH!?
WHAT FOR?
I HAVEN'T GOTTEN TO ASK RAL HOW I LOOKED IN IT...
...SO I WAS THINKING I'D ASK HIM THE NEXT TIME HE TURNS BACK INTO HUMAN FORM.
...SO YOU'RE GONNA GO TO THE TROUBLE OF PUTTING IT ON AGAIN?
I MADE SURE TO GET YOUR COSTUME TOO, RYUKA.
WHA—! I DON'T WANT IT!!
WHY ARE YOU SO STUBBORN? WE BOTH LOOKED GOOD, DIDN'T WE?
PUT IT ON AND SHOW IT TO THAT MOON SPIRIT.
YOUNG RYUKA AND HIS COMRADES, HAVING SUCCESSFULLY OBTAINED THE SPRIG OF PEACH PEARLS...
...NOW SET OUT FOR THE TIMLUS RESIDENCE TO SECURE THE NEXT ITEM, THE BREATH OF THE FIRE DRAGON.
SAY, WHO'D THOSE GIRLS MILLIA BROUGHT WITH HER TURN OUT TO BE?
EVERYONE WAS SAYING "I LOVE MILLIA-ONEE-SAMA!♡"-NYAN!
I BET ONCE THEY GET THEIR HANDS ON THE TREASURE, THEY'RE GONNA LIVE TOGETHER, ALL LOVEY-DOVEY-NYAN!
......
SO THE TWINS ARE BEING FORCED TO HELP MAKE THAT DREAM A REALITY, HUH?
MAYBE THE TWO AREN'T INTERESTED IN WOMEN 'COS OF MILLIA......

Tale of the Waning Moon

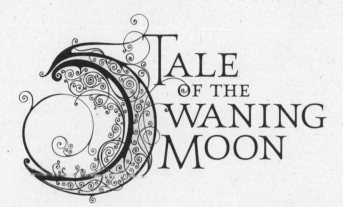

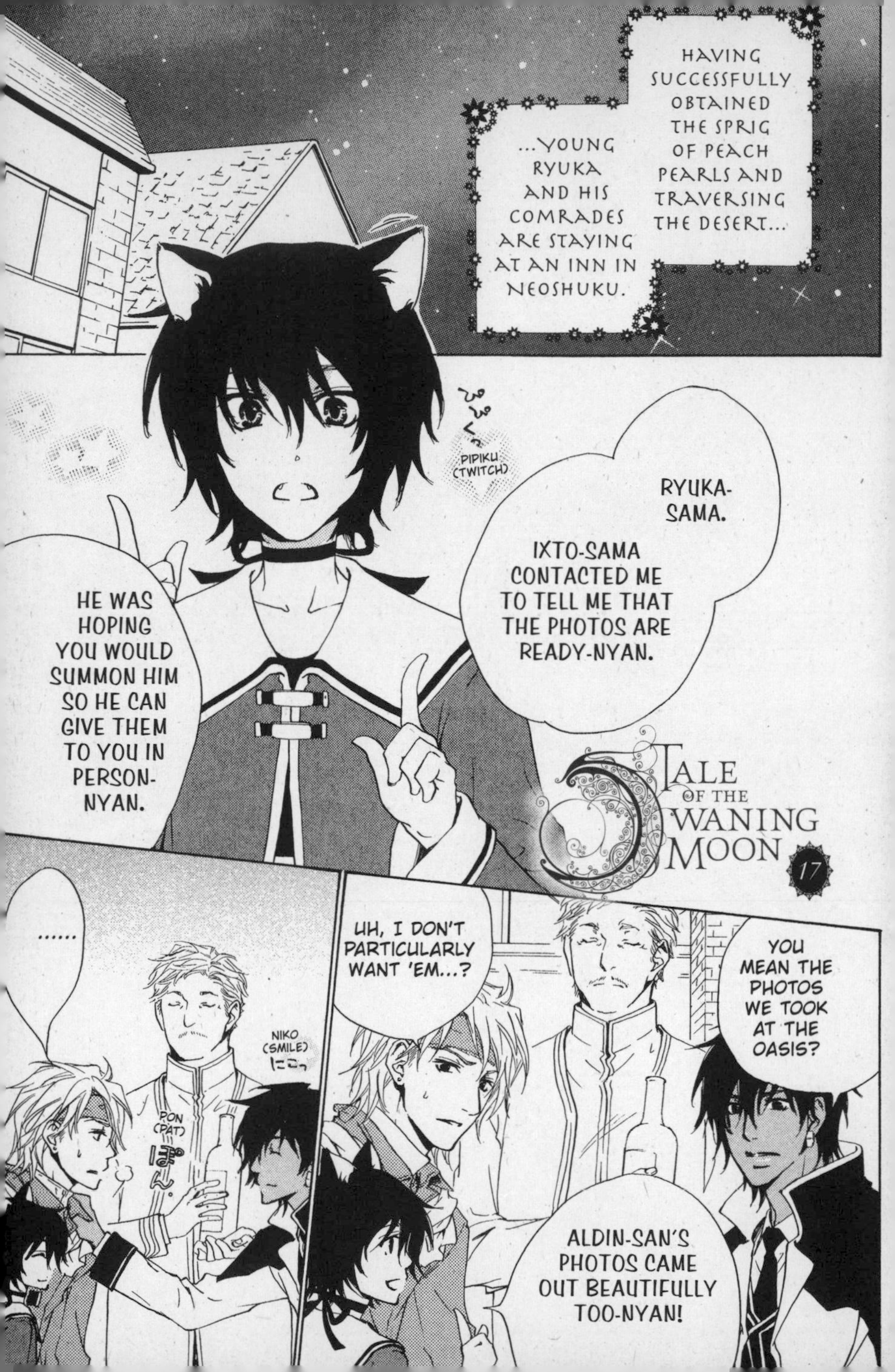
HAVING SUCCESSFULLY OBTAINED THE SPRIG OF PEACH PEARLS AND TRAVERSING THE DESERT...
...YOUNG RYUKA AND HIS COMRADES ARE STAYING AT AN INN IN NEOSHUKU.
ぴぴくっ
PIPIKU (TWITCH)
RYUKA-SAMA.
IXTO-SAMA CONTACTED ME TO TELL ME THAT THE PHOTOS ARE READY-NYAN.
HE WAS HOPING YOU WOULD SUMMON HIM SO HE CAN GIVE THEM TO YOU IN PERSON-NYAN.
TALE OF THE WANING MOON
17
YOU MEAN THE PHOTOS WE TOOK AT THE OASIS?
UH, I DON'T PARTICULARLY WANT 'EM...?
ALDIN-SAN'S PHOTOS CAME OUT BEAUTIFULLY TOO-NYAN!
NIKO (SMILE)
にこっ
PON (PAT)
ぽん。
......

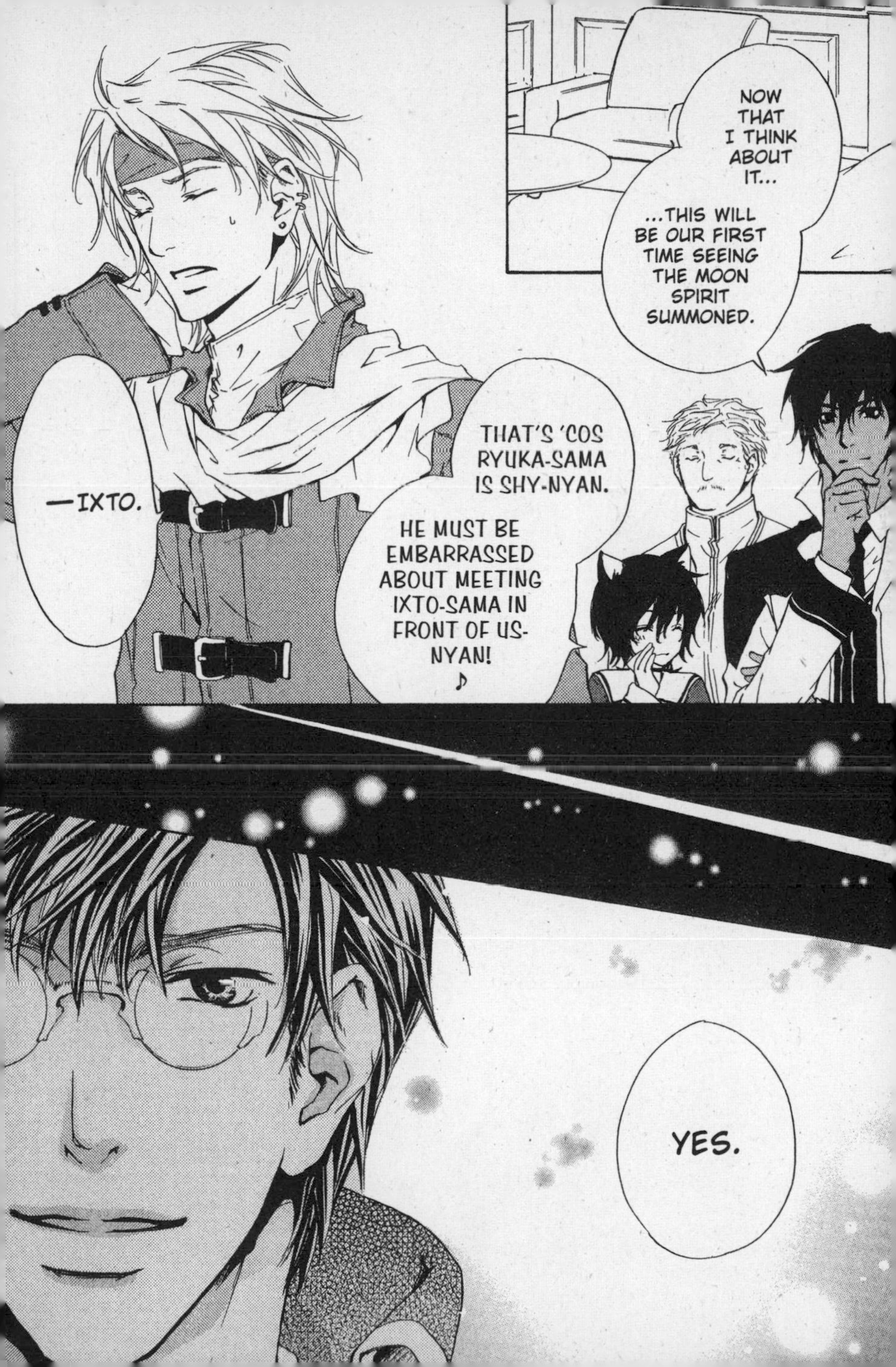
NOW THAT I THINK ABOUT IT...
...THIS WILL BE OUR FIRST TIME SEEING THE MOON SPIRIT SUMMONED.
THAT'S 'COS RYUKA-SAMA IS SHY-NYAN.
HE MUST BE EMBARRASSED ABOUT MEETING IXTO-SAMA IN FRONT OF US-NYAN! ♪
—IXTO.
YES.

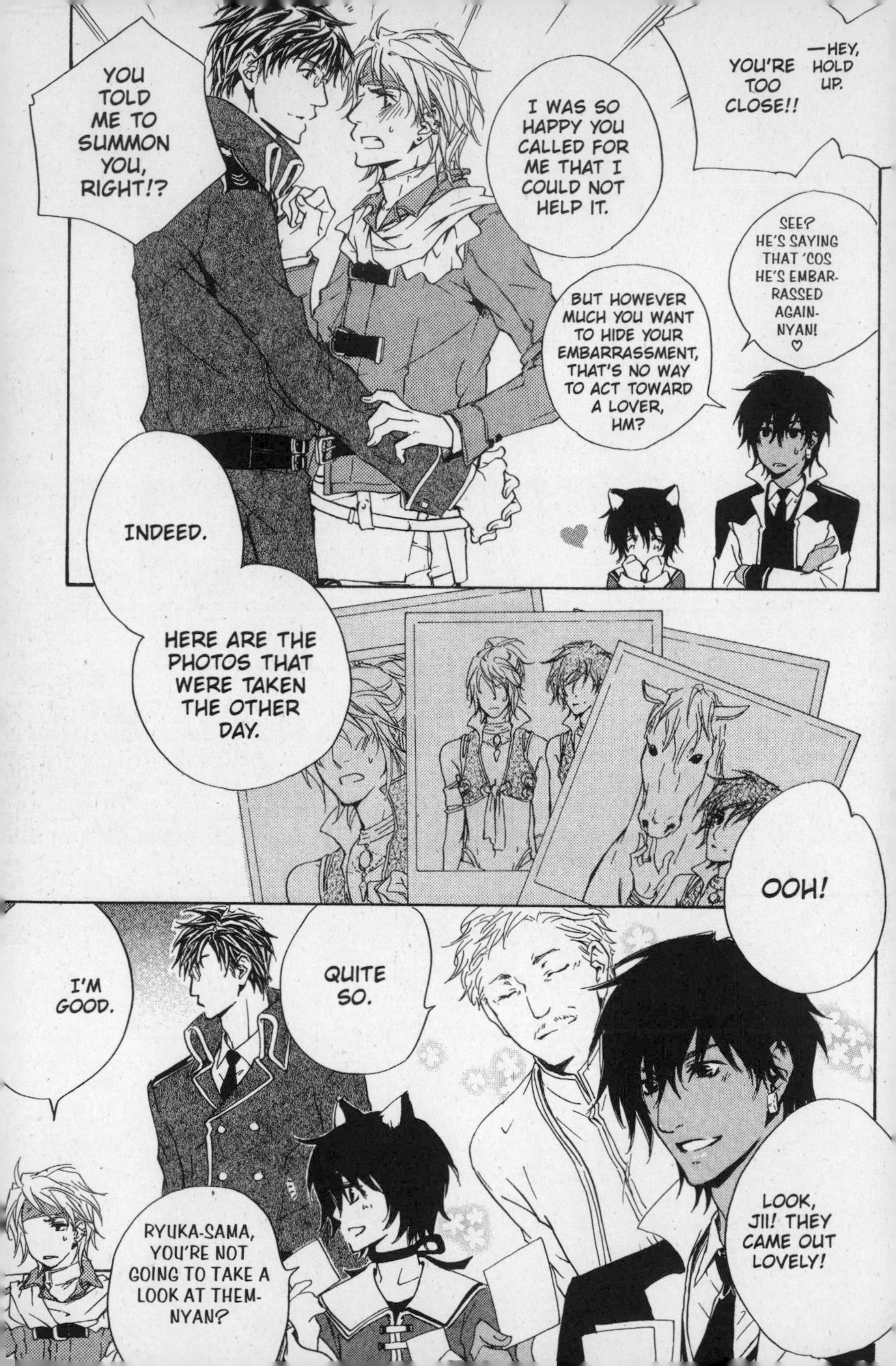
—HEY, HOLD UP.
YOU'RE TOO CLOSE!!
I WAS SO HAPPY YOU CALLED FOR ME THAT I COULD NOT HELP IT.
YOU TOLD ME TO SUMMON YOU, RIGHT!?
SEE? HE'S SAYING THAT 'COS HE'S EMBARRASSED AGAIN-NYAN! ♡
BUT HOWEVER MUCH YOU WANT TO HIDE YOUR EMBARRASSMENT, THAT'S NO WAY TO ACT TOWARD A LOVER, HM?
INDEED.
HERE ARE THE PHOTOS THAT WERE TAKEN THE OTHER DAY.
OOH!
QUITE SO.
I'M GOOD.
LOOK, JII! THEY CAME OUT LOVELY!
RYUKA-SAMA, YOU'RE NOT GOING TO TAKE A LOOK AT THEM-NYAN?

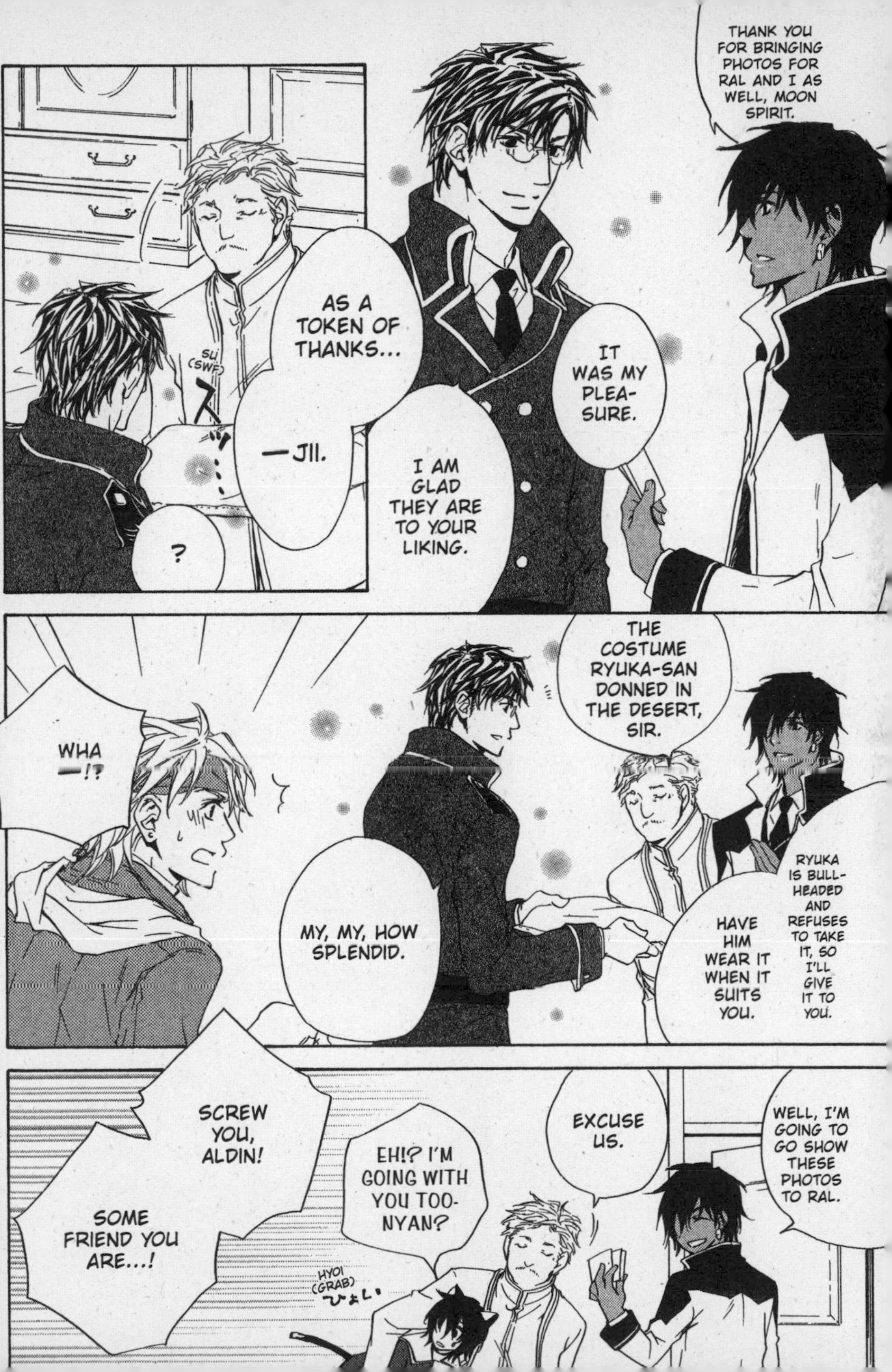
THANK YOU FOR BRINGING PHOTOS FOR RAL AND I AS WELL, MOON SPIRIT.
IT WAS MY PLEASURE.
I AM GLAD THEY ARE TO YOUR LIKING.
AS A TOKEN OF THANKS...
SU (SWF)
—JII.
?
THE COSTUME RYUKA-SAN DONNED IN THE DESERT, SIR.
RYUKA IS BULL-HEADED AND REFUSES TO TAKE IT, SO I'LL GIVE IT TO YOU.
HAVE HIM WEAR IT WHEN IT SUITS YOU.
MY, MY, HOW SPLENDID.
WHA—!?
WELL, I'M GOING TO GO SHOW THESE PHOTOS TO RAL.
EXCUSE US.
EH!? I'M GOING WITH YOU TOO-NYAN?
HYOI (GRAB)
SCREW YOU, ALDIN!
SOME FRIEND YOU ARE...!

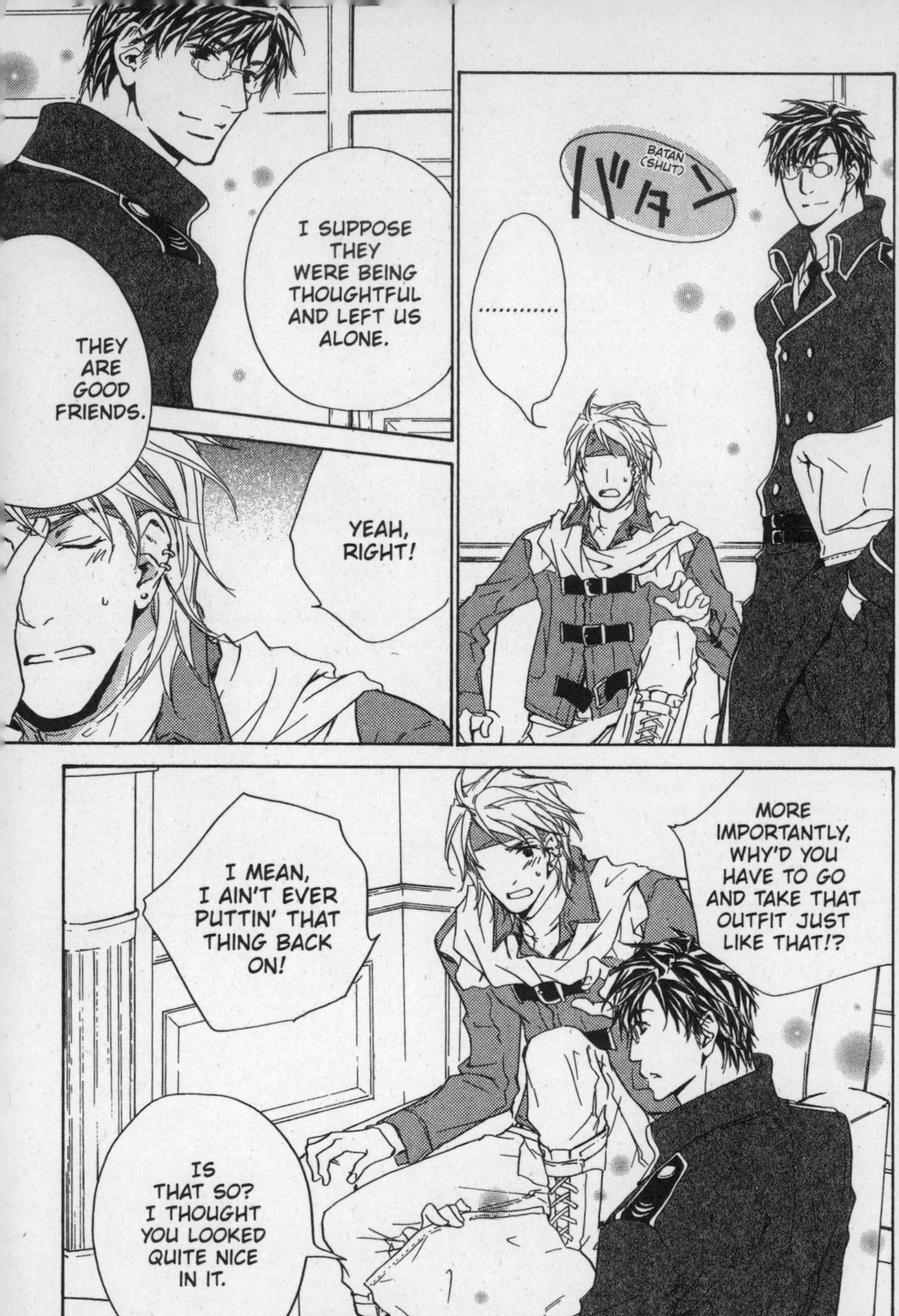
BATAN (SHUT)
....
I SUPPOSE THEY WERE BEING THOUGHTFUL AND LEFT US ALONE.
THEY ARE GOOD FRIENDS.
YEAH, RIGHT!
MORE IMPORTANTLY, WHY'D YOU HAVE TO GO AND TAKE THAT OUTFIT JUST LIKE THAT!?
I MEAN, I AIN'T EVER PUTTIN' THAT THING BACK ON!
IS THAT SO? I THOUGHT YOU LOOKED QUITE NICE IN IT.

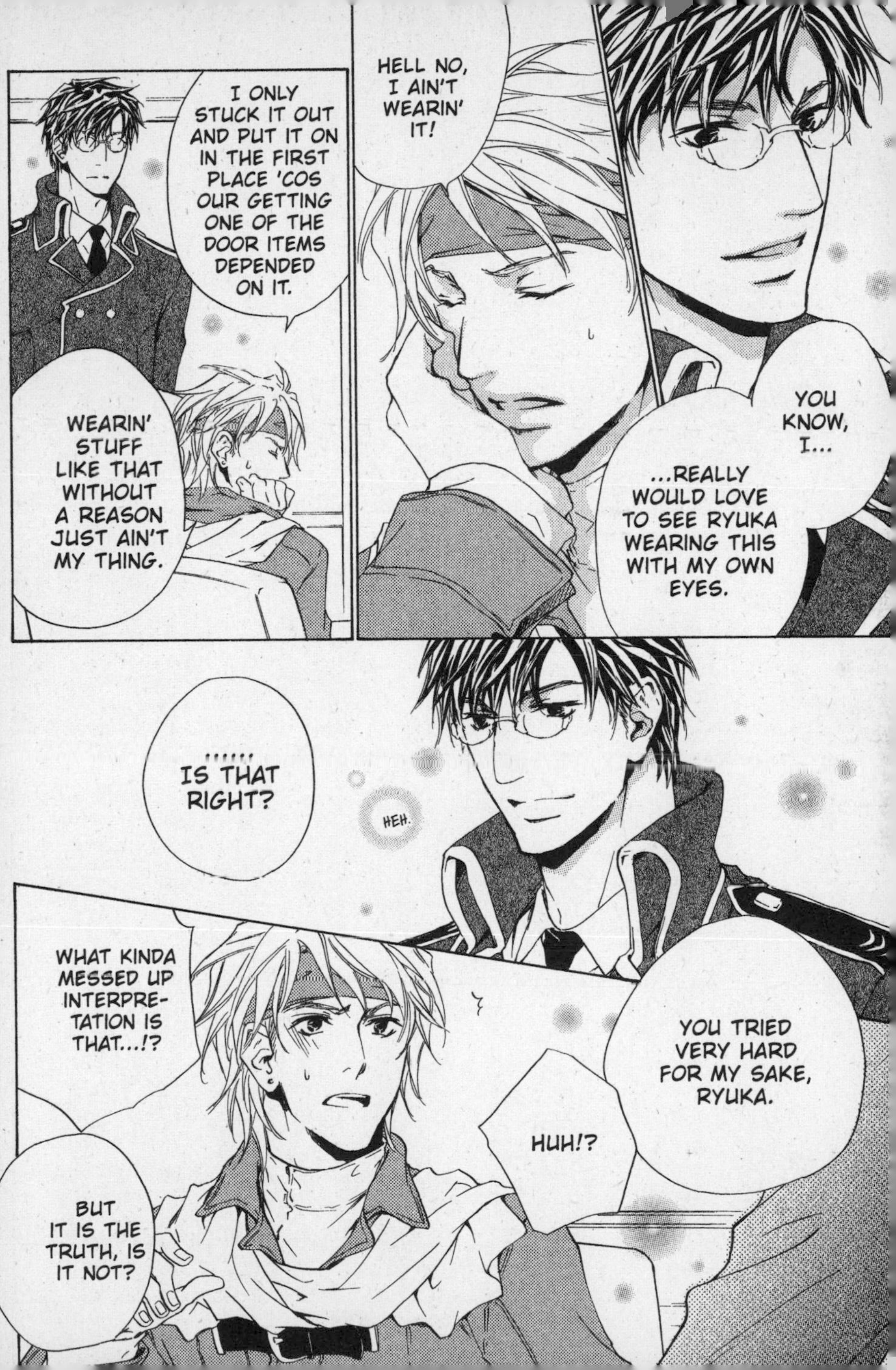
YOU KNOW, I...
...REALLY WOULD LOVE TO SEE RYUKA WEARING THIS WITH MY OWN EYES.
HELL NO, I AIN'T WEARIN' IT!
I ONLY STUCK IT OUT AND PUT IT ON IN THE FIRST PLACE 'COS OUR GETTING ONE OF THE DOOR ITEMS DEPENDED ON IT.
WEARIN' STUFF LIKE THAT WITHOUT A REASON JUST AIN'T MY THING.
......IS THAT RIGHT?
HEH.
YOU TRIED VERY HARD FOR MY SAKE, RYUKA.
HUH!?
WHAT KINDA MESSED UP INTERPRETATION IS THAT...!?
BUT IT IS THE TRUTH, IS IT NOT?

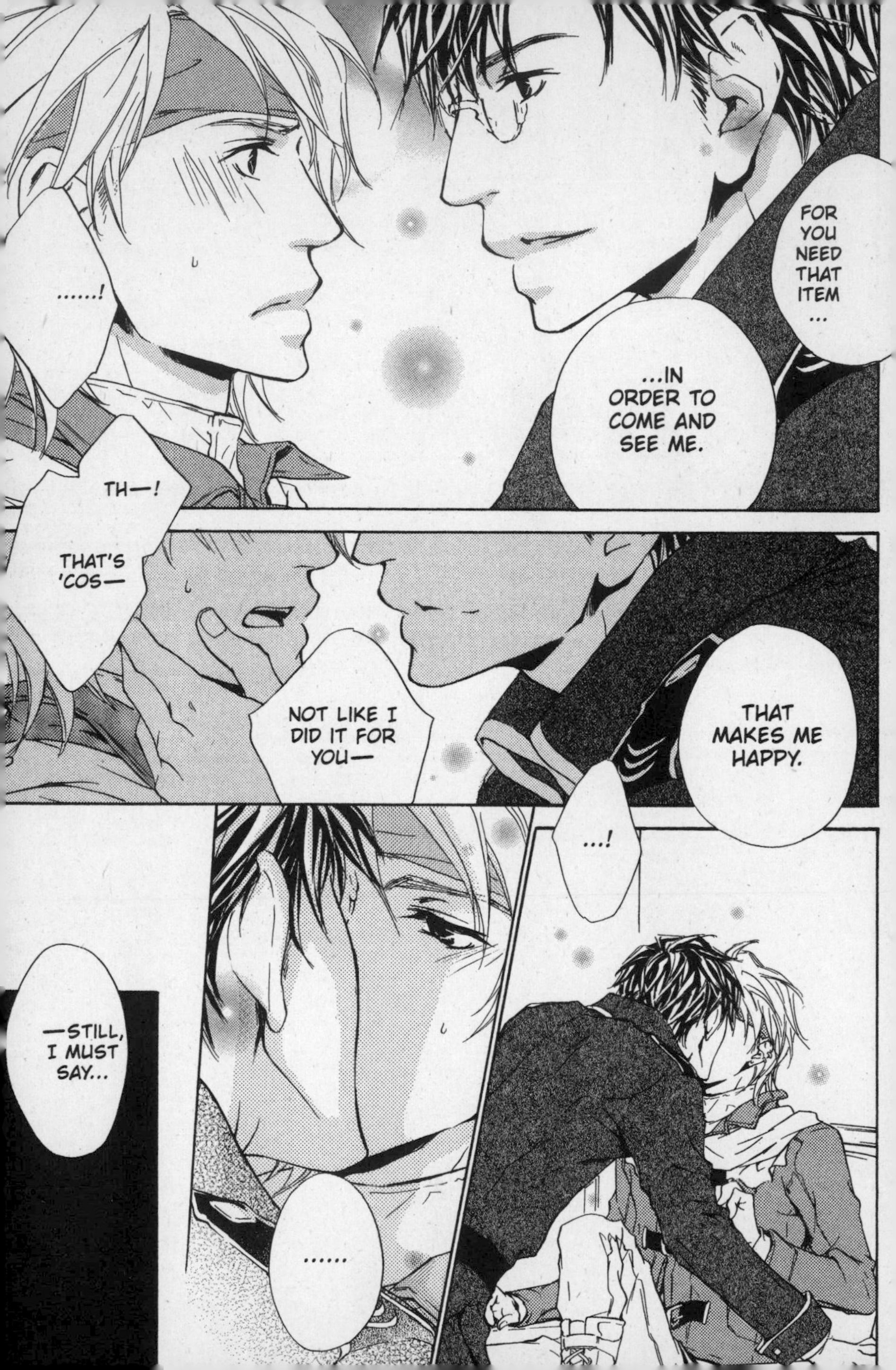
FOR YOU NEED THAT ITEM ...
...IN ORDER TO COME AND SEE ME.
......!
THAT MAKES ME HAPPY.
TH—!
THAT'S 'COS—
NOT LIKE I DID IT FOR YOU—
...!
—STILL, I MUST SAY...
......

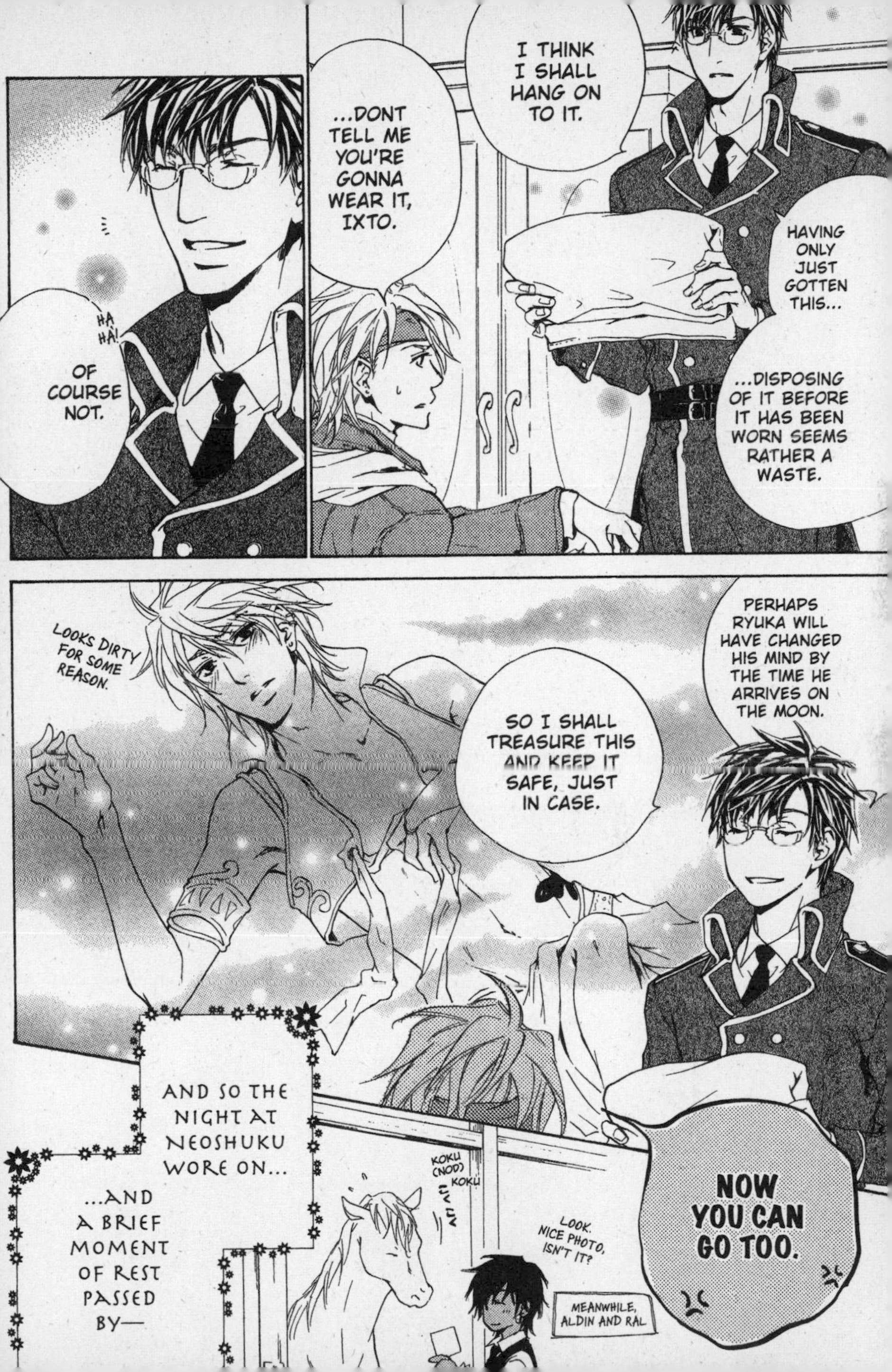
I THINK I SHALL HANG ON TO IT.
HAVING ONLY JUST GOTTEN THIS...
...DISPOSING OF IT BEFORE IT HAS BEEN WORN SEEMS RATHER A WASTE.
...DONT TELL ME YOU'RE GONNA WEAR IT, IXTO.
HA HA!
OF COURSE NOT.
PERHAPS RYUKA WILL HAVE CHANGED HIS MIND BY THE TIME HE ARRIVES ON THE MOON.
SO I SHALL TREASURE THIS AND KEEP IT SAFE, JUST IN CASE.
LOOKS DIRTY FOR SOME REASON.
NOW YOU CAN GO TOO.
LOOK. NICE PHOTO, ISN'T IT?
MEANWHILE, ALDIN AND RAL
KOKU (NOD) KOKU
AND SO THE NIGHT AT NEOSHUKU WORE ON...
...AND A BRIEF MOMENT OF REST PASSED BY—

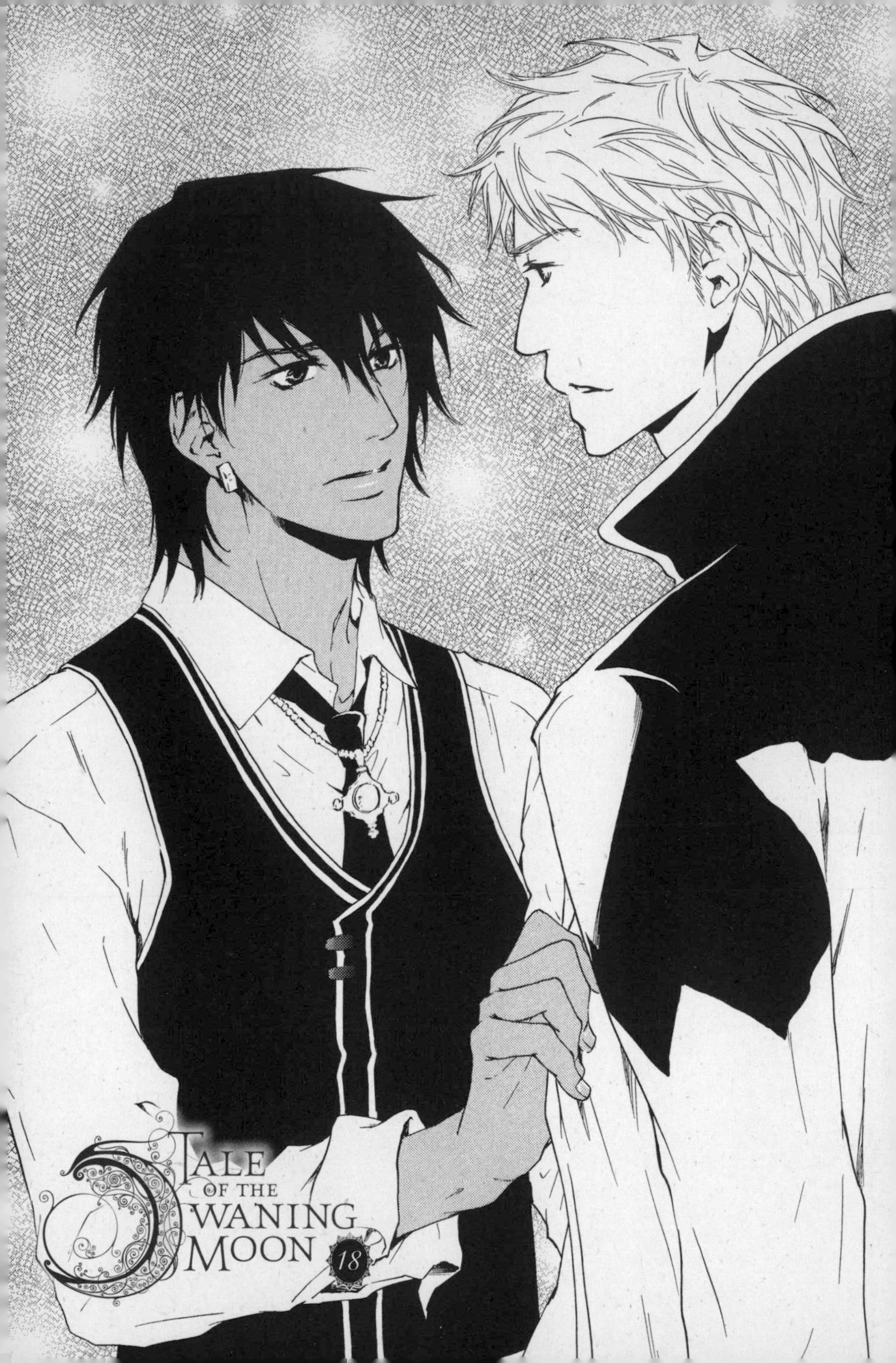
TALE OF THE WANING MOON
18

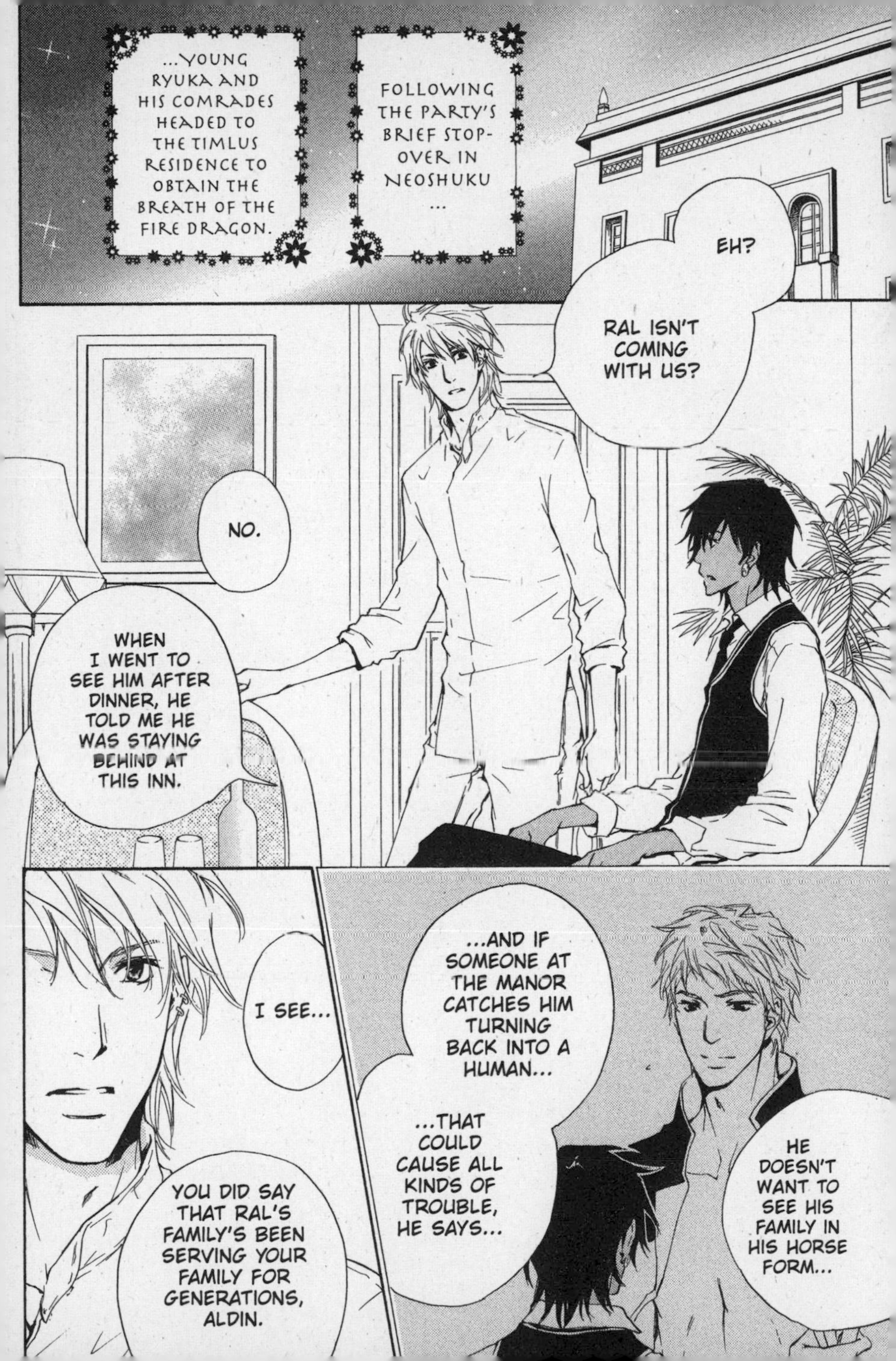
FOLLOWING THE PARTY'S BRIEF STOP-OVER IN NEOSHUKU ...
...YOUNG RYUKA AND HIS COMRADES HEADED TO THE TIMLUS RESIDENCE TO OBTAIN THE BREATH OF THE FIRE DRAGON.
EH?
RAL ISN'T COMING WITH US?
NO.
WHEN I WENT TO SEE HIM AFTER DINNER, HE TOLD ME HE WAS STAYING BEHIND AT THIS INN.
HE DOESN'T WANT TO SEE HIS FAMILY IN HIS HORSE FORM...
...AND IF SOMEONE AT THE MANOR CATCHES HIM TURNING BACK INTO A HUMAN...
...THAT COULD CAUSE ALL KINDS OF TROUBLE, HE SAYS...
I SEE...
YOU DID SAY THAT RAL'S FAMILY'S BEEN SERVING YOUR FAMILY FOR GENERATIONS, ALDIN.

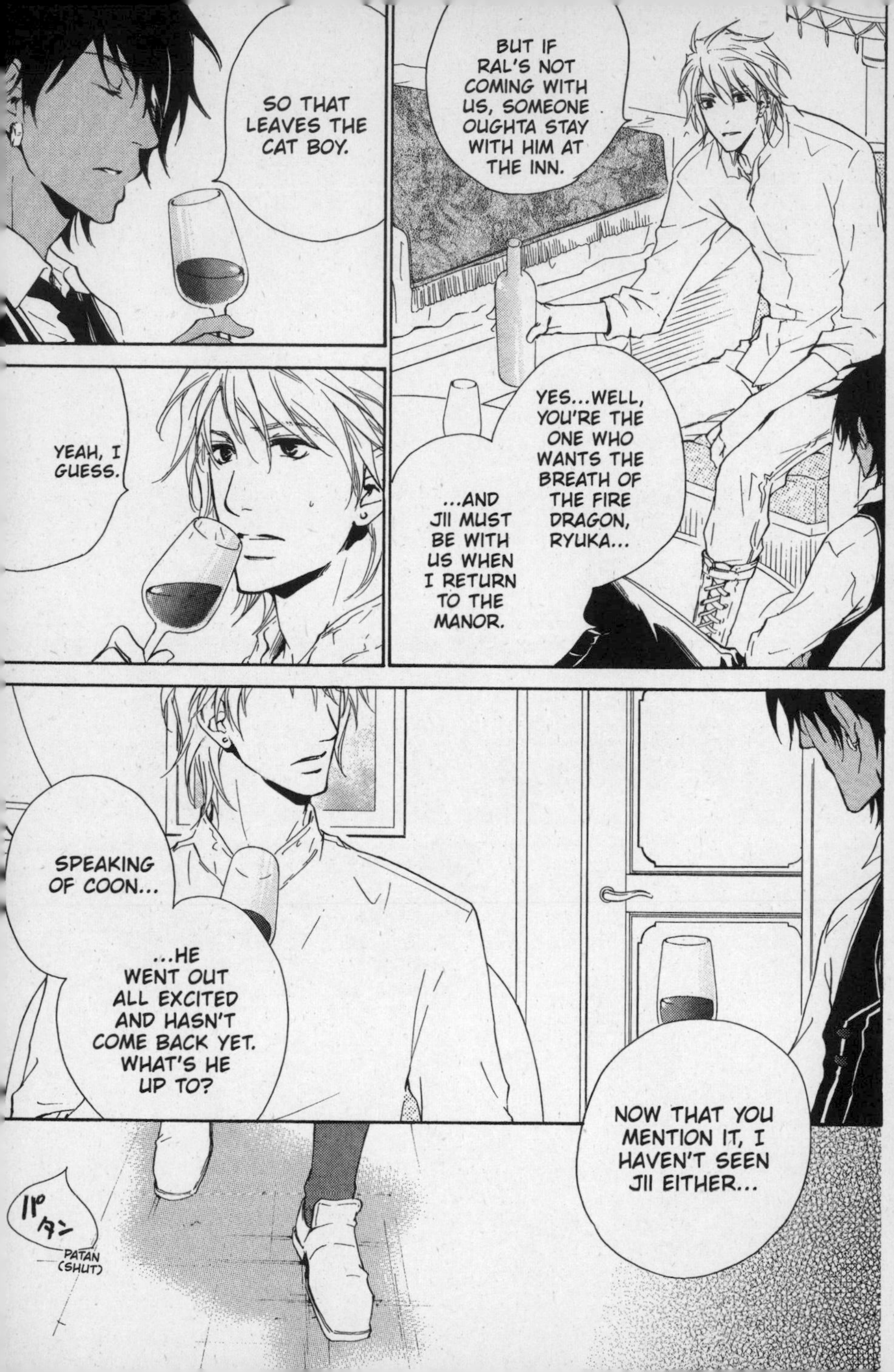
BUT IF RAL'S NOT COMING WITH US, SOMEONE OUGHTA STAY WITH HIM AT THE INN.
YES...WELL, YOU'RE THE ONE WHO WANTS THE BREATH OF THE FIRE DRAGON, RYUKA...
...AND JII MUST BE WITH US WHEN I RETURN TO THE MANOR.
SO THAT LEAVES THE CAT BOY.
YEAH, I GUESS.
SPEAKING OF COON...
...HE WENT OUT ALL EXCITED AND HASN'T COME BACK YET. WHAT'S HE UP TO?
NOW THAT YOU MENTION IT, I HAVEN'T SEEN JII EITHER...
パタン
PATAN (SHUT)

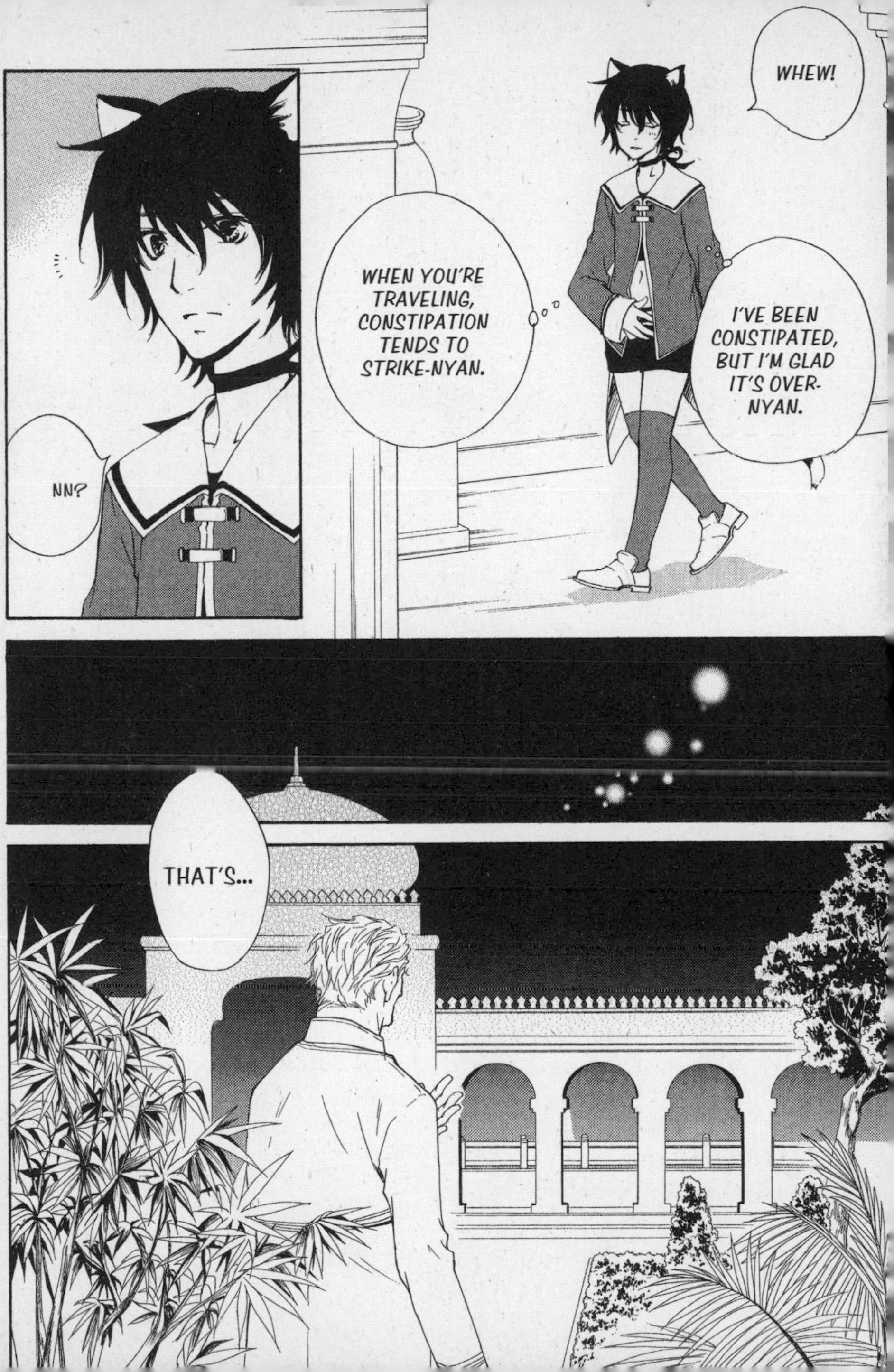
WHEW!
I'VE BEEN CONSTIPATED, BUT I'M GLAD IT'S OVER-NYAN.
WHEN YOU'RE TRAVELING, CONSTIPATION TENDS TO STRIKE-NYAN.
NN?
THAT'S...

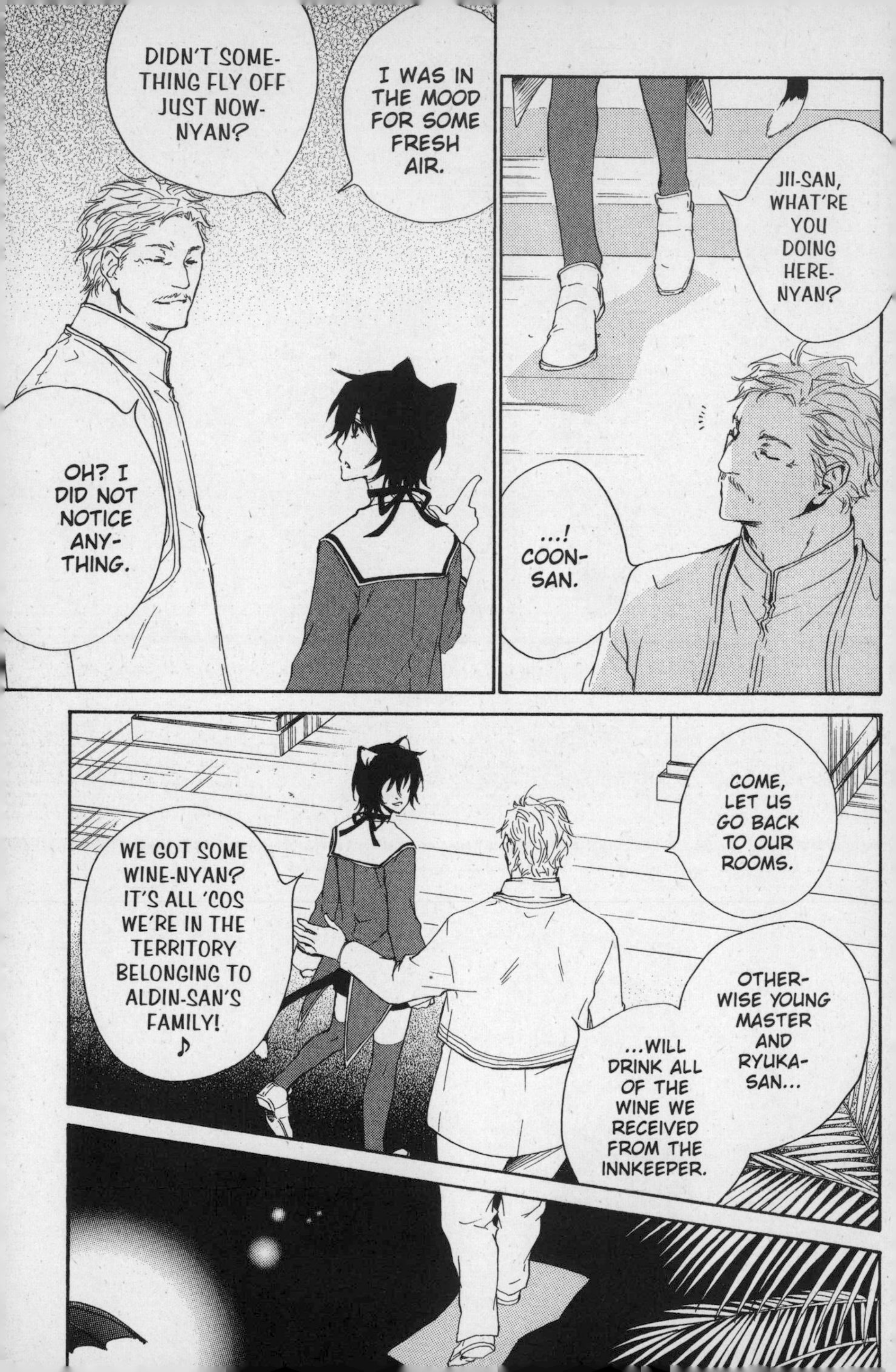
JII-SAN, WHAT'RE YOU DOING HERE-NYAN?
...! COON-SAN.
I WAS IN THE MOOD FOR SOME FRESH AIR.
DIDN'T SOME-THING FLY OFF JUST NOW-NYAN?
OH? I DID NOT NOTICE ANY-THING.
COME, LET US GO BACK TO OUR ROOMS.
OTHER-WISE YOUNG MASTER AND RYUKA-SAN...
...WILL DRINK ALL OF THE WINE WE RECEIVED FROM THE INNKEEPER.
WE GOT SOME WINE-NYAN? IT'S ALL 'COS WE'RE IN THE TERRITORY BELONGING TO ALDIN-SAN'S FAMILY! ♪

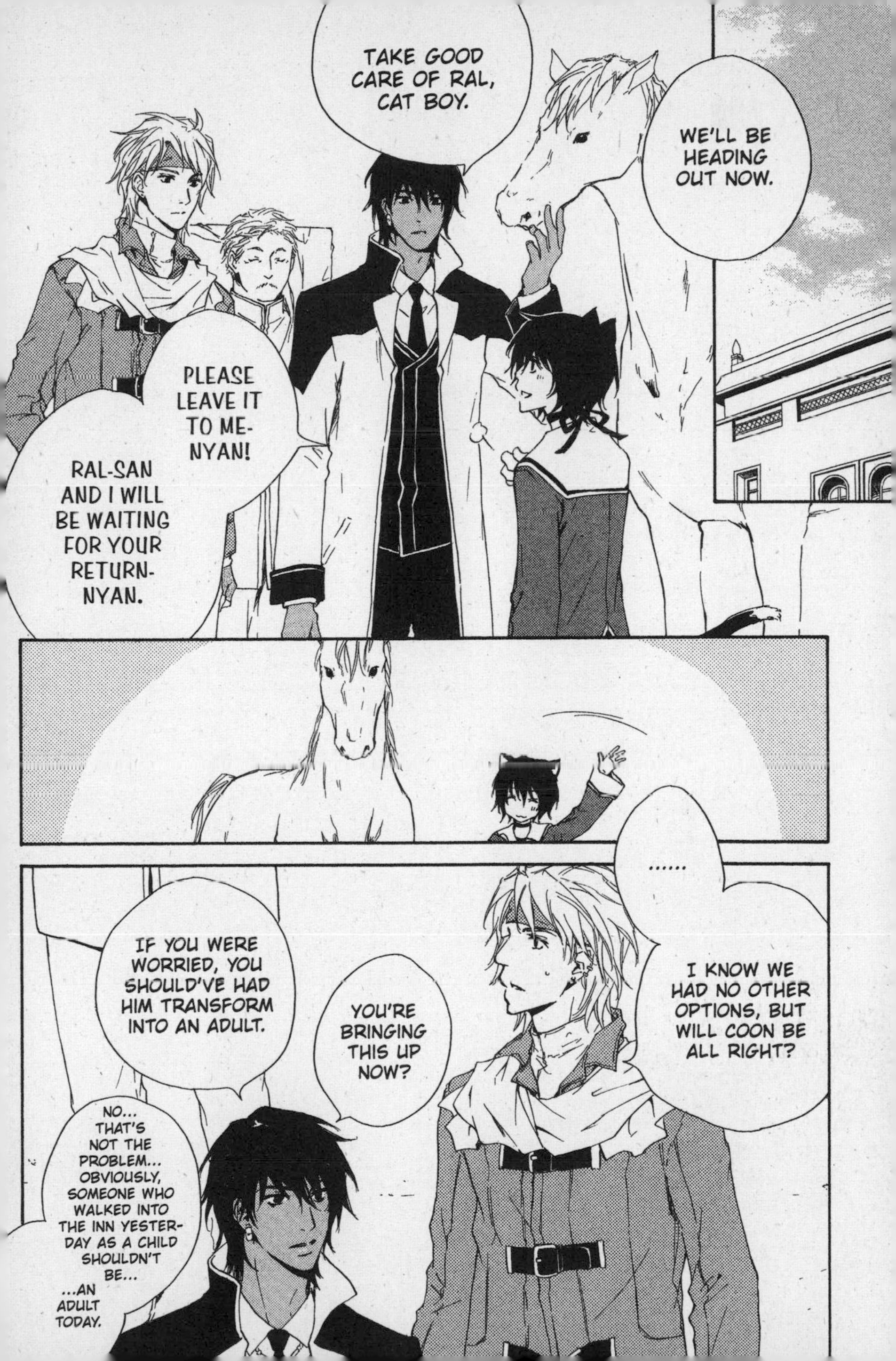
WE'LL BE HEADING OUT NOW.
TAKE GOOD CARE OF RAL, CAT BOY.
PLEASE LEAVE IT TO ME-NYAN!
RAL-SAN AND I WILL BE WAITING FOR YOUR RETURN-NYAN.
......
I KNOW WE HAD NO OTHER OPTIONS, BUT WILL COON BE ALL RIGHT?
IF YOU WERE WORRIED, YOU SHOULD'VE HAD HIM TRANSFORM INTO AN ADULT.
YOU'RE BRINGING THIS UP NOW?
NO... THAT'S NOT THE PROBLEM... OBVIOUSLY, SOMEONE WHO WALKED INTO THE INN YESTERDAY AS A CHILD SHOULDN'T BE... ...AN ADULT TODAY.

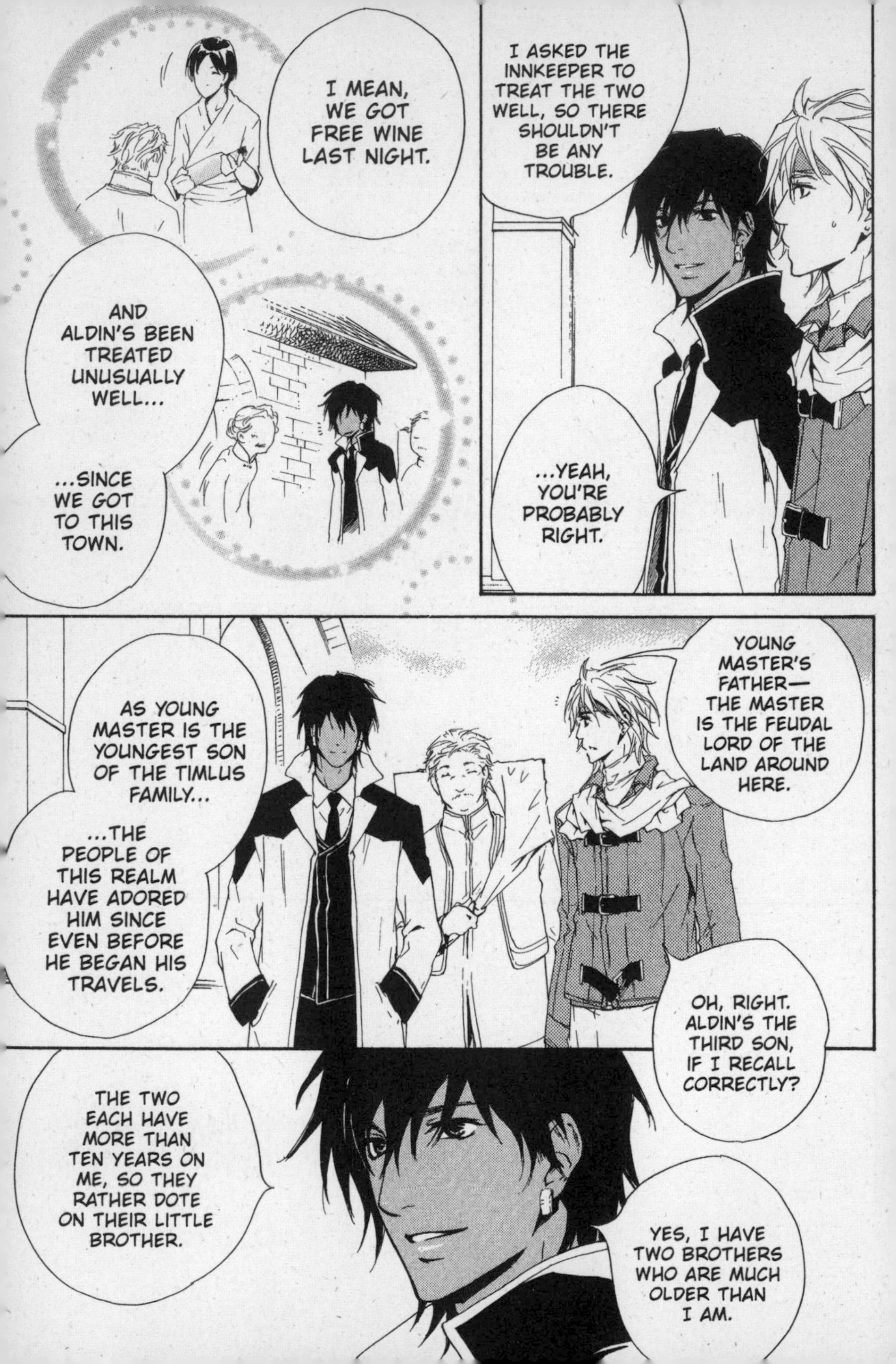
I ASKED THE INNKEEPER TO TREAT THE TWO WELL, SO THERE SHOULDN'T BE ANY TROUBLE.
...YEAH, YOU'RE PROBABLY RIGHT.
I MEAN, WE GOT FREE WINE LAST NIGHT.
AND ALDIN'S BEEN TREATED UNUSUALLY WELL...
...SINCE WE GOT TO THIS TOWN.
YOUNG MASTER'S FATHER—THE MASTER IS THE FEUDAL LORD OF THE LAND AROUND HERE.
AS YOUNG MASTER IS THE YOUNGEST SON OF THE TIMLUS FAMILY...
...THE PEOPLE OF THIS REALM HAVE ADORED HIM SINCE EVEN BEFORE HE BEGAN HIS TRAVELS.
OH, RIGHT. ALDIN'S THE THIRD SON, IF I RECALL CORRECTLY?
YES, I HAVE TWO BROTHERS WHO ARE MUCH OLDER THAN I AM.
THE TWO EACH HAVE MORE THAN TEN YEARS ON ME, SO THEY RATHER DOTE ON THEIR LITTLE BROTHER.

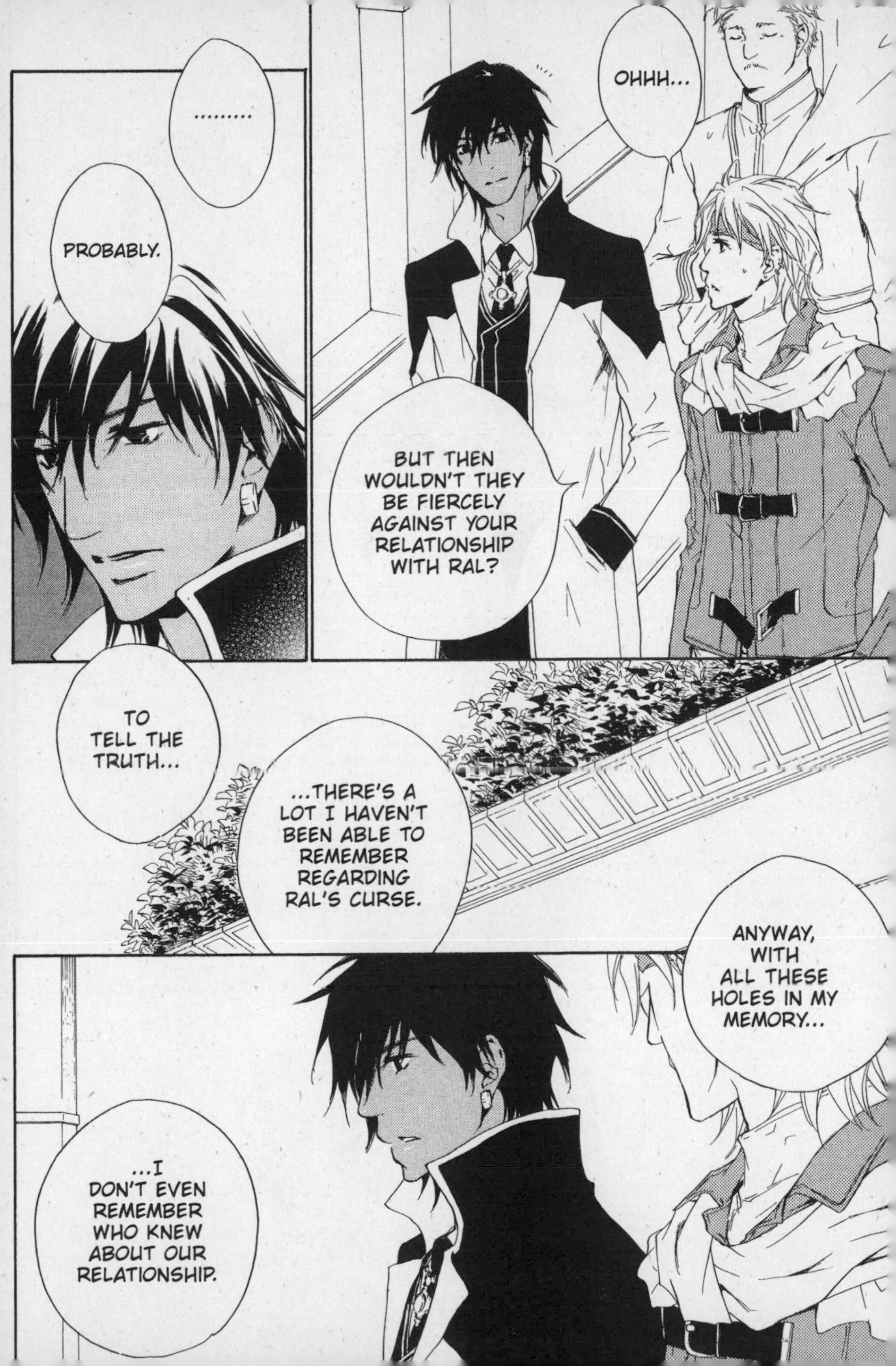
OHHH...
BUT THEN WOULDN'T THEY BE FIERCELY AGAINST YOUR RELATIONSHIP WITH RAL?
....
PROBABLY.
TO TELL THE TRUTH...
...THERE'S A LOT I HAVEN'T BEEN ABLE TO REMEMBER REGARDING RAL'S CURSE.
ANYWAY, WITH ALL THESE HOLES IN MY MEMORY...
...I DON'T EVEN REMEMBER WHO KNEW ABOUT OUR RELATIONSHIP.

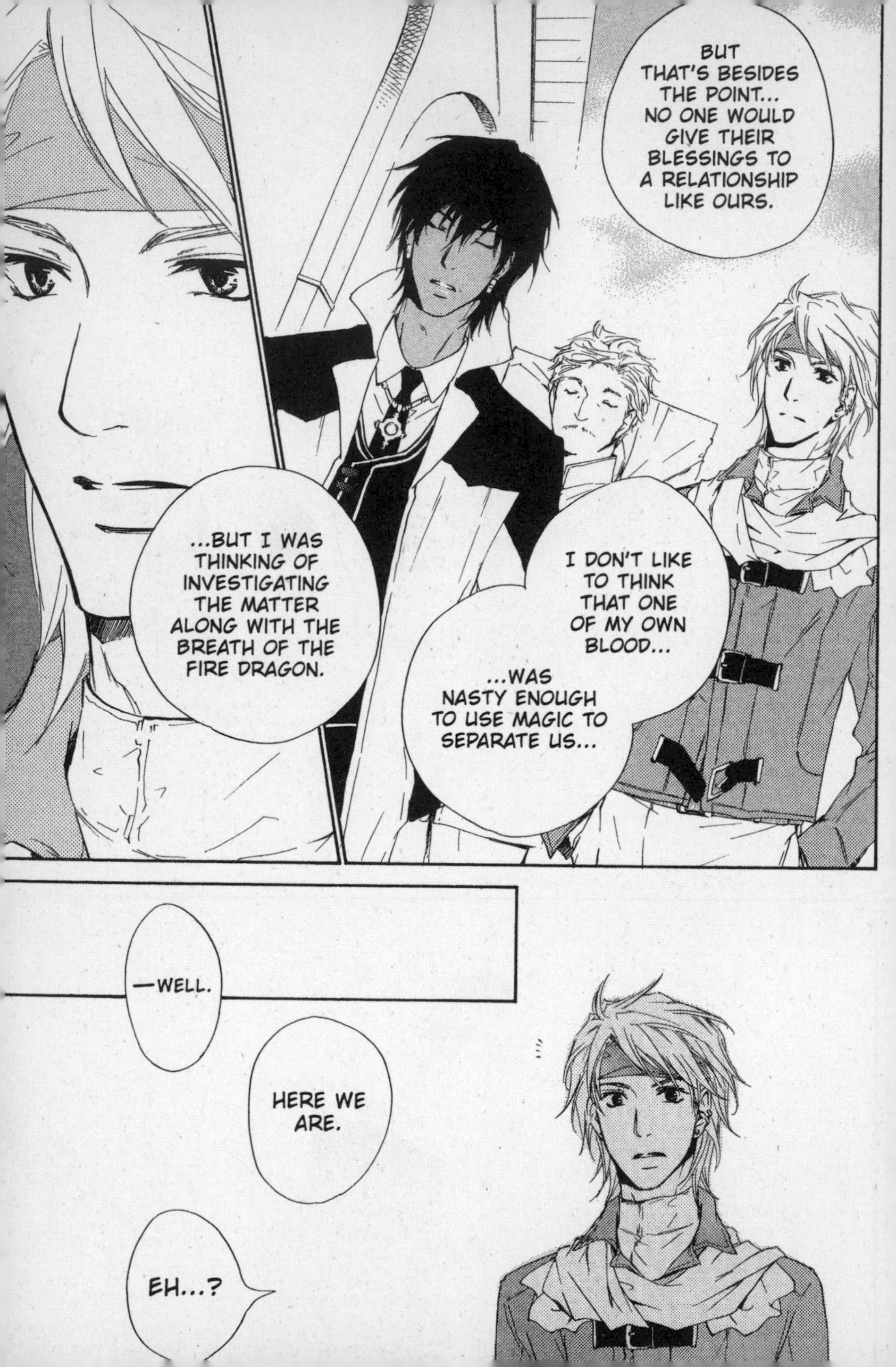
BUT THAT'S BESIDES THE POINT... NO ONE WOULD GIVE THEIR BLESSINGS TO A RELATIONSHIP LIKE OURS.
I DON'T LIKE TO THINK THAT ONE OF MY OWN BLOOD...
...WAS NASTY ENOUGH TO USE MAGIC TO SEPARATE US...
...BUT I WAS THINKING OF INVESTIGATING THE MATTER ALONG WITH THE BREATH OF THE FIRE DRAGON.
—WELL.
HERE WE ARE.
EH...?

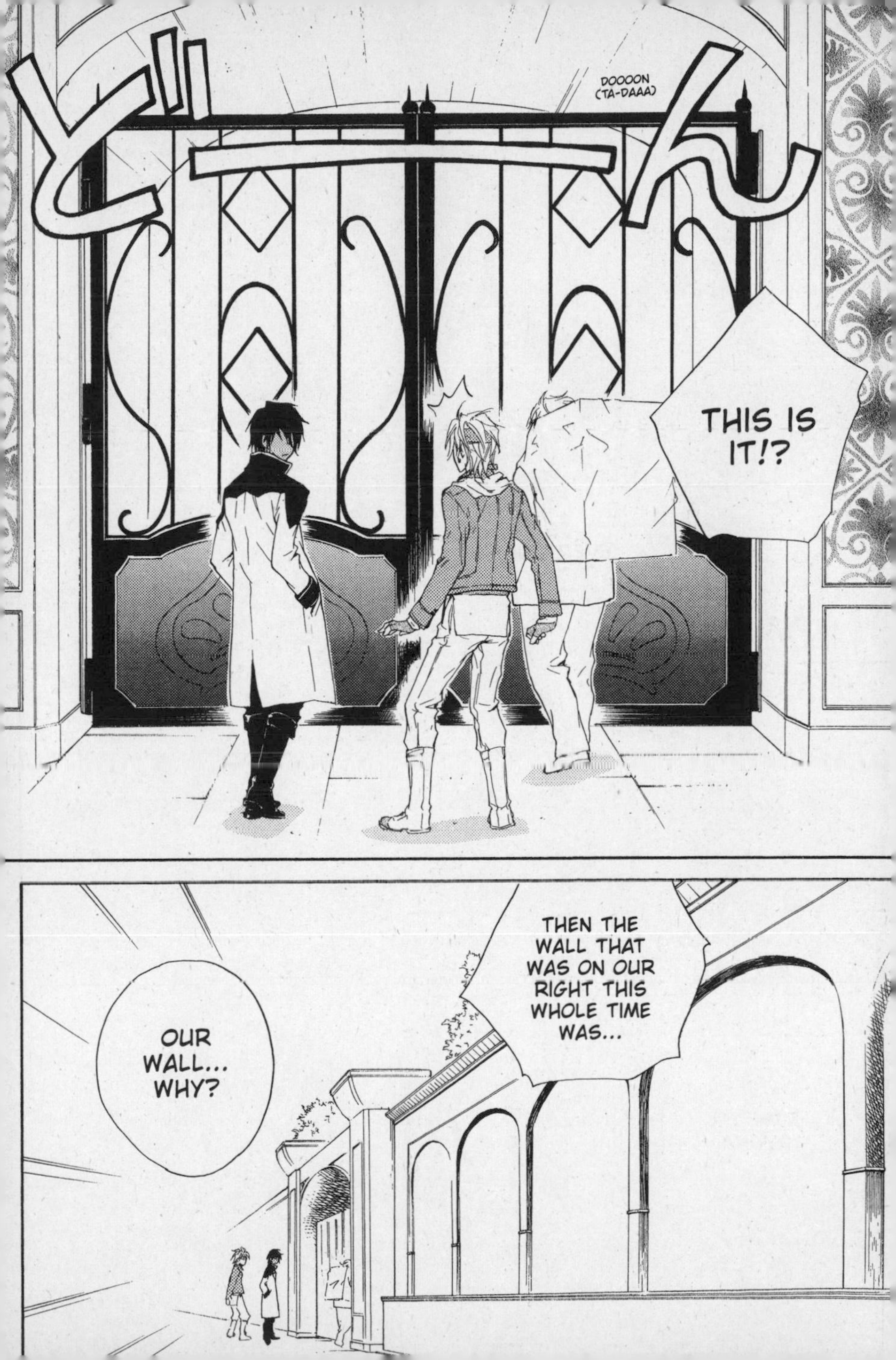

どーん
DOOOON (TA-DAAA)
THIS IS IT!?
THEN THE WALL THAT WAS ON OUR RIGHT THIS WHOLE TIME WAS...
OUR WALL... WHY?

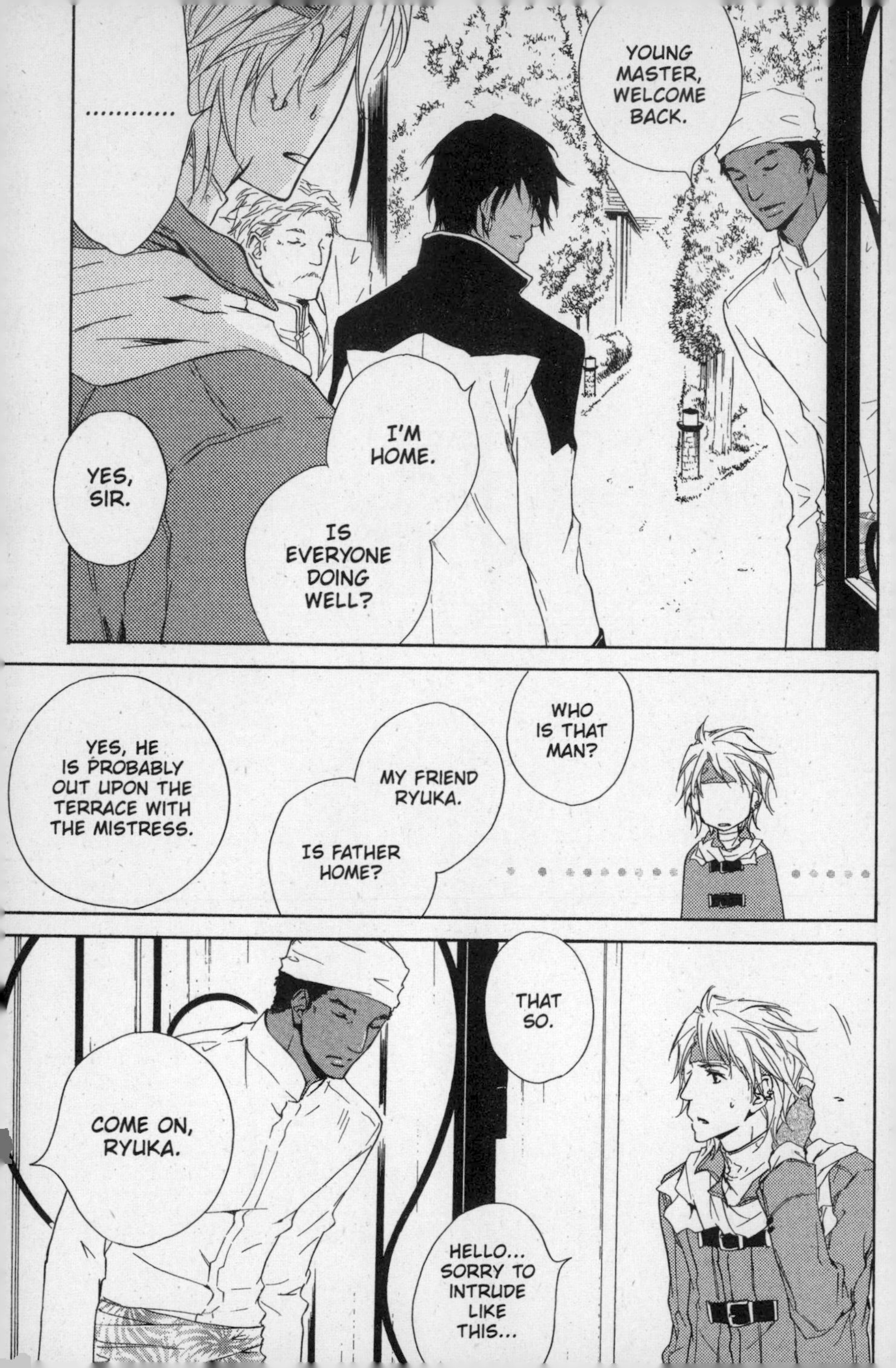
YOUNG MASTER, WELCOME BACK.
I'M HOME.
IS EVERYONE DOING WELL?
....
YES, SIR.
WHO IS THAT MAN?
MY FRIEND RYUKA.
IS FATHER HOME?
YES, HE IS PROBABLY OUT UPON THE TERRACE WITH THE MISTRESS.
THAT SO.
HELLO... SORRY TO INTRUDE LIKE THIS...
COME ON, RYUKA.

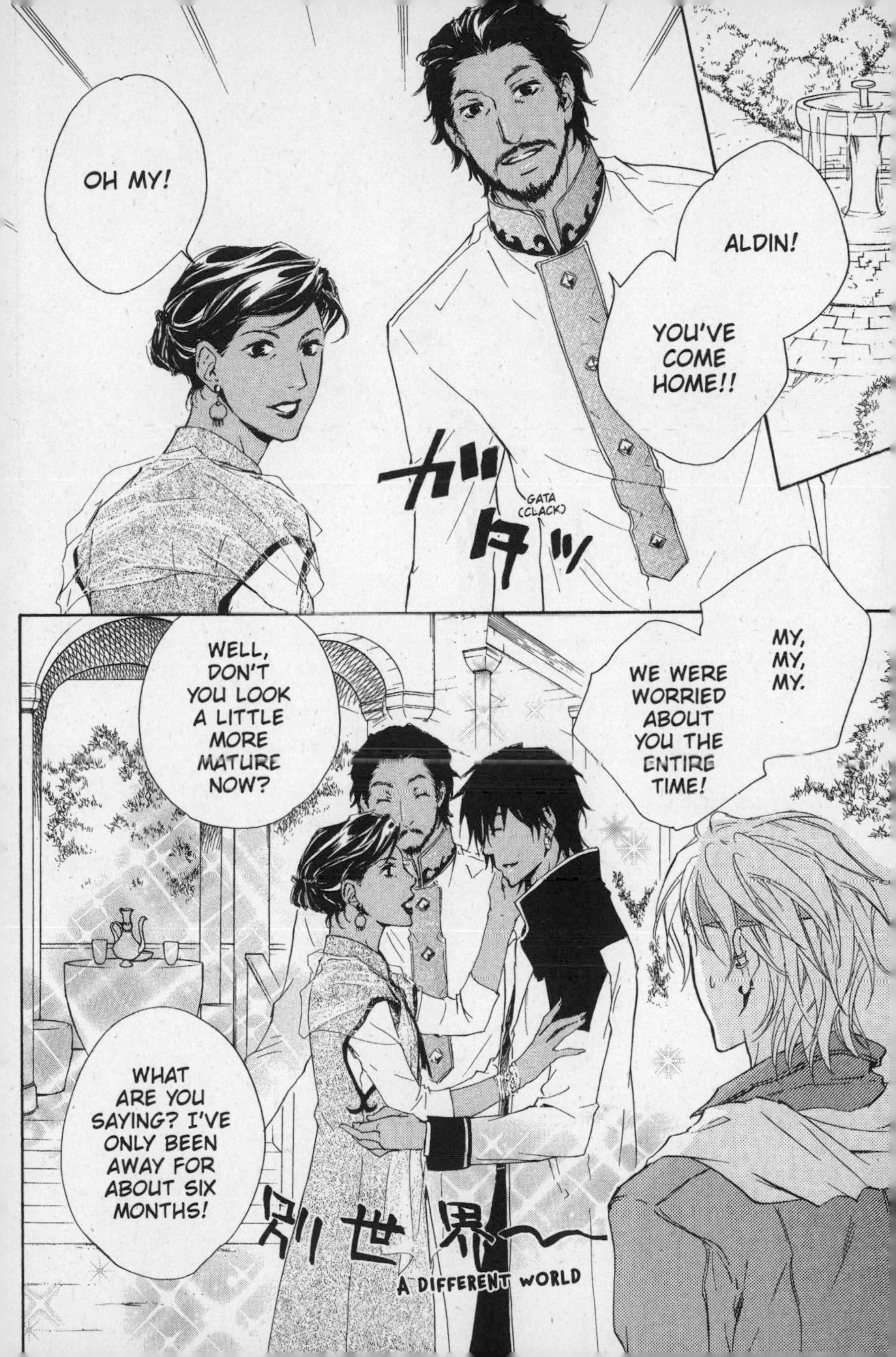
ALDIN!
YOU'VE COME HOME!!
ガタッ
GATA (CLACK)
OH MY!
MY, MY, MY.
WE WERE WORRIED ABOUT YOU THE ENTIRE TIME!
WELL, DON'T YOU LOOK A LITTLE MORE MATURE NOW?
WHAT ARE YOU SAYING? I'VE ONLY BEEN AWAY FOR ABOUT SIX MONTHS!
別世界
A DIFFERENT WORLD

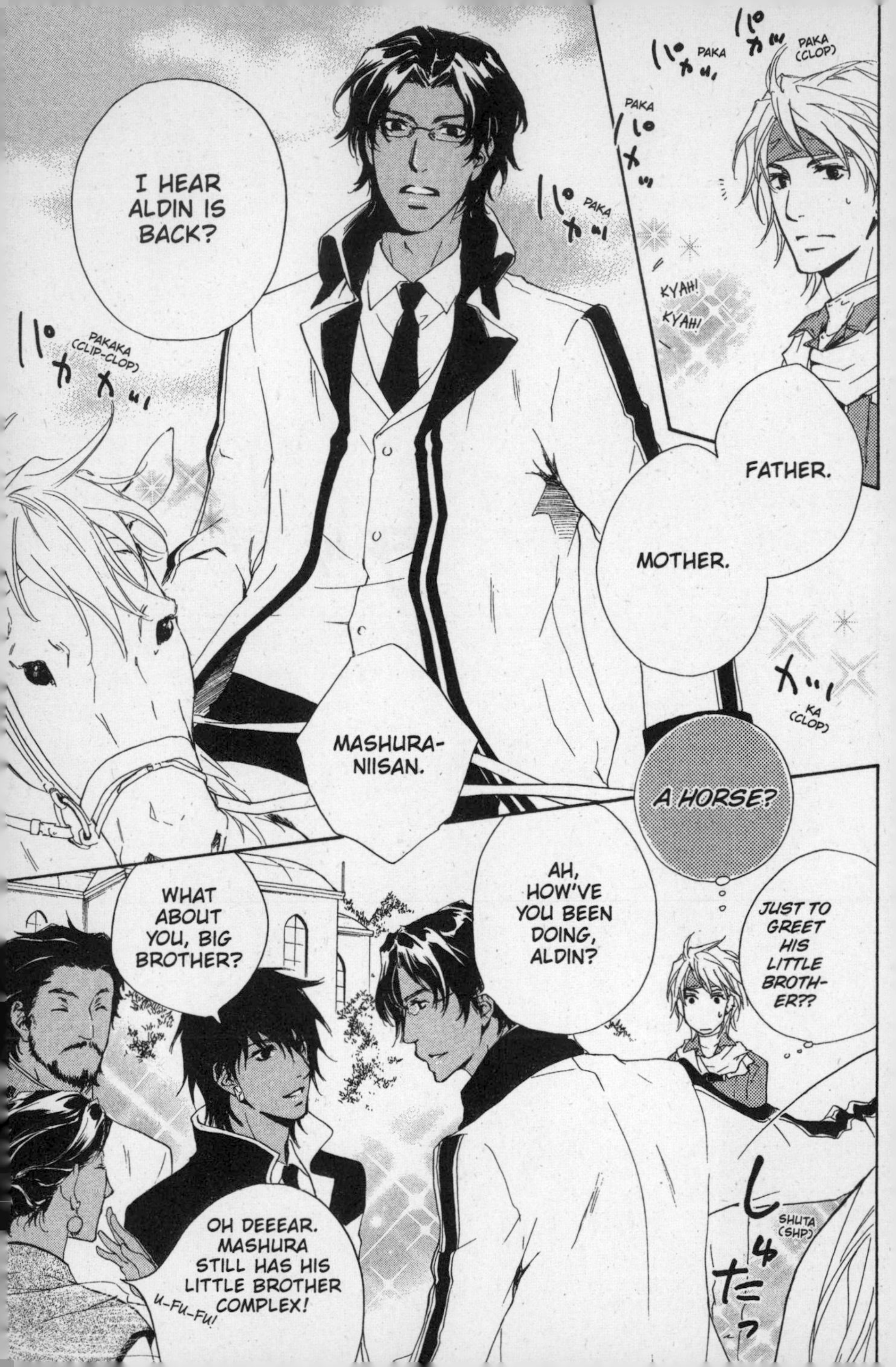
PAKA
PAKA (CLOP)
PAKA
KYAH!
KYAH!
FATHER.
MOTHER.
I HEAR ALDIN IS BACK?
PAKA
PAKAKA (CLIP-CLOP)
KA (CLOP)
MASHURA-NIISAN.
A HORSE?
JUST TO GREET HIS LITTLE BROTHER??
AH, HOW'VE YOU BEEN DOING, ALDIN?
WHAT ABOUT YOU, BIG BROTHER?
SHUTA (SHP)
OH DEEEAR. MASHURA STILL HAS HIS LITTLE BROTHER COMPLEX!
U-FU-FU!

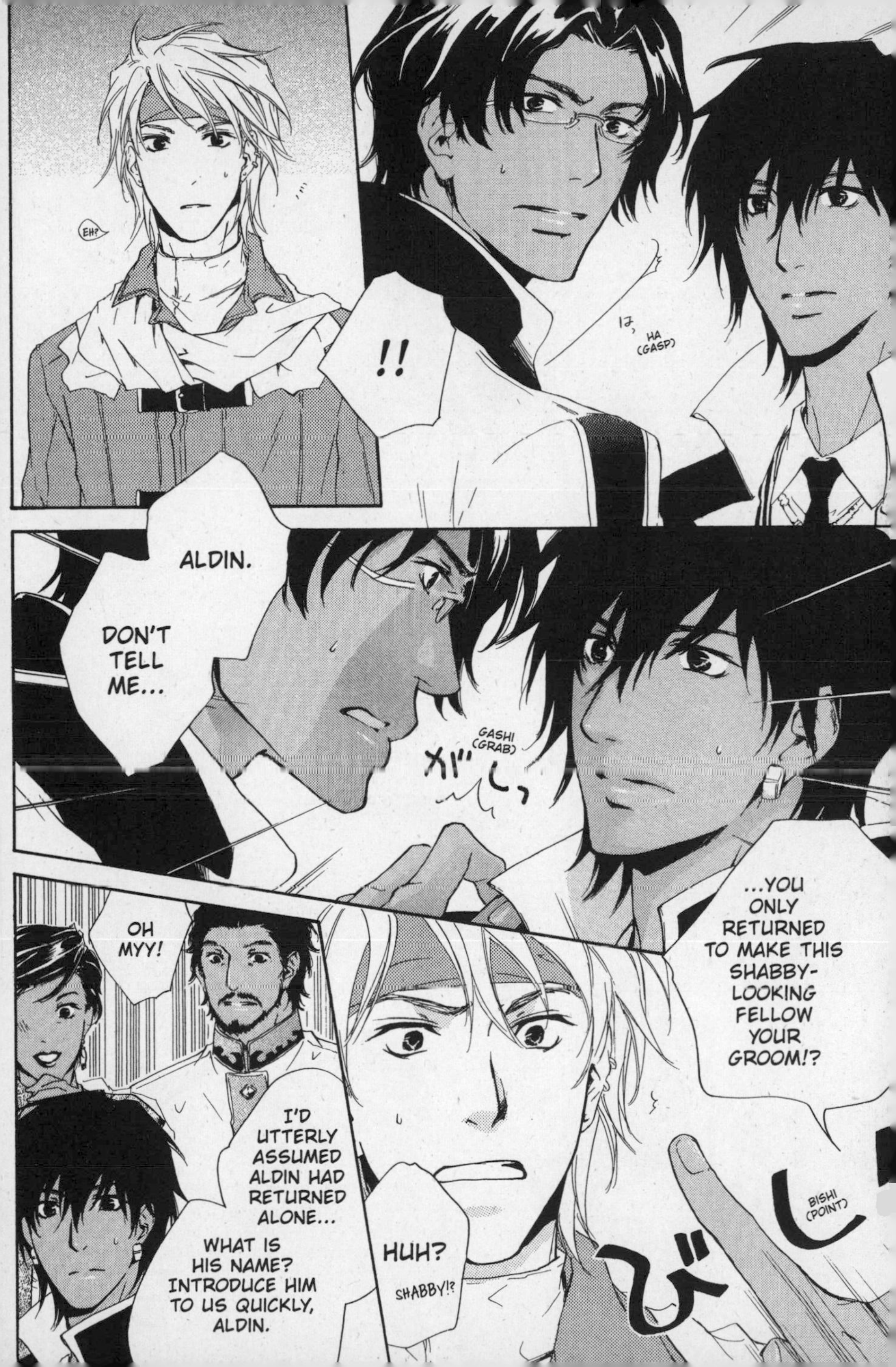
!!
HA (GASP)
EH?
ALDIN.
DON'T TELL ME...
GASHI (GRAB)
...YOU ONLY RETURNED TO MAKE THIS SHABBY-LOOKING FELLOW YOUR GROOM!?
BISHI (POINT)
HUH?
SHABBY!?
OH MYY!
I'D UTTERLY ASSUMED ALDIN HAD RETURNED ALONE...
WHAT IS HIS NAME? INTRODUCE HIM TO US QUICKLY, ALDIN.

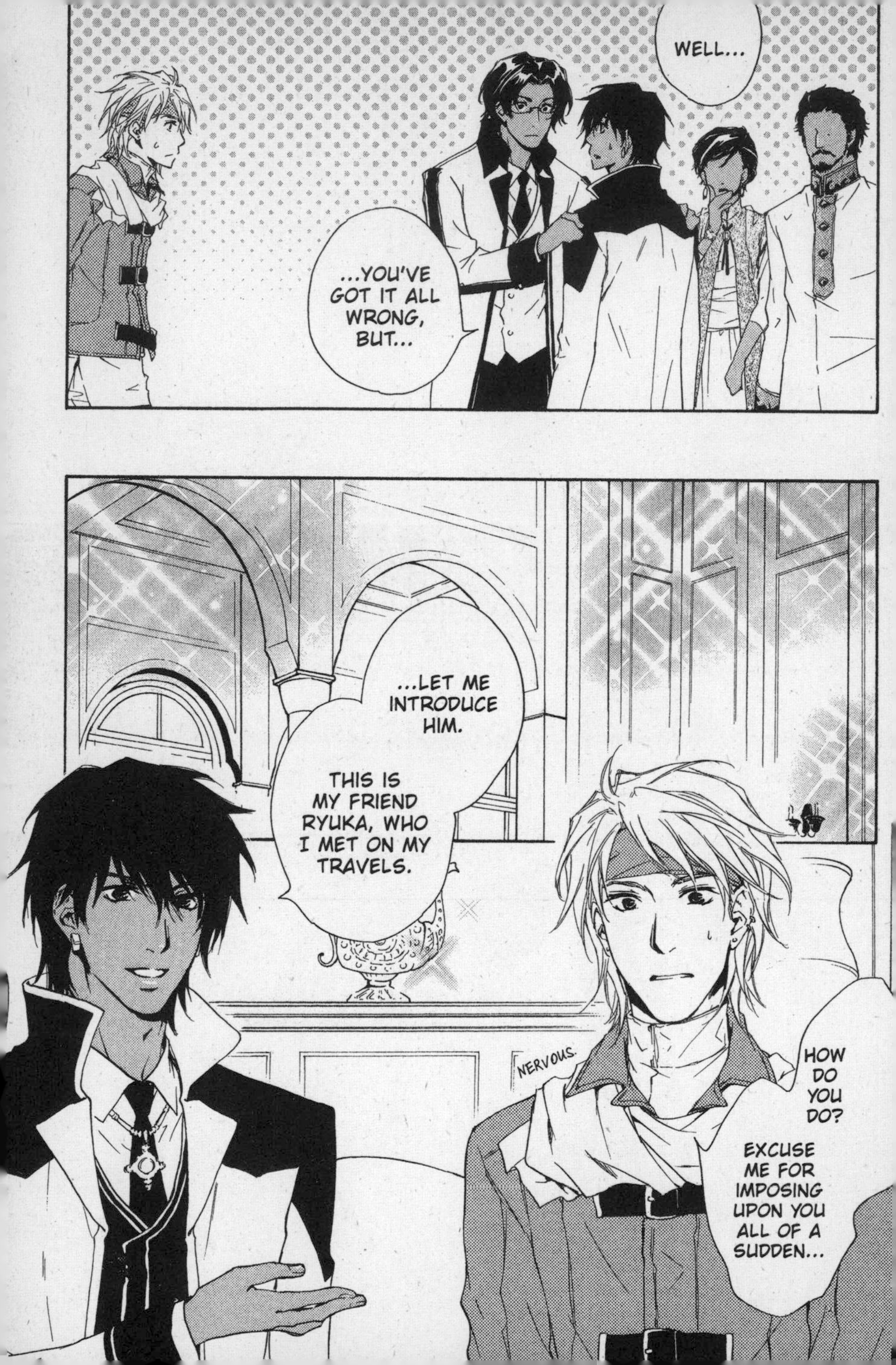
WELL...
...YOU'VE GOT IT ALL WRONG, BUT...
...LET ME INTRODUCE HIM.
THIS IS MY FRIEND RYUKA, WHO I MET ON MY TRAVELS.
HOW DO YOU DO?
EXCUSE ME FOR IMPOSING UPON YOU ALL OF A SUDDEN...
NERVOUS.

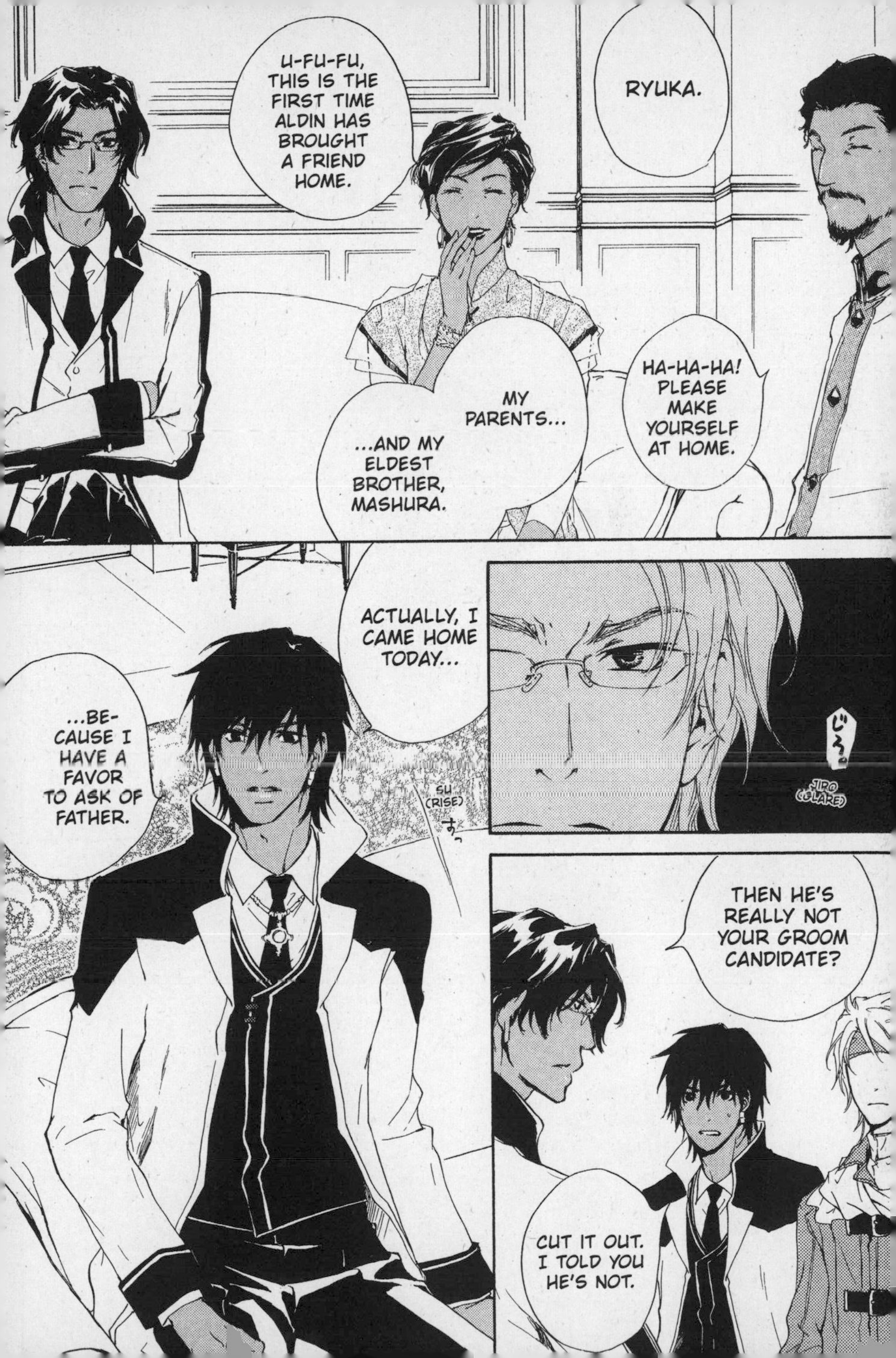
RYUKA.
U-FU-FU, THIS IS THE FIRST TIME ALDIN HAS BROUGHT A FRIEND HOME.
HA-HA-HA! PLEASE MAKE YOURSELF AT HOME.
MY PARENTS...
...AND MY ELDEST BROTHER, MASHURA.
JIRO (GLARE)
THEN HE'S REALLY NOT YOUR GROOM CANDIDATE?
CUT IT OUT. I TOLD YOU HE'S NOT.
ACTUALLY, I CAME HOME TODAY...
...BE-CAUSE I HAVE A FAVOR TO ASK OF FATHER.
SU (RISE)

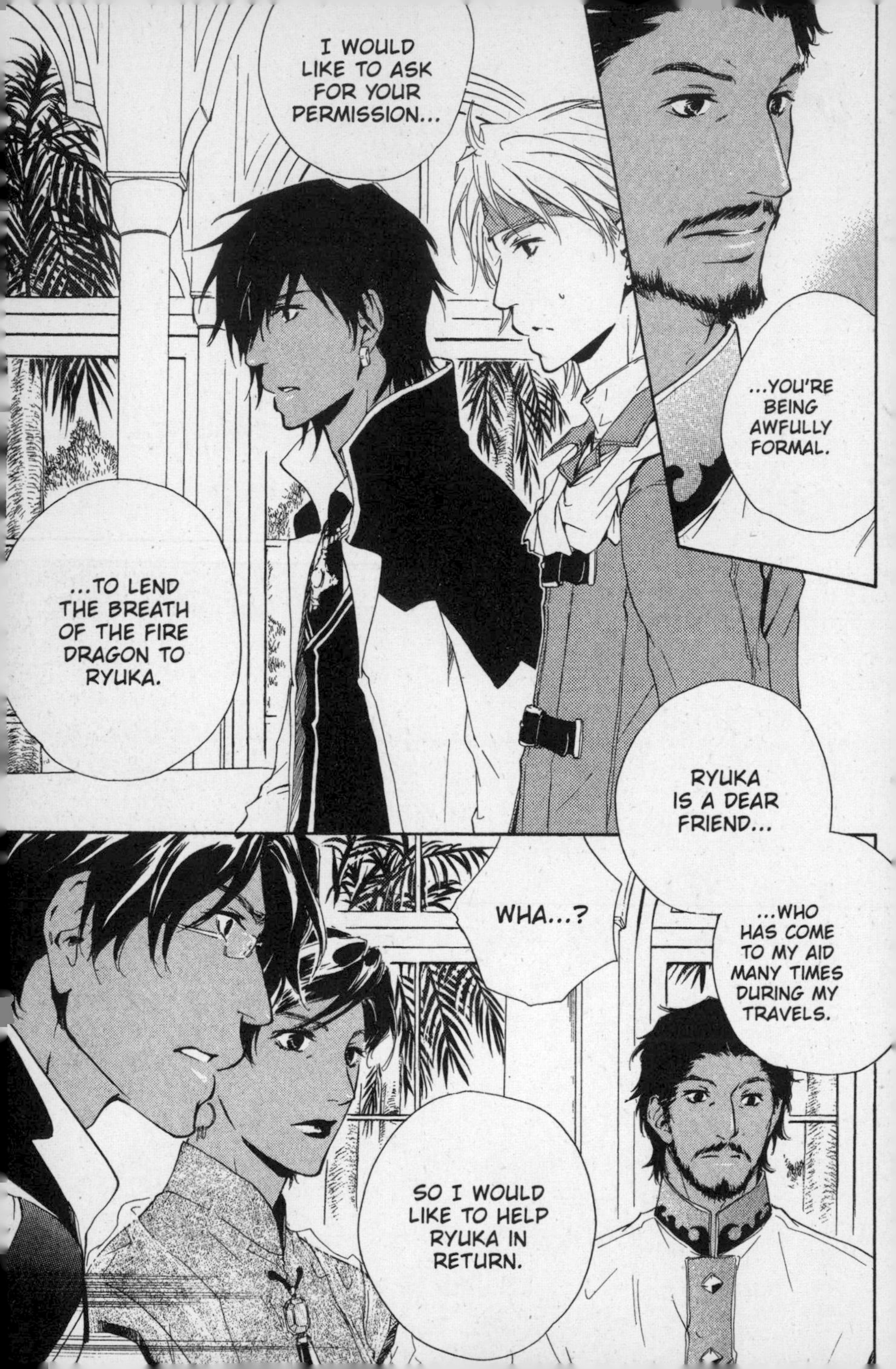
I WOULD LIKE TO ASK FOR YOUR PERMISSION...
...TO LEND THE BREATH OF THE FIRE DRAGON TO RYUKA.
...YOU'RE BEING AWFULLY FORMAL.
RYUKA IS A DEAR FRIEND...
...WHO HAS COME TO MY AID MANY TIMES DURING MY TRAVELS.
WHA...?
SO I WOULD LIKE TO HELP RYUKA IN RETURN.

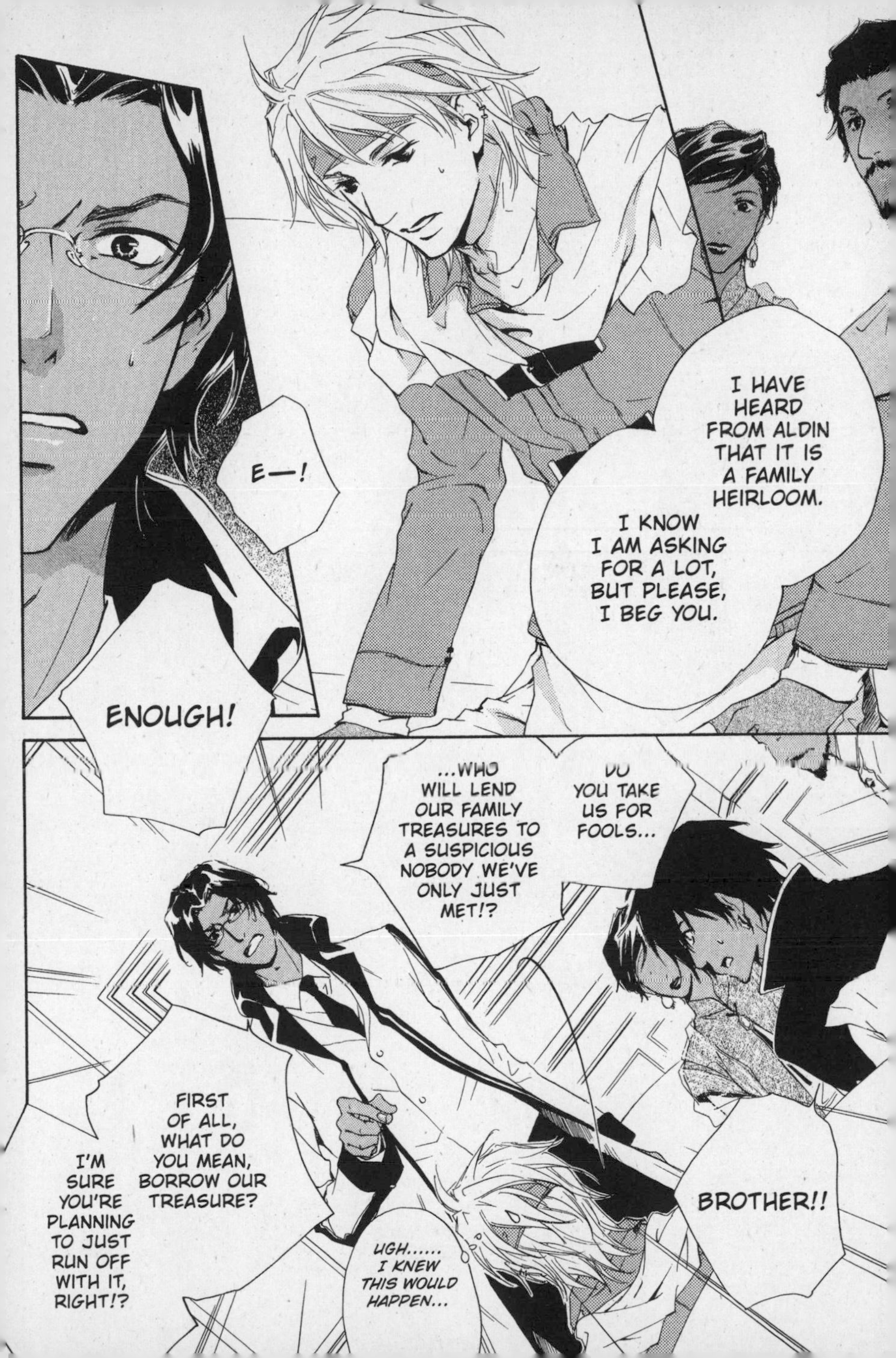

I HAVE HEARD FROM ALDIN THAT IT IS A FAMILY HEIRLOOM.
I KNOW I AM ASKING FOR A LOT, BUT PLEASE, I BEG YOU.
E—!
ENOUGH!
DO YOU TAKE US FOR FOOLS...
...WHO WILL LEND OUR FAMILY TREASURES TO A SUSPICIOUS NOBODY WE'VE ONLY JUST MET!?
FIRST OF ALL, WHAT DO YOU MEAN, BORROW OUR TREASURE?
I'M SURE YOU'RE PLANNING TO JUST RUN OFF WITH IT, RIGHT!?
BROTHER!!
UGH...... I KNEW THIS WOULD HAPPEN...

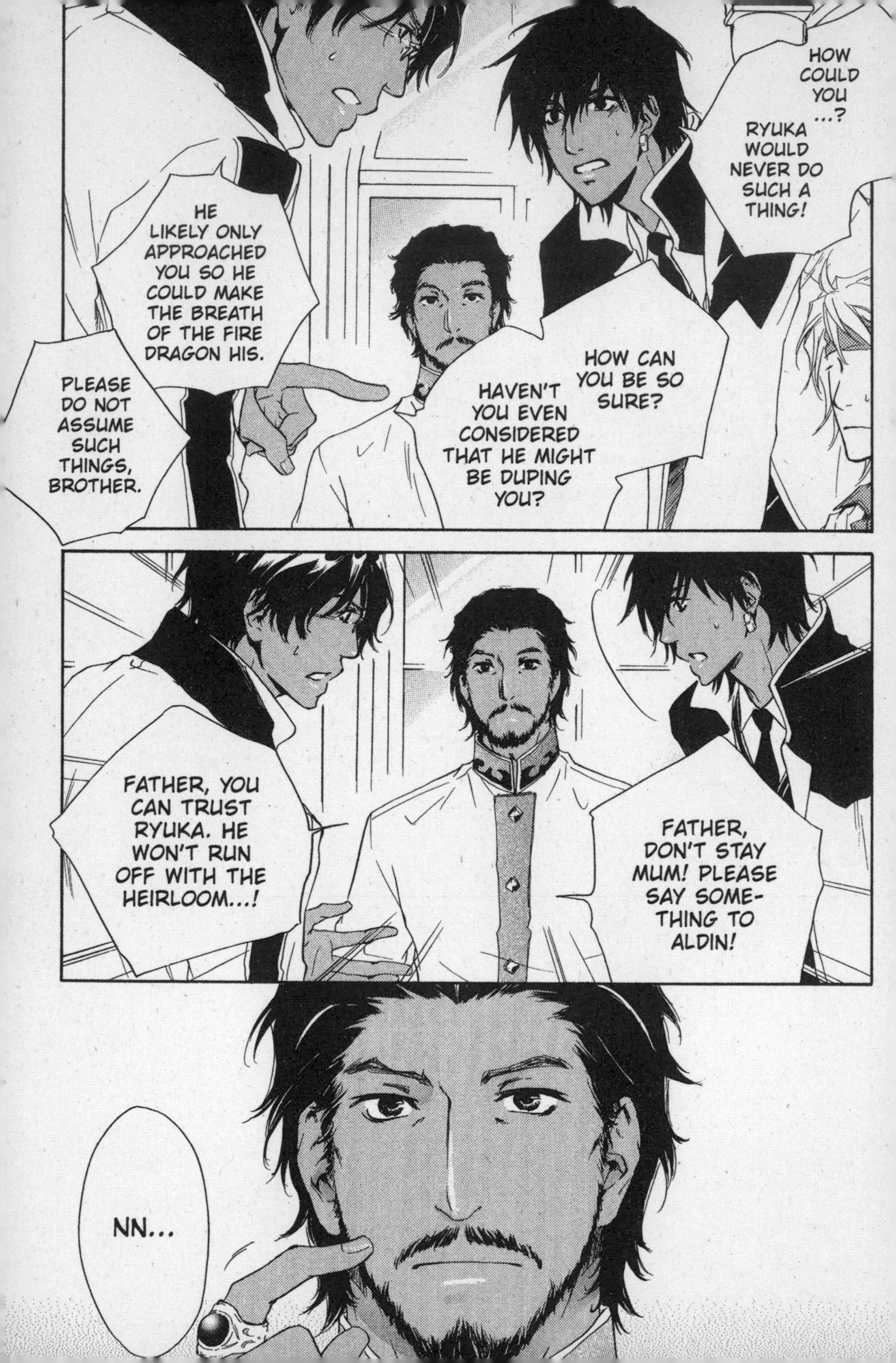
HOW COULD YOU ...?
RYUKA WOULD NEVER DO SUCH A THING!
HOW CAN YOU BE SO SURE?
HAVEN'T YOU EVEN CONSIDERED THAT HE MIGHT BE DUPING YOU?
HE LIKELY ONLY APPROACHED YOU SO HE COULD MAKE THE BREATH OF THE FIRE DRAGON HIS.
PLEASE DO NOT ASSUME SUCH THINGS, BROTHER.
FATHER, DON'T STAY MUM! PLEASE SAY SOME-THING TO ALDIN!
FATHER, YOU CAN TRUST RYUKA. HE WON'T RUN OFF WITH THE HEIRLOOM...!
NN...

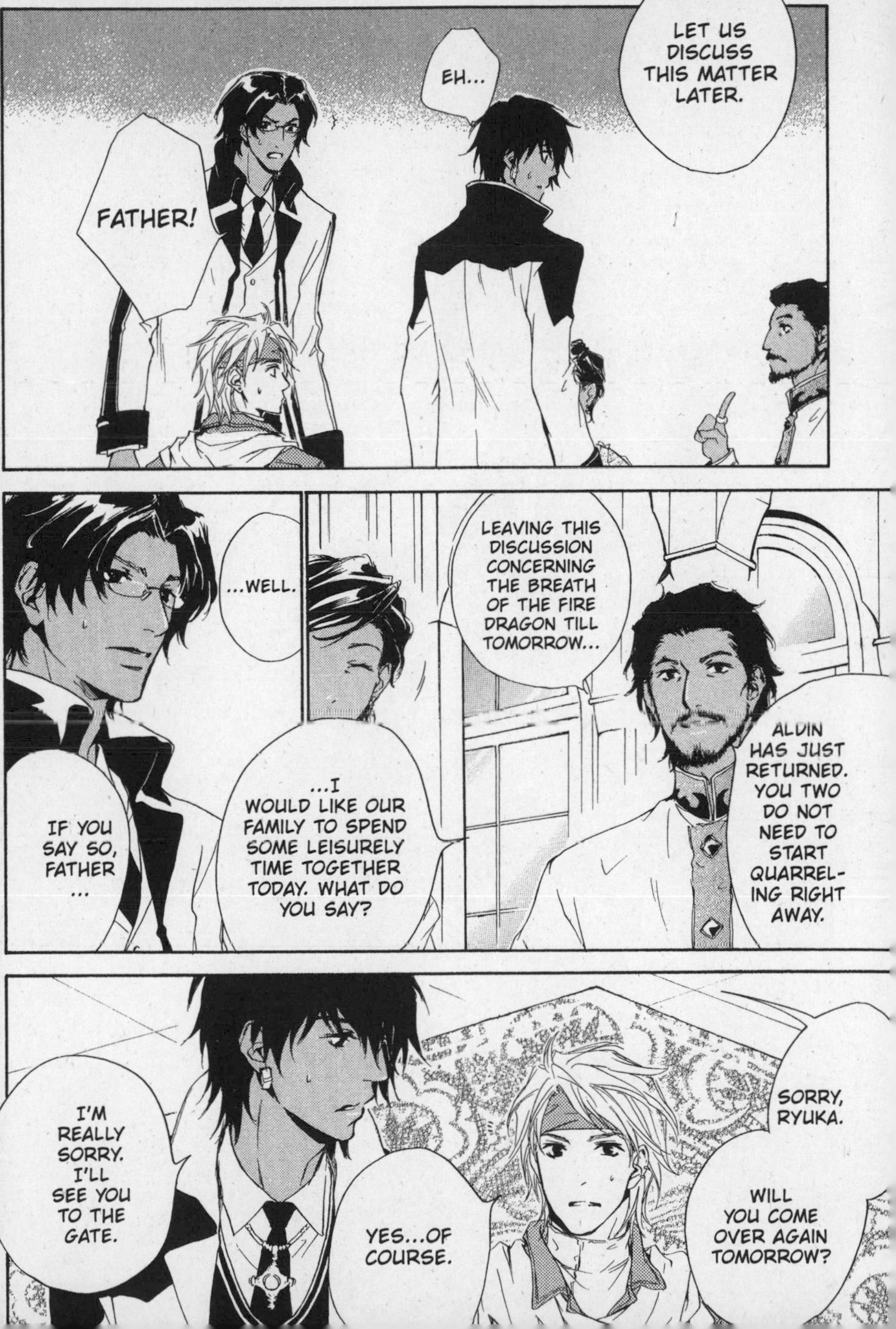
LET US DISCUSS THIS MATTER LATER.
EH...
FATHER!
LEAVING THIS DISCUSSION CONCERNING THE BREATH OF THE FIRE DRAGON TILL TOMORROW...
ALDIN HAS JUST RETURNED. YOU TWO DO NOT NEED TO START QUARREL-ING RIGHT AWAY.
...I WOULD LIKE OUR FAMILY TO SPEND SOME LEISURELY TIME TOGETHER TODAY. WHAT DO YOU SAY?
...WELL.
IF YOU SAY SO, FATHER ...
SORRY, RYUKA.
WILL YOU COME OVER AGAIN TOMORROW?
YES...OF COURSE.
I'M REALLY SORRY. I'LL SEE YOU TO THE GATE.

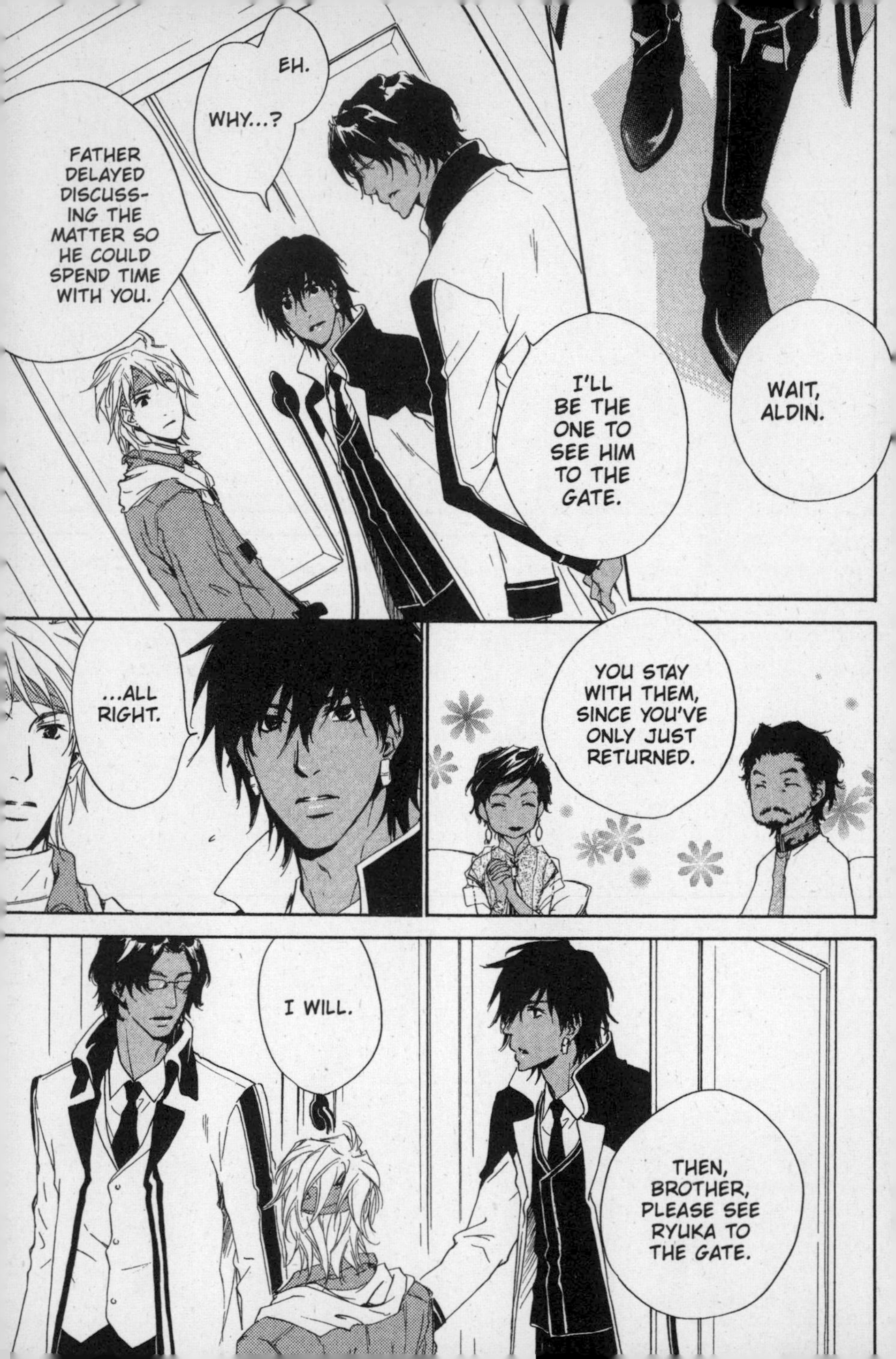
WAIT, ALDIN.
I'LL BE THE ONE TO SEE HIM TO THE GATE.
EH.
WHY...?
FATHER DELAYED DISCUSS-ING THE MATTER SO HE COULD SPEND TIME WITH YOU.
YOU STAY WITH THEM, SINCE YOU'VE ONLY JUST RETURNED.
...ALL RIGHT.
THEN, BROTHER, PLEASE SEE RYUKA TO THE GATE.
I WILL.

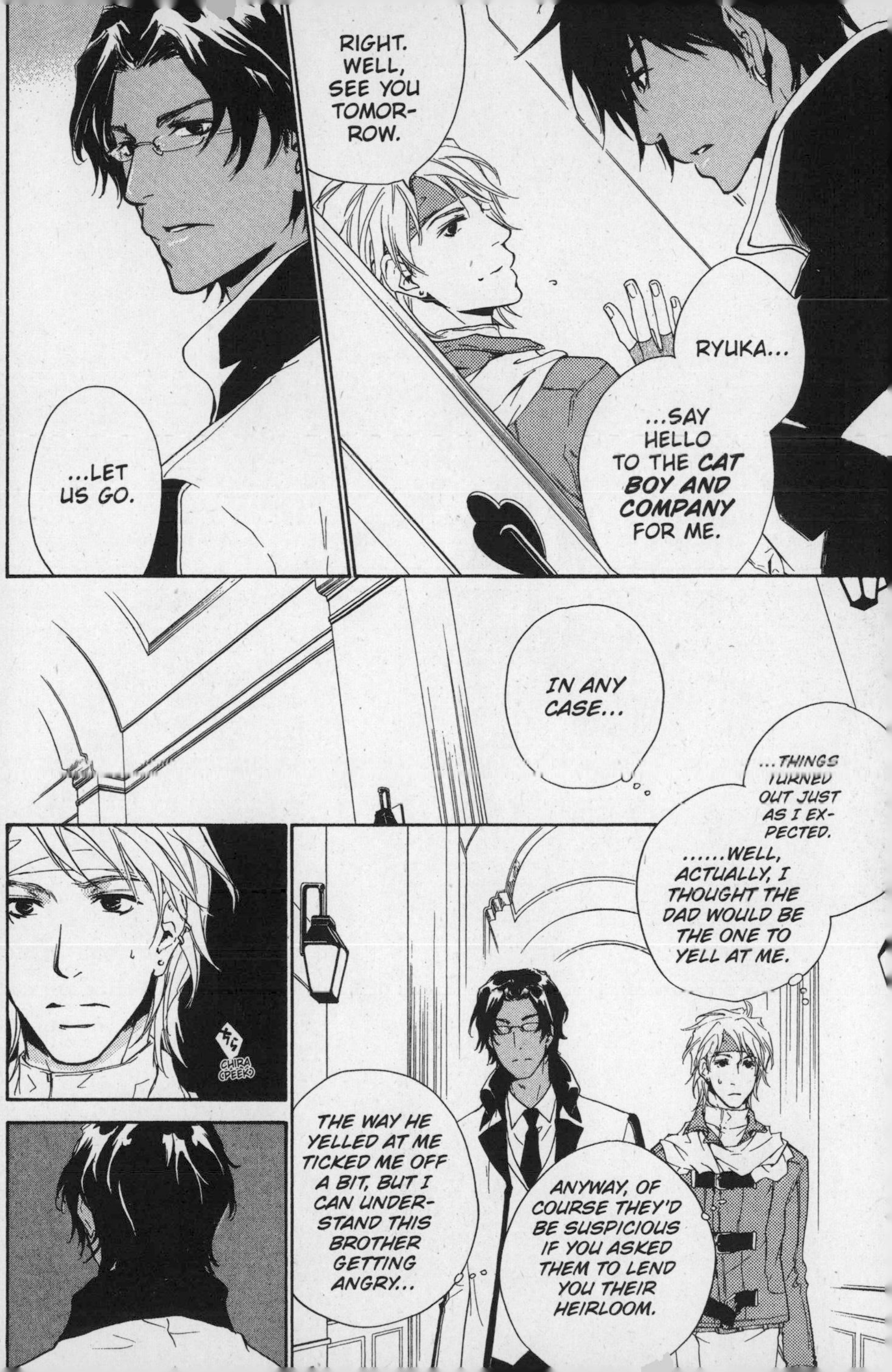
RYUKA...
...SAY HELLO TO THE CAT BOY AND COMPANY FOR ME.
RIGHT. WELL, SEE YOU TOMORROW.
...LET US GO.
IN ANY CASE...
...THINGS TURNED OUT JUST AS I EXPECTED.
......WELL, ACTUALLY, I THOUGHT THE DAD WOULD BE THE ONE TO YELL AT ME.
THE WAY HE YELLED AT ME TICKED ME OFF A BIT, BUT I CAN UNDERSTAND THIS BROTHER GETTING ANGRY...
ANYWAY, OF COURSE THEY'D BE SUSPICIOUS IF YOU ASKED THEM TO LEND YOU THEIR HEIRLOOM.
ちら
CHIRA (PEEK)

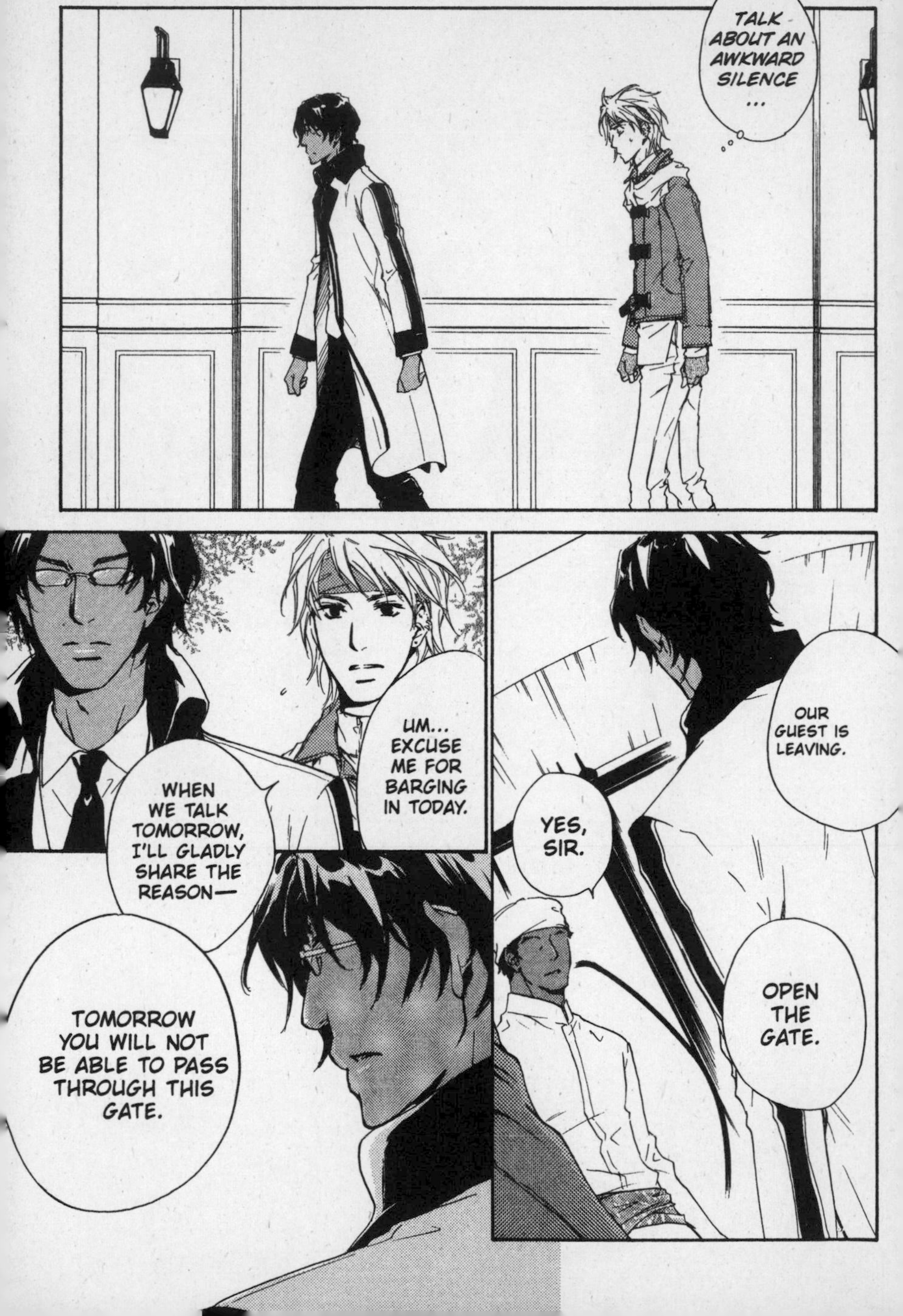
TALK ABOUT AN AWKWARD SILENCE ...
OUR GUEST IS LEAVING.
YES, SIR.
OPEN THE GATE.
UM... EXCUSE ME FOR BARGING IN TODAY.
WHEN WE TALK TOMORROW, I'LL GLADLY SHARE THE REASON—
TOMORROW YOU WILL NOT BE ABLE TO PASS THROUGH THIS GATE.

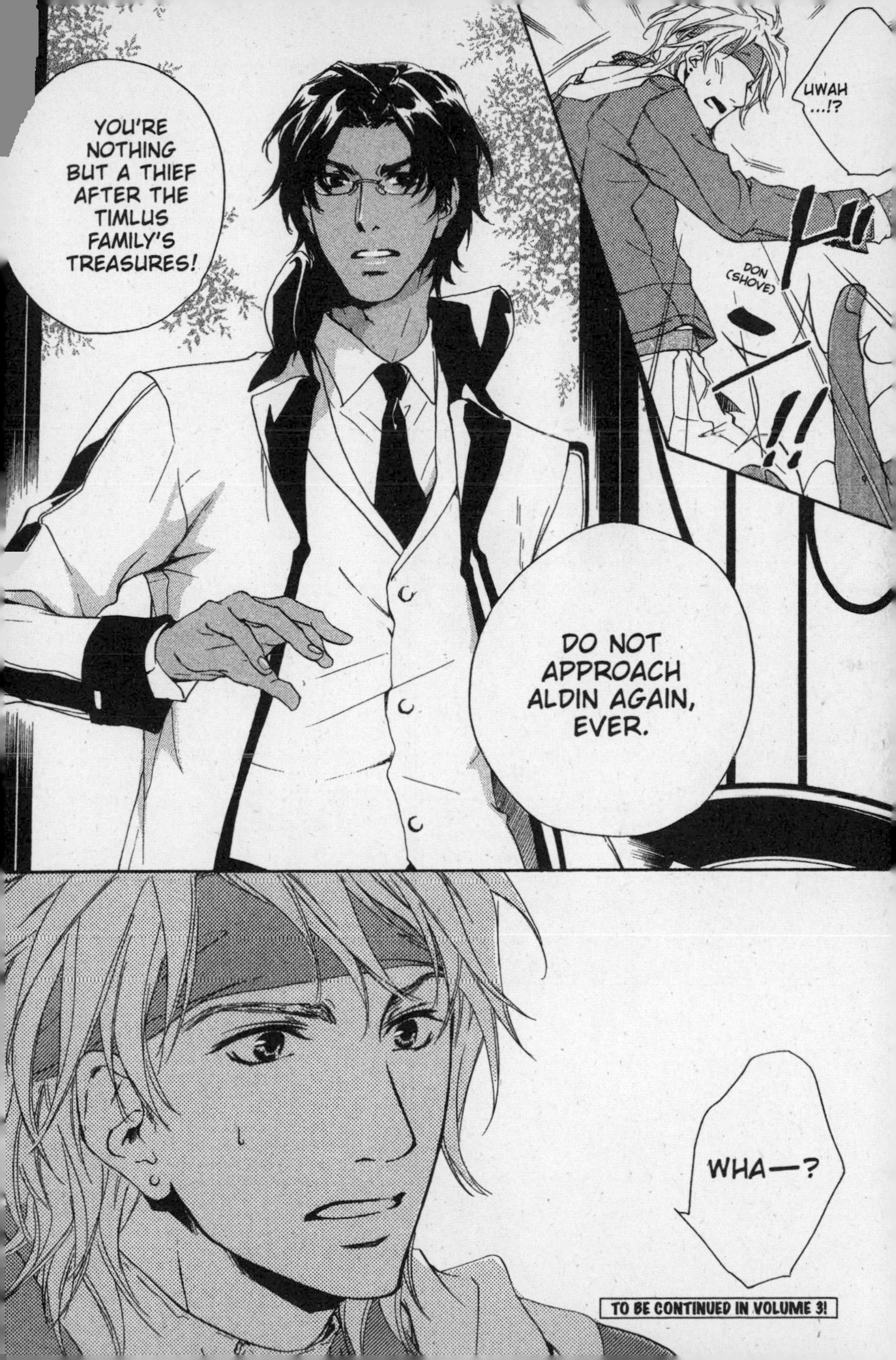
UWAH ...!?
DON (SHOVE)
YOU'RE NOTHING BUT A THIEF AFTER THE TIMLUS FAMILY'S TREASURES!
DO NOT APPROACH ALDIN AGAIN, EVER.
WHA—?
TO BE CONTINUED IN VOLUME 3!

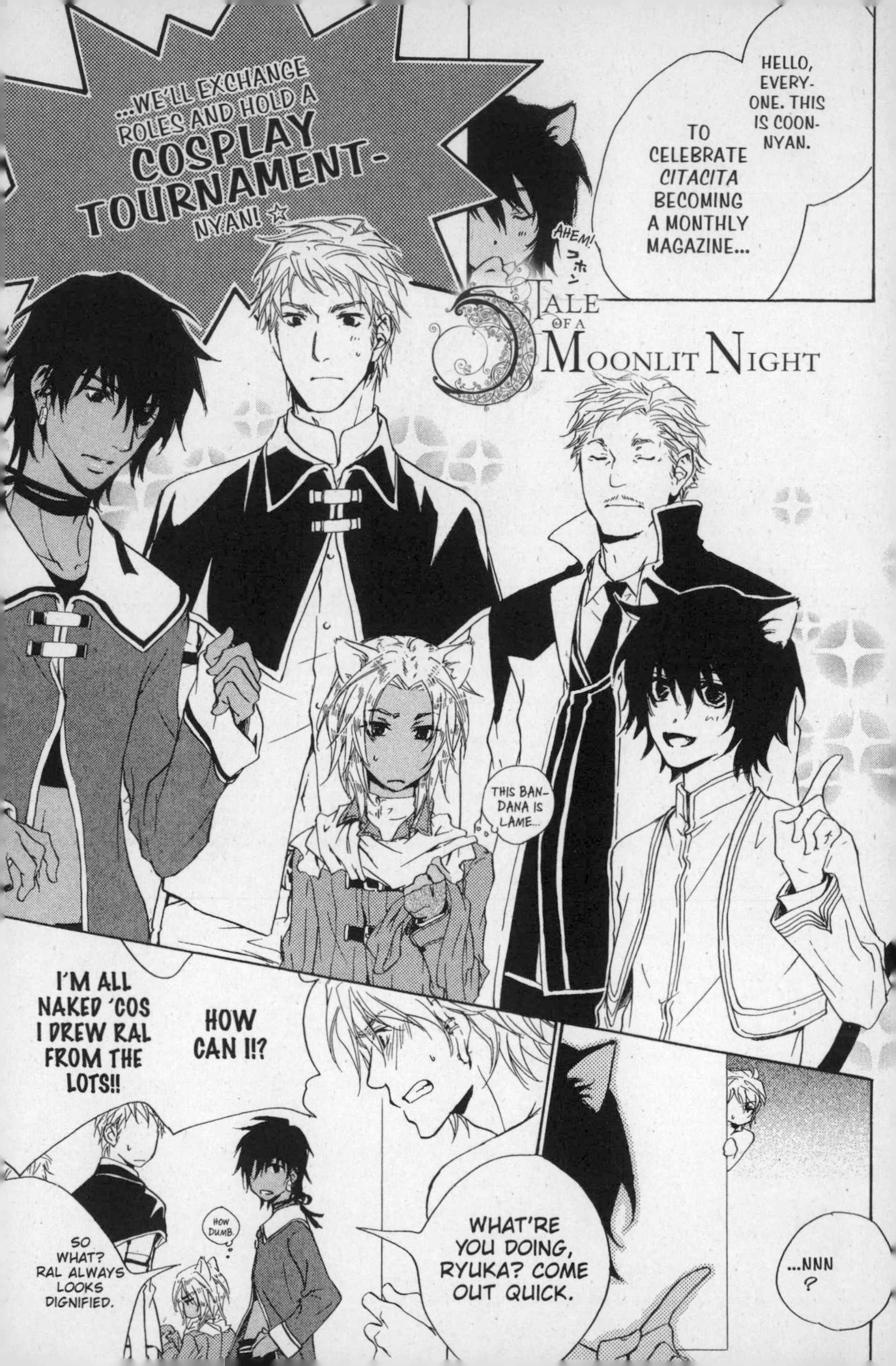
HELLO, EVERY-ONE. THIS IS COON-NYAN.
TO CELEBRATE CITACITA BECOMING A MONTHLY MAGAZINE...
AHEM!
コホン
TALE OF A MOONLIT NIGHT
...WE'LL EXCHANGE ROLES AND HOLD A COSPLAY TOURNAMENT-NYAN! ☆
THIS BAN-DANA IS LAME...
...NNN ?
WHAT'RE YOU DOING, RYUKA? COME OUT QUICK.
HOW CAN I!?
I'M ALL NAKED 'COS I DREW RAL FROM THE LOTS!!
HOW DUMB.
SO WHAT? RAL ALWAYS LOOKS DIGNIFIED.

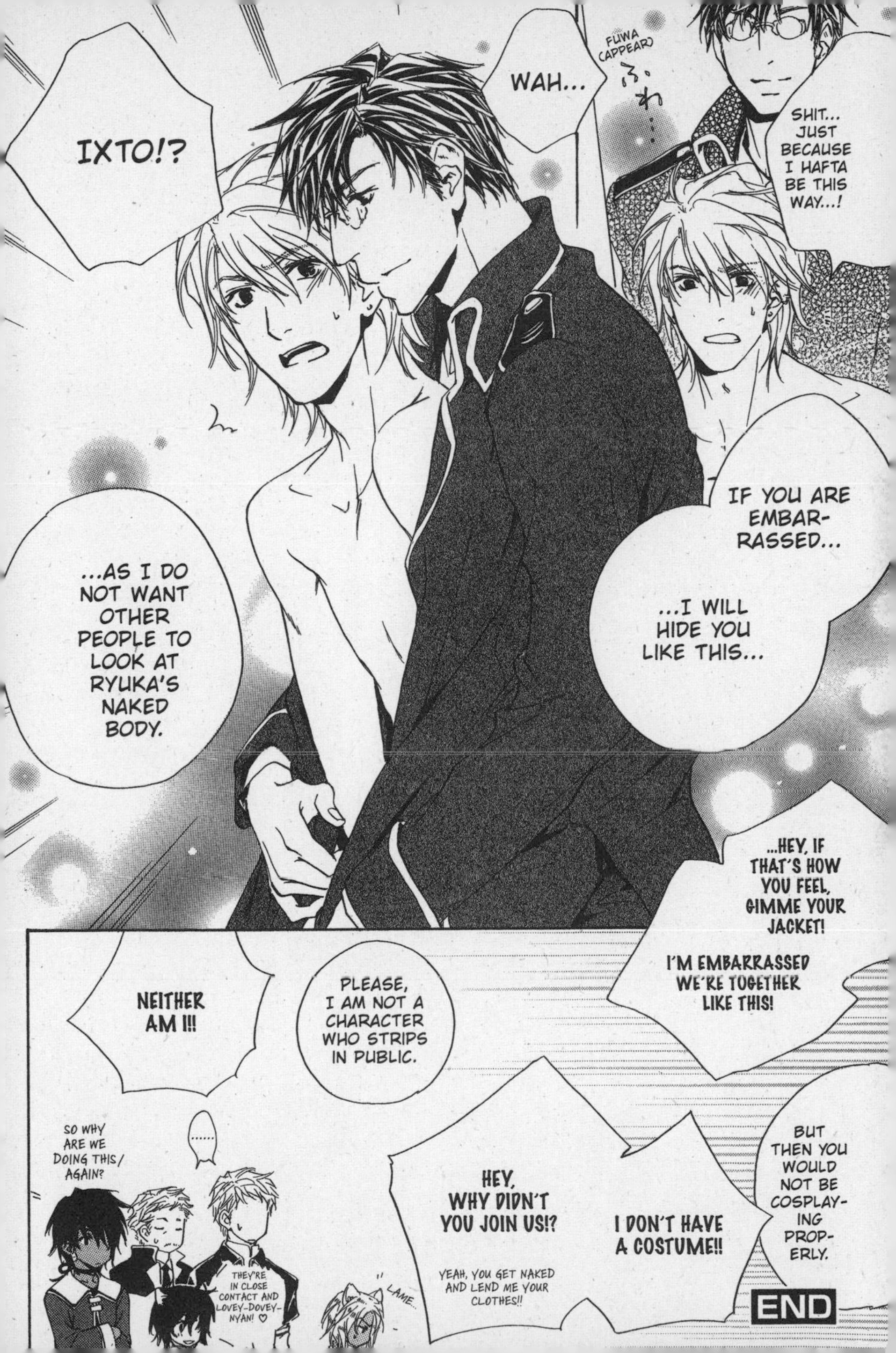
SHIT... JUST BECAUSE I HAFTA BE THIS WAY...!
FUWA (APPEAR)
ふわ…
WAH...
IXTO!?
IF YOU ARE EMBARRASSED...
...I WILL HIDE YOU LIKE THIS...
...AS I DO NOT WANT OTHER PEOPLE TO LOOK AT RYUKA'S NAKED BODY.
...HEY, IF THAT'S HOW YOU FEEL, GIMME YOUR JACKET!
I'M EMBARRASSED WE'RE TOGETHER LIKE THIS!
PLEASE, I AM NOT A CHARACTER WHO STRIPS IN PUBLIC.
NEITHER AM I!!!
BUT THEN YOU WOULD NOT BE COSPLAYING PROPERLY.
I DON'T HAVE A COSTUME!!
HEY, WHY DIDN'T YOU JOIN US!?
YEAH, YOU GET NAKED AND LEND ME YOUR CLOTHES!!
LAME..
THEY'RE IN CLOSE CONTACT AND LOVEY-DOVEY-NYAN! ♡
......
SO WHY ARE WE DOING THIS/ AGAIN?
END

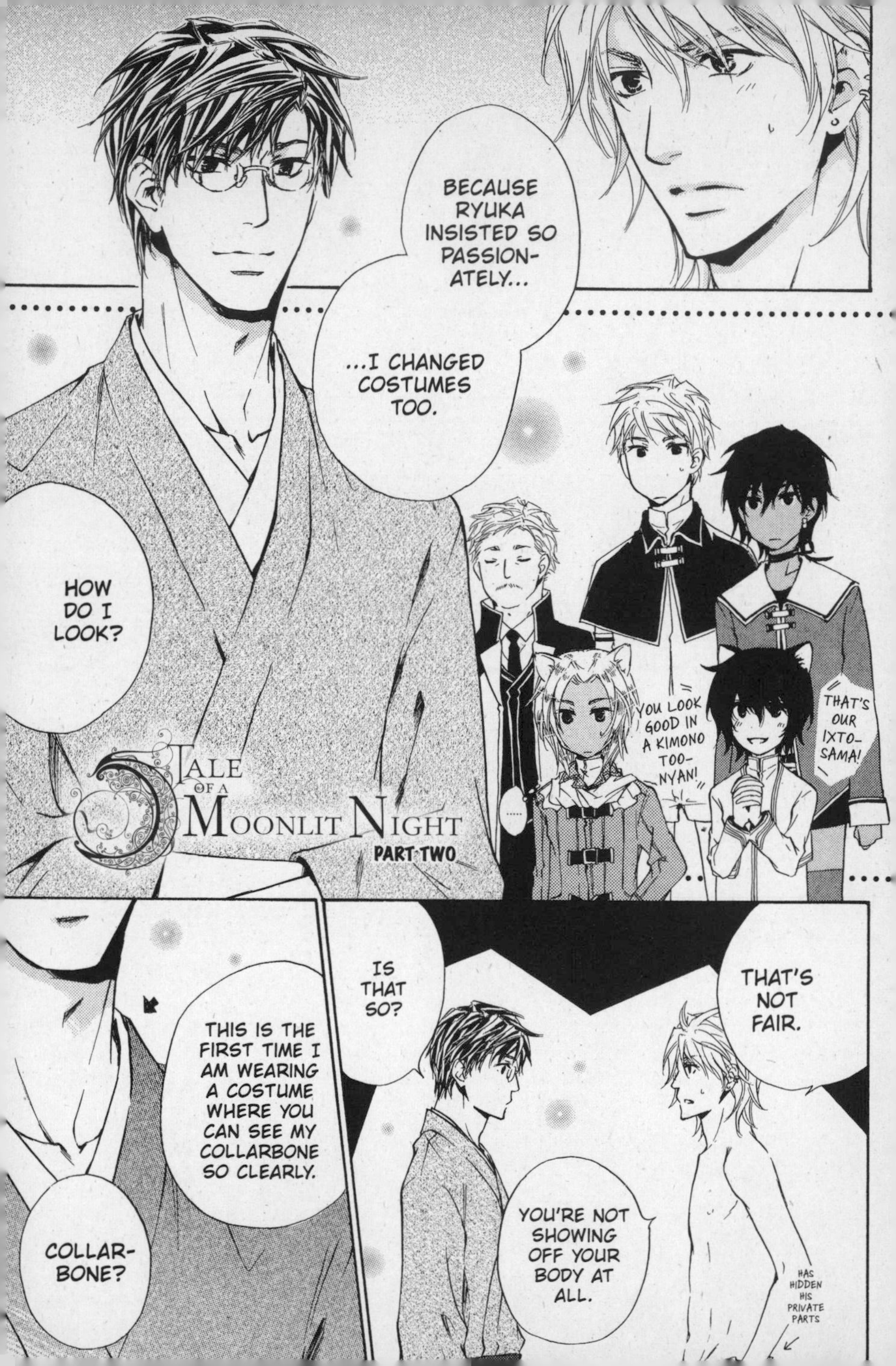
BECAUSE RYUKA INSISTED SO PASSION-ATELY...
...I CHANGED COSTUMES TOO.
THAT'S OUR IXTO-SAMA!
YOU LOOK GOOD IN A KIMONO TOO-NYAN!
......
HOW DO I LOOK?
TALE OF A MOONLIT NIGHT
PART TWO
THAT'S NOT FAIR.
IS THAT SO?
YOU'RE NOT SHOWING OFF YOUR BODY AT ALL.
HAS HIDDEN HIS PRIVATE PARTS
THIS IS THE FIRST TIME I AM WEARING A COSTUME WHERE YOU CAN SEE MY COLLARBONE SO CLEARLY.
COLLAR-BONE?

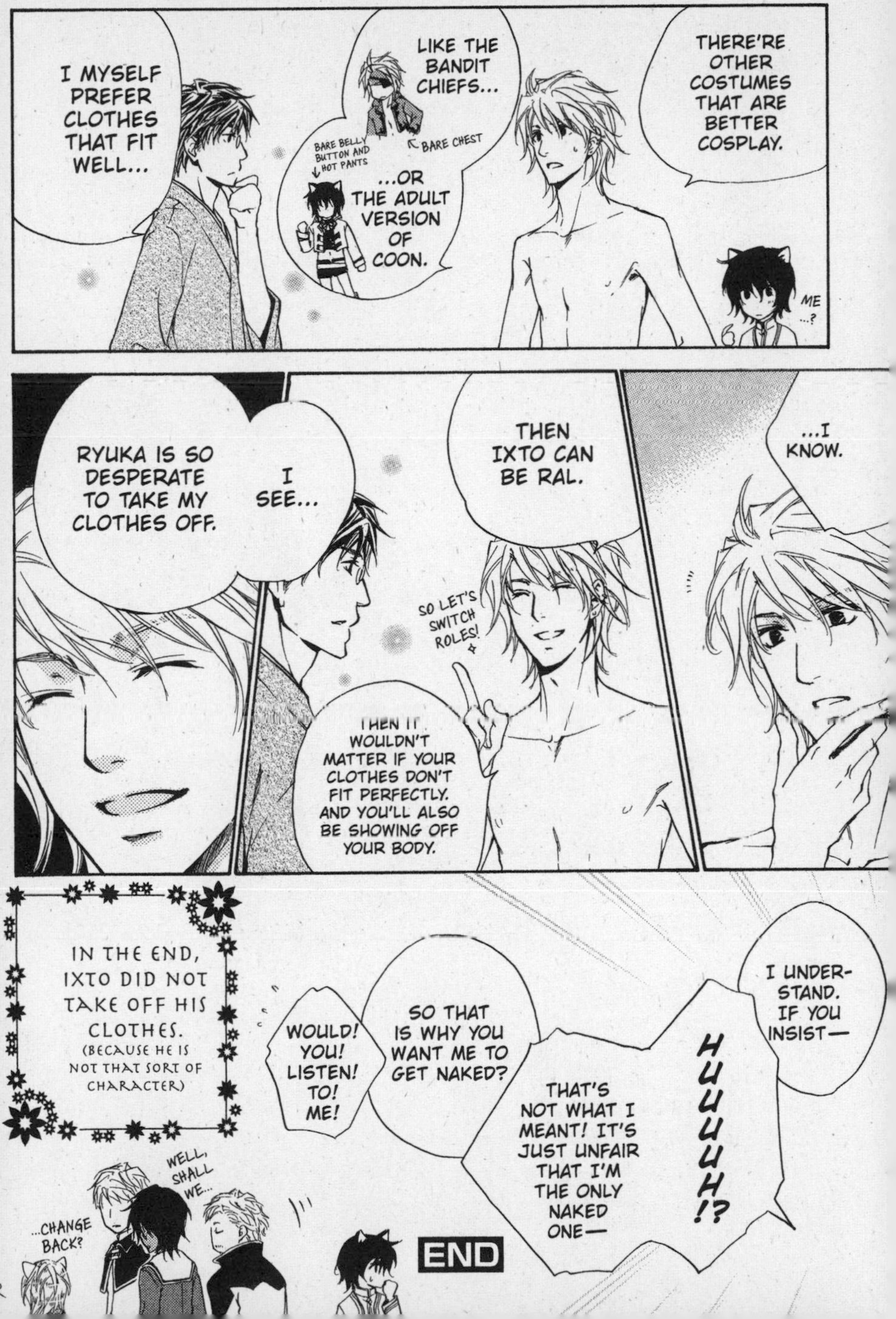
THERE'RE OTHER COSTUMES THAT ARE BETTER COSPLAY.
ME ...?
LIKE THE BANDIT CHIEFS...
BARE CHEST
BARE BELLY BUTTON AND HOT PANTS
...OR THE ADULT VERSION OF COON.
I MYSELF PREFER CLOTHES THAT FIT WELL...
...I KNOW.
THEN IXTO CAN BE RAL.
SO LET'S SWITCH ROLES!
THEN IT WOULDN'T MATTER IF YOUR CLOTHES DON'T FIT PERFECTLY. AND YOU'LL ALSO BE SHOWING OFF YOUR BODY.
I SEE...
RYUKA IS SO DESPERATE TO TAKE MY CLOTHES OFF.
I UNDER-STAND. IF YOU INSIST—
HUUUUH!?
THAT'S NOT WHAT I MEANT! IT'S JUST UNFAIR THAT I'M THE ONLY NAKED ONE—
SO THAT IS WHY YOU WANT ME TO GET NAKED?
WOULD! YOU! LISTEN! TO! ME!
IN THE END, IXTO DID NOT TAKE OFF HIS CLOTHES. (BECAUSE HE IS NOT THAT SORT OF CHARACTER)
WELL, SHALL WE...
...CHANGE BACK?
END

THANK FOR READING VOLUME 2 OF "TALE OF THE WANING MOON." DID YOU ENJOY IT? TWO YEARS HAVE PASSED SINCE VOLUME 1 CAME OUT... IT HAS BEEN A WHILE, BUT I'M GLAD YOU'RE STILL READING THE SERIES.

VOLUME 2 SEEMS TO CONTAIN FEWER NAKED BODIES AND FEWER DIRTY FACTORS...BUT I FEEL THAT IXTO AND RYUKA'S LOVE RELATIONSHIP IS STEADILY MOVING FORWARD...!

THE PARTY'S TAKING SOME TIME TO GET TO THE MOON, BUT THEY'LL GO TO THE MOON IN THE NEXT VOLUME!!...I HOPE.

I WANT TO ADD MORE SEXINESS TO THE STORY AS WELL...
IN ANY CASE, THANK YOU FOR READING THIS FAR! I PRAY THAT WE'LL BE ABLE TO MEET AGAIN IN THE NEXT VOLUME...AND SEE WHAT HAPPENS TO RYUKA, ALDIN, AND THE REST...

2010年 1月、藤山ひょうた
JANUARY 2010, HYOUTA FUJIYAMA

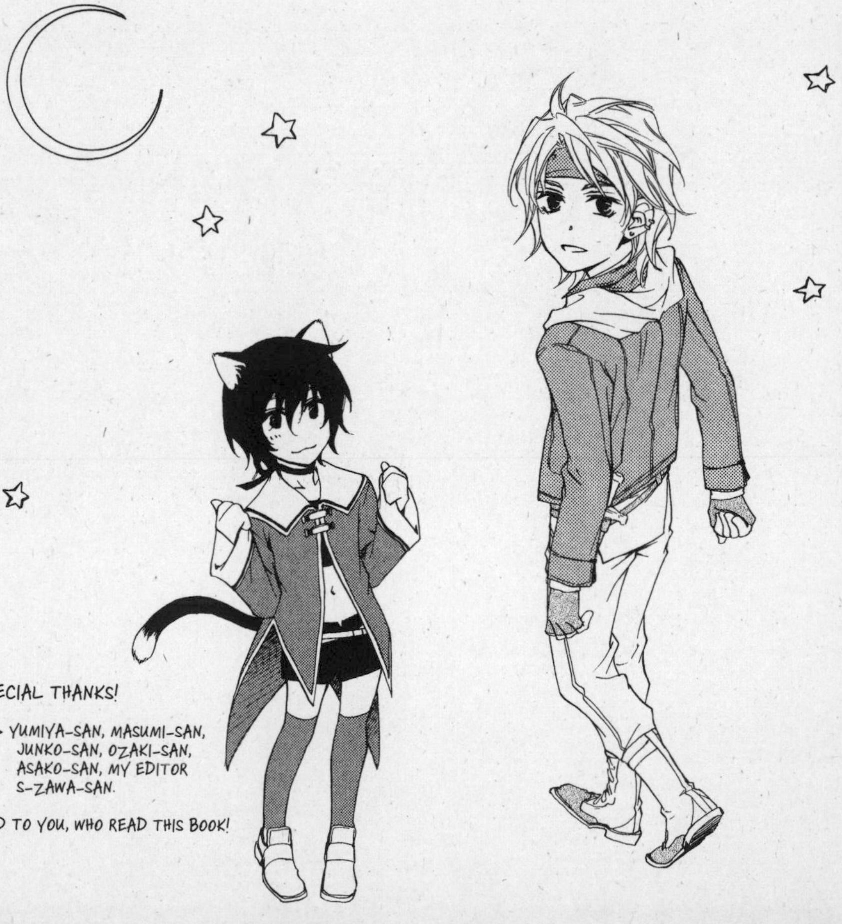

SPECIAL THANKS!

-> YUMIYA-SAN, MASUMI-SAN, JUNKO-SAN, OZAKI-SAN, ASAKO-SAN, MY EDITOR S-ZAWA-SAN.

AND TO YOU, WHO READ THIS BOOK!

Tale of the Waning Moon

TRANSLATOR'S NOTES

COMMON HONORIFICS

no honorific: Indicates familiarity or closeness; if used without permission or reason, addressing someone in this manner would constitute an insult.

-san: The Japanese equivalent of Mr./Mrs./Miss. If a situation calls for politeness, this is the fail-safe honorific.

-sama: Conveys great respect; may also indicate that the social status of the speaker is lower than that of the addressee.

-kun: Used most often when referring to boys, this indicates affection or familiarity. Occasionally used by older men among their peers, but it may also be used by anyone referring to a person of lower standing.

-chan: An affectionate honorific indicating familiarity used mostly in reference to girls; also used in reference to cute persons or animals of either gender.

-niisan, onii-san: Used to address an older brother or older brother figure.

-neesan, onee-san: Used to address an older sister or older sister figure.

PAGE 28
Four-dimensional box
A reference to the popular manga/anime character Doraemon. One of Doraemon's tools is the "four-dimensional pocket," where you can store an infinite number of items.

PAGE 107
Millia-neesan
Here "*neesan*" is used in the yakuza sense, not in the ordinary "big sister" sense. "Sibling" titles are often used among yakuza comrades, and a woman in a position of superiority is commonly addressed thusly.

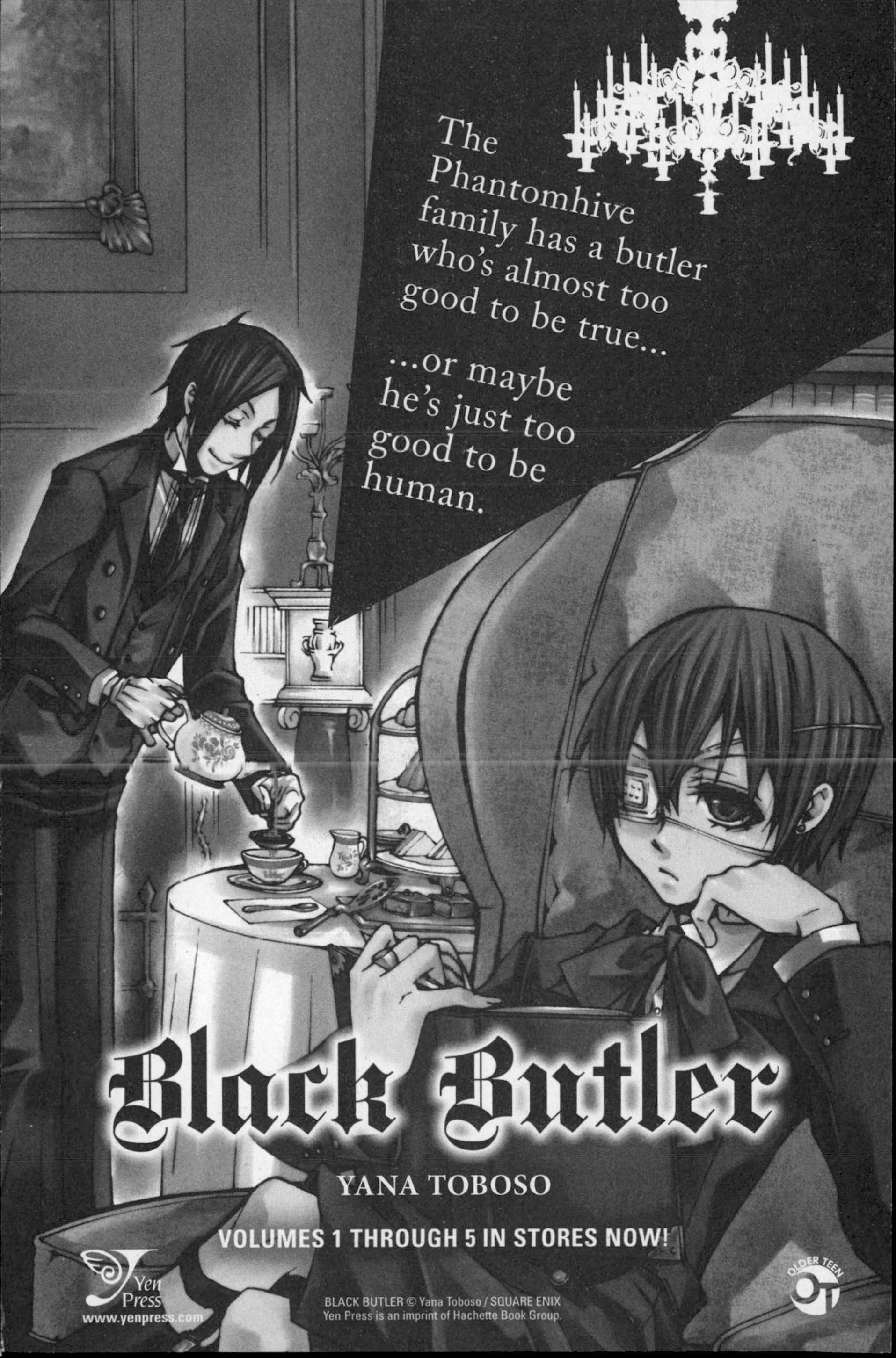